This book belongs to
Name / School:

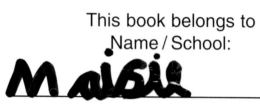

Jolly Dictionary

Sara Wernham and Sue Lloyd

Lexicography by Michael Janes   Illustrated by Lib Stephen

Jolly Learning Ltd

This hardback edition published June 2010

Jolly Learning Ltd
Tailours House
High Road
Chigwell
Essex
IG7 6DL
United Kingdom

Tel: (+44 or 0) 20 8501 0405
Fax: (+44 or 0) 20 8500 1696

www.jollylearning.co.uk
info@jollylearning.co.uk

Edited and designed by Angela Hockley.

Printed and bound in Singapore.

ISBN 978-1-84414-171-5

Acknowledgements

Our sincere thanks go to Toby Wernham for all his hard work in developing this dictionary. His dedication and effort has had a profound influence on this project.

We would also like to thank Caren Ewers and Gilbert Jolly for their detailed help and as ever we are grateful to Rachel Stadlen for her expertise and advice.

Lastly our thanks go to John Cunningham for the hours spent typing in the pronunciations.

Contents

All about the dictionary

Picture pages

The dictionary

Introduction

The *Jolly Dictionary* aims to teach young children how to use a dictionary, as well as being useful in its own right.

When children have been taught to read using a phonic method, such as *Jolly Phonics*, they are generally capable of reading words that they may not be familiar with and whose meanings they may not know. Being able to use a dictionary enables children to find out the meanings of those words and pronounce them correctly. It makes them truly independent readers and writers.

In order for this to happen, children must be familiar with using a dictionary and be able to look up the words they require without difficulty.

Children need to feel that a dictionary is fun and useful to them, not just something that grown-ups use.

To encourage this, the *Jolly Dictionary* begins with a number of illustrated pages where words are arranged by topic or theme. These Picture Pages provide an easy reference point for young children, showing them how to spell useful words such as days of the week, numbers and the names of animals.

Young children should also begin to learn simple dictionary skills by playing games such as finding a particular letter. With two or more children, this can be turned into a race. Once they are able to read and write with reasonable fluency, the children can move on to looking up words in the main body of the text. Some games and practice for this are in the *Jolly Grammar Handbooks 1* and *2*.

In particular, children need to feel confident about finding their way around a dictionary. A dictionary can be divided into four sections, made up of words beginning with the letters a–e, f–m, n–s and t–z. Each of these sections contains about a quarter of the words in the dictionary. In the *Jolly Dictionary* each of these sections has a different colour – red, yellow, green and blue. So if children know which quarter a letter is in, they can look up a word more quickly. For example, if they are looking up the word 'potato', the words beginning with 'p' are in the third quarter and the dictionary should be opened at the green section. They can then use the alphabet across the top of the page to help them find the words beginning with 'p'.

Each entry in this dictionary includes a guide to how the word is pronounced. It uses the joined digraphs familiar from *Jolly Phonics* and a few new symbols for clarity. The pronunciation guide also uses bolder type to show where to put the stress in a word. There is more information on how to use the pronunciation guide on pages 8 to 11.

Each entry also indicates which parts of speech the word may be, depending on how it is used in a sentence. The names of the different parts of speech are colour coded, so for example, 'noun' is black, 'verb' is red and 'adjective' is blue. This element of the dictionary becomes more interesting to the children as they learn more about parts of speech and how our language works.

All about the dictionary

About this dictionary

Colour band
The colour band at the edge of each page helps you find the section of the dictionary you want more quickly.

Alphabet
The alphabet across the top of each page reminds you of the order of the letters in the alphabet. This helps you when you are looking up a word.

Letter indicator
The alphabet letter in the colour band tells you that the words on the page begin with that letter.

Letter section
A picture next to a large capital and lower case letter tells you where each letter section begins.

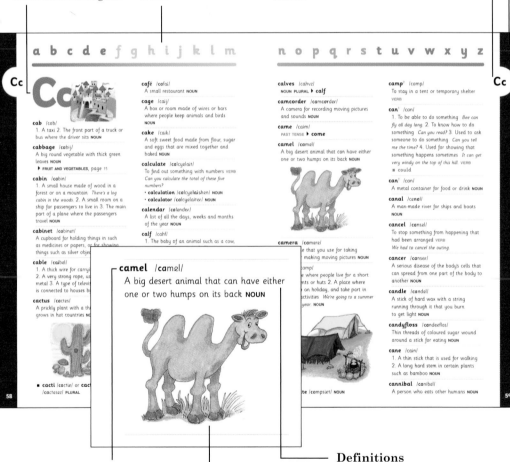

Headwords
Each headword is clearly written at the top of each entry to help you find it more easily.

Pictures
Some entries have a colourful picture to show you what the word may look like or help you understand its meaning.

Definitions
A definition is the meaning of a word. The definitions have been specially written to make them as clear and as easy for you to understand as possible.

How to use this dictionary

If you want to look up the word **mouse**:

1. Think about which letter the word begins with – **m**.

2. Think about which part of the dictionary **m** is in.

   ▸ Find the letter **m** on the front cover. It is in the yellow section.
   ▸ Put your thumb on the letter **m.**
   ▸ Run your thumb down the pages of the dictionary until you reach the yellow section.

3. The letter **m** is near the end of the yellow section, so open the dictionary near the end of the yellow pages.

4. Check that the words on the page begin with **m**. If not, think about which letter the words do begin with. Does this letter come before or after **m**? Use the alphabet at the top of the page to help you. Turn the pages to find the **m** section.

5. Now you need to look at the next letter in the word – **o**. Find the words that begin with **mo**.

6. Look at the next letter, **u**, and then the next, **s**, and use them to help you find the word **mouse**.

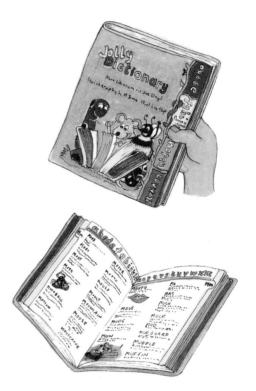

---

mouse /maʊs/
  1. A little furry animal with a long tail
  2. A small object that you move around on your desk to help you work a computer **NOUN**
  ■ **mice** /miːs/ **PLURAL**
  • **mousehole** /maʊshəʊl/ **NOUN**
  • **mousetrap** /maʊstrap/ **NOUN**

The definitions

Headword
The headword is the main word for each entry. It shows you how a word is spelt. All the headwords are in alphabetical order so that you can find them quickly.

Pronunciation guide
The letter sounds inside the slashes /wel/ show you how to say the word. This is called the pronunciation guide. You can find out more about how to use it on pages 8 to 11.

well[1] /wel/

1. If you do something well, you do it properly and in a very good way *I can swim very well.* 2. Very much *Inky finished the lesson well before three o'clock.* 3. **as well as** Used to include something or someone else in what you say *Snake reads comics as well as books.* ADVERB
■ better, best

Numbers
Many words have more than one meaning, so each meaning in the entry has a number. Make sure you read all of them to help you decide which is the one you want.

Examples
Examples are often given to help you understand how the word is used. They come at the end of a meaning and are in *italics*. Many of the examples include the characters from *Jolly Phonics*.

Phrases

Some headwords are used in common phrases. A phrase is written in bold, and comes before its meaning.

Numbered headwords

If a headword has a number, it means that there is more than one entry for the word. This is because some words in English are spelt the same but are different in meaning, grammar or pronunciation. Make sure you look at all the entries for a headword to help you decide which is the one you want.

lead[1] /leed/
1. To go in front and show people the way 2. To go somewhere *This path leads straight to our school.* 3. To be in charge of a group VERB
■ led
• **leader** /leeder/ NOUN

lead[2] /leed/
1. **in the lead** Ahead of everyone else in a race or competition 2. A strap for holding a dog NOUN

lead[3] /led/
A soft but very heavy metal NOUN

leaf /leef/
Leaves are the flat green or plant that grow from the stem NOUN
■ **leaves** /leevz/ PLURAL

Key to Symbols

• Other words connected to the headword

▪ Tricky or irregular verbs

■ Tricky or irregular plurals

■ Tricky or irregular forms of the comparative and superlative

▶ Go to the headword or Picture Page mentioned for more information

Parts of speech

Parts of speech are the special names that help us talk and write about the words we use. Some words can be more than one part of speech, depending on how you use them. In 'I walk to school' the word *walk* is a verb, but in 'I went for a walk' the word *walk* is a noun. There is more information about parts of speech on pages 6 and 7.

Parts of speech

NOUN

A noun is a word used to name a person, place or thing.

Common nouns are the names for things we can see and touch, for example 'chair' and 'mouse'.

Proper nouns are the special names used for a particular person, place or thing, for example 'Ben', 'Scotland' and 'Tuesday'. A proper noun starts with a capital letter.

PRONOUN

A pronoun is a word that can take the place of a noun. 'I', 'you', 'he', 'she', 'it', 'we' and 'they' are all pronouns.

INTERJECTION

An interjection is a word or phrase used to show a strong feeling such as surprise, pain or pleasure. 'Hello', 'thanks' and 'hooray' are interjections.

VERB

A verb is a word that is used to say what a person or thing does, for example 'sing', 'eat' and 'be'. Verbs change according to who is involved, so we say 'I *like* swimming', but 'He *likes* swimming'.

Verbs also change according to when they take place, so we say 'They *play* football', 'They *played* football yesterday', and 'They *will play* football next week'.

ADJECTIVE

An adjective is a word that describes a noun or pronoun. It can also describe who the noun or pronoun belongs to, or how many of them there are. 'Sad', 'big' and 'furry' are all adjectives. Numbers and colours can be adjectives too.

ADVERB

An adverb is a word that describes a verb. Usually it describes how, where, when or how often something happens. 'Quickly', 'happily' and 'carefully' are all adverbs.

PREPOSITION

A preposition is a word that links one noun or pronoun to another one. Prepositions often describe where someone or something is, or where it is moving towards. In 'A frog is sitting *on* a rock *in* the river', the words 'on' and 'in' are prepositions.

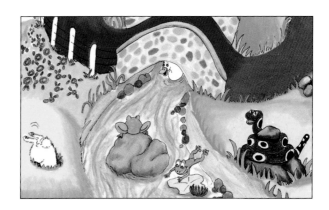

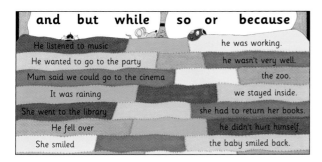

CONJUNCTION

A conjunction is a word that is used to join parts of a sentence together. The most common conjunction is the word 'and'. Other conjunctions are 'but', 'or' and 'because'.

Pronunciation guide

Children need to be able to find out how words are spoken, as well as what they mean. In adult dictionaries the pronunciation of words is generally provided by the International Phonetic Alphabet (IPA). This is too complicated for children. Instead, for this dictionary a simple Jolly Pronunciation Code has been developed, which mainly uses the known letter sounds.

Children learning with *Jolly Phonics* are initially taught 42 letter sounds and one way to write these sounds. These have been used in the Jolly Pronunciation Code. The digraphs – sounds represented by two letters – have been joined so that each sound is represented by one symbol. For example, the long *'a'* sound is first taught as *'ai'*, so in a word like ‹brave› the pronunciation is written as /braiv/. To help make the distinction clear in this and the following examples, pronunciations are given in slanted brackets, // and spellings are given in angled brackets, ‹ ›.

Two new letter sounds and some extra symbols have been introduced for clarity, in addition to those normally used in *Jolly Phonics*.

The first new letter sound is the schwa, or neutral vowel, that you hear in a word such as ‹begin›, /bəgin/. It is a very common sound in English and is represented by the symbol /ǝ/. Other examples of this sound are found in words like ‹table›, /**tai**bǝl/ and ‹mechanic›, /mǝ**ca**nic/.

Another new letter sound and joined digraph /zh/ has been introduced for the sound you hear in ‹television›, /**te**lǝvizhǝn/.

The joined digraph /ah/ is used in the pronunciation of words such as ‹father›, /**fah**ther/. Where the spelling of this sound is followed by the letter ‹r›, the joined digraph /ar/ is used, as in /cart/ for ‹cart›.

The symbol /a/ is used to represent the vowel sound in the pronunciation of words like ‹bath› and ‹fast›. These words are spoken with /ah/ in southern British English, but with /a/ in both northern British English and American English. While still using the one symbol, children and teachers can identify their own pronunciation for this vowel. This can be particularly helpful where teachers with different accents are teaching together, for instance in countries where English is a foreign language.

Similarly, the symbol /aw/ is used to represent the vowel sound in words such as ‹saw›, ‹jaw› and ‹law›. These words are spoken with an /or/ in British English, but with an /ah/ in American English.

At the end of a word such as ‹happy›, the sound of the letter ‹y› is given as /ee/ rather than /i/. In practice, the sound is somewhere between the two, and the use of /ee/ was considered the best option.

Where possible, the pronunciation shown follows the spelling. In a word such as ‹sack›, for example, the pronunciation uses the letter ‹c› in preference to ‹k›, to give /sac/, while for the word ‹lake› the ‹k› is used to give /laik/.

In words with more than one syllable, the pronunciation guide shows where to put the stress. The stress is shown by bolder type, as in /**chi**ldrǝn/. It is important that children know where the stress is in these longer words.

The pronunciation shown for a particular word is called its ‘sounding’. A word has a spelling, such as ‹snake› and a sounding, /snaik/. Children may misspell a word by writing ‘snaik’, in which case you can tell them that they have written the ‘sounding’ and ask them for the ‘spelling’.

The Jolly Pronunciation Code symbols

Spelling	*Sounding*
a ....ant, sand, catch	/ant/ /sand/ /cach/
a ....bath, fast, castle	/bath/ /fast/ /**cas**ᴧl/
ai ....aim, play, late	/aim/ /plai/ /lait/
ah ....father, llama, palm	/**fah**ther/ /**lah**mᴧ/ /pahm/
ar ....art, arm, start	/art/ /arm/ /start/
aw ....saw, all, pause	/saw/ /awl/ /pawz/
b ....bat, bend, crab	/bat/ /bend/ /crab/
c ....cat, cut, duck	/cat/ /cut/ /duc/
ch ....chop, chick, much	/chop/ /chic/ /much/
d ....dad, dip, sudden	/dad/ /dip/ /**sud**ᴧn/
e ....egg, end, shed	/eg/ /end/ /shed/
ee ....eel, dream, tree	/eel/ /dreem/ /tree/
ᴧ ....begin, grateful, total	/bᴧ**gin**/ /**grai**tfᴧl/ /**toa**tᴧl/
er ....her, bird, turn	/her/ /berd/ /tern/
f ....fog, lift, fluff	/fog/ /lift/ /fluf/
g ....goat, gap, giggle	/goat/ /gap/ /**gi**gᴧl/
h ....hop, hit, hill	/hop/ /hit/ /hil/
i ....ink, igloo, drink	/ingk/ /ig**loo**/ /dringk/
ie ....pie, night, line	/pie/ /niet/ /lien/
j ....jar, jet, jacket	/jar/ /jet/ /**ja**cit/
k ....king, kind, kettle	/king/ /kiend/ /**ke**tᴧl/
l ....leg, lap, shell	/leg/ /lap/ /shel/
m ....man, mill, shrimp	/man/ /mil/ /shrimp/
n ....nut, nod, spin	/nut/ /nod/ /spin/
ng ....flung, bang, string	/flung/ /bang/ /string/
o ....odd, on, spot	/od/ /on/ /spot/
oa ....oak, snow, stone	/oak/ /snoa/ /stoan/
oo ....look, hood, foot, (little oo)	/look/ /hood/ /foot/
oo ....moon, spoon, shoot (long oo)	/moon/ /spoon/ /shoot/
oi ....oil, ointment, boy	/oil/ /**oi**ntmᴧnt/ /boi/
or ....order, corn, storm	/**or**der/ /corn/ /storm/

ou ....out, cloud, brown	/out/	/cloud/	/broun/
p ....pet, pack, step	/pet/	/pac/	/step/
qu ....queen, quick, quiz	/queen/	/quic/	/quiz/
r ....run, rip, bread	/run/	/rip/	/bred/
s ....sand, sun, twist	/sand/	/sun/	/twist/
sh ....ship, shop, wish	/ship/	/shop/	/wish/
t ....top, tug, mat	/top/	/tug/	/mat/
th ....this, then, with (voiced th)	/this/	/then/	/with/
th ....thin, thick, mouth (unvoiced th)	/thin/	/thic/	/mouth/
u ....up, under, lung	/up/	/under/	/lung/
ue ....cue, few, cube	/cue/	/fue/	/cueb/
v ....van, vest, give	/van/	/vest/	/giv/
w ....wind, went, swim	/wind/	/went/	/swim/
x ....x-ray, ox, flex	/**ex** rai/	/ox/	/flex/
y ....yell, yes, yellow	/yel/	/yes/	/**ye**lou/
z ....zoo, zigzag, buzz	/zoo/	/**zig**zag/	/buz/
zh ....measure, treasure, television	/**me**zher/	/**tre**zher/	/**tele**vizhen/

In the pronunciation guide for the word 'insult', why is the 'i' darker in the noun /insult/ than in the verb /insult/?

When we say words, we say some bits of the word louder than others. This is called the stress in a word. In the pronunciation guide, the darker bit shows where the stress is.

insult /insult/
To say rude and nasty things to someone VERB
• **insult** /insult/ NOUN

If we look up the word 'insult', the noun and verb are spelt the same, but the stress is different.

Picture pages

Numbers

1	one		1st	first
2	two		2nd	second
3	three		3rd	third
4	four		4th	fourth
5	five		5th	fifth
6	six		6th	sixth
7	seven		7th	seventh
8	eight		8th	eighth
9	nine		9th	ninth
10	ten		10th	tenth
11	eleven		11th	eleventh
12	twelve		12th	twelfth
13	thirteen		13th	thirteenth
14	fourteen		14th	fourteenth
15	fifteen		15th	fifteenth
16	sixteen		16th	sixteenth
17	seventeen		17th	seventeenth
18	eighteen		18th	eighteenth
19	nineteen		19th	nineteenth
20	twenty		20th	twentieth
21	twenty-one		21st	twenty first
30	thirty		30th	thirtieth
40	forty		40th	fortieth
50	fifty		50th	fiftieth
60	sixty		60th	sixtieth
70	seventy		70th	seventieth
80	eighty		80th	eightieth
90	ninety		90th	ninetieth
100	hundred		100th	hundredth
1000	thousand		1000th	thousandth
1,000,000	million		1,000,000th	millionth

Calendar

Months of the year	Days of the week	Seasons
January	Monday	Spring
February	Tuesday	Summer
March	Wednesday	Autumn
April	Thursday	Winter
May	Friday	
June	Saturday	
July	Sunday	
August		
September		
October		
November		
December		

Picture pages

World map

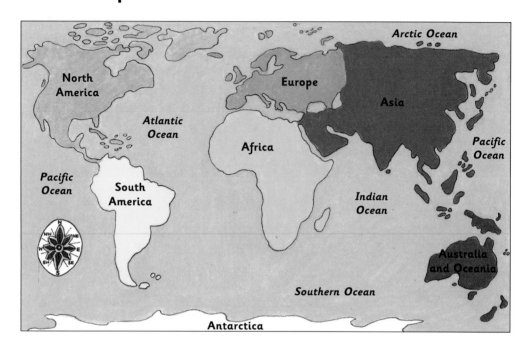

Insects

Fruit and vegetables

Picture pages

Animals

Colours

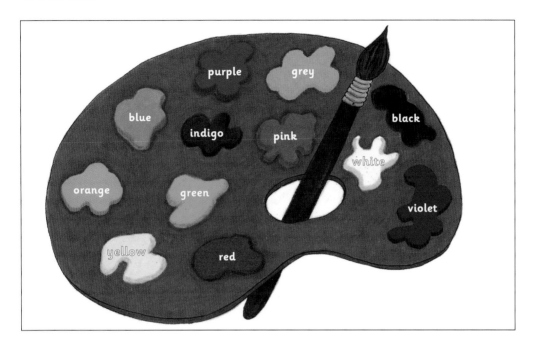

Shapes

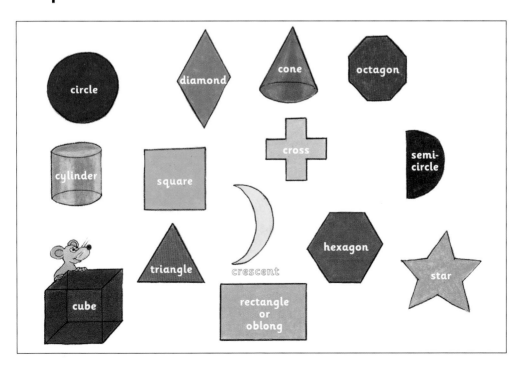

Parts of the body

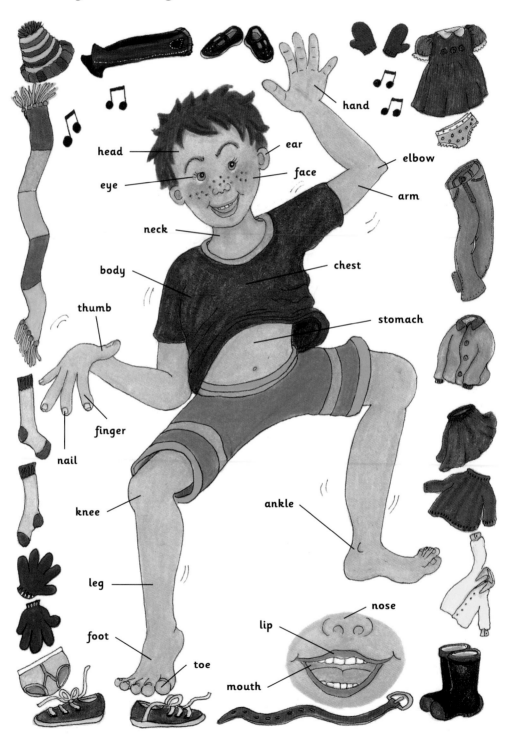

a

a, an /ai, an/
A word used before a noun 1. One
We waited an hour. 2. Any *Take a card.*
3. Every, each *We go swimming twice a
week.* INDEFINITE ARTICLE

aardvark /ardvark/
An animal with a long nose and tongue
that eats ants NOUN

abandon /ebanden/
1. To deliberately leave someone or
something behind 2. To give up on
something, especially an idea or plan VERB

abbreviate /ebreeveeait/
To make a word or phrase shorter by
leaving out some of the letters, such as
Dr for 'doctor', Mr for 'mister' VERB
• **abbreviation** /ebreeveeaishen/ NOUN

able /aibel/
Having the knowledge or skill to do
something ADJECTIVE
• **ability** /ebiletee/ Skill NOUN

abnormal /abnormel/
Different from normal, and usually
strange or worrying ADJECTIVE

aboard /ebord/
On or onto a ship or aircraft ADVERB,
PREPOSITION

What time do we go aboard?

abominable /ebominebel/
Very very bad ADJECTIVE
the abominable snowman

Aborigine /aberijenee/
A man or woman in Australia that
belongs to a group of people who have
lived there for thousands of years NOUN
• **aboriginal** /aberijenel/ ADJECTIVE

about /ebout/
1. On the subject of *This book is
about dinosaurs.* 2. Slightly more or
less *It happened about 15 years ago.*
3. All over the place *Snake left his
pencils lying about.* ADVERB, PREPOSITION

above /ebuv/
1. Higher or greater than *The plane flew
high above the clouds.* • above average
2. Over *Write in the space above the
picture.* ADVERB, PREPOSITION

abroad /ebrawd/
In or to a different country ADVERB

abrupt /ebrupt/
1. Rude and not friendly *He was very
abrupt with me.* 2. Sudden *an abrupt
change* ADJECTIVE

absent /absent/
Not in a place, away ADJECTIVE
Tom is absent from school today.
• **absence** /absens/ NOUN

absolute /abseloot/
Complete ADJECTIVE
an absolute disaster
absolutely /abselootlee/ ADVERB

absurd /ebserd/
Very silly ADJECTIVE

abundance /ebundens/
A great amount, lots of NOUN
There was an abundance of ants.
• **abundant** /ebundent/ ADJECTIVE

A

academy /ɐcadɘmee/
A school or college **NOUN**
an academy of music

accelerate /acselɘrait/
To go faster **VERB**
• **acceleration** /acselɘraishɘn/ **NOUN**

accent /acsɘnt/
The special way people say their words that shows where they come from **NOUN**
an American accent

accept /acsept/
1. To take something that someone gives you 2. To say you will do something, or say yes to something *Bee accepted Inky's invitation to her birthday party.* **VERB**
• **acceptable** /acseptɘbɘl/ **ADJECTIVE**

access¹ /acses/
A way to or into a place **NOUN**

access² /acses/
To go into a computer program or to find and use information on a computer **VERB**

accident /acsidɘnt/
1. An event when something bad or harmful happens unexpectedly *Tony broke a plate but it was an accident.* 2. A crash with one or more vehicles *a road accident* 3. **by accident** Not on purpose, by chance *Bee and Inky met by accident.* **NOUN**
• **accidentally** /acsidentɘlee/
By accident **ADVERB**

accompany /ɐcumpɘnee/
1. To go with someone 2. To play a musical instrument while someone sings or dances **VERB**

according to /ɐcording too/
Based on what someone or something says **PREPOSITION**
According to my dad, we're really late.

accordion /ɐcordee ɘn/
A musical instrument shaped like a box that you play by pulling the box in and out and pressing the buttons on the side **NOUN**

account /ɐcount/
1. A description of something that has happened *Judy gave us an amusing account of her holiday.* 2. Money you keep in a bank *Inky put some of her money into her bank account.* 3. **on account of** Because of *He's late on account of very bad traffic.* **NOUN**

accountant /ɐcountɘnt/
Someone who checks that people's money records are correct **NOUN**

accurate /acyɘrɘt/
Completely correct **ADJECTIVE**

accuse /ɐcuez/
To blame someone for doing something wrong **VERB**
David accused me of stealing his pencil.

ace /ais/
1. A playing card with just one symbol or mark on it *the ace of diamonds* 2. An expert *a flying ace* **NOUN**

ache¹ /aic/
A pain in your body that keeps on hurting **NOUN**

ache² /aic/
To hurt **VERB**
When Bee flies a long way, her wings ache.

a

achieve /əcheev/
To be successful in doing something VERB
• **achievement** /əcheevmənt/ NOUN

acid[1] /asid/
A type of chemical that can burn NOUN

acid[2] /asid/
Sour or bitter-tasting, like lemons
ADJECTIVE

acorn /aicorn/
A small nut that grows on oak trees
NOUN

acre /aicer/
A measurement of land NOUN

acrobat /acrəbat/
An entertainer who performs difficult jumps or balancing tricks, usually in the circus NOUN

• **acrobatic** /acrəbatic/ ADJECTIVE

across /əcros/
1. From one side of something to the other *Do you think you'll be able to swim across?* 2. On the opposite side of something *My aunt lives across the street.*
ADVERB, PREPOSITION

act[1] /act/
1. An action *What a generous act!*
2. One of the parts that a play is divided into *I really enjoyed Act Three.* NOUN

act[2] /act/
1. To do something or behave in a special way *He was acting strangely.*
2. To play a part in a film or play VERB

action /acshen/
1. Something that is done *His actions were very brave.* 2. Something happening, especially in a story *I liked the book, it had lots of exciting action.* 3. A strong or clear movement *The actions to this song are easy to learn.* NOUN

active /activ/
Always doing lots of things ADJECTIVE
I've had a very active day.

activity /activətee/
1. Something you spend your time doing *Inky organized lots of interesting activities for Bee and Snake.* 2. Being busy doing lots of things NOUN

actor /acter/
Someone who plays a part in a play or film NOUN

actor

actress

actress /actres/
A woman playing a part in a play or film NOUN

A

actual /acchooel/
Real ADJECTIVE
Were these his actual words?
• **actually** /acchooelee/ ADVERB

adapt /edapt/
1. To change something so it can
be used for a different purpose
2. To change, as you become more
familiar with a new situation *It might
take a few weeks to adapt to your new
school.* VERB
• **adaptable** /edaptebel/ ADJECTIVE

add /ad/
1. To put numbers or things together
Beat the eggs, then add milk and sugar.
2. To say something else VERB

addict /adict/
Someone who cannot stop doing
something, such as a drug addict NOUN

addition /edishen/
Putting things or numbers together NOUN
• **additional** /edishenel/ Extra
ADJECTIVE

address /edres/
1. The number or name of your house
and other details of the place where you
live 2. A speech NOUN

Kate Stephen,
25 Tree Lane,
LONDON
NW3 U.K.

adequate /adequet/
Just enough ADJECTIVE

adhesive /edheesiv/
Another word for glue NOUN
• **adhesive** /edheesiv/ Sticky
ADJECTIVE *adhesive tape*

adjacent /ejaisent/
Next to something ADJECTIVE
Inky was singing in the adjacent room.

adjective /ajectiv/
A word that tells you more about
someone or something NOUN
▶ PARTS OF SPEECH, pages 6 and 7

adjust /ejust/
1. To change something slightly so it is
better or more accurate 2. To change,
as you become more familiar with a new
situation *Unfortunately, John just can't
seem to adjust to his new school.* VERB
• **adjustment** /ejusment/ NOUN

admiral /admerel/
An important person in the navy who is
in charge of a group of ships NOUN

admire /edmieer/
1. To like and respect someone or
something very much 2. To look at
something with pleasure *Bee and Inky
admired the view.* VERB

admit /edmit/
1. To say that something is true
2. To let someone in VERB

adopt /edopt/
1. To take someone else's child into your
family 2. To start using new methods or
ideas that you have been shown VERB

a

adore /ədor/
To love someone or something very much
VERB
• **adorable** /ədorrəbəl/ ADJECTIVE

adrift /ədrift/
Not fixed to anything and carried along by the wind or water ADVERB, **ADJECTIVE**
The boat was adrift.

adult /adult/
A fully grown person or animal NOUN

advance /ədvans/
To move forward VERB

advantage /ədvantij/
Something that makes you more likely to succeed, or makes a situation easier or more pleasant NOUN

adventure /ədvencher/
An exciting or dangerous event NOUN

adverb /adverb/
A word that describes a verb and tells you when, where or how something happens NOUN
▶ PARTS OF SPEECH, pages 6 and 7

advertise /advertiez/
To tell lots of people about something, especially something you would like them to buy VERB
• **advert** /advert/ or **advertisement** /advertisment/ NOUN

advice /ədvies/
Something you say to someone to help them decide what to do NOUN
• **advise** /ədviez/ VERB

aerial /eəreeəl/
A piece of wire that is used to receive and send out radio and television programmes NOUN

aeroplane /eərəplain/
A vehicle with wings and an engine that flies in the air NOUN

affect /əfect/
To change or influence someone or something in some way VERB
These problems affect many people.

affection /əfecshən/
Another word for love or liking NOUN

afford /əford/
To have enough money to buy something VERB

afloat /əfloat/
Floating on water ADVERB

afraid /əfraid/
1. Frightened 2. Sorry *I'm afraid I can't help you.* ADJECTIVE

after /after/
1. Later than *You eat dessert after your meal.* 2. Behind someone or something *I ran after the dog.* 3. Following *Friday is the day after Thursday.*
PREPOSITION, ADVERB, CONJUNCTION

afternoon /afternoon/
The part of the day between midday and evening NOUN

afterwards /afterwerdz/
After that ADVERB
I'm at work, but I can meet you afterwards.

A

again /əgain/
One more time **ADVERB**

against /əgainst/
1. Touching *Inky was leaning against the wall.* 2. On the opposite side of a game or argument *The teams are playing against each other today.* **PREPOSITION**

Inky was leaning against the wall.

age /aij/
1. The number of years that someone has lived or that something has existed 2. A long period of time **NOUN**

agent /aijent/
Someone who organizes things for people **NOUN**

aggravate /agrəvait/
To annoy someone or make something worse **VERB**

aggressive /əgresiv/
Very angry and ready to fight **ADJECTIVE**

agile /ajiel/
Able to move quickly and easily **ADJECTIVE**
• **agility** /ajilətee/ **NOUN**

ago /əgoa/
In the past **ADVERB**
I started playing tennis two years ago.

agony /agənee/
Great pain **NOUN**

agree /əgree/
1. To say yes to something 2. To have the same opinion as someone else
I hope you agree with me. **VERB**
• **agreement** /əgreemənt/ **NOUN**

agriculture /agriculcher/
Growing fruit and vegetables on the land **NOUN**

aground /əground/
Stuck on the bottom of the sea or a river because the water is not deep enough **ADVERB**

The ship ran aground and was badly damaged.

ahead /əhed/
1. In front 2. In or into the future
We must plan ahead. **ADJECTIVE, ADVERB**

ahoy /əhoi/
A word that a sailor shouts to call for attention **INTERJECTION**
Ship ahoy!

aid /aid/
Another word for help **NOUN, VERB**

ail /ail/
An old-fashioned word meaning to make someone sick **VERB**

aim[1] /aim/
An intention or plan **NOUN**
• **aimless** /aimləs/ **ADJECTIVE**

a

aim[2] /aim/
1. To point an object at something that you are trying to hit 2. To try to achieve something *We should all aim to do well in the exams.* VERB

air /eer/
The different gases that we breathe, and that make up the atmosphere on earth NOUN
• **airborne** /eerborn/ Moving in the air ADJECTIVE

aircraft /eercraft/
Any flying vehicle NOUN
■ **aircraft** /eercraft/ PLURAL

air force /eer fors/
The part of an army that uses planes NOUN

airmail /eermail/
1. Letters sent by plane 2. A way of sending letters by plane NOUN

airport /eerport/
A place where people can get on or off planes NOUN

aisle /iel/
A space to walk between rows of seats or shelves NOUN

ajar /ejar/
Slightly open ADVERB, ADJECTIVE
Inky left the door ajar so Bee could come in.

alarm /elarm/
1. Something that warns you about danger, usually by making a loud noise *Listen, it's the fire alarm!* 2. A sudden feeling of fear NOUN

alarm clock /elarm cloc/
A clock that sounds a bell to wake you up at a certain time NOUN

albatross /albetros/
A big white sea bird with very long wings NOUN

album /albem/
A book in which collections of things like photos or stamps can be kept NOUN

alcohol /alcehol/
A strong drink such as wine or beer NOUN
• **alcoholic** /alceholic/ ADJECTIVE

alcove /alcoav/
A space in the wall of a room where you can put things such as a chair NOUN

ale /ail/
A type of beer NOUN

alert /elert/
Wide awake and ready to act ADJECTIVE

algae /algee/
A type of simple water plant such as seaweed NOUN

alien /aileeen/
A creature from another planet NOUN
The book was about aliens from Mars.

alike /eliek/
Very similar to one another ADJECTIVE, ADVERB *Margaret and her sister look alike.*

alive /əliev/
Living now and not dead **ADJECTIVE**

all /awl/
1. The whole of something *Snake ate all the cake.* 2. Everyone or everything *Let's all go together.* 3. Completely *My shoes are all dirty.* **ADJECTIVE, ADVERB, PRONOUN**

allergy /alerjee/
A bad reaction that your body has to something you eat, drink or touch **NOUN**
• **allergic** /əlerjic/ **ADJECTIVE**

alley /alee/
A narrow path between buildings **NOUN**

alligator /aligaiter/
An animal like a crocodile that has short legs and a long mouth with very sharp teeth **NOUN**

allotment /əlotment/
A small piece of land that someone rents to grow vegetables **NOUN**

allow /əlou/
To let happen **VERB**
Inky allowed Bee to use her computer.

all right /awl riet/
Or **alright**. 1. Good, but not excellent
2. Safe and well *Are you all right?*
3. Another way of saying yes
4. Used when you want someone to give permission for something, or to agree with what you do *Is it all right to open the window?* **ADJECTIVE, ADVERB, INTERJECTION**

almond /ahmend/
A type of flat pale nut that tastes slightly sweet **NOUN**

almost /awlmoast/
Very nearly **ADVERB**
It's almost eight o'clock.

alone /əloan/
Without anyone or anything else
ADJECTIVE, ADVERB

along /əlong/
1. Moving forward *We're driving along a very narrow road.* 2. From one end of something to the other *The road runs along the river.* **PREPOSITION, ADVERB**

aloud /əloud/
In a loud voice so people can hear **ADVERB**

alphabet /alfəbet/
All the letters used in a language, placed in order **NOUN**
• **alphabetical** /alfəbeticəl/ Arranged in the order of the alphabet **ADJECTIVE**

already /awlredee/
1. By or before a particular time
Snake had already eaten when Bee arrived.
2. Sooner than expected *Have you finished already?* **ADVERB**

alright /awlriet/
▶ **all right**
ADJECTIVE, ADVERB, INTERJECTION

also /awlsoa/
Used to include something or someone else in what you say **ADVERB**
Can I come also?

altar /awlter/
A special table used in religious ceremonies **NOUN**

alter /awlter/
To change **VERB**
• **alteration** /awlteraishen/ **NOUN**

a

alternate /awlternait/
If things alternate, one thing comes first and then the other, in a regular pattern
VERB

• **alternate** /awlternet/ ADJECTIVE

alternative[1] /awlternetiv/
Another choice or possibility NOUN

alternative[2] /awlternetiv/
Another ADJECTIVE
Is there an alternative road we can take?

although /awlthoa/
Used for saying something that makes another part of the sentence surprising
CONJUNCTION *Although it's late, I'm not tired.*

altogether /awltegether/
In total, counting everything or everyone
ADVERB *Bee has six pots of honey altogether.*

aluminium /alemineeem/
A silver-coloured metal that is not very heavy NOUN

always /awlwaiz/
1. All the time *Snake is always hungry.*
2. Every time *I always remember to brush my teeth.* 3. For ever *Inky will always love reading and writing.* ADVERB

am /am/
▶ **be** VERB

a.m. /ai em/
Used to show the time in the morning. It is short for 'ante meridiem', which means 'before midday' *We start school at 9 a.m.*

amateur /ameter/
Someone who does an activity for enjoyment, not for payment NOUN

amaze /emaiz/
To surprise someone very much VERB
• **amazing** /emaizing/ ADJECTIVE

amber /amber/
1. A yellow-brown substance often used in jewellery 2. A yellow-brown colour
NOUN

ambition /ambishen/
1. A strong wish to be or to do something *My ambition is to be a teacher.*
2. A strong wish for success *I have a lot of ambition.* NOUN
• **ambitious** /ambishes/ ADJECTIVE

ambulance /ambyelens/
A vehicle for taking sick or injured people to the hospital NOUN

ambush /amboosh/
To make a surprise attack on someone from a hiding place VERB
• **ambush** /amboosh/ NOUN

ammunition /amyenishen/
Something that can be fired from a weapon, such as bullets NOUN

amoeba /emeebe/
A tiny creature with only one cell NOUN

among /emung/
Or **amongst** /emungst/ 1. Surrounded by, or in the middle of, something *Inky sat among the flowers.* 2. Included in a group of people or things *Tim is among the best readers in his class.* 3. Between
Let's share the cake amongst us. PREPOSITION

A

amount[1] /əmount/
1. A quantity or value 2. The total of
a number of things added together
Do you have the full amount? NOUN

amount[2] /əmount/
amount to To add up to a particular
total VERB

amphibian /amfibeeən/
An animal that lives both on land and in
water, such as a frog NOUN

ample /ampəl/
More than enough, plenty ADJECTIVE
We had ample time to finish our game.

amuse /əmuez/
To make someone laugh or smile VERB
• **amusement** /əmuezmənt/ NOUN
• **amusement park** /əmuezmənt park/
  NOUN
• **amusing** /əmuezing/ ADJECTIVE

an /an/
Used instead of 'a' before words starting
with a vowel sound or a silent 'h'
INDEFINITE ARTICLE   *an ant • an hour*

anaesthetic /anəsthetic/
A drug that stops you feeling pain NOUN

anagram /anəgram/
A word with the same letters as another
word, but in a different order NOUN
'Last' is an anagram of 'salt'.

analyse /anəliez/
To examine something very carefully to
find out how it is made or put together
VERB

anatomy /ənatəmee/
1. All the parts of the body and how
they work together 2. The study of
the body, and how it is built NOUN

ancestor /ansester/
A person in your family who lived a long
time ago NOUN

anchor /angcer/
A heavy piece of metal that is fixed
to a ship by a chain. It is dropped into
the water to stop the ship from floating
away NOUN

anchovy /anchevee/
A small fish with a salty taste NOUN

ancient /ainshent/
Very old ADJECTIVE

and /and/
1. A word used to join words or
sentences *Go upstairs and brush your hair.*
2. Plus *Add two and two.* 3. Used to
include something or someone else in
what you say *I'm buying tea and coffee.*
CONJUNCTION

angel /ainjel/
1. A messenger from God
2. A person who does good things NOUN

anger /angger/
A strong feeling you get that makes
you want to say or do bad things
when something bad happens NOUN
• **angry** /anggree/ ADJECTIVE

angle /anggel/
The space between two straight lines
that join each other at a point NOUN

angler /anggler/
Someone who catches fish with a
fishing rod NOUN

a

anguish /anggwish/
Great pain or suffering NOUN

animal /animəl/
Any living creature that can move around. Birds, fish, snakes and insects are all animals but plants are not NOUN

animation /animaishən/
A film in which drawings appear to be moving NOUN
• **animated** /animaitid/ ADJECTIVE

ankle /angkəl/
The place where your foot and leg are connected NOUN
▶ **PARTS OF THE BODY**, page 18

anniversary /aniversəree/
A day when people remember a special event that happened on the same day in another year NOUN
Today is our wedding anniversary.

announce /ənouns/
To tell everyone about something VERB
• **announcement** /ənounsmənt/ NOUN

annoy /ənoi/
To make someone rather angry VERB
• **annoyed** /ənoid/ ADJECTIVE
• **annoying** /ənoiing/ ADJECTIVE

annual /anuel/
Happening once every year ADJECTIVE

anonymous /ənonimes/
By someone who does not give their name or is not known ADJECTIVE
We found some old anonymous letters.

anorak /anerak/
A short warm raincoat with a hood NOUN

another /ənuther/
1. One more *Snake wanted another egg sandwich.* 2. Different, or a different one *Bee wanted another sort of sandwich.*
ADJECTIVE, PRONOUN

answer /anser/
1. A reply to a question or letter
2. A solution to a problem NOUN
• **answer** /anser/ VERB

ant /ant/
A small insect that lives in a large group NOUN

Antarctic /antarctic/
The very cold part of the world around the South Pole NOUN
▶ **WORLD MAP**, page 14

anteater /anteeter/
An animal with a long nose that eats ants NOUN

antelope /anteloap/
An animal like a deer that can run very fast NOUN

antenna¹ /antene/
An aerial NOUN

antenna² /antene/
One of the two long thin parts on the head of insects or animals such as snails NOUN

■ **antennae** /antenie/ PLURAL

A

anthem /anthem/
A song of praise NOUN
Many countries have a national anthem.

antibiotic /anteebieotic/
A drug used to kill bacteria in your body when you have an infection
NOUN

antibody /anteebodee/
A substance people make in their blood that fights disease NOUN

anticipate /antisipait/
To be ready and waiting for something to happen VERB

anticlockwise /anteeclocwiez/
Moving in the opposite direction to the hands of a clock ADVERB, ADJECTIVE

antidote /anteedoat/
A substance that fights against a poison
NOUN

antique /anteec/
Something very old and valuable such as a piece of furniture NOUN
• **antique** /anteec/ ADJECTIVE

antiseptic /anteeseptic/
A substance that kills germs NOUN

antler /antler/
A horn that grows on the head of a male deer NOUN

antonym /antenim/
A word that means the opposite of another word NOUN
'Big' is the antonym of 'small'.

anvil /anvil/
A big block of iron used for hammering hot pieces of metal into shape NOUN

anxious /angkshes/
1. Very worried *I feel anxious about the exam.* 2. Eager *I'm anxious to get home.*
ADJECTIVE
• **anxiety** /angzieetee/ NOUN

any /enee/
1. Some *Do you have any money?*
2. Every *Any teacher will tell you.*
3. One *Take any card you like.*
4. **any more** If something does not happen any more, it stops happening
ADJECTIVE, PRONOUN, ADVERB

anybody /eneebodee/
Any person PRONOUN

anyhow /eneehou/
Another word for anyway ADVERB

anymore /eneemor/
Or **any more**. If something does not happen anymore, it stops happening
ADVERB

anyone /eneewun/
Another word for anybody PRONOUN

anything /eneething/
Something of any kind PRONOUN

anyway /eneewai/
1. No matter what happens, in any case *I'm feeling tired but I'll go anyway.*
2. Used in a conversation when you want to change the subject *Anyway, let's sit down and eat.* ADVERB

anywhere /eneeweer/
In, at or to any place ADVERB
I didn't go anywhere, I stayed at home.

a

apart[1] /əpart/
1. With an amount of space or time in between *The school and the library are far apart.* · *I'm seeing two plays. They are one week apart.* 2. To or into pieces *take apart* · *fall apart* ADVERB

apart[2] /əpart/
apart from Except for PREPOSITION
The dog was black apart from a white ear.

apartment /əpartmənt/
Another word for a flat NOUN

ape /aip/
A large monkey with long arms and no tail, such as a chimpanzee or gorilla NOUN

apologize /əpoləjiez/
To say sorry for something VERB
· **apology** /əpoləjee/ NOUN

apostrophe /əpostrəfee/
1. A punctuation mark (') that shows where a letter or letters have been left out of a word *I've is short for 'I have'.*
2. The same mark, used to show that something belongs to someone *I like that girl's dress.* NOUN

apparatus /apəraitəs/
Equipment used for a particular purpose NOUN *They got the gym apparatus out.*

appeal /əpeel/
1. To ask for something such as help or information 2. If something appeals to you, you like it very much VERB
· **appeal** /əpeel/ NOUN

appear /əpier/
1. If something or someone appears somewhere, you begin to see them
2. To seem *Nobody appears to be at home.*
3. To stand in front of a group of people to entertain them or to answer questions VERB

appearance /əpierəns/
1. The way something or someone looks
2. When you appear somewhere NOUN

appetite /apətiet/
A wish for food NOUN

applaud /əplawd/
To show that you like something by clapping your hands VERB
· **applause** /əplawz/ NOUN

apple /apəl/
A round red, green or yellow fruit NOUN
▶ FRUIT AND VEGETABLES, page 15

appliance /əpliəns/
A machine used in the home, such as a toaster or dishwasher NOUN

application /aplicaishən/
When you ask for something in writing such as a job NOUN

apply /əplie/
1. To put or spread one thing on another *Apply a thin layer of paint.* 2. To ask for something in writing such as a job VERB

appointment /əpointmənt/
A time you arrange to see someone NOUN
· **appoint** /əpoint/ VERB

appreciate /əpreesheeait/
1. To be grateful for something *I really appreciate your help.* 2. To like or value something very much *Snake appreciates good food.* 3. To understand something *I appreciate why you did it.* VERB
· **appreciation** /əpreesheeaishən/ NOUN

A

apprentice /əprentis/
A person who is working for someone and learning a skill from them NOUN
• **apprenticeship** /əprentiship/ NOUN

approach /əproach/
To get nearer to something or someone VERB

appropriate /əprɔɑpree ət/
Suitable ADJECTIVE

approve /əprɔɔv/
If you approve of someone or something, you have a good opinion of them VERB
• **approval** /əprɔɔvəl/ NOUN

approximate /əproximət/
Slightly more or less than a number or amount ADJECTIVE
What's the approximate time he arrives?

apricot /aipricot/
A small soft yellow or orange fruit NOUN
▶ **FRUIT AND VEGETABLES**, page 15

April /aipril/
The fourth month of the year NOUN
▶ **CALENDAR**, page 13

apron /aiprən/
Something you wear over the front of your clothes to stop them getting dirty NOUN

aquarium /əquɛɛree əm/
1. A large glass container for keeping fish 2. A building where you can go to see fish and other water animals NOUN

aquatic /əquatic/
Living, growing or happening in water ADJECTIVE

arachnid /əracnid/
An animal belonging to a group that includes spiders and scorpions NOUN

arc /arc/
A curved line, or a part of a circle NOUN

arch /arch/
The curved part at the top of a door or window, or under a bridge NOUN

archaeology /arceeolɘjee/
The study of those things left in or on the ground by people who lived in the past NOUN
• **archaeological** /arcee ɘlojicəl/ ADJECTIVE

archery /archeree/
The skill of using a bow and arrow NOUN
• **archer** /archer/ NOUN

architect /arcitect/
Someone who designs buildings NOUN

Arctic /arctic/
The very cold part of the world around the North Pole NOUN
▶ **WORLD MAP**, page 14

are /ar/
▶ **be** VERB

a

area /eɐreeɐ/
1. Any place, or piece of ground
2. The size of a surface NOUN

arena /ɐreenɐ/
A large open space surrounded by seats where sports or concerts take place NOUN

argue /argue/
To talk with someone in an angry way because you do not agree with them VERB
• **argument** /argyemɐnt/ NOUN
• **argumentative** /argyementɐtiv/ Always arguing ADJECTIVE

arid /arid/
Very dry ADJECTIVE
Deserts are arid places.

arise /ɐriez/
1. To happen *A problem may arise.*
2. Another way of saying rise VERB
■ arose, arisen

arithmetic /ɐrithmetic/
The skill of adding, subtracting, multiplying and dividing numbers NOUN

ark /ark/
A large boat described in the Bible that was built by Noah to save people and animals from the flood NOUN

arm /arm/
The part of your body between your shoulder and your hand NOUN
▶ PARTS OF THE BODY, page 18

armada /armardɐ/
A large group of ships ready for war NOUN

armadillo /armedilɒɐ/
An animal with a long nose and tail and a very hard shell NOUN

armchair /armcheer/
A big chair with parts at the side to rest your arms on NOUN

armed /armd/
Carrying a weapon such as a gun ADJECTIVE

armour /armer/
1. A metal covering to protect a soldier's body in past times 2. A metal layer that protects things such as tanks and battleships NOUN
• **armoury** /armeree/ A place where weapons are kept NOUN

army /armee/
The men and women of a country who are ready to fight in a war NOUN

aroma /ɐroɐmɐ/
A strong and usually pleasant smell of things like food and coffee NOUN

arose /ɐroɑz/
PAST TENSE ▶ **arise**

around /ɐroʊnd/
1. Going all the way round something *We are putting up a fence around the field.*
2. In the opposite direction *Let's turn around and go home.* 3. In or to several places *She's always rushing around.* · *Don't leave your things lying around.* 4. About *There are around 600 children in the school.*
PREPOSITION, ADVERB

arrange /ɐrainj/
1. To put things in a special order
2. To make plans for something to happen VERB
• **arrangement** /ɐrainjment/ NOUN

A

arrest /ɐrest/
If the police arrest someone, they take them prisoner VERB
• **arrest** /ɐrest/ NOUN

arrive /ɐriev/
1. To get where you are going to
2. To come or happen   *Your birthday has arrived!* VERB
• **arrival** /ɐrievɐl/ NOUN

arrow /arɒɐ/
1. A long thin stick with a sharp point that is shot from a bow 2. A shape (➜) that points to the direction of something, often used on maps and road signs NOUN

arsenal /arsɐnɐl/
A place where many weapons are stored NOUN

arson /arsɐn/
A crime in which someone sets fire to a building NOUN

art /art/
1. Drawing, painting and sculpture
2. A skill in doing or making something NOUN

artefact /artifact/
An object made by people in the past, such as a tool or some jewellery NOUN

artery /artɐree/
A tube that carries blood from your heart to the rest of your body NOUN

article /articɐl/
1. Any particular or separate thing   *an article of clothing* 2. Something that someone has written in a newspaper or magazine   *Did you read that fashion article?*
3. A grammar word for referring to 'the' (the definite article) or 'a' (the indefinite article) NOUN

artificial /artifishɐl/
Looking natural or real but made by people or machines ADJECTIVE
The artificial flowers were made of paper.

artist /artist/
A person who creates art, especially paintings NOUN
• **artistic** /artistic/ ADJECTIVE

as /az/
1. At the same time   *Steve left just as I was walking through the door.* 2. In a particular way   *He works as an English teacher.*
3. Used when comparing things   *His hair was as white as snow.* 4. What   *Can we do as we like?* 5. Because   *Let's stay in as it's raining.* CONJUNCTION, PREPOSITION

ascend /ɐsend/
1. To go up in the air 2. To climb up VERB
• **ascent** /ɐsent/ NOUN

ash[1] /ash/
A powder left over after something has burnt NOUN

ash[2] /ash/
A type of tall tree with hard wood NOUN

ashamed /ɐshaimd/
Feeling bad because you have done something wrong ADJECTIVE

ashore /ɐshɒr/
From the sea towards or onto the land ADVERB   *The sailor pulled the boat ashore.*

aside /ɐsied/
On or to one side ADVERB

a

ask /ask/
1. To say something so you get an answer to a question 2. To tell someone you want them to give you something or do something 3. To invite *Inky asked Snake and Bee to the party.* VERB

asleep /əsleep/
Sleeping ADJECTIVE

asphalt /asfawlt/
A black substance for making hard surfaces such as roads and paths NOUN

aspire /əspieer/
To aim to be or to do something, or hope to have something VERB
He aspires to be a doctor.

ass /as/
1. A donkey 2. A very stupid person NOUN

assault /əsawlt/
An attack NOUN
• **assault** /əsawlt/ VERB

assemble /əsembəl/
1. To meet all together in one place *Please assemble outside the school gates at three o'clock.* 2. To put together the parts of something *Where are the instructions to assemble the book shelves?* 3. To put together a group of people or things *We need to assemble a football team.* VERB
• **assembly** /əsemblee/ NOUN

assist /əsist/
To help someone do something VERB
• **assistance** /əsistens/ NOUN

assistant /əsistent/
1. A person who serves customers
2. A person who helps someone else do their job NOUN

associate /əsoasheeait/
1. **associate with** To spend time with a group of people 2. To connect something with something else in your mind VERB
• **association** /əsoaseeaishen/ NOUN

assume /əsuem/
To think that something is true, that may not be VERB

asterisk /asterisk/
A shape like a small star (*) used in writing, usually to draw someone's attention to something NOUN

asteroid /asteroid/
One of the thousands of rocks, much smaller than a planet, that moves around the sun NOUN

asthma /asme/
An illness that makes it hard to breathe NOUN
• **asthmatic** /asmatic/ ADJECTIVE, NOUN

astonish /əstonish/
To surprise someone very much VERB
• **astonished** /əstonisht/ ADJECTIVE
• **astonishing** /əstonishing/ ADJECTIVE
• **astonishment** /əstonishment/ NOUN

astray /əstrai/
go astray To become lost ADVERB

astronaut /astrenawt/
Someone who travels in space NOUN

A

astronomy /əstronəmee/
The study of the stars and planets NOUN

at /at/
1. Used for showing the position or direction of something *Someone's at the door. • Look at me!* 2. Used for showing time *Lunch is at one o'clock.* PREPOSITION

ate /ait/
PAST TENSE ▶ **eat**

athlete /athleet/
A person who has trained in a sport NOUN
• **athletic** /athletic/ ADJECTIVE

atlas /atləs/
A book of maps NOUN

atmosphere /atməsfier/
1. The air and gases that surround the earth 2. The feeling a place gives you *It has a warm friendly atmosphere.* NOUN

attach /ətach/
To join or fasten two things together VERB

attack /ətac/
To start to hit someone or fight with them VERB
• **attack** /ətac/ NOUN

attempt /ətempt/
To try very hard to do something VERB
• **attempt** /ətempt/ NOUN

attend /ətend/
To go to or be present at something VERB
to attend school
• **attendance** /ətendəns/ NOUN

attention /ətenshən/
Taking notice of something, interest NOUN
Pay attention, please! • Do I have your attention?

attic /atic/
A room just under the roof of a house NOUN

attitude /atitued/
What you think and feel about something NOUN

attract /ətract/
1. To make someone interested or cause them to like something *Bee attracted Inky's attention.* 2. To make something come nearer *Magnets attract metal.* VERB
• **attraction** /ətracshən/ NOUN

attractive /ətractiv/
Very pleasant, or nice to look at ADJECTIVE

audible /awdəbəl/
Easy to hear ADJECTIVE

audience /awdeeəns/
All the people who watch and listen to something NOUN
The whole audience enjoyed the play.

audio /awdeeoa/
Connected with sound ADJECTIVE
We need audio tapes for the tape recorder.

August /awgəst/
The eighth month of the year NOUN
▶ CALENDAR, page 13

aunt /ant/
1. The sister of your father or mother 2. The wife of your uncle NOUN
• **auntie** /antee/ NOUN

author /awther/
The writer of something such as a book or article NOUN

autograph /awtəgraf/
The name of someone famous in their own handwriting NOUN
• **autograph** /awtəgraf/ VERB

automatic /awtəmatic/
Working by itself without someone having to operate it ADJECTIVE
an automatic door
• **automatically** /awtəmaticəlee/ ADVERB

a

autumn /awtem/

The season between summer and winter

NOUN

▶ CALENDAR, page 13

available /evailebel/

1. Ready for you to get or use

The book will be available in the summer.

2. Free to do something Are you available this afternoon? ADJECTIVE

avalanche /avelanch/

A large amount of snow that falls down the side of a mountain NOUN

avenue /avenue/

A street, often with trees growing on each side NOUN

average /averij/

Normal or typical ADJECTIVE

avocado /avecahdoa/

A fruit shaped like a pear with a hard green skin NOUN

avoid /evoid/

To keep away from something or someone VERB

awake /ewaik/

Not sleeping ADJECTIVE

award /eword/

A prize, or special honour NOUN

aware /eweer/

Knowing about something ADJECTIVE

away /ewai/

1. From a place When I went up to him, he walked away. 2. Not in a place Joe must be away for the weekend. 3. From now or from here Summer is months away. · How far away is your house? ADVERB

awesome /awsem/

An informal way of saying excellent

ADJECTIVE

awful /awfel/

Very bad ADJECTIVE

awfully /awflee/

1. Very It's awfully late. 2. Very badly

ADVERB

awkward /awkwerd/

1. Clumsy 2. Difficult to deal with

3. Uncomfortable or embarrassed

ADJECTIVE

axe /ax/

A tool with a long handle and a big blade for chopping wood NOUN

axle /axel/

A metal bar connecting two wheels, for example on a car NOUN

B

baa /bah/
The sound made by a sheep or lamb
NOUN

baboon /bɐboon/
A big monkey with a long face that lives in Africa NOUN

baby /baibee/
A very young child NOUN
• **babysit** /baibeesit/ VERB

back[1] /bac/
1. In the opposite direction *Try not to look back.* 2. Where you were before *It's time to go back home.* 3. Again, or in return *Can you phone back later? · Give it back to me!* 4. Away from something *Stand back!*
ADVERB

back[2] /bac/
1. The part opposite the front *the back of your hand* 2. The part of your body from the back of your neck to the top of your legs NOUN

back[3] /bac/
At the back, behind something ADJECTIVE
the back door

backbone /bacbɒan/
The bones going down your back NOUN

background /bacground/
1. The back part of a picture or scene
2. Used about a sound that is not the main sound you are listening to *Music was playing in the background.* NOUN

backwards /bacwerdz/
In the opposite way or direction to usual
ADVERB

bacon /baicɐn/
Meat from a pig that is dried and salted
NOUN

bacteria /bactiereeɐ/
Tiny creatures that can cause disease
NOUN PLURAL

bad /bad/
1. Not good 2. Serious *There was a bad accident yesterday.* ADJECTIVE
■ worse, worst
• **badly** /badlee/ ADVERB

badge /baj/
A piece of cloth, plastic or metal that you wear as a sign of something, such as a school badge NOUN

badger[1] /bajer/
A grey animal with black and white stripes on its face that comes out at night NOUN

b

badger[2] /bajer/
To keep annoying someone because you want something VERB

bag /bag/
A container made of soft material for carrying things NOUN

bake /baik/
1. To cook something in the oven
2. To make bread or cakes VERB
• **baker** /baiker/ NOUN

balaclava /baleclahve/
A hat made of wool that covers the neck and head except for the face NOUN

balance /balens/
1. To keep something steady without letting it fall over 2. To keep yourself steady without falling VERB
• **balance** /balens/ NOUN

bald /bawld/
With no hair on your head ADJECTIVE

ball /bawl/
1. A round object used in games
2. An important event with dancing where people wear special clothes NOUN

balloon /beloon/
1. A small rubber container filled with air used as a toy 2. A big container filled with air used to travel in the sky NOUN

ballpoint /bawlpoint/
A pen that uses a tiny ball at the end to write with NOUN

banana /benane/
A tropical yellow fruit that is long and curved NOUN
▶ FRUIT AND VEGETABLES, page 15

band /band/
1. A group of musicians or people
2. A thin piece of cloth that goes around something 3. A thick line, or stripe NOUN

bandage /bandij/
A piece of cloth you put around a cut to protect it NOUN
• **bandage** /bandij/ VERB

bang[1] /bang/
A sudden loud noise NOUN

bang[2] /bang/
1. To hit something
2. To make a loud noise VERB

bank /bangk/
1. The ground along the side of a river
2. A place where money is kept NOUN

banner /baner/
A long piece of cloth with a message on it NOUN

bar[1] /bar/
1. A piece of something solid such as a bar of soap 2. A length of metal such as an iron bar 3. A place where people can buy drinks NOUN

bar[2] /bar/
To prevent someone from doing something or getting somewhere VERB

B

barbecue¹ /barbicue/
To cook food outside over hot coals
VERB

barbecue² /barbicue/
1. A container of hot coals for cooking food outside 2. A party outside where you eat barbecued food NOUN

barber /barber/
Someone who cuts men's hair NOUN

bare /beer/
1. Not covered with anything *If you have bare feet, you have no socks or shoes on.*
2. Empty *The room is bare.* ADJECTIVE

bargain /bargin/
Something you buy cheaply and is good value NOUN

bark¹ /bark/
The outer covering of a tree trunk NOUN

bark² /bark/
The short loud noise a dog makes NOUN
• **bark** /bark/ VERB

barley /barlee/
A plant with seeds that people use for food NOUN

barn /barn/
A large building used by farmers for storing crops NOUN

base /bais/
1. The bottom of something 2. A place where soldiers or sailors live and work NOUN

baseball /baisbawl/
A game played by two teams with a bat and ball NOUN

bash /bash/
To hit someone or something hard VERB

basic /baisic/
1. Most important or necessary
2. Very simple ADJECTIVE

basket /baskit/
A container for carrying or storing things, usually made from pieces of wire, plastic or wood woven together NOUN

basketball /baskitbawl/
A game in which two teams of people try to throw a ball into a high net NOUN

bat /bat/
1. A small flying animal with a body like a mouse 2. A piece of wood used to hit a ball in a game NOUN

bath¹ /bath/
1. A large water container that you sit in to wash your whole body
2. **have a bath** To sit in the bath and wash your body NOUN
• **bathroom** /bathroom/ NOUN

bath² /bath/
To wash someone in a bath VERB

b

battery /batree/
1. An object that stores electricity. Batteries are used to make things such as watches or radios work 2. A car battery is like a big square box that gives power to the car to make it start **NOUN**

battle /batəl/
A fight, usually between armies **NOUN**

bay /bai/
A part of the coast where the sea goes in towards the land and forms a curve **NOUN**

bazaar /bəzar/
1. A street market, usually in the Middle East 2. An event where things are sold to raise money **NOUN**

be /bee/
1. To exist *There may be a problem.*
2. To have a particular purpose or job *I want to be an actor.* 3. To have a particular feeling or quality *Don't be sad.* **VERB**
■ **am, are, is · being · was, were · been**

beach /beech/
An area of sand or stones where the land meets the sea **NOUN**

beads /beedz/
Small round balls of glass, plastic or wood with a hole in them that you can wear on a string around your neck or arm **NOUN PLURAL**

beak /beek/
The hard part of a bird's mouth **NOUN**

beam /beem/
1. A thick line of light that shines from something such as the sun 2. A long piece of wood or metal for building houses or bridges **NOUN**

bean /been/
One of many different types of seed that you can eat as a vegetable or use to make drinks. Beans include kidney beans and coffee beans **NOUN**
▶ **FRUIT AND VEGETABLES**, page 15

beanstalk /beenstawk/
The part of a plant that grows beans **NOUN**

bear¹ /beer/
A big wild animal with thick fur **NOUN**

bear² /beer/
1. To carry 2. If you cannot bear someone or something, you do not like them 3. To suffer **VERB**
■ **bore, borne**

beard /bierd/
The hair that grows on a man's chin **NOUN**

beat¹ /beet/
A regular musical rhythm **NOUN**

beat² /beet/
1. To hit many times 2. To do better than someone, usually in a competition 3. To move with a regular musical rhythm *My heart was beating fast.* **VERB**
■ **beat, beaten**

beautiful /buetifel/
1. Very nice to look at 2. Extremely pleasant *What beautiful music!* ADJECTIVE
• **beauty** /buetee/ NOUN

became /becaim/
PAST TENSE ▶ **become**

because /becoz/
1. Used for giving a reason for something *Snake was happy because it was his birthday.*
2. **because of** As a result of something CONJUNCTION

become /becum/
To start to be something, or to change into something VERB
■ **became, become**

bed /bed/
Something that you sleep on NOUN
• **bedbug** /bedbug/ NOUN
• **bedclothes** /bedcloathz/ Sheets and blankets NOUN
• **bedroom** /bedroom/ NOUN

bee /bee/
A flying insect that has a sting and makes honey NOUN

beech /beech/
A tall tree that is smooth and silvery with shiny leaves NOUN

beef /beef/
Meat from a cow NOUN
• **beefburger** /beefberger/ NOUN

beehive /beehiev/
A place where bees live NOUN

B

been /been/
PAST PARTICIPLE ▶ **be**

beep /beep/
A high sound made by an electronic machine such as a computer, or a car horn NOUN
• **beep** /beep/ VERB

beer /bier/
A drink containing alcohol, made from grain NOUN

beetle /beetel/
An insect with a round hard body and wings NOUN
▶ INSECTS, page 14

beetroot /beetroot/
A vegetable with a dark red root NOUN

before /befor/
1. Earlier than something *Brush your teeth before bed. · I've never seen her before.*
2. In front of something or someone *They played before a crowd of many thousands.*
PREPOSITION, ADVERB, CONJUNCTION

beg /beg/
1. To ask for food or money 2. To ask for something you want very much VERB
• **beggar** /beger/ NOUN

b

began /bɛgan/
PAST TENSE ▶ **begin**

begin /bɛgin/
To start VERB
- ■ began, begun
- **beginner** /bɛginer/ NOUN
- **beginning** /bɛgining/ NOUN

begun /bɛgun/
PAST TENSE ▶ **begin**

behave /bɛhaiv/
1. To do or say things in a certain way *Stop behaving like an idiot!* 2. To do or say things in a polite and proper way *I want you to behave yourself.* VERB
- **behaviour** /bɛhaivyer/ NOUN

behind[1] /bɛhiend/
1. At the back of something or someone *Stand right behind me.* 2. Not doing as well as someone *Jake is a bit behind now but he'll catch up.* 3. Late *I'm behind with my homework.* PREPOSITION, ADVERB

behind[2] /bɛhiend/
Another word for your bottom
NOUN

belch /belch/
To let air out noisily from your stomach through your mouth VERB
- **belch** /belch/ NOUN

believe /bɛleev/
1. To think something is true 2. To feel sure that something exists *Do you believe in ghosts?* VERB
- **belief** /bɛleef/ NOUN

bell /bel/
A metal cup that makes a ringing sound when hit NOUN

belly /belee/
Another word for your stomach NOUN

belong /bɛlong/
1. To be owned by someone or something *The umbrella belongs to Bee.* 2. To be a part of something *I belong to the Scouts.* 3. To be in the right place *The chair belongs under the table.* VERB

below /bɛloʊ/
1. In a lower place 2. Less than something *It is below freezing point.* PREPOSITION, ADVERB

belt /belt/
A piece of cloth that goes around your waist to hold your clothes up or in NOUN

bench /bench/
A long chair for more than one person, usually made of wood NOUN

bend /bend/
1. To make something curved, or to become curved 2. To lean over so that your head is nearer the ground *Inky bent down to pick a flower.* VERB
- ■ bent
- **bend** /bend/ A curve NOUN
- **bent** /bent/ Not straight ADJECTIVE

berry /beree/
Berries are little soft fruits with seeds NOUN

beside /bɛsied/
Next to, by the side of PREPOSITION

besides[1] /bɛsiedz/
Used to include something or someone else in what you say PREPOSITION
Do we need to buy anything besides eggs?

besides[2] /bɛsiedz/
Used for giving another reason for what you are saying ADVERB
I like walking. Besides, it's good exercise.

best[1] /best/
Better than anything else, most excellent
ADJECTIVE, ADVERB

B

best[2] /best/
1. Something or someone that is better than anything else 2. The biggest effort *I'll do my best to be good.* **NOUN**

bet /bet/
1. To risk some money by guessing what will happen in a game or race. If you win you get more money but if not you lose the money 2. To say you are fairly sure of something *I bet you're tired.* **VERB**
■ **bet** or **betted**
• **bet** /bet/ **NOUN**

betray /betrai/
To harm someone by giving secret information to an enemy or by not keeping a promise **VERB**

better /beter/
1. Of a higher quality than something else 2. More able 3. Not sick any more
ADJECTIVE, **ADVERB**

between /between/
1. In the space separating two things or times *Bee is standing between Snake and Inky.* 2. Used to show a connection or choice *There's a strong friendship between the two boys.* • *Snake must choose between chocolate or coffee cake.* 3. Among *Let's divide the money between us.*
PREPOSITION, **ADVERB**

Bee is standing between Snake and Inky.

beware /beweer/
To be careful about something **VERB**

beyond /beyond/
Further than, or later than **PREPOSITION**, **ADVERB** *The rocket flew beyond the moon.*

bib /bib/
Something that babies wear around their necks to protect their clothes while eating **NOUN**

bible
The holy book of the Christian or Jewish religion **NOUN**

bicycle /biesicel/
A vehicle with two wheels **NOUN**

big /big/
Large or important **ADJECTIVE**

bike /biek/
Short for bicycle **NOUN**

bikini /bikeenee/
A piece of clothing in two separate pieces that girls and women wear for swimming **NOUN**

bill /bil/
A piece of paper showing the amount you have to pay for something **NOUN**

billion /bileeen/
A thousand million **NOUN**

bin /bin/
1. A container you put rubbish in
2. A container you store things in such as bread **NOUN**

bingo /binggoa/
A game in which numbers are called out and you match them to the numbers on your card. Bingo is often played for money or prizes **NOUN**

b

binoculars /binocyelerz/
A special pair of glasses, like short telescopes, for looking at things far away
NOUN PLURAL

bird /berd/
An animal with feathers, wings and two legs **NOUN**

birth /berth/
The time when a baby is born **NOUN**
· **birthday** /berthdai/ **NOUN**

biscuit /biscit/
A small dry flat cake **NOUN**

bit[1] /bit/
1. A small piece or amount of something
2. Slightly *Sally was a bit tired.* **NOUN**

bit[2] /bit/
PAST TENSE ▶ **bite**[1]

bite[1] /biet/
To cut into something with your teeth
VERB
■ bit, bitten

bite[2] /biet/
1. The action of biting
2. A small amount to eat **NOUN**

bitten /biten/
PAST PARTICIPLE ▶ **bite**[1]

bitter /biter/
Strong and not tasting very pleasant
ADJECTIVE
· **bitterly** /biterlee/ Very **ADVERB**
  Today it's bitterly cold.

black /blac/
A very dark colour, like coal
NOUN, ADJECTIVE

blackbird /blacberd/
A common bird that is black with a yellow beak **NOUN**

blackboard /blacbord/
A big black board that you write on with chalk **NOUN**

bladder /blader/
A part of the body shaped like a bag that holds liquid waste **NOUN**

blade /blaid/
1. The part of a knife or tool that cuts
2. A single piece of grass **NOUN**

blame[1] /blaim/
To say that something bad is the fault of someone or something **VERB**

blame[2] /blaim/
The responsibility for doing something bad **NOUN**

blank /blangk/
With nothing written or recorded on it **ADJECTIVE**
a blank page

blanket /blangkit/
A warm cover for a bed **NOUN**

blast /blast/
A loud explosion **NOUN**

B

blaze /blaiz/
To burn very brightly VERB
• **blaze** /blaiz/ A bright fire NOUN

blazer /blaizer/
A jacket, usually part of a school uniform
NOUN

bleak /bleek/
1. Cold and unpleasant *It's a bleak day today.* 2. Sad and without any hope *a bleak time* ADJECTIVE

bled /bled/
PAST TENSE ▶ **bleed**

bleed /bleed/
To lose blood from your body VERB
■ **bled**

blend /blend/
To mix things together VERB
• **blender** /blender/ A machine that mixes foods and makes them liquid
NOUN

blew /bloo/
PAST TENSE ▶ **blow**[1]

blind[1] /bliend/
Not able to see ADJECTIVE

blind[2] /bliend/
A type of screen made of cloth or plastic that you pull down over a window
NOUN

blindfold /bliendfoald/
To cover someone's eyes VERB
• **blindfold** /bliendfoald/ NOUN

blink /blingk/
To close your eyes and open them again quickly VERB

blister /blister/
A small bubble on your skin filled with liquid NOUN

blizzard /blizerd/
A storm of wind and snow NOUN

blob /blob/
A drop of something thick or sticky such as paint or glue NOUN

block[1] /bloc/
1. A big hard lump of something such as wood or stone 2. A big building containing flats or offices NOUN

block[2] /bloc/
To stop anything passing by, usually by putting something in the way VERB

blond /blond/
A blond boy or man has light yellow hair
ADJECTIVE
• **blond** /blond/ NOUN

blond

blonde

blonde /blond/
A blonde girl or woman has light yellow hair ADJECTIVE
• **blonde** /blond/ NOUN

blood /blud/
The red liquid that your heart pumps around your body NOUN

b

bloom /bloom/
To come into flower VERB
• **bloom** /bloom/ NOUN

blossom /blosəm/
The flowers on a tree in spring NOUN
• **blossom** /blosəm/ VERB

blot /blot/
A dirty mark such as an ink blot
NOUN

blouse /blouz/
A shirt for a girl or woman NOUN

blow[1] /bloa/
1. To force air to come out of your
mouth 2. To force air into or along
The wind is blowing. 3. To move along
in the wind *My hat blew away.* VERB
■ **blew, blown**
• **blowy** /bloaee/ Windy ADJECTIVE

blow[2] /bloa/
A hard knock NOUN
a blow with a hammer

blown /bloan/
PAST PARTICIPLE ▶ **blow**[1]

blue /bloo/
The colour of the sky on a sunny day
with no clouds NOUN, ADJECTIVE

bluebell /bloobel/
A wild plant with blue flowers like bells
NOUN

blunder /blunder/
A big mistake NOUN

blunt /blunt/
Not pointed or sharp ADJECTIVE

blurred /blerd/
Or **blurry** /blerree/ Not very clear
ADJECTIVE *The photo was blurry.*

blush /blush/
To go red in the face because you are
shy or embarrassed VERB

board /bord/
1. A flat piece of something such as
wood 2. Short for blackboard or
noticeboard NOUN

boast /boast/
To say good things about yourself
because you want other people to
have a high opinion of you VERB
He's boasting about how clever he is.

boat /boat/
Something in which people travel on
water, that is smaller than a ship NOUN

bob /bob/
To move up and down quickly VERB

body /bodee/
1. Your complete shape, including head,
arms and legs *Snake has spots all over
his body.* 2. Your shape, not including
the head, arms and legs *I have long
legs but a short body.* ▶ PARTS OF THE BODY,
page 18 NOUN

B

bogeyman /bʊɑgeeman/
A frightening person that exists in the imagination and makes children afraid
NOUN

boil /bɔil/
1. If you boil a liquid or if the liquid boils, it becomes hot and starts to bubble and steam 2. To cook something in boiling water **VERB**

• **boiler** /bɔiler/ A container of hot water for heating a house **NOUN**
• **boiling** /bɔiling/ **ADJECTIVE**

bold /bɔuld/
Not afraid to do dangerous things
ADJECTIVE

bomb /bom/
A weapon that explodes, killing people and causing damage **NOUN**
• **bomb** /bom/ **VERB**

bone /bɔun/
One of the hard parts inside your body. All your bones together form your skeleton **NOUN**

bonfire /bonfieer/
A big fire that you make outside **NOUN**

bonnet /bonit/
1. A hat that is tied under the chin, usually worn by babies or women
2. The front part of a car that covers the engine and can be lifted open **NOUN**

bony /bɔunee/
1. Without much flesh covering the bones *She had bony hands.* 2. With lots of little bones *I don't like bony fish.* **ADJECTIVE**

book[1] /bʊk/
Printed sheets of paper with words or pictures, fastened together inside a cover **NOUN**
• **bookcase** /bʊkcais/
Shelves for putting books on **NOUN**
• **bookshelf** /bʊkshelf/ **NOUN**
• **bookshop** /bʊkshop/ **NOUN**

book[2] /bʊk/
To arrange to have something you want such as a hotel room for the time that you want it **VERB**

boom /bɔom/
A deep loud noise **NOUN**

boot /bɔot/
1. A strong type of shoe that covers your ankle 2. The part of a car where you keep the luggage **NOUN**

border[1] /bɔrder/
1. The line between two countries where one country ends and the other begins
2. The edge of something *Inky drew flowers on the border of her picture.*
NOUN

border[2] /bɔrder/
If one country borders another, it lies next to it **VERB**

b

bore /bɔr/
PAST TENSE ▶ **bear**²

bored /bɔrd/
Feeling tired and in a bad mood because
what you are doing is not interesting,
or because you have nothing to do
ADJECTIVE
• **bore** /bɔr/
To make someone feel bored VERB
• **boring** /bɔrring/
Not interesting ADJECTIVE

born /bɔrn/
be born To come into life as a baby
ADJECTIVE

borne /bɔrn/
PAST PARTICIPLE ▶ **bear**²

borrow /borɒa/
To take something from someone with
their permission, then use it and give it
back to them later VERB

boss¹ /bos/
The person in charge of people at work
NOUN

boss² /bos/
To tell someone what to do all the time
VERB
• **bossy** /bosee/ ADJECTIVE

both /boath/
The two together ADJECTIVE, PRONOUN
Use both hands. · I saw both of them.

bother¹ /bother/
1. To annoy someone by interrupting
them or not leaving them alone
2. To take the trouble to do something
Don't bother to come if you're too busy.
3. To worry VERB

bother² /bother/
Trouble or difficulty NOUN

bottle /botel/
A container for liquids with a narrow
opening NOUN

bottom¹ /botem/
1. The lowest part of something
2. The part underneath something
The ship sank to the bottom of the sea.
3. The part of the body that you sit on
NOUN

bottom² /botem/
1. At the lowest part of something It's in
the bottom drawer. 2. Worse than all the
others Nobody wants to be bottom of the
class. ADJECTIVE

bought /bɔt/
PAST TENSE ▶ **buy**

boulder /boalder/
A big round rock NOUN

bounce /bouns/
1. To jump up and down 2. To move
away after hitting a surface VERB
• **bounce** /bouns/ NOUN
• **bouncy** /bounsee/ ADJECTIVE

bound /bound/
Certain or likely to happen ADJECTIVE
He's bound to catch you sooner or later.

bounds /boundz/
out of bounds Somewhere you are not
allowed to go NOUN PLURAL

bouquet /boʊcai/
A bunch of flowers that you give to someone **NOUN**

bow[1] /boʊ/
1. A knot of something like ribbon or string with two loops in it *Can you tie your laces in a bow?* 2. A curved piece of wood for shooting arrows 3. A thin piece of wood with a kind of string fixed to it for playing musical instruments like the violin **NOUN**

bow[2] /boʊ/
To bend your head or body forward to show respect when greeting an important person **VERB**
• **bow** /boʊ/ **NOUN**

bowels /boʊelz/
The parts of your body like long tubes where food slowly passes from the stomach and out of the body. They are also called intestines **NOUN PLURAL**

bowl /0 l/
A deep round dish mainly for holding liquids or food **NOUN**

bowling /boʊling/
A game you play indoors. You roll a heavy ball along the ground and try to knock down some standing sticks called pins **NOUN**
• **bowling alley** /boʊling alee/ The building where people go bowling **NOUN**

box[1] /box/
Any container with hard sides **NOUN**

box[2] /box/
In a sport, to fight someone using big leather gloves **VERB**
• **boxer** /boxer/ **NOUN**
• **boxing** /boxing/ **NOUN**

boy /boi/
A male child **NOUN**

boyfriend /boifrend/
Someone's boyfriend is the boy or man they are going out with **NOUN**

bra /brah/
Underwear girls or women wear to support their breasts **NOUN**

brace /brais/
1. A brace or braces are wires on your teeth to make them straight
2. Braces are straps over the shoulders for holding up trousers **NOUN**

bracelet /braislet/
A chain or band that you wear around your wrist as jewellery **NOUN**

brag /brag/
To say good things about yourself because you want other people to have a high opinion of you **VERB**

brain /brain/
The part inside your head that controls the body's activities, such as thinking and feeling **NOUN**
• **brainy** /brainee/ Clever **ADJECTIVE**

brake /braik/
The part of a car or other vehicle that slows down and stops the wheels **NOUN**
• **brake** /braik/ **VERB**

b

bran /bran/
The skin of grain that is left over after making flour NOUN

branch /branch/
1. Branches are the parts of a tree that have leaves on them 2. A shop or office that is part of a group of shops or offices NOUN

brass /bras/
A hard yellow metal NOUN

brave /braiv/
Willing to do something difficult or dangerous even if it frightens you ADJECTIVE

bread /bred/
A baked food made from flour and water, with yeast to make it rise NOUN

• **breadcrumbs** /bredcrumz/ NOUN PLURAL

break[1] /braik/
1. To damage something and knock it into smaller pieces, for example by hitting it or dropping it 2. To become damaged and fall into smaller pieces 3. **break a promise** To not do what you said you would do VERB
■ broke, broken

break[2] /braik/
A short period of time when you have a rest from something NOUN

breakfast /brekfəst/
The first meal of the day that you eat in the morning NOUN

breast /brest/
The upper part of the chest NOUN

breath /breth/
The air that goes in and out of your lungs through your nose and mouth when you breathe NOUN
• **breathe** /breeth/ VERB
• **breathless** /brethləs/ ADJECTIVE

bred /bred/
PAST TENSE ▶ **breed**[1]

breed[1] /breed/
1. To produce babies, especially baby animals 2. To keep animals so that they will produce babies VERB
■ bred

breed[2] /breed/
A type of animal NOUN
There are many breeds of dog.

breeze /breez/
A light wind NOUN
• **breezy** /breezee/ ADJECTIVE

brick /bric/
A small block of baked clay for building houses and walls NOUN

bride /bried/
A woman on her wedding day NOUN

bridegroom /briedgroom/
A man on his wedding day NOUN

bridesmaid /briedzmaid/
A girl who helps the bride on her wedding day NOUN

bridge /brij/
Something built over a river or road for people, cars or trains to cross from one side to the other **NOUN**

brief /breef/
Lasting for a short time only **ADJECTIVE**

briefcase /breefcais/
A small case with a handle for carrying papers **NOUN**

briefs /breefs/
Short underwear for the bottom half of the body **NOUN PLURAL**

bright /briet/
1. Shining *I saw a bright light.*
2. Strong and very noticeable in colour
3. Very clever 4. Cheerful *He gave a bright smile.* **ADJECTIVE**
• **brighten** /brieten/ **VERB**

brilliant /brileeent/
1. Very good or very clever *What a brilliant idea!* 2. Very bright in colour
ADJECTIVE

bring /bring/
1. To take something or someone with you when you go somewhere *Bring a friend to the party.* 2. To go and get something *Can you bring me a sandwich?*
3. To make something happen *His laziness brought him a lot of problems.* **VERB**
■ **brought**

brittle /britel/
Hard but easy to break **ADJECTIVE**
Be careful, the glass is brittle.

broad /brawd/
Wide **ADJECTIVE**
He has very broad shoulders.

broadcast /brawdcast/
A programme on the television or radio
NOUN
• **broadcast** /brawdcast/ **VERB**

broke /broak/
PAST TENSE ▶ **break**[1]

broken /broaken/
PAST PARTICIPLE ▶ **break**[1]
• **broken** /broaken/ **ADJECTIVE**

bronze /bronz/
A hard yellow-brown metal, made from copper and tin **NOUN**

brooch /broach/
A small piece of jewellery that is fastened to a dress or blouse with a pin **NOUN**

brook /brook/
A small stream **NOUN**

broom /broom/
A brush with a long handle for sweeping the floor **NOUN**
• **broomstick** /broomstic/ **NOUN**

brother /bruther/
A boy or man who has the same parents as you **NOUN**

brought /brawt/
PAST TENSE ▶ **bring**

brow /brou/
The part of your face below your hair and above your eyes **NOUN**

brown /broun/
The colour of mud or earth
NOUN, ADJECTIVE

b

browse /brouz/
To look through pages in a book or things in a shop to see if there is anything interesting VERB

bruise /brooz/
A dark mark that appears on your skin if it is hit hard NOUN
• **bruise** /brooz/ VERB

brunch /brunch/
A meal you eat instead of breakfast and lunch that combines both of them together NOUN

brush¹ /brush/
1. A tool with hairs and a handle used for making your hair tidy, cleaning or painting 2. A fox's tail NOUN

brush² /brush/
1. To clean something or smooth your hair with a brush *She was brushing her teeth.* 2. To touch something slightly *The cat's tail brushed against my leg.* VERB

brutal /brootel/
Violent and cruel ADJECTIVE

bubble /bubel/
A small ball of air on or in a liquid NOUN
soap bubbles
• **bubble** /bubel/ VERB

bubble

bucket

bucket /bucit/
A container with an open top and a handle for carrying things such as water NOUN

buckle¹ /bucel/
A metal fastener for a belt or strap NOUN

buckle² /bucel/
1. To fasten with a buckle
2. To get bent, for example in the heat *One of my bicycle wheels is buckled.* VERB

bud /bud/
A flower or a leaf before it is completely open NOUN
• **bud** /bud/ VERB

Buddhist /boodist/
Someone who believes in the religion of Bhudda, common in China and Japan NOUN

buddy /budee/
Another word for a friend NOUN

budge /buj/
To move slightly VERB
Be quiet and don't budge!

B

budgerigar /bujereegar/
Or **budgie** /bujee/ A brightly-coloured bird like a small parrot often kept as a pet NOUN

bug /bug/
1. Any small insect 2. A germ that causes illness 3. A fault in a computer program NOUN

buggy /bugee/
A light folding chair with wheels for pushing a baby in NOUN

build /bild/
To make something by putting together the different parts of it VERB
The king built a castle on the hill.
■ **built**
• **builder** /bilder/ NOUN
• **building** /bilding/ Anything built such as a house NOUN

built /bilt/
PAST TENSE ▶ **build**

bulb /bulb/
1. The round glass part of an electric light 2. The root of a plant such as a tulip that is shaped like a ball NOUN

bulge /bulj/
To swell or stick out VERB
• **bulge** /bulj/ NOUN

bull /bool/
A male cow, elephant or whale NOUN

bulldozer /booldoazer/
A type of big tractor for moving earth and knocking down buildings NOUN

bullet /boolit/
The pointed piece of metal fired from a gun NOUN

bull's-eye /boolz ie/
The small circle at the centre of a target NOUN

bully /boolee/
Someone who frightens or hurts a weaker person NOUN
• **bully** /boolee/ VERB

bump¹ /bump/
A raised part NOUN
a bump in the road • a bump on the head
• **bumpy** /bumpee/ ADJECTIVE

bump² /bump/
1. To hit something *Don't bump your head!* 2. **bump into** To meet someone somewhere by accident *Inky bumped into Bee in the forest.* VERB

Inky bumped into Bee in the forest.

b

bumper /bumper/
A bar at the front and back of a car that protects the car if it hits something **NOUN**

bun /bun/
A small round cake or bread roll **NOUN**

bunch /bunch/
1. A group of similar things joined or fastened together   *a bunch of grapes* · *a bunch of flowers* 2. A group of people *a bunch of friends* **NOUN**

bundle /bundel/
A collection of things fastened together such as a bundle of newspapers **NOUN**

bungalow /bunggeloa/
A house that has only one level or floor **NOUN**

bunk /bungk/
1. A bed on a ship 2. **bunk beds** Two beds that are built with one on top of the other **NOUN**

bunny /bunee/
Another word for a rabbit **NOUN**

burger /berger/
A flat round piece of minced meat that is fried and eaten in a bun **NOUN**

burglar /bergler/
Someone who forces their way into a building to steal things **NOUN**
· **burglar alarm** /bergler elarm/ **NOUN**

burn[1] /bern/
1. To be on fire   *The candle burnt brightly.*
2. To set fire to something 3. To hurt or damage something with fire or heat
VERB
■ **burnt** or **burned**

burn[2] /bern/
An injury to your body caused by fire or heat **NOUN**

burnt /bernt/
PAST TENSE ▶ **burn**[1]

burp /berp/
To let air out noisily from your stomach through your mouth **VERB**
· **burp** /berp/ **NOUN**

burst /berst/
1. To break open suddenly or into pieces because there is too much inside
2. To happen suddenly   *He burst into the room.* **VERB**
■ **burst**

bury /beree/
To dig a hole in the ground and put something or someone in it **VERB**

bus /bus/
A big vehicle for carrying passengers from place to place **NOUN**
· **bus stop** /bus stop/ **NOUN**

bush /boosh/
A big plant smaller than a tree with lots of thin branches **NOUN**
· **bushy** /booshee/ **ADJECTIVE**

business /biznes/
1. Work that people do buying and selling things   *Sam's uncle is in business.*
2. A company such as a shop or factory
3. Any activity or subject   *I've had enough of all this business.* **NOUN**

B

bust[1] /bust/
To break or damage something **VERB**

bust[2] /bust/
A model of someone's head and shoulders **NOUN**

busy /bizee/
1. Doing lots of things *I'll do it later, I'm busy now.* 2. Not available *The telephone is busy.* **ADJECTIVE**

but /but/
1. A word you use to show a difference between the two parts of a sentence *I'm tired but happy.* 2. Except *We have nothing to do but wait.*
CONJUNCTION, PREPOSITION

butcher /boocher/
A person who cuts up and sells meat **NOUN**

butter /buter/
A yellow food made from milk that you can spread on bread **NOUN**

buttercup /butercup/
A wild flower with small shiny yellow petals **NOUN**

butterfingers /buterfinggerz/
Someone who is clumsy with their fingers and drops things **NOUN**

butterfly /buterflie/
An insect with big colourful wings
NOUN

button /buten/
A small round object used for putting through holes in clothes to fasten them
NOUN
• **button** /buten/ **VERB**

buy /bie/
To get something by giving money for it
VERB
■ **bought**

buzz /buz/
The sound a bee makes **NOUN**
• **buzz** /buz/ **VERB**

by /bie/
1. Done or caused by someone or something *I was helped by my dad.* • *Helen was hit by a stone.* 2. Doing something in a particular way *I travel by car.* 3. Near to or past something or someone *Inky was standing by the window.* 4. Not later than *Be home by four o'clock.*
PREPOSITION

bye /bie/
Short for goodbye **INTERJECTION**

c

Cc

cab /cab/
1. A taxi 2. The front part of a truck or bus where the driver sits NOUN

cabbage /cabij/
A big round vegetable with thick green leaves NOUN
▶ FRUIT AND VEGETABLES, page 15

cabin /cabin/
1. A small house made of wood in a forest or on a mountain *There's a log cabin in the woods.* 2. A small room on a ship for passengers to live in 3. The main part of a plane where the passengers travel NOUN

cabinet /cabinet/
A cupboard for holding things in such as medicines or papers, or for showing things such as silver objects or vases NOUN

cable /caibel/
1. A thick wire for carrying electricity 2. A very strong rope, usually made of metal 3. A type of television system that is connected to houses by cables NOUN

cactus /cactes/
A prickly plant with a thick stem that grows in hot countries NOUN

■ **cacti** /cactie/ or **cactuses** /cactesez/ PLURAL

café /cafai/
A small restaurant NOUN

cage /caij/
A box or room made of wires or bars where people keep animals and birds NOUN

cake /caik/
A soft sweet food made from flour, sugar and eggs that are mixed together and baked NOUN

calculate /calcyelait/
To find out something with numbers VERB
Can you calculate the total of these five numbers?
• **calculation** /calcyelaishen/ NOUN
• **calculator** /calcyelaiter/ NOUN

calendar /calender/
A list of all the days, weeks and months of the year NOUN

calf /cahf/
1. The baby of an animal such as a cow, an elephant or a whale 2. The back part of your leg between your knee and your ankle NOUN
■ **calves** /cahvz/ PLURAL

call¹ /cawl/
1. To cry out to attract someone's attention *I heard someone calling for help.*
2. To give something or someone a name *What will your parents call the new baby?*
3. To ask someone to come *Bee called Snake over to have a look.* 4. To phone someone *I'll call you tomorrow.* VERB

call² /cawl/
1. When you speak to someone on the phone 2. A cry to attract someone's attention 3. A short visit to someone NOUN

calm /cahm/
1. Quiet and still 2. Not excited or upset *Try and stay calm.* ADJECTIVE

C

calves /cahvz/
NOUN PLURAL ▶ **calf**

camcorder /camcorder/
A camera for recording moving pictures and sounds **NOUN**

came /caim/
PAST TENSE ▶ **come**

camel /camel/
A big desert animal that can have either one or two humps on its back **NOUN**

camera /camera/
A machine that you use for taking photos or making moving pictures **NOUN**

camp[1] /camp/
1. A place where people live for a short time in tents or huts 2. A place where people go on holiday, and take part in outdoor activities *We're going to a summer camp this year.* **NOUN**

• **campsite** /campsiet/ **NOUN**

camp[2] /camp/
To stay in a tent or temporary shelter **VERB**

can[1] /can/
1. To be able to do something *Bee can fly all day long.* 2. To know how to do something *Can you read?* 3. Used to ask someone to do something *Can you tell me the time?* 4. Used for showing that something happens sometimes *It can get very windy on the top of this hill.* **VERB**
■ **could**

can[2] /can/
A metal container for food or drink **NOUN**

canal /cenal/
A man-made river for ships and boats **NOUN**

cancel /cansel/
To stop something from happening that had been arranged **VERB**
We had to cancel the outing.

cancer /canser/
A serious disease of the body's cells that can spread from one part of the body to another **NOUN**

candle /candel/
A stick of hard wax with a string running through it that you burn to get light **NOUN**

candyfloss /candeeflos/
Thin threads of coloured sugar wound around a stick for eating **NOUN**

cane /cain/
1. A thin stick that is used for walking
2. A long hard stem in certain plants such as bamboo **NOUN**

cannibal /canibel/
A person who eats other humans **NOUN**

C

cannon /canen/
A big heavy gun used in past times NOUN

cannot /canot/
Can not VERB
Snake and Inky cannot fly.

canoe /cenoo/
A small narrow boat that is moved through the water with a paddle NOUN

can't /cant/
A short way of saying 'cannot', especially when speaking VERB

canteen /canteen/
An eating place in an office, factory or school NOUN

canvas /canves/
A very strong cloth for making things such as tents or bags NOUN

cap /cap/
1. A soft hat with a flat curved part at the front 2. A cover that protects the top of something such as a bottle or pen NOUN

capable /caipebel/
1. Good at doing something *She is a very capable teacher.* 2. Being able to do something *Is Snake capable of lifting those weights?* ADJECTIVE

Is Snake capable of lifting those weights?

capital[1] /capetel/
The main town or city in a country where the government meets NOUN

capital[2] /capetel/
A capital letter is one of the alphabet letters written in the big shape used at the beginning of names and sentences, for example A or B ADJECTIVE

captain /capten/
1. The person in charge of a ship or plane 2. The person in charge of a sports team 3. An officer in the army or navy NOUN

capture /capcher/
1. To catch a person or animal and hold them so that they cannot escape 2. To get control of a place in a war VERB
• **capture** /capcher/ NOUN

car /car/
A small vehicle with wheels and an engine for carrying people NOUN

caravan /carevan/
A small home on wheels pulled by a car NOUN

card /card/
1. A type of stiff thick paper 2. A piece of card with a picture and a short message that is sent to people at special times *a birthday card* 3. A small piece of card with numbers or pictures on for playing games 4. A small piece of plastic with information on it *a library card* NOUN

a birthday card

C

cardboard /cardbord/
A type of very strong thick paper for making boxes **NOUN**

cardigan /cardigən/
A knitted jacket made of wool **NOUN**

care[1] /ceer/
1. **care about** To really like someone or be interested in something 2. **care for** To like or look after someone **VERB**

care[2] /ceer/
1. **take care of** To look after something or someone 2. Being careful *Take care!*
3. Another word for worry *Snake doesn't seem to have a care in the world.* **NOUN**

careful /ceerfəl/
Paying special attention to things to try and avoid danger or mistakes **ADJECTIVE**
• **carefully** /ceerfəlee/ **ADVERB**
• **careless** /ceerləs/ **ADJECTIVE**

caretaker /ceertaiker/
Someone who looks after a building **NOUN**

cargo /cargoʊ/
Goods carried by a ship or plane **NOUN**

carnation /carnaishən/
A plant with flowers that smell very sweet **NOUN**

carnival /carnivəl/
A celebration where people dress in costumes and dance through the streets **NOUN**

carol /carəl/
A special song sung at Christmas **NOUN**

carpenter /carpenter/
A person who makes things with wood **NOUN**

carpet /carpit/
A thick material for covering floors **NOUN**

carriage /carij/
1. One of the parts of a train where the passengers sit 2. A vehicle for carrying people, pulled by horses **NOUN**

carrier bag /careeer bag/
A plastic bag for carrying things **NOUN**

carrot /carət/
An orange-coloured vegetable that is long and pointed **NOUN**

carry /caree/
1. To take something or someone from one place to another 2. To have something with you *I carry money in my wallet.* 3. **carry on** To keep on doing something **VERB**

cart /cart/
A vehicle with two wheels used to carry heavy loads, usually pulled by a horse **NOUN**

carton /cartən/
1. A small cardboard container for drinks such as milk 2. A large cardboard box for carrying things **NOUN**

C

cartoon /cartoon/
1. A funny drawing or lots of funny drawings 2. A film where drawings appear to move **NOUN**

carve /carv/
1. To cut a shape out of something solid like a piece of wood, or to cut a pattern in it 2. To cut meat into slices **VERB**

case /cais/
1. A container for holding or carrying something 2. A particular event *In case of fire, press the fire alarm.* 3. An example of something *There are some cases of chickenpox in the school.* **NOUN**

cash /cash/
Coins and paper money **NOUN**

cassette /cɛset/
A plastic container with a special tape inside for playing and recording sounds and music, or for showing and recording pictures **NOUN**

cast¹ /cast/
1. To throw *The fisherman cast his net.* 2. To make something by pouring a liquid into a container shaped in a special way **VERB**
■ cast

cast² /cast/
1. An object made by pouring a liquid into a container shaped in a special way 2. All the actors in a play or film **NOUN**

castle /casɛl/
A big building with tall strong walls built to protect people against their enemies **NOUN**

casualty /cazhooltee/
1. The part of a hospital where people go if they are suddenly hurt or sick 2. Someone hurt or killed in an accident **NOUN**

cat /cat/
A small furry animal with whiskers that people keep as a pet **NOUN**

catalogue /catɛlog/
1. A magazine with pictures of things you can buy 2. A list of books or objects **NOUN**

catapult /catɛpult/
A small stick shaped like a 'Y' with an elastic tied to the ends for shooting stones **NOUN**

catch /cach/
1. To get hold of someone or something *Catch the ball!* 2. To get an illness 3. To be in time for something such as a train or plane 4. To surprise someone doing something **VERB**
■ caught
• **catching** /caching/ If an illness is catching, you can easily get it **ADJECTIVE**

caterpillar /caterpiler/
A little creature like a worm that turns into a butterfly or moth **NOUN**

cattle /catɛl/
Cows and bulls **NOUN PLURAL**

caught /cawt/
PAST TENSE ▶ **catch**

C

cauliflower /coleeflouer/
A round white vegetable with green
leaves **NOUN**

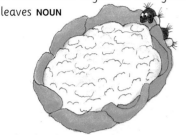

cause¹ /cawz/
To make something happen **VERB**

cause² /cawz/
The reason why something happens **NOUN**

cave /caiv/
A big hole in a rock or under the ground
NOUN
• **caveman** /caivman/ **NOUN**

CD /see dee/
Short for 'compact disc', a shiny disc
that can store music and different kinds
of information **NOUN**

CD-ROM /see dee rom/
Short for 'compact disc read-only
memory', a shiny computer disc that
can store lots of information **NOUN**

ceiling /seeling/
The part of a room above your head
NOUN

celebrate /selebrait/
To do something enjoyable because of a
special event **VERB**
Let's have a party to celebrate your birthday.
• **celebration** /selebraishen/ **NOUN**

celery /seleree/
A vegetable with long light green stems
NOUN

cell /sel/
1. The smallest part of a living thing
red blood cells 2. A very small room in
a prison **NOUN**

cellar /seler/
A room under a house **NOUN**

cello /cheloa/
A musical instrument like a big violin
NOUN

• **cellist** /chelist/ **NOUN**

cement /sement/
A material used for building. It is a grey
powder that is mixed with sand and
water and goes hard when it dries **NOUN**

cemetery /semetree/
A place where dead people are buried
NOUN

cent /sent/
A unit of money in many countries.
There are 100 cents in an American
dollar **NOUN**

centimetre /sentimeeter/
A measurement of length. There are 100
centimetres in a metre **NOUN**

centipede /sentepeed/
A small creature like a thin worm with
lots of legs **NOUN**

centre /senter/
1. The middle part of something
2. A building that can be used for
different activities *I'm going to the
sports centre.* **NOUN**
• **central** /sentrel/ **ADJECTIVE**

C

century /sencheree/
A hundred years NOUN

cereal /siereeel/
1. A food made from seeds called grain that you eat for breakfast 2. A plant such as wheat or rice that produces grain NOUN

ceremony /seremenee/
A very serious and important occasion when lots of special things must be done NOUN *a wedding ceremony*

certain /serten/
1. Completely sure about something and believing it is true *I'm certain she's telling the truth.* 2. Used about something or someone when you do not say exactly what or who they are *In certain countries they drive on the other side of the road.* ADJECTIVE
• **certainly** /sertenlee/ Of course ADVERB

certificate /sertificet/
A piece of printed paper that shows that something is true NOUN
a birth certificate

chaffinch /chafinch/
A small bird of the finch family NOUN

chain /chain/
Metal rings joined together usually in a line NOUN
• **chain** /chain/ VERB

chair /cheer/
A piece of furniture for sitting on, with a back and four legs NOUN

chalk /chawk/
1. A type of soft white rock 2. A small stick made of chalk used for writing or drawing, especially on blackboards NOUN
• **chalk** /chawk/ VERB
• **chalky** /chawkee/ ADJECTIVE

chamber /chaimber/
Another word for a room NOUN

chameleon /cemeeleeen/
A lizard that can change colour NOUN

champagne /shampain/
A white wine with lots of bubbles that people drink on special occasions NOUN

chance /chans/
1. Something that might happen *There's a chance you might fall, so be very careful.*
2. The opportunity to do something *I never get the chance to play tennis.* NOUN

change¹ /chainj/
1. To make something different, or to become different *Snake's always hungry. I don't think he'll ever change.* 2. To stop doing something, and start doing something else *Where do we change trains?*
3. To put on different clothes *Go upstairs and change.* VERB

C

change² /chainj/
1. A difference *What a change!* 2. Money that someone gives back to you when you buy something 3. Money as coins *Do you have any change on you?* **NOUN**

changing room /chainjing room/
A room where people can change their clothes **NOUN**

channel /chanel/
1. A TV station 2. An area of water between two seas *The English Channel separates England from France.* **NOUN**

chapter /chapter/
One of the main sections of a book **NOUN**

character /carecter/
1. Someone's special qualities that make them different from other people
2. A person in a film, play or book
3. A letter, number or symbol **NOUN**

charge¹ /charj/
1. **in charge** Looking after someone or something, or in control of them
2. The money you pay for something
3. A strong sudden attack **NOUN**

charge² /charj/
1. To ask an amount of money for something *How much do you charge for a pizza?* 2. To rush somewhere *The lion came charging towards us.* 3. To put energy into a battery so it can be used again **VERB**

charm¹ /charm/
1. Something thought to bring good luck *a lucky charm* 2. A special friendly quality that some people have **NOUN**

charm² /charm/
To make people like you because you have a special friendly quality **VERB**

charming /charming/
1. Pleasant and attractive
2. Very friendly and kind **ADJECTIVE**

chart /chart/
1. A picture with lots of information that explains something in a simple way
2. A map of the sea **NOUN**

chase /chais/
1. To run after someone or something *Bee chased after the butterfly.*
2. **chase away** To make a person or animal go away **VERB**

chat /chat/
To talk to someone in a friendly way **VERB**
• **chatty** /chatee/ **ADJECTIVE**

chatter /chater/
To talk a lot without stopping about things that are not very important **VERB**
• **chatterbox** /chaterbox/ **NOUN**

cheap /cheep/
Not costing much money **ADJECTIVE**

cheat /cheet/
1. To behave in a way that goes against the rules 2. To trick someone **VERB**
• **cheat** /cheet/ **NOUN**

check¹ /chec/
To look at something carefully to make sure it is correct or working properly **VERB** *Remember to check your answers.*

check² /chec/
1. Something done to make sure everything is correct or working properly *a health check* 2. A pattern of little squares **NOUN**

C

cheek /cheek/
1. One of the two soft parts of your face between your mouth and your ears
2. Rude behaviour NOUN
• **cheeky** /cheekee/ ADJECTIVE

cheer /chier/
1. To shout out loud to show your happiness *The audience cheered when the pop group came onto the stage.*
2. If someone cheers you up, they make you happy VERB
• **cheer** /chier/ NOUN

cheerful /chierfel/
Happy, or making you feel happy
ADJECTIVE *a cheerful room*

cheese /cheez/
A hard or soft type of food made from milk NOUN
• **cheesecake** /cheezcaik/ NOUN

cheetah /cheetel/
A big wild cat with spots that can run very fast NOUN

chef /shef/
A cook in a restaurant NOUN

chemical /cemicel/
A substance made by mixing other substances together in a scientific way
NOUN
• **chemical** /cemicel/ ADJECTIVE

chemist /cemist/
A person who prepares and sells medicines NOUN

cheque /chec/
Printed paper that people can write an amount of money on and use to buy things NOUN

cherry /cheree/
A small round fruit that is red or yellow, and has a stone inside NOUN
▶ **FRUIT AND VEGETABLES**, page 15

chess /ches/
A game for two people played on a board with squares. Each player has 16 pieces including a king and queen NOUN

chest /chest/
1. The front part of the body covering your ribs ▶ **PARTS OF THE BODY**, page 18
2. A big strong box for keeping things in
3. **chest of drawers** A piece of furniture with lots of drawers NOUN

chestnut /chesnut/
A red-brown nut you can eat NOUN

chew /choo/
To break things up with your teeth
VERB

chewing gum /chooing gum/
A soft sweet you chew for a long time but do not swallow NOUN

chick /chic/
A baby bird NOUN

chicken /chicin/
1. A bird that people keep on farms that gives us eggs and meat 2. The meat from chickens that we eat NOUN

chickenpox /chicinpox/
An illness that makes red spots appear all over your body NOUN

chief[1] /cheef/
Someone who is in charge of something, such as the leader of a tribe NOUN

C

chief² /cheef/
The most important ADJECTIVE
the chief reason for something

child /chield/
1. A boy or girl 2. Someone's son or daughter NOUN
- ■ **children** /children/ PLURAL
- **childhood** /chieldhood/ The time when you are a child NOUN
- **childish** /chieldish/ ADJECTIVE

chill /chil/
1. A feeling of being cold 2. A slight illness where you feel very cold NOUN
- **chilly** /chilee/ ADJECTIVE

chimney /chimnee/
A big tube going through a building that lets smoke from a fire get away through the roof NOUN

chimpanzee /chimpanzee/
An intelligent animal belonging to the ape family NOUN

chin /chin/
The bottom part of your face just below your mouth NOUN

china /chiene/
1. A type of clay used to make things such as cups and saucers 2. Things made out of china NOUN

chip¹ /chip/
If you chip something or if it chips, a tiny piece of it breaks off VERB
Be careful not to chip the plate.

chip² /chip/
1. A tiny hole in something where a piece has broken off *Don't use that glass, it has a chip.* 2. Chips are long pieces of potato fried in oil 3. A computer chip is a small piece of special material that helps the computer to deal with information NOUN
- **chipped** /chipt/ ADJECTIVE

chipmunk /chipmungk/
A small animal with stripes similar to a small squirrel NOUN

chirp /cherp/
A short high sound made by a bird VERB

chocolate /choclet/
1. A sweet food made from cocoa beans 2. A drink made from chocolate NOUN

choice /chois/
1. When you choose something *We have to make a choice.* 2. The thing you choose *Bee's choice was the red flower.* NOUN

choir /cwieer/
A group of people who sing together NOUN

choke /choak/
To find it hard to breathe because your throat is blocked VERB
The smoke made them choke.

choose /chooz/
1. To decide you want something or someone, and not something or someone else *Snake chose the biggest piece of cake.* 2. To decide to do something because you want to VERB
- ■ **chose, chosen**

C

chop[1] /chop/
To cut something into pieces such as with an axe or knife VERB

chop[2] /chop/
A small piece of meat from a sheep or pig NOUN
Let's have lamb chops for lunch.

chopstick /chopstic/
Chopsticks are thin sticks of wood or plastic for eating Chinese food NOUN

chord /cord/
Musical notes played at the same time to make a pleasant sound NOUN

chore /chor/
Things you have to do such as tidying your room NOUN

chorus /corres/
1. Part of a song that you sing between each verse 2. A group of singers NOUN

chose /choaz/
PAST TENSE ▶ **choose**
• **chosen** /choazen/
   PAST PARTICIPLE ▶ **choose**

Christian /crischen/
Someone who believes in Jesus Christ NOUN
• **Christian** /crischen/ ADJECTIVE

Christmas /crismes/
A festival on 25 December celebrating the birth of Jesus NOUN
• **Christmas Eve** /crismes eev/ NOUN
• **Christmas tree** /crismes tree/ NOUN

chuckle /chucel/
To laugh in a quiet way VERB

chunk /chungk/
A big thick piece of something NOUN

church /cherch/
A building where Christian people go to pray NOUN

churn[1] /chern/
1. To mix milk or cream together to make butter 2. If your stomach is churning, you feel nervous and upset VERB

churn[2] /chern/
A container for milk NOUN

cigar /sigar/
Something that people smoke made up of tobacco leaves rolled together like a thick tube NOUN

cigarette /sigeret/
Something that people smoke made of small pieces of tobacco inside a piece of paper NOUN

cinema /sineme/
A place you go to see films NOUN

circle /sercel/
A perfectly round shape NOUN
▶ SHAPES, page 17
• **circular** /sercyeler/ ADJECTIVE

circus /serces/
A show with clowns and acrobats, and sometimes animals. It goes from place to place to perform, often in a big tent NOUN

city /sitee/
A big town NOUN

c

clang /clang/
A loud ringing noise like a big bell being hit **NOUN**
• **clang** /clang/ **VERB**

clap /clap/
To quickly slap the palms of your hands together to show that you like something **VERB**

clarinet /clarinet/
A musical instrument like a long tube that you blow into and hold out in front of you **NOUN**

class /clas/
1. A group of students who are taught together 2. A period of time when students are taught *When is our next dancing class?* 3. A group of people or things of the same type **NOUN**
• **classroom** /clasroom/ **NOUN**

claw[1] /claw/
Claws are the pointed curved nails on the feet of birds or some animals **NOUN**

claw[2] /claw/
To scratch using claws **VERB**

clay /clai/
A sticky material that comes out of the ground and becomes hard when you bake it in a special oven **NOUN**

clean[1] /cleen/
If something or someone is clean, there is no dirt on them **ADJECTIVE**

clean[2] /cleen/
To get rid of dirt or dust from something **VERB**

• **cleaner** /cleener/ **NOUN**

clear[1] /clier/
1. Easy to see or understand *The picture isn't very clear.* • *a clear explanation* 2. Not blocked by anything *The road ahead is clear.* **ADJECTIVE**
• **clearly** /clierlee/ **ADVERB**

clear[2] /clier/
To get rid of things from something **VERB** *Can I clear the table?*

clever /clever/
Intelligent, and quick to learn **ADJECTIVE**

click[1] /clic/
A short sharp sound **NOUN**

click[2] /clic/
1. To make a clicking sound 2. To press the mouse button when you are using your computer **VERB**

cliff /clif/
A tall rock with a very steep side **NOUN**

climb /cliem/
To go up somewhere such as a tree or a ladder **VERB**
• **climb** /cliem/ **NOUN**
• **climber** /cliemer/ **NOUN**

c

cling /cling/
To hold on to something or someone very tightly **VERB**
■ **clung**

clip /clip/
Something that holds things together such as a paper clip **NOUN**
• **clip** /clip/ **VERB**

cloak /cloak/
Something that people wear around their shoulders like a loose coat without sleeves **NOUN**

cloakroom /cloakroom/
A room where people can leave their coat, hat, bag or umbrella **NOUN**

clock /cloc/
A machine that shows what time it is **NOUN**

clockwise /clocwiez/
Moving in the same direction as the hands of a clock **ADVERB, ADJECTIVE**

close¹ /cloaz/
To make something not open any more **VERB** *Close the window.*
• **closed** /cloazd/ **ADJECTIVE**

close² /cloas/
1. Not far away 2. Close weather is hot and without much fresh air **ADJECTIVE**
• **closely** /cloaslee/ **ADVERB**

cloth /cloth/
1. Woven material made from something such as cotton or wool 2. A piece of cloth for cleaning **NOUN**

clothes /cloathz/
The things that you wear to cover your body **NOUN PLURAL**
• **clothing** /cloathing/ **NOUN**

cloud /cloud/
1. One of the white or grey shapes that float in the sky and bring rain 2. A similar shape in the air containing dust or smoke **NOUN**
• **cloudy** /cloudee/ **ADJECTIVE**

clown /cloun/
Someone in a circus who wears funny clothes and makes people laugh **NOUN**

club /club/
1. A heavy stick used as a weapon 2. A thin stick for hitting the ball in golf 3. A group of people who meet together because they share the same ideas *I belong to the youth club.* **NOUN**

clue /cloo/
Anything that helps people to solve a mystery or a crime **NOUN**

clumsy /clumzee/
Careless in the way you move or do things **ADJECTIVE**
She's so clumsy, she keeps dropping things.

C

clung /clung/
PAST TENSE ▶ **cling**

coach[1] /coach/
1. A bus for taking people on long journeys 2. A person who teaches someone a sport 3. One of the parts of a train where the passengers sit 4. A vehicle with wheels, pulled by horses **NOUN**

coach[2] /coach/
To teach someone a sport or a school subject **VERB**

coal /coal/
A hard black rock from the ground that people burn to make heat **NOUN**

coast /coast/
The place where the land meets the sea **NOUN**

coat /coat/
1. Something you wear over your other clothes to keep you warm 2. The hair or wool that covers an animal's body **NOUN**

cobweb /cobweb/
The net made by a spider to catch insects **NOUN**

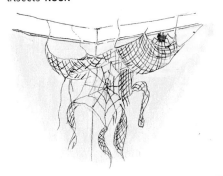

cockpit /cocpit/
The part of a plane where the pilot sits **NOUN**

cockroach /cocroach/
A big brown insect like a beetle that comes out at night **NOUN**

cocoa /coacoa/
1. A brown powder made from cocoa beans, used to make chocolate 2. A hot drink made from cocoa powder **NOUN**
• **cocoa beans** /coacoa beenz/ Seeds from a tropical tree used to make cocoa powder and chocolate **NOUN PLURAL**

coconut /coacenut/
1. The big brown nut of a palm tree 2. The thick white layer inside a coconut that you can eat **NOUN**

cod[1] /cod/
A sea fish with white flesh **NOUN**
■ **cod** /cod/ **PLURAL**

code /coad/
A secret way of writing a message so that only the person you are sending it to can understand it **NOUN**

coffee /cofee/
1. A hot drink made from coffee beans 2. The brown powder used for making this hot drink **NOUN**

coil[1] /coil/
A length of wire or rope twisted into small loops **NOUN**

coil[2] /coil/
To twist something into loops **VERB**

coin /coin/
A round piece of metal used as money **NOUN**

C

coincidence /cɔɑinsidens/
When two things happen at the same time by accident NOUN

cold[1] /cɔɑld/
At a low temperature ADJECTIVE

cold[2] /cɔɑld/
A slight illness with sneezing and a runny nose NOUN

collar /coler/
1. The stiff folded part around the neck of a shirt or coat 2. A piece of leather or plastic put around the neck of a dog or cat NOUN

collect /cɛlect/
1. To go and get things and bring them together *Lots of children collect stamps.* 2. To go and meet someone and bring them somewhere *Who's collecting you from school today?* VERB
• **collection** /cɛlecshen/ NOUN

college /colij/
A place where students study after they leave school NOUN

colour[1] /culer/
Red, blue, green and yellow are the names of some colours NOUN

▶ COLOURS, page 17

colour[2] /culer/
colour in To use pencils or paints to put colour into the shapes of a picture VERB
• **coloured** /culerd/ ADJECTIVE
• **colourful** /culerfel/ ADJECTIVE

column /colem/
1. A tall round post that is part of a building or holds up a statue *Nelson's Column* 2. A section of a printed page that is read from top to bottom *newspaper columns* NOUN

comb /cɔɑm/
A piece of plastic with little teeth that you use to make your hair neat NOUN
• **comb** /cɔɑm/ VERB

combine /cembien/
To join together VERB
• **combination** /combinaishen/ NOUN

come /cum/
1. To move in the direction where someone is *Come here!* 2. To reach something or someone *When does this TV show come to an end?* VERB
■ **came, come**

comfort /cumfert/
A feeling of being relaxed and enjoying things NOUN

comfortable /cumftebel/
Making you feel good or relaxed ADJECTIVE *a comfortable chair*

comic /comic/
A magazine with pictures that tell a story NOUN

comma /come/
A punctuation mark (**,**) used for showing words in a list or a short pause NOUN

command /cemand/
1. An order to be obeyed 2. Control of something NOUN
• **command** /cemand/ VERB

commit /cɛmit/
To do something bad **VERB**
to commit a crime

common[1] /comɛn/
1. Happening a lot or found in many places *It's common to see lots of traffic at this time of day.* 2. Shared *We have a common interest.* 3. Ordinary *It's only a common cold.* **ADJECTIVE**

common[2] /comɛn/
1. If two people have something in common, they share something such as ideas 2. If two things have something in common, they share some things that are very similar **NOUN**

communicate /cɛmuɛnicait/
To share information or ideas with someone **VERB**
• **communication** /cɛmuɛnicaishɛn/ **NOUN**

company /cumpɛnee/
1. The people you have with you *Snake and Bee enjoy each other's company.*
2. A shop or factory or some other business for making money **NOUN**

compare /cɛmpeɛr/
To look at things or people to see how different or how similar they are **VERB** *Compare Frank and Sam to see who's tallest.*
• **comparison** /cɛmparisɛn/ **NOUN**

compass /cumpɛs/
An instrument with a needle that always points north. It helps people find their way **NOUN**

compasses /cumpɛsɛs/
An instrument used for drawing circles **NOUN PLURAL**

compete /cɛmpeet/
To take part in a race or game **VERB**

competition /compɛtishɛn/
An activity or game that people take part in and try to win **NOUN**

complain /cɛmplain/
To say you are not happy about something or someone **VERB**
• **complaint** /cɛmplaint/ **NOUN**

complete[1] /cɛmpleet/
1. Whole and with nothing missing *Inky put the last piece in and the jigsaw was complete.* 2. Finished *Inky can leave now. Her work is complete.* **ADJECTIVE**

Inky put the last piece in and the jigsaw was complete.

complete[2] /cɛmpleet/
To finish **VERB**
Complete the sentence by choosing one of the following three words.

C

completely /cəmpleetlee/
Used to mean very, or to say something is true in every way ADVERB
Snake is completely happy. · Have you finished completely?

complicated /complicaitid/
Difficult to understand because there are lots of details ADJECTIVE

computer /cəmpueter/
A machine that stores information and lets you do many things such as write things, make calculations, play games or listen to music NOUN

Phonic is Inky's computer.

concentrate /consentrait/
To think very hard about something VERB
Bee's trying to concentrate on her homework.
· **concentration** /consentraishen/ NOUN

concern /cənsern/
1. To have something to do with someone *These problems concern everyone in the class.* 2. **be concerned about**
To be worried about something *Inky is concerned about Bee's sore throat.* VERB
· **concerning** /cənserning/ PREPOSITION

concert /consert/
A show by musicians NOUN

concrete /congcreet/
A hard material made by mixing sand and cement, used for building things
NOUN

condition /cəndishən/
1. What someone or something is like
The bike was old and in very bad condition.
2. Something that must happen first before something else is done NOUN

The bike was old and in very bad condition.

conduct[1] /conduct/
The way you behave NOUN

conduct[2] /cənduct/
To lead an orchestra by showing them how you want the music to be played
VERB

conductor /cənducter/
1. Someone in charge of an orchestra
2. Someone who sells tickets on a bus
NOUN

cone /coan/
A shape that has a circle at the bottom and comes to a point at the top NOUN
▶ SHAPES, page 17

confess /cənfes/
To say you have done something wrong or bad VERB
The thief confessed to the crime.
· **confession** /cənfeshen/ NOUN

confident /confidənt/
1. Certain that you have good skills or qualities, and you can do things well
2. Certain that something will happen or is true ADJECTIVE
· **confidence** /confidens/ NOUN

C

confiscate /confiscait/
To take something away from someone because they should not have it, or as a punishment VERB

confuse /cɛnfuez/
1. To make it hard for someone to understand something or know what is happening *Don't use such long words, you're confusing me.* 2. To get two things mixed up *People often confuse Jim and Tim because they are twins.* VERB
• **confused** /cɛnfuezd/ ADJECTIVE
• **confusing** /cɛnfuezing/ ADJECTIVE
• **confusion** /cɛnfuezhen/ NOUN

conjunction /cɛnjungcshen/
A word such as 'and' or 'but' that joins words together NOUN
▶ PARTS OF SPEECH, pages 6 and 7

conjurer /cunjerer/
A person who performs magical tricks NOUN
• **conjure** /cunjer/ VERB

conker /congker/
A shiny brown nut from the horse chestnut tree NOUN

connect /cɛnect/
To join things together VERB
• **connected** /cɛnectid/ ADJECTIVE
• **connection** /cɛnecshen/ NOUN

conquer /congcer/
To battle against something and win VERB

consider /cɛnsider/
1. To think about something carefully
2. To have an opinion about something *Robert considers Andy to be his best friend.* VERB

consist /cɛnsist/
To be made up of something VERB
Breakfast consisted of toast and an egg.

consonant /consenent/
A letter that is not a vowel NOUN

contain /cɛntain/
To have something inside VERB
The box contained Snake's lunch.
• **container** /cɛntainer/ NOUN

continent /contenent/
A very big area of land that usually has other countries in it NOUN
Africa and Asia are continents.
▶ WORLD MAP, page 14

continue /cɛntinue/
To keep on doing something VERB
Bee continued flying until she reached home.

continuous /cɛntinuees/
Continuing without stopping ADJECTIVE
Two days of continuous rain.

contradict /contredict/
To not agree with someone and say the opposite of what they say VERB

control[1] /cɛntroal/
1. When you are in charge of something and make things do what you want
2. If something is under control, people are dealing with it properly, and there is no need to be worried *The fire is under control.* 3. Controls are the levers and buttons used to operate a machine *a television remote control* NOUN

a television remote control

C

control² /centroal/
1. To make something or someone behave how you want them to 2. If you control your feelings, you behave in a normal way even though you are angry or upset VERB

convenient /cenveeneeent/
1. Good and useful because it makes things easier *The school is very convenient, it's just around the corner.* 2. A convenient time is a time when you are free to do something *Come to our party tomorrow, if it's convenient.* ADJECTIVE

conversation /conversaishen/
Another word for talking NOUN

cook /cook/
To prepare and heat food ready for eating VERB

• **cook** /cook/ NOUN
• **cooked** /cookt/ ADJECTIVE
• **cooking** /cooking/ NOUN

cooker /cooker/
A big machine that people use for heating up food NOUN

cool¹ /cool/
1. Cold but not too cold 2. Not excited or nervous but quiet and calm
3. Another way of saying 'very good'
I think helping other people is really cool.
ADJECTIVE

cool² /cool/
To become cooler with time VERB

copper /coper/
A red-brown metal used for making coins, wires and pipes NOUN

copy /copee/
1. To do or make something that is exactly the same as something else
2. To do something exactly like someone else does it VERB
• **copy** /copee/ NOUN

cord /cord/
A piece of thick string NOUN

core /cor/
The middle part of a fruit such as an apple NOUN

cork /cork/
1. The bark of the cork oak tree, used for making many things 2. A piece of cork used for putting in the tops of wine bottles NOUN

corkscrew /corkscroo/
A piece of twisted metal for pulling corks out of bottles NOUN

corn /corn/
1. A plant such as wheat, barley or oats
2. Or **sweetcorn** /sweetcorn/ The soft yellow seeds of the maize plant that people cook and eat ▶ FRUIT AND VEGETABLES, page 15 3. A piece of hard skin on your foot NOUN

corner /corner/
The meeting place of two lines or walls NOUN *The lamp is in the corner of the room.*

C

cornflakes /cornflaiks/
Small thin pieces of maize that you eat
for breakfast with milk NOUN PLURAL

correct[1] /cerect/
Right, or with no mistakes ADJECTIVE
Snake gave the correct answer.

correct[2] /cerect/
If someone corrects something such as
your spelling, they put the mistakes right
VERB
• **correction** /cerecshen/ NOUN
• **correctly** /cerectlee/ ADVERB

correspond /corespond/
1. To be similar to something else, or
similar to each other *These two drawings
don't correspond.* 2. If you correspond with
someone, you send them letters VERB

corridor /coridor/
A long passage in a building with lots of
doors leading to rooms such as
classrooms NOUN

cost[1] /cost/
The amount of money you have to pay
for something NOUN

cost[2] /cost/
If something costs a certain amount of
money, that is what people have to pay
for it VERB
▪ cost

costume /costuem/
Clothes that make you look like someone
or something else NOUN

cosy /coazee/
Comfortable, and nice and warm
ADJECTIVE

cot /cot/
A bed that a baby sleeps in NOUN

cottage /cotij/
A little house in the country NOUN

cotton /coten/
1. A type of cloth made from the white
hairs of the cotton plant 2. The sewing
thread made from the cotton plant
a reel of cotton NOUN

couch /couch/
Another word for a sofa or settee
NOUN

cough /cof/
To force air out of your throat with a
loud noise VERB
• **cough** /cof/ NOUN

could[1] /cood/
1. Used for saying you are able to do
something *You could easily win if you tried.*
2. Used when you ask someone politely
to do something *Could you tell me the
time, please?* 3. Used for showing that
something is possible *It could get very
windy on the top of this hill.* VERB

could[2] /cood/
PAST TENSE ▶ **can**[1]

c

count /count/
1. To name numbers in the correct order *Can you count up to 20, Inky?* 2. To add up things or people to find how many there are *Count how many people there are in your class.* VERB

counter /counter/
1. A kind of table where you are served in a shop or bank 2. A small round piece of plastic or cardboard that you use in some indoor games NOUN

country /cuntree/
1. A separate land with its own government *Mexico is a country.* 2. Another word for countryside NOUN

countryside /cuntreesied/
The land away from towns and cities that has not been built on NOUN

county /countee/
One of the smaller areas a country can be divided into NOUN
Essex is a county in England.

couple /cupel/
1. A way of saying two 2. A few *Wait a couple of minutes.* NOUN

courage /curij/
When you are able to do something difficult or dangerous even if it frightens you NOUN

courgette /corzhet/
A long green vegetable that looks like a small cucumber NOUN

course /cors/
1. A number of lessons to learn a certain subject *The French course is seven weeks long.* 2. A certain amount of medicine a doctor wants you to take *When my sister was sick, she had a course of antibiotics.* 3. A period of time when something gradually happens *In the course of the morning, the weather got warmer.* NOUN

court /cort/
1. A place where people such as criminals are taken so their crimes can be judged 2. A place where a king or a queen lives 3. A place where games are played *Where's the tennis court?* NOUN

cousin /cuzen/
The son or daughter of your aunt or uncle NOUN

cover[1] /cuver/
1. To put something on top of something else 2. To be on top of something *Look how the snow covers the ground.* VERB

cover[2] /cuver/
1. Anything that is on top of something, for example to protect it *Dad put a cover on the saucepan.* 2. The outside part of a book or magazine NOUN

cow /cou/
A female farm animal that gives us milk and meat NOUN

coward /couerd/
Someone who avoids doing anything difficult or dangerous because they are too frightened NOUN

cowboy /couboi/
A man who rides a horse and takes care of cows on a large farm NOUN
• **cowgirl** /cougerl/ NOUN

C

crab /crab/
A sea animal with claws and a round shell that covers its body **NOUN**

crack[1] /crac/
1. A line where something is slightly broken *Don't use this cup, it has a crack in it.* 2. A very narrow space such as a crack in the curtains 3. A loud noise such as the sound of something being broken **NOUN**

crack[2] /crac/
1. If you crack something or it cracks, it breaks and a line appears in it
2. To hit something quickly and strongly
3. To make a cracking noise **VERB**

cracker /cracer/
1. A tube with coloured paper over it that opens with a little exploding noise when two people pull it apart *Christmas crackers* 2. A small thin biscuit **NOUN**

cradle /craidel/
A baby's bed that can be rocked from side to side **NOUN**

craft /craft/
A skilled activity where you make things with your hands **NOUN**

crafty /craftee/
Someone who is crafty tricks people to get what they want **ADJECTIVE**

crane /crain/
A very tall machine for lifting heavy things **NOUN**

crash[1] /crash/
1. A very loud noise such as things hitting each other or breaking
2. An accident in which a car or plane hits something **NOUN**

crash[2] /crash/
1. If a vehicle crashes or if someone crashes a vehicle, it hits something
2. If someone or something crashes into something, they hit them while moving **VERB**
• **crash helmet** /crash helmet/ **NOUN**

crater /craiter/
A very big hole in the ground caused by an explosion or something hitting it from the sky **NOUN**

crawl /crawl/
1. To move along the ground on your hands and knees 2. If an insect crawls, it moves slowly along the ground **VERB**

C

crayon /craion/
A kind of coloured pencil made from wax **NOUN**

crazy /craizee/
1. Stupid or strange 2. Mad *Go away, you're driving me crazy.* **ADJECTIVE**

creak /creek/
To make a harsh squeaking noise **VERB**
• **creaky** /creekee/ **ADJECTIVE** .

cream[1] /creem/
1. The yellow-white fat substance that comes from milk 2. A soft substance you put on your skin to make it better or protect it **NOUN**
• **creamy** /creemee/ **ADJECTIVE**

cream[2] /creem/
A yellow-white colour **NOUN, ADJECTIVE**

• **creamy** /creemee/ **ADJECTIVE**

crease /crees/
A line made in paper or cloth when it is folded **NOUN**
• **crease** /crees/ **VERB**

create /creeait/
To make something **VERB**

creature /creecher/
A living thing, such as an animal **NOUN**

creep /creep/
To move along somewhere slowly and carefully **VERB**
■ **crept**

creepy /creepee/
An informal word that means very frightening **ADJECTIVE**

creepy-crawly /creepee crawlee/
An informal word for insect **NOUN**

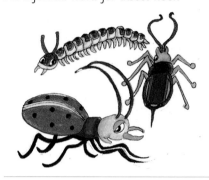

crept /crept/
PAST TENSE ▶ **creep**

crescent /crezent/
A curved shape like the shape of a new moon **NOUN**
▶ **SHAPES**, page 17

crew /croo/
A group of people who work together somewhere such as on a ship or plane **NOUN**

cricket /cricit/
1. A game where two teams of people try to hit a ball with a bat. They score points when they run between two places called wickets 2. A small insect that jumps like a grasshopper **NOUN**

crime /criem/
A very bad action that is against the law, such as stealing **NOUN**

criminal /criminel/
A person who has committed a crime **NOUN**
• **criminal** /criminel/ **ADJECTIVE**

crisp[1] /crisp/
Crisps are round thin pieces of potato that are fried and eaten cold **NOUN**

C

crisp² /crisp/
1. Hard, fresh and ready to eat, like a lettuce 2. Hard, and usually easy to break *The snow was deep and crisp.* **ADJECTIVE**

criticize /critesiez/
To complain about someone or something, and say what you think is wrong with them **VERB**
• **criticism** /critesizem/ **NOUN**

croak /croak/
To make a noise deep in your throat, like a frog **VERB**
• **croak** /croak/ **NOUN**

crockery /croceree/
Cups, plates and other dishes made from clay or china **NOUN**

crocodile /crocediel/
An animal with short legs and a long mouth with sharp teeth showing on the outside. Crocodiles live in rivers in hot countries **NOUN**

crocus /croaces/
A little purple, yellow or white flower that grows in spring **NOUN**

crook /crook/
1. Someone who is not honest such as a thief 2. A stick with a big hook shape at the top used by shepherds **NOUN**

crooked /crookid/
1. Not straight 2. Not honest **ADJECTIVE**

crop /crop/
Crops are plants that people grow for food such as wheat or potatoes **NOUN**

cross¹ /cros/
1. A shape that looks like ✖ or ✚
2. The shape ✖ that you use in writing to show that something is wrong **NOUN**

cross² /cros/
To go from one side of something to the other **VERB**
Inky and Snake must cross the river by boat.
• **crossroads** /crosroadz/ **NOUN**

cross³ /cros/
Another word for angry **ADJECTIVE**

crossing /crosing/
1. A place where it is safe to cross a road or railway line 2. A journey across the sea **NOUN**

crossword puzzle /croswerd puzel/
A word puzzle where you write the answers to questions in little squares **NOUN**

C

crouch /crouch/
To bend your legs and put your body close to the ground **VERB**

crow /croa/
A big black bird that makes a loud noise **NOUN**

crowd[1] /croud/
Lots of people together in one place as a big group **NOUN**
There was a crowd waiting to see the show.

crowd[2] /croud/
If people crowd somewhere, lots of them go there together at the same time **VERB**
It was so hot that hundreds of people crowded onto the beach.
• **crowded** /croudid/ **ADJECTIVE**

crown /croun/
A special hat made of gold and jewels worn by kings and queens **NOUN**
• **crowned** /cround/ **ADJECTIVE**

cruel /crooel/
Bad and making people suffer **ADJECTIVE**
• **cruelty** /crooeltee/ **NOUN**

crumb /crum/
Crumbs are tiny pieces of dry food such as the pieces that come off bread or cakes **NOUN**

crumble /crumbel/
To break or fall into little pieces **VERB**
• **crumbly** /crumblee/ **ADJECTIVE**

crumpet /crumpit/
A small round food like bread with holes in the top. People toast crumpets and eat them hot **NOUN**

crunch /crunch/
1. To eat something hard that makes a lot of noise, such as an apple 2. To make a noisy sound as if you are crushing something *The glass bottle crunched when I stepped on it.* **VERB**
• **crunch** /crunch/ **NOUN**
• **crunchy** /crunchee/ **ADJECTIVE**

crush /crush/
To squeeze something or hit it hard so that it breaks in many places or becomes much smaller **VERB**

crust /crust/
The hard brown part on the outside of bread **NOUN**
• **crusty** /crustee/ **ADJECTIVE**

crutches /cruchiz/
Special sticks that people put under their arms to help them walk if they have hurt one of their legs **NOUN PLURAL**

cry[1] /crie/
1. To let tears come out of your eyes
2. Another word for shout **VERB**

cry[2] /crie/
1. A shout 2. The high sound made by some animals **NOUN**

cub /cub/
1. A young animal such as a lion, fox or bear 2. A young boy who is a member of the Scout Association **NOUN**

C

cube /cueb/
A solid square with six sides that are all the same size **NOUN**

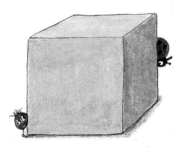

cuckoo /coocoo/
A grey-brown bird that lays its eggs in other birds' nests **NOUN**

cucumber /cuecumber/
A long dark green vegetable that is eaten raw in salads or sandwiches **NOUN**
▶ **FRUIT AND VEGETABLES**, page 15

cuddle /cudel/
To hold someone or something tight in your arms because you like or love them **VERB**
• **cuddle** /cudel/ **NOUN**
• **cuddly** /cudelee/ **ADJECTIVE**

cue /cue/
1. A long thin stick used to play snooker and pool 2. A sign for someone such as an actor to start speaking **NOUN**

cuff /cuf/
On a shirt or dress, the cuff is the part at the end of the sleeve near your wrist **NOUN**

culprit /culprit/
The person who is to blame for doing something wrong **NOUN**

cultivate /cultivait/
To prepare land for growing plants on **VERB**

cunning /cuning/
Good at planning things and getting what you want, often by tricking other people **ADJECTIVE**

cup /cup/
1. A small container with a handle for drinking hot drinks such as tea or coffee
2. A prize shaped like a big silver or metal cup, given to the winners of a game or competition **NOUN**

cupboard /cuberd/
A piece of furniture or a kind of small room with doors and shelves for storing things in **NOUN**

cure /cyooer/
To make a sick person better **VERB**
Inky is sick but the doctor can easily cure her.
• **cure** /cyooer/ **NOUN**

curious /cyooreees/
1. Very strange *What's that curious sound?*
2. Wanting to know more *Snake is curious to know how Bee makes her honey.* **ADJECTIVE**

Snake is curious to know how Bee makes her honey.

• **curiosity** /cyooreeosetee/ **NOUN**

curl[1] /cerl/
A circle or curve of hair **NOUN**

curl[2] /cerl/
1. To bend in a spiral shape 2. If a person or animal curls up, they put their body into a round shape **VERB**
• **curly** /cerlee/ **ADJECTIVE**

C

curler /cerler/
Curlers are small tubes for making your hair curl NOUN

current[1] /curent/
A flow of something like water or air NOUN *The river has a strong current.*

current[2] /curent/
Most recent or modern ADJECTIVE
I bought the current issue of my comic today.

curry /curee/
Vegetables or meat cooked with spices that have a very strong taste NOUN

curtain /certen/
1. Curtains are the pieces of cloth that hang down in front of a window
2. In a theatre, the curtain is the big piece of cloth that hangs down in front of the stage NOUN

curve /cerv/
A line with a bend in it, like the edge of a circle NOUN
• **curve** /cerv/ VERB
• **curvy** /cervee/ ADJECTIVE

cushion /cooshen/
A little pillow put on chairs or sofas to make them more comfortable NOUN

custard /custerd/
A sweet yellow sauce made from eggs, milk and sugar NOUN

custom /custem/
A special way of doing things that people have always had NOUN
It's the custom to give someone a present on their birthday.

customer /custemer/
Someone who buys something NOUN

cut[1] /cut/
1. To separate something into smaller pieces or take a piece out of it using scissors or a knife *Phil cut the paper into different shapes.* 2. To accidentally hurt a part of your body with something sharp *Poor Snake cut himself trying to squeeze under the rose bushes.* VERB
■ **cut**

cut[2] /cut/
An injury to your body, or a hole made in something caused by something sharp NOUN

cute /cuet/
Very pretty ADJECTIVE
What a cute little baby!

cutlery /cutleree/
The knives, forks and spoons that you eat with NOUN

cycle /siecel/
To ride a bicycle VERB
• **cyclist** /sieclist/ NOUN

cylinder /silinder/
An object shaped like a tube. It has circles at both ends that are the same size NOUN

Dd

dad /dad/
Another word for father NOUN
• **daddy** /dadee/ NOUN

daddy long legs /dadee long legz/
An insect that flies and has very long legs NOUN

daffodil /dafɛdil/
A yellow flower with long thin leaves that grows in the spring. The centre of the flower is shaped like a trumpet NOUN

dagger /dager/
A small pointed knife used as a weapon NOUN

daily /dailee/
Happening every day ADJECTIVE, ADVERB

daisy /daizee/
A small wild flower with a yellow centre and white petals NOUN

damage[1] /damij/
Something broken or spoilt NOUN
The storm caused a lot of damage.

damage[2] /damij/
To break or spoil something, or harm it in some way VERB

damp /damp/
Slightly wet ADJECTIVE
• **dampness** /dampnɛs/ NOUN

dance[1] /dans/
To move your feet and body in time to music VERB

• **dancer** /danser/ NOUN

dance[2] /dans/
1. A time when people dance *Let's have another dance!* 2. A party where people go to dance NOUN

dandelion /dandɛlieɛn/
A wild plant with yellow flowers. Its seeds grow in white fluffy balls NOUN

danger /dainjer/
1. The chance that somone can be hurt or killed *You're in danger, Inky. Here comes a cat!* 2. Something or someone that can hurt or kill *Don't be afraid, he's no danger.* 3. The chance that something bad can happen *She's in danger of failing the exam if she doesn't study.* NOUN
• **dangerous** /dainjɛrɛs/ ADJECTIVE

dare /deer/
1. To do something even though it is dangerous or frightening *You wouldn't dare!* 2. To try to get someone to do something even though it is dangerous or frightening *I dare you to climb that tree.* VERB
• **daredevil** /deerdevɛl/ NOUN
• **daring** /deering/ ADJECTIVE

D

d

dark¹ /dark/
1. With not enough light to see clearly *The room was very dark.* 2. Black or brown in colour *Ruth has dark hair.* 3. Strong in colour, not pale *Jenny was wearing a dark red dress.* **ADJECTIVE**

dark² /dark/
When there is no light or it is night-time **NOUN** *Bee doesn't like flying in the dark.*
• **darkness** /darknəs/ **NOUN**

darling /darling/
A word people use to call someone they love **NOUN**

dart¹ /dart/
A small pointed object like an arrow that people throw at a target **NOUN**

dart² /dart/
To move somewhere quickly or suddenly **VERB**

dash /dash/
To go somewhere quickly, to hurry **VERB** *Linda dashed into the classroom.*

date¹ /dait/
1. To put a date on something such as a letter 2. To go out with a boyfriend or girlfriend **VERB**

date² /dait/
1. The words and numbers showing the day, month and year *25 October 2010* 2. The particular day something happens *We've set a date for the wedding.* 3. A time for meeting someone such as a boyfriend or girlfriend 4. A sticky brown fruit with a stone inside **NOUN**

daughter /dawter/
The female child of a mother or father **NOUN**

dawdle /dawdəl/
To take too much time walking or doing something **VERB**

dawn /dawn/
The time at the beginning of the day when it starts to get light **NOUN**

day /dai/
1. A period of time lasting 24 hours 2. The time during the morning, afternoon and evening when it is light 3. Any time in the past or future *In my grandmother's day the city was very different.* • *One day, I'll finish that book.* **NOUN**
• **daylight** /dailiet/ **NOUN**
• **daytime** /daitiem/ **NOUN**

daydream /daidreem/
To imagine that pleasant things are happening instead of paying attention to what you are doing **VERB**

D

daze /daiz/
A feeling when you are not able to think clearly **NOUN**
Bee was in a daze all day.

dazzle /dazel/
If a light dazzles you, it is so bright that you cannot see properly **VERB**
The sun dazzled Bee as she flew.
• **dazzling** /dazeling/ **ADJECTIVE**

dead /ded/
1. Not living any more 2. If somewhere like a town is dead, there is nothing interesting happening *Our street is dead after six o'clock.* 3. Exact or exactly *The arrow landed dead in the centre of the target.* 4. Complete or completely *dead silence* • *Inky stopped dead.*
ADJECTIVE, ADVERB

The arrow landed dead in the centre of the target.

deaf /def/
Not able to hear **ADJECTIVE**
My aunt is deaf.

deal[1] /deel/
1. **deal with** To give something all your attention, and try to solve any problems *Inky Mouse was dealing with all of Bee's questions.* 2. **deal with** To be about a subject *This book deals with reading and writing.* 3. To share out something to a group of people *Deal the cards.* **VERB**
■ **dealt**

deal[2] /deel/
1. **a great deal** A large amount
Bee has a great deal of books to read.
2. **it's a deal** Used for saying yes to something **NOUN**

dealt /delt/
PAST TENSE ▶ **deal**[1]

dear /dier/
1. A word you use about someone or something you love *My dear mother told me that.* 2. A word used to start a letter *Dear Inky...* 3. Costing a lot of money *I can't afford this bike. It's too dear.*
ADJECTIVE

• **dear** /dier/ **NOUN**

death /deth/
The end of life **NOUN**

decade /decaid/
A period of ten years **NOUN**

decay /decai/
1. When the condition of something gets worse 2. The bad part of something *tooth decay* **NOUN**
• **decay** /decai/ **VERB**

deceive /deseev/
To trick someone by making them believe something that is not true **VERB**

December /desember/
The twelfth month of the year **NOUN**
▶ **CALENDAR**, page 13

d

decide /dəsied/
If you decide to do something, you think carefully about it before saying you will do it VERB

Finally, Snake decided to take the left turn.

• **decision** /dəsizhən/ NOUN

decimal¹ /desiməl/
A way of numbering things using units of ten ADJECTIVE
the decimal system

decimal² /desiməl/
A fraction that is written by using numbers after a dot NOUN
The decimal 0.5 is another way of writing 'half.
• **decimal point** /desiməl point/ NOUN

deck /dec/
One of the floors or levels on a ship NOUN

deckchair /deccheer/
A folding chair with a cloth seat, for sitting outside NOUN

declare /dəcleer/
To say something clearly and firmly, or in an official way VERB

decorate /decərait/
1. To make something look nice *Inky decorated her bedroom with lots of pictures.*
2. To paint the inside of a building, or put paper on the walls VERB
• **decorator** /decəraiter/ NOUN

decoration /decəraishən/
Decorations are pretty things you put on something for a special occasion NOUN

Christmas decorations

deduct /dəduct/
To take away one amount from another VERB

deep /deep/
1. Going a long way down or into
deep under the sea · deep into the forest
2. Very strong *deep feelings*
ADJECTIVE, ADVERB
• **deeply** /deeplee/ ADVERB

deer /dier/
A big wild animal that eats grass and can run fast. The male has big horns on its head like branches NOUN
■ **deer** /dier/ PLURAL

defend /dəfend/
To protect someone or something from being harmed or attacked VERB
• **defence** /dəfens/ NOUN

define /dəfien/
To explain what something means VERB
• **definition** /defənishən/ NOUN

definite /definət/
1. Clear and easy to see *That's a definite improvement.* 2. Certain and not likely to change *Inky has a definite plan.* ADJECTIVE
• **definitely** /definətlee/ Used to mean something is completely true ADVERB
It's definitely snowing!

D

deformed /dəf, u0254rmd/
Having a shape that is not normal
ADJECTIVE

delay /dəlai/
1. To do something later instead of doing it now 2. To make someone or something late VERB
• **delay** /dəlai/ NOUN

delete /dəleet/
1. To cross out or remove something that has been written down 2. To get rid of something on a computer VERB

deliberate /dəlibərət/
Not happening or not done by accident
ADJECTIVE *a deliberate mistake*
• **deliberately** /dəlibərətlee/ ADVERB

delicate /delicət/
1. Easily damaged *A butterfly has delicate wings.* 2. Small and pretty *She has delicate hands.* 3. Done with a lot of skill, or with lots of detail *Look at this delicate pattern.*
ADJECTIVE

delicious /dəlishəs/
Very good to taste or smell ADJECTIVE

deliver /dəliver/
To take or send something to where it should go VERB
Please deliver this message.

demand /dəmand/
To ask something in a very strong or angry voice VERB
• **demand** /dəmand/ NOUN

demonstrate /demənstrait/
To show or explain something very clearly VERB
• **demonstration** /demənstraishən/ NOUN

dense /dens/
Very thick or crowded ADJECTIVE
dense fog · a dense forest

dent /dent/
To hit something hard enough to push in part of the surface VERB
• **dent** /dent/ NOUN
• **dented** /dentid/ ADJECTIVE

dentist /dentist/
Someone who takes care of people's teeth NOUN

depart /dəpart/
To leave a place VERB
• **departure** /dəparcher/ NOUN

depend /dəpend/
depend on 1. To happen in a certain way only if something else happens or has a particular effect *What time they get home will depend on the traffic.* 2. To be sure someone or something will do what you want them to *I'm depending on you to help me.* VERB

depth /depth/
How deep something is NOUN

descend /dəsend/
To go down from a higher level VERB

describe /dəscrieb/
1. To write or say what something or someone is like 2. To explain or give details about something *Describe what happened next.* VERB
• **description** /dəscripshən/ NOUN

d

desert /dezert/
A very hot place with lots of sand and almost no water NOUN

deserve /dezerv/
If you deserve something, you should have it because of the way you have behaved or done something VERB
You deserve a treat for being so good.

design[1] /dezien/
To make a drawing of something so that it can be made VERB

design[2] /dezien/
1. The way something is made
2. A drawing of something to be made or built 3. A pattern NOUN

desk /desk/
A table where you sit to do your work NOUN

desktop /desktop/
The computer screen that allows you to reach any of your programs NOUN

desperate /desperet/
1. Ready to do anything even if it is dangerous *He's a desperate man.*
2. Needing something very much ADJECTIVE
• **desperately** /desperetlee/ ADVERB

despite /despiet/
Used to show that something mentioned in one part of a sentence makes no difference to what is mentioned in the other part PREPOSITION
Despite the rain, Inky and her friends decided to go out.

dessert /dezert/
Sweet food or fruit that people eat at the end of a meal NOUN

destination /destinaishen/
The place where someone or something is going NOUN

destroy /destroi/
To cause so much damage to something that it does not exist or work any more VERB
• **destruction** /destrucshen/ NOUN

detail /deetail/
1. One small part of the information about something *Do you have all the details?* 2. One small part of a picture or design NOUN
• **detailed** /deetaild/ ADJECTIVE

detective /detectiv/
Someone such as a police officer who finds things out and tries to solve crimes NOUN

determined /determind/
With a firm idea of doing something, no matter how difficult ADJECTIVE
determined to win
• **determination** /determinaishen/ NOUN

detest /detest/
To hate someone or something very much VERB

develop /dɛvelɒp/
1. To grow into something bigger or stronger *Caterpillars develop into butterflies.* 2. To make something better or stronger *develop your mind* 3. To make photos from the film in a camera VERB

Caterpillars develop into butterflies.

devil /dɛvill/
An evil spirit or person NOUN

dew /duːe/
Tiny drops of water that form on things outside during the night as the air gets cooler NOUN

diagonal /dieaɡenel/
A straight line that joins the two opposite corners of a square or rectangle NOUN
• **diagonal** /dieaɡenel/ ADJECTIVE

diagram /dieeɡram/
A drawing that shows what something looks like or how it works NOUN

dial[1] /diel/
To enter a telephone number by pressing the buttons and making a call VERB

dial[2] /diel/
A round part on the front of a machine that shows measurements. On a clock the dial is the part that shows the time NOUN

diameter /dieameter/
A straight line that goes through the middle of a circle from one side to the other NOUN

diamond /dieemend/
1. A very hard jewel with no colour *a diamond ring* 2. A shape that is like a square that stands on one of its corners and has sloping sides ▶ SHAPES, page 17

a diamond ring

diary /dieeree/
1. A book with spaces for every day of the year where you write down the things you plan to do 2. A book where you write down important things that happen every day NOUN

dice /dies/
A small cube of plastic or wood with a different number of spots on each side, that is used in games NOUN

■ **dice** /dies/ PLURAL

d

dictionary /dicshənəree/
A book of words shown in alphabetical order, with all their meanings explained NOUN

did /did/
PAST TENSE ▶ **do**

die /die/
1. To stop living 2. **die away** To become less strong and gradually disappear *The thunder died away.* VERB

diet /dieət/
1. The food that people usually eat *Inky has a healthy diet.* 2. If someone is on a diet, they only eat certain kinds of food, because they are sick or want to become thinner NOUN

different /difərənt/
1. Not like someone or something *Snake and Bee are very different.* 2. Not like someone or something was in the past *The classroom looks different.* ADJECTIVE
• **difference** /difərəns/ NOUN

difficult /dificəlt/
1. Not easy to do or understand *That's a difficult question.* 2. Not easy to please *a difficult customer* ADJECTIVE
• **difficulty** /dificəltee/ NOUN

dig /dig/
1. To make a hole in the ground 2. If someone digs something into something else, they push it in very hard *Snake dug his teeth into a juicy tomato.* VERB
■ **dug**

digit /dijit/
1. A finger or toe 2. Any number from 0 to 9 NOUN

digital /dijetəl/
1. **digital camera** A camera that takes pictures that you can put directly onto your computer 2. **digital watch** A watch that shows the time as a row of numbers ADJECTIVE

a digital watch

dim¹ /dim/
Not bright ADJECTIVE
a dim light

dim² /dim/
To make or become darker VERB
Dim the lights.

din /din/
A loud long noise NOUN

dinghy /dingee/
A small open boat NOUN

dingy /dinjee/
Dark and dirty ADJECTIVE
The old shed is very dingy.

dining room /diening room/
A room in a house where people eat their meals NOUN

dinner /diner/
The main meal of the day NOUN

D

dinosaur /dienesor/
A giant reptile that lived millions of years ago NOUN

dip¹ /dip/
1. To put something into a liquid and take it out again quickly
2. To go downwards VERB

dip² /dip/
1. A short swim 2. A slope that goes downwards 3. A soft or liquid snack that you dip other food into NOUN

direct¹ /dierect/
1. As straight and quick as possible *a direct flight* 2. Clear or honest *Give me a direct answer.* ADJECTIVE

direct² /dierect/
1. To tell someone which way to go
2. To point or aim something
3. To control something *Our teacher directed the school play.* VERB

direction /dierecshen/
1. The way in which someone or something goes or points 2. If you give someone directions, you show them which way to go or tell them how to do something NOUN

directly /dierectlee/
1. Exactly *Inky stood directly opposite Bee.*
2. Immediately *Bee went to Inky's house directly after lunch.* ADVERB

dirt /dert/
Anything that makes something dirty such as dust or mud NOUN

dirty /dertee/
If something or someone is dirty, they have marks on them that can come from many things such as dust, earth or sweat ADJECTIVE

disabled /disaibeld/
Someone who is disabled cannot use a part of their body properly because of illness or injury ADJECTIVE

disadvantage /disedvantij/
Something that makes you less likely to succeed, or makes a situation more difficult or less pleasant NOUN

disagree /disegree/
To have different ideas or opinions about something VERB
I must disagree with you about that.
• **disagreement** /disegreement/ NOUN

disappear /disepier/
If something or someone disappears, they go away so that you cannot see them any more VERB
I can't find Bee, she's disappeared.

disappoint /disepoint/
To make someone sad or upset because you do not do what they expected VERB
• **disappointed** /disepointid/ ADJECTIVE
• **disappointing** /disepointing/ ADJECTIVE
• **disappointment** /disepointment/ NOUN

disapprove /diseproov/
If you disapprove of someone or something, you do not have a good opinion of them VERB
He disapproves of smoking.
• **disapproval** /diseproovel/ NOUN

disaster /dizaster/
Something very bad that happens NOUN
• **disastrous** /dizastres/ ADJECTIVE

d

disc /disc/
An object that is round and flat **NOUN**

discipline /diseplin/
Making people obey the rules **NOUN**
• **disciplined** /diseplind/ **ADJECTIVE**

disco /discoa/
A place or party where people go to dance to pop music **NOUN**

discover /discuver/
1. To find something out 2. To find something, especially for the first time **VERB**
• **discovery** /discuveree/ **NOUN**

discuss /discus/
To talk about something with someone **VERB**
• **discussion** /discushen/ **NOUN**

disease /dizeez/
An illness **NOUN**

disguise /disgiez/
Things people wear so that other people will not recognize them **NOUN**

Snake was wearing a disguise.

• **disguise** /disgiez/ **VERB**

disgust /disgust/
To make someone feel very shocked or upset about something **VERB**
• **disgust** /disgust/ **NOUN**
• **disgusting** /disgusting/ **ADJECTIVE**

dish /dish/
1. A plate or bowl for food   *a butter dish*
2. Food cooked or prepared as a meal
3. Dishes are the plates, cups and other things that people use for eating meals
Inky was busy washing the dishes. **NOUN**
■ **dishes** /dishiz/ **PLURAL**

dishonest /disonest/
Not honest **ADJECTIVE**
• **dishonesty** /disonestee/ **NOUN**

dishwasher /dishwosher/
A machine for washing dirty dishes **NOUN**

disinfectant /disinfectent/
A chemical that kills germs **NOUN**

disintegrate /disintegrait/
To fall apart in very small pieces **VERB**

disk /disk/
A flat round object that stores music, films or computer information **NOUN**
Save your work on a floppy disk.

disk drive /disk driev/
The part in a computer that holds the disk and makes it work **NOUN**

dislike /disliek/
To not like someone or something **VERB**
• **dislike** /disliek/ **NOUN**

dismal /dizmel/
Sad or dark **ADJECTIVE**

D

disobey /disǝbai/
To not do what someone tells you to do
VERB
• **disobedient** /disǝbeedeeǝnt/ ADJECTIVE

disorganized /disorgǝniezd/
1. Not good at organizing things
He's very disorganized. 2. Badly planned
ADJECTIVE

display /displai/
To show something clearly so that
everyone can see it VERB
• **display** /displai/ NOUN

disposable /dispoazǝbǝl/
If something is disposable, it is made
so that you can throw it away after
you have used it ADJECTIVE
a disposable camera

disrupt /disrupt/
To stop something from happening or
continuing in the usual way VERB
• **disruption** /disrupshǝn/ NOUN

dissatisfied /dissatisfied/
Not pleased with something ADJECTIVE

dissolve /dizolv/
If something solid dissolves or you
dissolve it, it is put into a liquid so
that it becomes part of the liquid VERB
Sugar dissolves in tea.

distance /distǝns/
1. The amount of space between two
places *What's the distance between your
house and school?* 2. **in the distance**
Far away NOUN
• **distant** /distǝnt/ Far away ADJECTIVE

distinct /distingct/
1. Very different *All the children have
distinct handwriting.* 2. Noticeable
There's a distinct smell of gas. ADJECTIVE
• **distinction** /distingcshǝn/
A difference NOUN
• **distinctly** /distingctlee/ Clearly ADVERB

distinctive /distingctiv/
Very different and easy to recognize
ADJECTIVE *Snake has a distinctive look.*

district /district/
A part of a town, city or country NOUN

disturb /disterb/
1. To annoy or interrupt someone, for
example by making a noise *Don't disturb
me while I'm working.* 2. To worry or upset
someone 3. To move things out of place
VERB
• **disturbance** /disterbǝns/ NOUN

ditch /dich/
A long hole in the ground, such as by
the side of the road NOUN

dive /diev/
1. To jump head first into water
2. To move down very quickly VERB

• **dive** /diev/ NOUN
• **diver** /dievǝr/ NOUN

divide /divied/
1. To separate something into smaller
parts or groups 2. To find out how
many times a smaller number can go
into a bigger number *Ten divided by
five equals two.* VERB
• **division** /divizhǝn/ NOUN

divorced /divorst/
Not married any more ADJECTIVE

dizzy /dizee/
Feeling as if everything is going around
and around, and you might fall over
ADJECTIVE

d

do /doo/
1. To perform an action *What is Inky doing?* 2. To be enough *That will do.* 3. **do up** To fasten something *Do up your coat.* VERB
■ **does, did, done**

doctor /docter/
A person who treats people who are sick NOUN

document /docyement/
1. A piece of paper with important information on it 2. A piece of work created on a computer NOUN

dodge /doj/
To move quickly to try and avoid something VERB

does /duz/
▶ **do** VERB

dog /dog/
An animal that has a fur coat and barks, that lots of people keep as a pet NOUN

doll /dol/
A toy that looks like a person or baby NOUN

dollar /doler/
A unit of money used in many countries such as the USA, Canada and Australia. There are a hundred cents in a dollar NOUN

dolphin /dolfin/
An intelligent sea animal that swims in groups NOUN

dome /doam/
A special type of roof that is shaped like the top half of a ball NOUN

dominoes /domenoaz/
A game that people play using long flat pieces of wood or plastic with different numbers of spots on them NOUN PLURAL

done[1] /dun/
PAST PARTICIPLE ▶ **do**

done[2] /dun/
1. Finished *I'm done!* 2. Cooked *Are the potatoes done yet?* ADJECTIVE

donkey /dongkee/
An animal like a small furry horse with long ears NOUN

don't /doant/
A short way of saying 'do not', especially when speaking VERB
Don't forget your homework!

door /dor/
A flat object that you open or close to go into or out of somewhere, such as a room or building NOUN
• **doorbell** /dorbel/ NOUN
• **doorknob** /dornob/ NOUN
• **doormat** /dormat/ NOUN
• **doorstep** /dorstep/ NOUN
• **doorway** /dorwai/ NOUN

dormitory /dormetree/
A big room with lots of beds in it, such as in a school NOUN

Dd

dose /doʊs/
An amount of medicine that you take at one time NOUN

dot /dot/
A small spot or mark NOUN

double[1] /dubəl/
1. Twice as many, twice as much, or twice the normal size *Your apple is double the size of mine!* 2. For two people *Is there room for a double bed?* 3. Made up of two things of the same type *You spell 'door' d–double o–r.* ADJECTIVE, ADVERB, **NOUN**

double[2] /dubəl/
To make something twice as big, or to become twice as many, or twice as much VERB *Take any number, and then double it.*
• **double-decker** /dubəl decer/
A bus that has two levels NOUN

doubt /doʊt/
To not be sure of something VERB
• **doubt** /doʊt/ NOUN
• **doubtful** /doʊtfəl/ ADJECTIVE

dough /doʊ/
A mixture of flour and water for baking bread or cakes NOUN

doughnut /doʊnut/
A small round cake often shaped like a ring NOUN

dove /duv/
A bird like a small pigeon NOUN

down[1] /doʊn/
1. Towards or in a lower position or level *Walk down the stairs. • I'm down here!*
2. Along *I was walking down the street.*
ADVERB, PREPOSITION
• **downhill** /doʊnhil/ ADVERB
• **downstairs** /doʊnsteerz/ ADVERB
• **downwards** /doʊnwerds/ ADVERB

down[2] /doʊn/
Soft feathers on a young bird NOUN

doze /doʊz/
To sleep for a little while VERB

dozen /duzen/
1. A group of twelve *I'll have a dozen eggs, please.* 2. **dozens of** Lots of NOUN

drag /drag/
To pull something along the ground, often something heavy VERB

dragon /dragen/
In stories, a dragon is an animal with wings and a long tail that makes fire come out of its mouth NOUN

dragonfly /dragenflie/
A colourful insect with a long thin body and wings, often seen over water NOUN

drain[1] /drain/
A pipe that takes away waste liquids NOUN

drain[2] /drain/
1. To make or let water flow away from something *Drain the dishes.* 2. To flow away *The water drained away.* VERB
• **drainpipe** /drainpiep/ NOUN

Dd

draining board /draining bord/
A place on a kitchen sink where people put dishes until they are dry NOUN

drama /drahmə/
1. A play that people act in
2. Any event that is exciting or very serious NOUN

drank /drangk/
PAST TENSE ▶ **drink**

drastic /drastic/
Very strong or extreme ADJECTIVE
drastic action

draught /draft/
Cold air that comes into a room NOUN
• **draughty** /draftee/ ADVERB

draughts /drafts/
A game for two people played on a board with squares, using small round pieces NOUN PLURAL

draw /draw/
1. To make a picture with a pencil or pen
2. To attract *The race will draw a crowd.*
3. To move somewhere *The car drew closer.* 4. To pull something *Can you draw the curtains?* 5. To finish a game with the same score on both sides VERB
■ **drew, drawn**

drawbridge /drawbrij/
A bridge in front of a castle or over a river, that can be lifted up and down
NOUN

drawer /dror/
An open box for putting things in that slides in and out of a piece of furniture
NOUN

drawing /drawing/
1. A picture done with a pencil or pen
2. The making of pictures *Ann is very good at drawing.* NOUN

drawn /drawn/
PAST PARTICIPLE ▶ **draw**

dread /dred/
To feel frightened or worried about something that might happen VERB

dreadful /dredfəl/
Very bad ADJECTIVE
a dreadful mess

dreadfully /dredfəlee/
Very, or very bad ADVERB
Let's go home now, it's dreadfully late.

dream[1] /dreem/
1. The images and thoughts that you have when you are asleep 2. Something you really want to happen in the future that you often think about *My dream is to have a new yellow bike.* NOUN

dream[2] /dreem/
1. To have a dream when you are asleep
2. To think a lot about something that you really want to happen VERB
■ **dreamt** or **dreamed**
• **dreamer** /dreemer/ NOUN

dreamt /dremt/
PAST TENSE ▶ **dream**²

dreary /driｱree/
Not pleasant or interesting ADJECTIVE

drenched /drencht/
Very wet ADJECTIVE
*Inky got caught in the rain
and was drenched.*

dress¹ /dres/
1. A top and a skirt in one piece
2. Someone's way of dressing NOUN

dress² /dres/
1. To put clothes on 2. **dress up**
To put on special clothes VERB
• **dressing-up** /dresing up/ NOUN

dressing gown /dresing goun/
A kind of thin loose coat people wear
over their pyjamas NOUN

drew /droo/
PAST TENSE ▶ **draw**

dribble /dribel/
1. To let liquid flow from the mouth
The baby is dribbling. 2. To keep a football
moving along with you as you run VERB
• **dribble** /dribel/ NOUN

drift /drift/
To float along slowly on the wind or
water VERB
• **drift** /drift/ A big pile of snow or
sand made by the wind NOUN

drill /dril/
A machine for making holes in something
hard NOUN

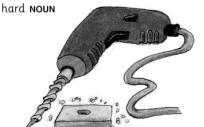

• **drill** /dril/ VERB

drink /dringk/
To put a liquid in your mouth and
swallow it VERB
■ **drank, drunk**
• **drink** /dringk/ NOUN
• **drinkable** /dringkebel/ ADJECTIVE

drip /drip/
1. To fall in small drops *Water dripped
from the roof.* 2. To let liquid fall in small
drops *Inky dripped paint all over the carpet.*
VERB
• **drip** /drip/ NOUN

drive¹ /driev/
1. To control a vehicle or an animal and
make it go somewhere 2. To take
someone somewhere by car 3. To make
someone go somewhere or behave in a
certain way *The rain drove Bee inside.*
• *You're driving me crazy!* VERB
■ **drove, driven**
• **driver** /driever/ NOUN

drive² /driev/
1. A ride in a car
2. Or **driveway** /drievwai/ A small
area for someone's car between their
house and the street NOUN

driven /driven/
PAST PARTICIPLE ▶ **drive**¹

drizzle /drizel/
To rain very slightly VERB
• **drizzle** /drizel/ NOUN

droop /droop/
To hang down VERB

drop¹ /drop/
1. A tiny amount of liquid 2. A fall
or reduction *There's been a drop in
temperature.* NOUN

d

drop[2] /drop/
1. To fall, or to let something fall
2. To go down to a lower amount or level   *The wind has dropped.*
3. **drop in** To visit VERB

drought /drout/
A long period of very dry weather when there is not enough water NOUN

drove /droav/
PAST TENSE ▶ **drive**[1]

drown /droun/
To die from being under water with no air to breathe VERB

drowsy /drouzee/
Very sleepy ADJECTIVE

drug /drug/
A type of medicine for treating an illness NOUN
• **drug** /drug/ VERB

drum /drum/
A big round musical instrument that you hit with sticks to make sounds NOUN

• **drum** /drum/ VERB
• **drummer** /drumer/ NOUN
• **drumstick** /drumstic/ NOUN

drunk[1] /drungk/
PAST PARTICIPLE ▶ **drink**

drunk[2] /drungk/
Having drunk too much alcohol
ADJECTIVE

dry[1] /drie/
Without water or liquid ADJECTIVE

dry[2] /drie/
To make or become dry VERB
Dad was drying the dishes.
• **dryer** /drieer/ A machine for drying things such as your hair or clothes
NOUN

duchess /duches/
The wife of a duke NOUN

duck[1] /duc/
A bird with short legs and a big round beak that swims on water NOUN

• **duckling** /ducling/ A young duck NOUN

duck[2] /duc/
To move your head or body down very quickly to avoid something VERB

due[1] /due/
due to Because of PREPOSITION

due[2] /due/
1. Expected *My plane is due in an hour.*
2. If money is due, someone must pay it to someone else ADJECTIVE

dug /dug/
PAST TENSE ▶ **dig**

duke /duek/
A man of great importance in society
NOUN

D

dull /dul/
1. Not interesting *a dull story*
2. Cloudy *a dull day*
3. Not bright or strong in colour
4. Not sharp *a dull sound* **ADJECTIVE**

dumb /dum/
1. Not able to speak
2. Stupid *That's a dumb idea!* **ADJECTIVE**

dummy /**du**mee/
1. The model of a person for showing clothes 2. A rubber object that babies suck **NOUN**

dump¹ /dump/
1. To put something down heavily or in a careless way 2. To get rid of something that you do not want any more **VERB**

dump² /dump/
1. A place to leave rubbish or unwanted things 2. An untidy or dirty place **NOUN**

dungeon /dunjen/
An old dark prison built underground **NOUN**

during /**du**ering/
1. All through a period of time *People sleep during the night.* 2. At one point in a period of time *Inky woke up during the night.* **PREPOSITION**

dusk /dusk/
The time of the day when it starts to get dark **NOUN**

dust¹ /dust/
A powder that is made up of tiny pieces of something such as dirt or sand **NOUN**

Inky drove across the field in a cloud of dust.

• **dusty** /**du**stee/ **ADJECTIVE**

dust² /dust/
To wipe or brush the dust off something **VERB**

dustbin /**du**sbin/
A large container with a lid for storing rubbish **NOUN**

duster /**du**ster/
A cloth for getting rid of dust **NOUN**

duty /**du**etee/
1. The things people must do, or feel that they should do 2. A tax **NOUN**

duvet /**doo**vai/
A bed cover filled with feathers or other warm material that people use instead of a blanket **NOUN**

dwarf /dworf/
1. Someone or something that is much smaller than usual 2. A magic creature in stories like a small man **NOUN**

dye /die/
A special substance for changing the colour of something such as cloth **NOUN**
• **dye** /die/ **VERB**

dying /**die**ing/
▶ **die** **VERB**

e

Ee

each /eech/
All of the people or things you are
talking about **ADJECTIVE**, PRONOUN
Each person is different. • *Snake, Bee and
Inky each had an apple.*

eager /eeger/
Really happy about something that is
going to happen soon **ADJECTIVE**
Snake and Bee are eager to play.

eagle /eegəl/
A big bird with a curved beak that eats
small animals **NOUN**

ear /ier/
One of the two parts on either side of
your head used for hearing **NOUN**
▶ **PARTS OF THE BODY**, page 18
• **earache** /iɛraic/ **NOUN**
• **earphones** /ierfoɑnz/ **NOUN PLURAL**

early /erlee/
1. Getting somewhere before you expected
to 2. Near the beginning of something
in the early evening • *This happened early in
the book.* **ADJECTIVE**, ADVERB

earn /ern/
1. To get money for the work you do
2. To get something because you deserve
it **VERB**

earring /iɛring/
Earrings are jewels that people wear on
their ears **NOUN**

earth /erth/
1. The soil that plants and trees grow in
2. Earth is the planet we live on **NOUN**

earthquake /erthquaik/
An occasion when the ground suddenly
shakes **NOUN**

earwig /ierwig/
A long thin brown insect **NOUN**
▶ **INSECTS**, page 14

easel /eezəl/
A frame people use for putting paintings
on while they are painting them **NOUN**

easily /eezilee/
Without any problems **ADVERB**
Bee found the answer easily.

east /eest/
The direction from which the sun rises.
If someone is looking north, the east
is on their right **NOUN**
• **east** /eest/ **ADJECTIVE**, ADVERB
▶ **WORLD MAP**, page 14

easy /eezee/
If something is easy, it does not cause
you any problems or need much effort
ADJECTIVE

eat /eet/
To put food into your mouth, chew it
and swallow it **VERB**
■ ate, eaten
• **eatable** /eetəbəl/ **ADJECTIVE**
• **eater** /eeter/ **NOUN**

echo /ecoa/
A sound that can be heard again and again because it is reflected from a surface such as the wall of a cave **NOUN**
■ **echoes** /ecoaz/ **PLURAL**
• **echo** /ecoa/ **VERB**

eclipse /eclips/
When the moon moves between the earth and the sun and blocks out the light **NOUN**

edge /ej/
The line on the outside of something where it stops **NOUN**

edgy /ejee/
Nervous, and getting annoyed quickly **ADJECTIVE**

edible /edibel/
Able to be eaten **ADJECTIVE**

educate /eduecait/
To teach someone, or to help them to learn **VERB**
• **educated** /eduecaitid/ **ADJECTIVE**
• **education** /eduecaishen/ **NOUN**
• **educational** /eduecaishenel/ **ADJECTIVE**

eel /eel/
A very long and thin fish like a snake **NOUN**

effect /efect/
If something has an effect on something else, it changes it in some way **NOUN**

efficient /efishent/
Working well, and not wasting any time or money **ADJECTIVE**

effort /efert/
When you try very hard to do something **NOUN**

egg /eg/
1. A round or oval object with a shell that contains the baby of a bird, fish, reptile or insect 2. The egg of a chicken used for food **NOUN**

• **eggcup** /egcup/ **NOUN**
• **eggshell** /egshel/ **NOUN**

either¹ /iether/
1. Only one thing or the other, not both *Either Bee or Snake can go with Inky.*
2. Both *You can go either this way or that way to get to the forest.*
ADJECTIVE, CONJUNCTION, PRONOUN

either² /eether/
Also **ADVERB**
I can't ride a bike either.

elastic /elastic/
A rubber material that stretches **NOUN**
• **elastic band** /elastic band/

elbow /elboa/
The joint in the middle of your arm **NOUN**
▶ **PARTS OF THE BODY**, page 18

elderly /elderlee/
Another way of saying old **ADJECTIVE**
The elderly man had white hair and walked with a limp.

eldest /eldist/
Another way of saying oldest **ADJECTIVE**
Victor is the eldest boy in his family.

e

electric /electric/
Using electricity or connected with it
ADJECTIVE
• **electrical** /electrical/ ADJECTIVE

electricity /electrisetee/
A type of energy that flows down wires
NOUN

electronic /electronic/
Using computer chips or connected with computers ADJECTIVE

elephant /elifent/
A very heavy animal with big ears, tusks and a long trunk NOUN

elf /elf/
In stories, an elf is a magic creature like a little person NOUN
■ **elves** /elvz/ PLURAL

elk /elk/
A very large deer with big horns NOUN

else /els/
1. Instead *Would you like something else?*
2. More, also *Can you see anything else?*
3. If not *Be quiet, or else I can't hear what the teacher is saying.* ADVERB

elsewhere /elsweer/
In or to another place ADVERB

elves /elvz/
NOUN PLURAL ▶ **elf**

email /eemail/
Short for 'electronic mail'. 1. A way of sending messages using computers
2. The message you send NOUN
• **email** /eemail/ VERB

embarrass /embares/
To make someone feel uncomfortable with other people, or ashamed about something VERB
• **embarrassed** /embarest/ ADJECTIVE
• **embarrassing** /embaresing/ ADJECTIVE

emergency /emerjensee/
Something dangerous or unexpected that must be dealt with very quickly NOUN

emotion /emoashen/
A very strong feeling such as love or fear
NOUN
• **emotional** /emoashenel/ ADJECTIVE

employ /emploi/
To give work to someone, and pay them for doing it VERB
• **employer** /emploier/ NOUN

employment /emploiment/
Work NOUN
Marie's looking for employment.

empty¹ /emptee/
Without anything inside it or on it
ADJECTIVE *an empty box* • *an empty chair*

empty² /emptee/
To take everything out of something VERB

E

emu /eemue/
A big bird from Australia that cannot fly
NOUN

enclose /enclɑuz/
To put something inside or around
something else VERB
Dad enclosed some money with his letter.
• **enclosed** /enclɑuzd/ ADJECTIVE

encounter /encounter/
To meet someone or something VERB
• **encounter** /encounter/ NOUN

encourage /encurij/
To say or do things that help or support
someone with what they are doing VERB
*Inky Mouse encouraged Snake and Bee to
learn to read.*
• **encouragement** /encurijment/ NOUN
• **encouraging** /encurijing/ ADJECTIVE

encyclopaedia /ensieclepeedeee/
A book containing information about
many different subjects, arranged in
alphabetical order NOUN

end¹ /end/
1. The last part of something
2. **at an end** Finished or stopped
The lesson is at an end. NOUN

end² /end/
If something ends or you end something,
it comes to its final part and is finished
VERB
• **ending** /ending/ The final part of
something such as a book NOUN
• **endless** /endles/ Not stopping, having
no end ADJECTIVE

enemy /enemee/
1. Someone who hates you
2. The people or country on the
other side in a war NOUN

energetic /enerjetic/
Very active, and full of energy ADJECTIVE

energy /enerjee/
1. The strength or power to do things
2. Things such as oil and electricity that
people use for heat or for making
machines work NOUN

engaged /engaijd/
1. If a man and a woman are engaged,
they have decided to get married
2. If the phone is engaged, someone
is already using it ADJECTIVE

• **engagement** /engaijment/ NOUN

engine /enjin/
1. A machine that uses energy such as
electricity or oil to make something move
2. The big vehicle that pulls a train NOUN

engineer /enjinier/
1. Someone who repairs things such
as televisions 2. Someone who designs
things such as machines and roads NOUN

enjoy /enjoi/
To like something very much VERB
• **enjoyable** /enjoiebel/ ADJECTIVE
• **enjoyment** /enjoiment/ NOUN

enormous /inormes/
Very very big ADJECTIVE

e

enough /ɘnuf/
As much as is needed
ADJECTIVE, ADVERB, PRONOUN

enter /enter/
1. To go in or come in 2. To take part
in something like a competition 3. To do
something like press the Enter key to put
information in a computer VERB

entertain /entertain/
1. To make people happy and interested
2. To have guests come to your home
VERB
• **entertainer** /entertainer/ NOUN
• **entertaining** /entertaining/ ADJECTIVE
• **entertainment** /entertainment/ NOUN

enthusiastic /enthoozeeastic/
Very interested about something
or about doing something ADJECTIVE
• **enthusiasm** /enthoozeeazm/ NOUN

entire /entieer/
All of something, the whole of something
ADJECTIVE

entirely /entieerlee/
In every way, completely ADVERB

entrance /entrens/
The place where you go into a building
NOUN

entry /entree/
1. When you go into a building
2. What you send in for a competition
NOUN

envelope /enveloap/
The paper cover that a letter or card is
put into NOUN

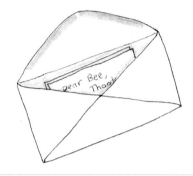

envious /enveees/
If you are envious of someone, you want
the same things that someone else has
ADJECTIVE
• **envy** /envee/ NOUN, VERB

environment /envierenment/
1. The conditions that influence people's
lives 2. The air, water and land where
people, animals and plants live NOUN

episode /episoad/
An episode of a TV or radio programme
is one of the parts it is divided into NOUN

equal[1] /eequel/
The same in size or quantity ADJECTIVE

equal[2] /eequel/
1. To be the same *Three plus three equal
six.* 2. To be as good as someone or
something else VERB
• **equally** /eequelee/ ADVERB
• **equals sign** /eequelz sien/ NOUN

equator /equaiter/
An imaginary line around the middle of
the earth NOUN

equipment /equipment/
All the machines and tools that people use for an activity NOUN

equivalent /equivelent/
The same as something else NOUN
• **equivalent** /equivelent/ ADJECTIVE

erase /eraiz/
1. To get rid of something written in pencil by using an eraser 2. To get rid of information stored in the memory of a computer VERB

eraser /eraizer/
A little piece of rubber for getting rid of pencil marks NOUN

errand /erend/
A short journey to do or get something for someone NOUN

error /erer/
1. Another word for a mistake
2. A computer problem NOUN

erupt /erupt/
To come out suddenly and violently VERB
The volcano erupted.

escalator /escelaiter/
Moving stairs that carry people from one level to another NOUN

escape /escaip/
To get away from somewhere VERB
He escaped from prison.
• **escape** /escaip/ NOUN

especially /espeshelee/
1. A word you use to give special importance to something 2. Another way of saying most of all Snake especially likes to eat eggs. ADVERB

essential /esenshel/
Very very important, or necessary ADJECTIVE

establish /establish/
1. To begin something 2. To prove something The police established the facts before arresting the man. VERB

estimate /estimait/
To guess a value as accurately as you can VERB
• **estimate** /estimet/ NOUN

etc /etsetre/
Short for etcetera, a word used at the end of a list to show that there are more things in it ADVERB
At the shop Snake had to buy bread, milk, tea etc.

eve /eev/
The day before something NOUN
Christmas Eve

even[1] /eeven/
1. A word used to say something in the sentence is surprising We've all made mistakes, even Phonic. 2. More than something else, or more than before This book is even better than that one. ADVERB

even[2] /eeven/
1. Completely flat The road has an even surface. 2. Not changing The car drove at an even speed. 3. An even number can be divided by two ADJECTIVE
• **evenly** /eevenlee/ ADVERB

e

evening /eevning/
The part of the day between the afternoon and night **NOUN**

event /ɛvent/
Something that happens **NOUN**

eventually /ɛvenchooɛlee/
Happening after a long time **ADVERB**

ever /ever/
1. At any time *Don't ever do that again!*
2. Always *I'll love you for ever.*
3. Very *You're ever so lucky!*
ADVERB

evergreen /evergreen/
A tree that keeps its leaves even in winter **NOUN**

every /evɛree/
1. All of the things or people you are talking about *Every boy and girl in our class can read.* 2. Used to say that something keeps happening *We go swimming every week.* **ADJECTIVE**
• **everybody** /evɛreebodee/ **PRONOUN**
• **everyone** /evɛreewun/ **PRONOUN**
• **everything** /evɛreething/ **PRONOUN**

everywhere /evɛreeweer/
In every place **ADVERB**

evil /eevil/
Very very bad **ADJECTIVE**
• **evil** /eevil/ **NOUN**

ewe /ue/
A female sheep **NOUN**

exact /egzact/
1. Completely correct in every way *an exact copy of something* 2. This and no other *At that exact time I turned on the TV.* **ADJECTIVE**
• **exactly** /egzactlee/ **ADVERB**

exaggerate /egzajɛrait/
To say that something is, for example, bigger, better or worse than it really is **VERB**
• **exaggeration** /egzajɛraishɛn/ **NOUN**

exam /egzam/
A test of someone's knowledge **NOUN**

examination /egzaminaishɛn/
1. Another word for exam 2. When you look at something carefully **NOUN**

examine /egzamin/
To look at something carefully **VERB**

example /egzampel/
1. Something that shows what you mean or explains something *I'll show you how to answer the questions by doing an example.* 2. Something that is typical of something else *Here's a good example of Snake's work.* 3. A pattern that other people should follow because it is good *We should all follow John's example because he always works hard.* **NOUN**

excellent /exelent/
Very very good **ADJECTIVE**

except /eksept/
Used to show there is something that is not included in what you say
PREPOSITION, CONJUNCTION
Everyone's coming on the trip except Frank.
• *There's nothing to do except wait.*
• **exception** /eksepshen/ **NOUN**

exceptional /eksepshenel/
Very unusual **ADJECTIVE**
• **exceptionally** /eksepshenelee/ **ADVERB**

exchange /exchainj/
To give someone something and get another thing in return **VERB**
The two girls exchanged addresses.
• **exchange** /exchainj/ **NOUN**

excite /eksiet/
If something excites you, it makes you feel happy and eager to do something
VERB *I'm really excited about the trip.*
• **excitement** /eksietment/ **NOUN**
• **exciting** /eksieting/ **ADJECTIVE**

exclamation mark
/exclemaishen mark/
A punctuation mark (**!**) that people use at the end of a sentence to show a strong feeling like anger or surprise **NOUN**

excuse[1] /ekscuez/
1. To forgive someone for doing something bad *We'll excuse you for being late this time.* 2. To let someone not do something *Please excuse Zack from swimming today.* 3. Used to attract someone's attention *Excuse me, can you tell me the way to the station?*
VERB

excuse[2] /ekscues/
1. A reason that explains something you did so that people will forgive you
2. A reason you give to avoid doing something **NOUN**

execute /execuet/
To kill someone as a punishment
VERB

exercise[1] /exersiez/
1. Things you do such as running or swimming to keep your body healthy
2. A test of someone's knowledge using a number of questions **NOUN**
• **exercise book** /exersiez book/
NOUN

exercise[2] /exersiez/
To move your body in different ways to keep healthy **VERB**

exhausted /egzawstid/
Very very tired **ADJECTIVE**

exhibit[1] /egzibit/
To show something **VERB**

exhibit[2] /egzibit/
Something that is being shown
NOUN

exhibition /exibishen/
An event where people show things such as paintings **NOUN**

e

exist /egzist/
1. To live or survive *In some places people have to exist on bread and water.*
2. To be real *Some people believe ghosts exist.* VERB
• **existence** /egzistens/ NOUN
• **existing** /egzisting/ ADJECTIVE

exit¹ /exit/
The door or place you go through to leave somewhere such as a building NOUN

exit² /exet/
1. To leave or go out of somewhere
2. To leave a computer program VERB

expand /ekspand/
To become bigger, or make something bigger VERB

expect /ekspect/
1. To think something may happen in the future *I expect they will work it out eventually.* 2. To think something will happen at a particular time *I expect Snake here for tea at eleven o'clock.* VERB
• **expectation** /expectaishen/ NOUN

expel /ekspel/
To tell someone they must leave VERB
He was so naughty they expelled him from school.

expenses /ekspensiz/
Money spent on doing your work NOUN

expensive /ekspensiv/
Costing a lot of money ADJECTIVE

experience¹ /ekspiereeens/
1. Knowledge that people get from doing things 2. Something that happens to you NOUN

experience² /ekspiereeens/
To have something happen to you VERB

experiment¹ /eksperiment/
A scientific test to try and discover something NOUN

experiment² /eksperiment/
To try different things, or to do experiments VERB

expert /expert/
Someone who knows a lot about something NOUN

expire /ekspieer/
1. To come to an end 2. To die VERB

explain /eksplain/
1. To tell people something clearly so that they can understand it 2. To give the reasons for something *Bee explained why she was late.* VERB
• **explanation** /explenaishen/ NOUN

explode /eksploʊd/
If something such as a bomb explodes,
it breaks up into small pieces and makes
a very loud noise VERB
• **explosion** /eksploʊzhen/ NOUN

explore /eksplor/
1. To travel in a place you do not know
2. To search or examine something to
find out what it is like VERB

express[1] /ekspres/
To say your feelings or ideas VERB

express[2] /ekspres/
A train that goes very fast NOUN
• **express** /ekspres/ Going fast ADJECTIVE

expression /ekspreshen/
1. A look on someone's face
2. A group of words NOUN

extend /ekstend/
1. To continue over a bigger distance
The town extends as far as the river.
2. To make something bigger or longer
VERB
• **extension** /ekstenshen/ NOUN

exterminate /eksterminait/
To destroy something entirely VERB

extinct /ekstingct/
Not living any more ADJECTIVE
Dinosaurs are extinct.

extra[1] /extre/
More of something ADJECTIVE
Bee needs extra time to finish her work.

extra[2] /extre/
1. More money *That costs extra.*
2. More than before *Be extra careful!*
ADVERB

extra[3] /extre/
An extra is something more added to
something NOUN

extract /ekstract/
To take or pull something out of
somewhere VERB

extreme /ekstreem/
Used to mean the greatest possible
amount of something ADJECTIVE
Some people live in extreme poverty.
• **extremely** /ekstreemlee/ Very ADVERB

eye /ie/
1. One of the two parts of your body
you use for seeing 2. **keep an eye on**
To watch or pay attention to someone
or something NOUN
• **eyeball** /iebawl/ NOUN
• **eyebrows** /iebrouz/ NOUN PLURAL
• **eyelashes** /ielashiz/ NOUN PLURAL
• **eyelids** /ielidz/ NOUN PLURAL

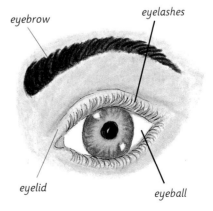

eyebrow   *eyelashes*

eyelid   *eyeball*

Ff

fabulous /fabyeles/
Wonderful **ADJECTIVE**
Bee is a fabulous flyer.

face¹ /fais/
The front part of your head **NOUN**
▶ **PARTS OF THE BODY**, page 18

face² /fais/
1. To look or be looking in the direction of someone or something *Turn and face the front.* 2. To deal with something bad *You must face this problem.* **VERB**
• **facing** /faising/ Opposite **PREPOSITION**

fact /fact/
Something that is true, or that really happened **NOUN**

factory /factree/
A big place where people make things **NOUN**

fade /faid/
1. To gradually lose colour and become less bright *Look how my jeans have faded!*
2. To gradually disappear **VERB**

fail /fail/
1. To try and do something but not be able to 2. To not do something that you should *Zack failed to tell his teacher that he would be late.* 3. To not happen *The letter failed to arrive.* 4. To not pass an exam **VERB**
• **failure** /failyer/ **NOUN**

faint¹ /faint/
To feel very weak suddenly and not know what is happening around you because you cannot see or hear for a short time **VERB**

faint² /faint/
Not very clear **ADJECTIVE**

fair¹ /feer/
1. Light in colour 2. Treating all people the same *Everyone was given a fair share of cake.* **ADJECTIVE**
• **fairly** /feerlee/ **ADVERB**

fair² /feer/
1. An outside event with games and machines to ride on 2. An exhibition where people show things from different companies or countries *We're going to a book fair.* **NOUN**

fairy /feeree/
A small person in stories with wings and magical powers **NOUN**

faith /faith/
A strong feeling of belief in something or someone **NOUN**
• **faithful** /faithfel/ **ADJECTIVE**

fake¹ /faik/
If something is fake, it looks real but is not **ADJECTIVE**
• **fake** /faik/ **NOUN**

fake² /faik/
To pretend to do or feel something **VERB**

falcon /fawlcen/
A big bird like a hawk that kills other birds and animals **NOUN**

fall[1] /fawl/
To move down from a higher position to a lower one VERB
Inky tripped and fell over. · The vase fell down onto the floor.
■ **fell, fallen**

fall[2] /fawl/
A fall in something such as the temperature means it goes down NOUN

fallen /fawlen/
PAST PARTICIPLE ▶ **fall**[1]

false /fawls/
Not true or not real ADJECTIVE
false teeth

fame /faim/
When lots of people know about someone NOUN

familiar /femileeer/
1. If someone is familiar, you recognize or know them 2. If you are familiar with something, you know it well ADJECTIVE

family /familee/
1. People who are related to each other *My family is made up of my mother, father, grandparents, aunts, uncles, etc.* 2. A group of things such as animals or plants *Lions and tigers belong to the cat family.* NOUN

famine /famin/
When lots of people do not have enough food to eat NOUN

famous /faimes/
Known to lots of people ADJECTIVE

fan /fan/
1. A machine with blades that go around for making the air cooler 2. Something flat that people wave in their hand to keep cool 3. Someone who likes someone famous or likes watching sports or music NOUN
• **fan** /fan/ VERB

fantastic /fantastic/
Very very good ADJECTIVE

far /far/
1. Used when you are talking about a big distance or something that is a long way away *Bee was sitting at the far end of the table.* 2. Very much *Snake's reading is far better than it used to be.*
ADVERB, ADJECTIVE
■ **farther, farthest**
• **faraway** /farewai/ ADJECTIVE

fare /feer/
The money you pay to travel somewhere NOUN *bus fare*

farm /farm/
Land people use for keeping animals like cows or sheep, or growing plants for food NOUN

• **farm** /farm/ VERB
• **farmer** /farmer/ NOUN
• **farmyard** /farmyard/ NOUN

Ff

Ff

farther /farther/
Used when you are talking about a bigger distance than something else ADVERB, ADJECTIVE
Bee threw the ball, but Inky threw it farther.

farthest /farthest/
Used when you are talking about the biggest distance ADVERB, ADJECTIVE
Bee threw the ball, Inky threw it farther, but Snake threw it farthest.

fascinate /fasinait/
To interest someone greatly VERB

fascinating /fasinaiting/
Very interesting ADJECTIVE
• **fascination** /fasinaishen/ NOUN

fashion /fashen/
1. The type of clothes people wear that are popular at a particular time 2. A way of doing things NOUN
• **fashionable** /fashenebel/ ADJECTIVE

fast[1] /fast/
1. Quick or quickly 2. If a clock or watch is fast, the time it shows is later than it should be ADJECTIVE, ADVERB

fast[2] /fast/
To eat no food for a short time VERB

fasten /fasen/
1. To close something or join two ends of something together *Fasten your seatbelts!* 2. To fix something to something else VERB

fat[1] /fat/
Big and heavy ADJECTIVE
• **fatten** /faten/ VERB

fat[2] /fat/
1. The substance under the skin of people and animals that keeps them warm 2. An oily substance such as butter that is used in cooking NOUN

father /fahther/
A man who has children NOUN

fault /fawlt/
1. If something is your fault, people blame you for it *It's her fault the cup got knocked over.* 2. Something that is wrong with someone or something *The machine had a fault and would not work properly.* NOUN

faulty /fawltee/
Broken, not working properly ADJECTIVE

favour /faiver/
1. A kind action that someone does to help someone 2. **in favour of** Wanting something or supporting something NOUN

favourable /faiverebel/
Something favourable is good, and you like it ADJECTIVE

favourite /faivrit/
Your favourite thing or person is the one you like the best ADJECTIVE
• **favourite** /faivret/ NOUN

fax /fax/
1. A machine for sending and receiving messages on paper, using a telephone line 2. A message you send or receive using a fax machine NOUN
• **fax** /fax/ VERB

fear[1] /fier/
A very strong unpleasant feeling people have when they are in danger NOUN

fear[2] /fier/
1. To feel frightened that something bad will happen 2. To be afraid of someone or something VERB

feast /feest/
A big and delicious meal for lots of people NOUN

feather /fether/
One of the soft parts that cover a bird's body **NOUN**

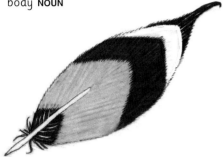

feature /feecher/
An important quality or special part of something **NOUN**
The statue is a feature of our town.

February /febrooeree/
The second month of the year **NOUN**
▶ **CALENDAR**, page 13

fed /fed/
PAST TENSE ▶ **feed**
• **fed up** /fed up/
Unhappy or bored **ADJECTIVE**

feeble /feebel/
Another word for weak **ADJECTIVE**

feed /feed/
1. To give food to someone or an animal
2. To eat a certain food *Cats sometimes feed on mice.* **VERB**
■ **fed**

feel /feel/
1. To think or have an emotion *Bee feels very happy.* 2. To touch something
3. To have a feeling when you touch something, or to give a feeling when you are touched *The water feels cold.* **VERB**
■ **felt**

feeling /feeling/
1. Feelings are such things as happiness or sadness, joy or anger, love or hate
2. A thought or idea about something
NOUN

feet /feet/
NOUN PLURAL ▶ **foot**

fell /fel/
PAST TENSE ▶ **fall**[1]

fellow /felooa/
1. Another word for a man or boy
2. Used to describe someone you share an activity with *These are my school fellows.* **NOUN**

felt /felt/
PAST TENSE ▶ **feel**

felt-tip pen /felt tip pen/
A special pen with a soft thick end **NOUN**

female /feemail/
A girl or a woman **NOUN**
• **female** /feemail/ **ADJECTIVE**

fence /fens/
Something made of wood or metal that is put around land to keep people out or animals in **NOUN**

fern /fern/
A type of plant with no flowers **NOUN**

ferocious /feroashes/
Violent and frightening **ADJECTIVE**
a ferocious lion

ferry /feree/
A boat that carries people and things short distances **NOUN**

fertile /fertiel/
Good for growing things **ADJECTIVE**
This is fertile land.

Ff

Ff

festival /festivəl/
1. An occasion when people organize special shows of something *Are you going to the music festival?* 2. A special time for celebrating something, usually a religious event *Diwali is a religious festival.* NOUN

fetch /fech/
To go and get something VERB

fever /feevər/
An illness when you have a high temperature NOUN
• **feverish** /feevərish/ ADJECTIVE

few¹ /fuel/
Not many ADJECTIVE

few² /fuel/
A small number NOUN

fiction /ficshən/
Something that has been made up and is not real or true NOUN
Novels and fairy stories are fiction.

fiddle¹ /fidəl/
To keep moving something with your fingers VERB
Stop fiddling with your pencil.

fiddle² /fidəl/
Another word for a violin NOUN

fidget /fijit/
If you fidget, you cannot keep still and keep moving your body all the time VERB
• **fidget** /fijit/ NOUN
• **fidgety** /fijətee/ ADJECTIVE

field /feeld/
1. A piece of land where people grow plants and keep animals 2. A small area of land where people play sports NOUN

fiend /feend/
A very cruel and evil person NOUN

fierce /fiers/
Frightening and violent ADJECTIVE
The dog was fierce.

fight /fiet/
1. To try and hit and hurt each other *The boys were fighting in the playground.*
2. To argue *I wish you two boys would stop fighting!* VERB
■ **fought**
• **fight** /fiet/ NOUN
• **fighter** /fietər/ NOUN

figure¹ /figer/
1. Another word for a number
2. A shape in mathematics
A hexagon is a six-sided figure.
3. The shape of a person's body NOUN

figure² /figer/
To think about something and understand it VERB

file /fiel/
1. Information on a computer that is grouped together under a special name 2. A folder to keep papers in
3. **in single file** One at a time NOUN
• **file** /fiel/ VERB

fill /fil/
To take up all the space in a container VERB *Inky filled the bottle with water.*

film /film/
1. A moving picture that you watch in the cinema 2. The plastic material in a camera for taking photos or making moving pictures NOUN
• **film** /film/ VERB

Ff

filthy /filthee/
Very dirty ADJECTIVE

fin /fin/
One of the parts of a fish that stick out and help it to balance and swim
NOUN

final /fienel/
1. The very last of something
2. If a decision is final, it cannot be changed ADJECTIVE

finally /fienelee/
1. After a long period of time
2. Used when talking about the very last thing ADVERB

finch /finch/
A small bird that eats seeds NOUN

find /fiend/
1. To get or see something that you have been looking for 2. To see something by chance 3. **find out** To learn something *We found out all about insects today.*
VERB
■ found

fine[1] /fien/
1. Good *The weather is fine today.*
2. Another way of saying yes
3. Very thin ADJECTIVE, ADVERB

fine[2] /fien/
Money paid as a punishment for doing something wrong NOUN
• **fine** /fien/ VERB

finger /fingger/
One of the long thin parts at the end of your hand NOUN
▶ PARTS OF THE BODY, page 18
• **fingernail** /finggernail/ NOUN
• **fingerprint** /finggerprint/ NOUN
• **fingertip** /finggertip/ NOUN

finish /finish/
1. To come to an end
2. To stop doing something VERB
• **finished** /finisht/ ADJECTIVE

fir /fer/
A tree with leaves shaped like needles that stay green all the year NOUN

fire[1] /fieer/
1. Flames and heat caused by something burning *Be careful, there's a house on fire!*
2. A heater for a room *Turn on the gas fire.* NOUN
• **fire engine** /fieer enjin/ NOUN
• **fire fighter** /fieer fieter/ NOUN
• **fireman** /fieermen/ NOUN
• **fireplace** /fieerplais/ NOUN
• **fire station** /fieer staishen/ NOUN

fire[2] /fieer/
1. To shoot bullets from a gun
2. To make someone leave their job VERB

firework /fieerwerk/
Fireworks are small objects containing chemicals that explode brightly that people use for fun NOUN

Ff

firm /ferm/
1. Hard but not completely hard
2. Strong, and not likely to change
I've made a firm decision. **ADJECTIVE**

first[1] /ferst/
Before all the others **ADJECTIVE**, **ADVERB**

first[2] /ferst/
1. The thing or person who comes or finishes before all the others *Snake was the first to finish the race.* 2. **at first** At the beginning **PRONOUN**, **NOUN**

fish[1] /fish/
An animal with fins that lives in the water **NOUN**
■ **fish** /fish/ or **fishes** /fishiz/ **PLURAL**

fish[2] /fish/
To try to catch fish **VERB**
• **fisherman** /fishermen/ **NOUN**
• **fishing** /fishing/ **NOUN**

fist /fist/
A tightly closed hand **NOUN**

fit[1] /fit/
1. To be the right size or shape *Does the dress fit you?* 2. To make something go in a certain space *Inky had to fit a new lock in the door.* **VERB**

fit[2] /fit/
1. Suitable for something *This is a meal fit for a king!* 2. In very good health **ADJECTIVE**

fit[3] /fit/
A sudden attack of something that is difficult to control **NOUN**
a fit of coughing

fix /fix/
1. To repair something *My watch is broken, can you fix it?* 2. To arrange something *Shall we fix a date for the meeting?* 3. To put something somewhere so that it cannot move, using something such as nails or glue *Inky fixed a picture to the wall.* **VERB**

fixture /fixcher/
Something fixed inside a building, such as a bath **NOUN**

fizz /fiz/
If a liquid fizzes, it makes lots of bubbles **VERB**
• **fizzy** /fizee/ **ADJECTIVE**

flag /flag/
A piece of cloth with a special pattern that represents a country or group **NOUN**

• **flag pole** /flag pol/ **NOUN**

flame /flaim/
A small bit of fire that comes from something burning **NOUN**

flannel /flanel/
1. A small cloth for washing yourself
2. A kind of soft cloth made from wool or cotton **NOUN**

Ff

flap¹ /flap/
To move something quickly up and down
VERB *The bird was flapping its wings.*

flap² /flap/
A thin flat part of something that is
loose and can move NOUN
the flap of an envelope

flash¹ /flash/
1. To shine brightly for a moment and
then stop, or to keep doing this *The light
flashed on and off.* 2. To show something
quickly or suddenly *A message flashed on
the screen.* 3. To move quickly *The car
flashed past.* VERB

flash² /flash/
1. A light that suddenly shines then
stops 2. A very quick look at someone
or something 3. A short length of time
NOUN

flask /flask/
A special bottle for keeping liquids hot or
cold NOUN

flat¹ /flat/
1. Level, not sloping or upright *It's on flat
ground.* 2. Smooth, not bumpy *We need a
flat piece of wood.* ADJECTIVE, ADVERB

flat² /flat/
A room or group of rooms where people
live in a large building, all on one level
NOUN

flatten /flaten/
To make something flat VERB

flavour¹ /flaiver/
The special taste of food or drink NOUN

flavour² /flaiver/
To give food a special taste by adding
something to it VERB

flaw /flaw/
A mark or break in something that
means it is not perfect NOUN
There's a slight flaw in this glass.

flea /flee/
A tiny insect that jumps and feeds on
blood NOUN
▶ INSECTS, page 14

fleece /flees/
1. The coat of wool that covers a sheep
2. A warm jacket or sweater made from
a special soft material NOUN
• **fleecy** /fleesee/ ADJECTIVE

flesh /flesh/
1. The soft part of your body that covers
your bones 2. The soft part of a fruit
such as a peach NOUN
• **fleshy** /fleshee/ ADJECTIVE

flew /floo/
PAST TENSE ▶ **fly**¹

flex /flex/
To bend and move something VERB

flick /flic/
To make something move with a small,
quick movement VERB
• **flick** /flic/ NOUN

flight /fliet/
1. A journey by plane 2. The flying
of a bird *Look at the eagle in flight.*
3. A number of stairs between one
level and the next in a building NOUN

119

Ff

fling /fling/
To throw something quickly or suddenly
VERB *Inky was so happy she flung her arms around Phonic.*
■ **flung**

flip /flip/
To turn over or put into another position
VERB *Can you flip a pancake? · The car hit a tree and flipped over.*

float /float/
1. To stay on the surface of a liquid without sinking *I saw pieces of wood floating in the sea.* 2. To stay up in the air like clouds or balloons VERB

flock[1] /floc/
A group of animals such as sheep or birds NOUN

flock[2] /floc/
To go somewhere with lots of other people or animals VERB

flood[1] /flud/
Water that overflows and covers land that is usually dry NOUN

flood[2] /flud/
1. To cover something with water
2. If people or things flood somewhere, lots of them go there *Letters flooded in from all over the world.* VERB

floor /flor/
1. The bottom part of a room that people walk on 2. One of the levels in a building NOUN
• **floorboard** /florbord/ NOUN

floppy[1] /flopee/
Hanging down, not stiff ADJECTIVE
Look at that dog's floppy ears.

floppy[2] /flopee/
Short for 'floppy disk', a square piece of plastic put into a computer to store information on NOUN

flour /flouer/
A powder made from wheat for making bread or cakes NOUN
• **floury** /floueree/ ADJECTIVE

flourish /flurish/
To be healthy or successful VERB

flow /floa/
To move along smoothly VERB
The river flowed gently by.
• **flow** /floa/ NOUN

flower /flouer/
The colourful part of a plant surrounded by petals NOUN

• **flower** /flouer/ VERB
• **flowerpot** /flouerpot/ NOUN

flown /floan/
PAST PARTICIPLE ▶ **fly**[1]

flu /floo/
Short for influenza, a type of heavy cold and fever NOUN

fluff /fluf/
Small soft lumps of dust or hair NOUN
• **fluffy** /flufee/ ADJECTIVE

flung /flung/
PAST TENSE ▶ **fling**

flush /flush/
1. To turn red in the face 2. To pour water down something to clean it VERB

Ff

flute /floot/

A musical instrument like a long thin tube that you blow into and hold sideways to your mouth NOUN

flutter /fluter/

To move or flap quickly but gently VERB *Birds flutter their wings.*

fly[1] /flie/

1. To travel through the air
2. To move or go very quickly VERB
■ **flew, flown**
• **flyover** /flieoaver/ A road bridge going over another road NOUN

fly[2] /flie/

A small flying insect with wings NOUN

foal /foal/

A young horse NOUN

foam /foam/

1. The many small white bubbles formed on the surface of a liquid 2. A type of soft rubber used in cushions NOUN
• **foam** /foam/ VERB

focus /foaces/

1. To pay attention to one thing
2. To make a picture clear on a camera VERB

fog /fog/

A cloud of tiny drops of water that hangs in the air and makes it hard to see NOUN
• **foggy** /fogee/ ADJECTIVE

foil /foil/

Very thin sheets of metal NOUN

fold /foald/

1. To bend something over *Fold the paper in half.* 2. To bend or move parts of something so it takes up less space *Fold the chairs up and put them away.* VERB
• **fold** /foald/ NOUN

folder /foalder/

1. A thin cardboard cover for papers
2. The place on a computer where information or a file is stored NOUN

folk /foak/

Another word for people NOUN

follow /foloa/

1. To go along behind someone or something *Snake followed Bee through the forest.* 2. To come after something *Day follows night.* 3. To obey rules or instructions *Follow the instructions carefully.* 4. To understand VERB
• **follower** /foloaer/ NOUN
• **following** /foloaing/ ADJECTIVE

fond /fond/

If you are fond of something or someone, you like them very much ADJECTIVE

font /font/

The design or style of the letters used in printing or on a computer screen NOUN

food /food/

What people and animals eat NOUN

121

Ff

fool /fool/
1. A stupid person
2. A sort of clown NOUN

• **foolish** /foolish/ ADJECTIVE

foot /foot/
1. The part of the body at the end of your leg that you stand on ▶ PARTS OF THE BODY, page 18 2. The lowest part of something *I'm at the foot of the mountain.*
3. A measurement of length. A foot is made up of twelve inches NOUN
■ **feet** /feet/ PLURAL
• **footprint** /footprint/ NOUN
• **footstep** /footstep/ NOUN

football /footbawl/
1. A game where two teams of players kick a ball to try and score goals
2. The big round ball used in football
NOUN
• **footballer** /footbawler/ NOUN

for /for/
1. Used to say where something is to go *This letter is for Inky Mouse.* 2. Used to show the reason for something *I need a jacket for keeping warm.* 3. So as to help someone, or instead of someone *Bee did the washing up for Snake.* 4. During a certain period of time *It rained for two hours.* PREPOSITION

forbade /ferbad/
PAST TENSE ▶ **forbid**

forbid /ferbid/
To tell someone they are not allowed to do something VERB
Our teacher has forbidden us to talk in the classroom.
■ **forbade, forbidden**
• **forbidden** /ferbiden/ ADJECTIVE

force¹ /fors/
1. To make someone do something they do not want to do 2. To use strength to push or open something VERB

force² /fors/
1. A lot of strength 2. A strong influence
3. A group of people who are trained as soldiers or police officers *Seth's dad is in the police force.* NOUN
• **forceful** /forsfel/ ADJECTIVE

forehead /forhed/
The part of your face below your hair and above your eyes NOUN

foreign /foren/
From or in another country ADJECTIVE
• **foreigner** /forener/ NOUN

forest /forest/
A place where lots of trees grow thickly over a very big area NOUN

forever /ferever/
If something continues forever, it will never end ADVERB

forgave /fergaiv/
PAST TENSE ▶ **forgive**

forget /ferget/
1. To not remember any more *I've forgotten how to do that.* 2. To not remember to do something *Inky forgot to take her book with her.* VERB
■ **forgot, forgotten**
• **forgetful** /fergetfel/ ADJECTIVE

Ff

forgive /fergiv/
1. To stop being angry with someone even though they have done something wrong or bad 2. Used to say sorry
Forgive me, but I must go home now.
VERB
- forgave, forgiven

forgot /fergot/
PAST TENSE ▶ **forget**
• **forgotten** /fergoten/
PAST PARTICIPLE ▶ **forget**

fork /fork/
1. A small handle with two or more points at one end used for eating
2. A tool with a big handle and points at one end used for digging earth
NOUN

form¹ /form/
1. Another word for the shape of something *The jug is in the form of a cow.*
2. A piece of paper with questions on it and spaces for the answers NOUN

The jug is in the form of a cow.

form² /form/
1. If something forms or someone forms it, it starts to exist *Ice is forming on the window.* 2. Another way of saying to be *This forms part of my plan.* VERB

fort /fort/
A strong building where soldiers live NOUN

fortnight /fortniet/
Another way of saying two weeks NOUN

fortunate /forchenet/
Lucky ADJECTIVE
• **fortunately** /forchenetlee/ ADVERB

fortune /forchoon/
1. A lot of money
2. Good fortune is good luck NOUN

forward /forwerd/
Or **forwards** /forwerdz/
1. Towards the front *The car moved forward.* 2. **from that time forward** Starting from that time ADVERB

fossil /fosel/
The body of an animal or plant that died thousands of years ago and has turned to rock NOUN

Ff

fought /fort/
PAST TENSE ▶ **fight**

found /found/
PAST TENSE ▶ **find**

fountain /founten/
A jet of water going up in to the air
NOUN

fowl /foul/
A bird such as a chicken, usually found
in farmyards NOUN
■ **fowl** /foul/ or **fowls** /foulz/ PLURAL

fox /fox/
A wild animal like a dog with red-brown
fur and a thick tail NOUN

fraction /fracshen/
1. A tiny amount of something
2. A number that is less than a
whole number *A half is a fraction.*
NOUN

fracture /fraccher/
To break or crack VERB
Inky fractured her arm.
• **fracture** /fraccher/ NOUN

fragile /frajiel/
Easily broken ADJECTIVE

frame /fraim/
1. Something that goes around a
window or picture 2. A support for
something NOUN

frank[1] /frangk/
Honest in what you say, even if people
do not like it ADJECTIVE

frank[2] /frangk/
The mark put on an envelope that has
been sent through the post NOUN

frantic /frantic/
1. Doing things in a hurry, and with a
lot of energy *There was a frantic search for
clues.* 2. Very worried about something
ADJECTIVE

freak /freek/
1. Someone who looks or behaves
strangely 2. Someone who does or
thinks about something all the time
He's a health freak. NOUN

freckle /frecel/
One of the small brown spots on your
skin NOUN

• **freckled** /freceld/ ADJECTIVE

free /free/
1. Not costing any money
2. Able to do what you like
3. Available *Is this chair free?*
ADJECTIVE
• **freedom** /freedem/ NOUN
• **freely** /freelee/ ADVERB

freeze /freez/
1. To be very cold 2. To reach a
temperature where water turns to ice
3. To make food very cold so that it lasts
longer 4. To stay very still VERB
■ **froze, frozen**
• **freezer** /freezer/ NOUN
• **freezing** /freezing/ ADJECTIVE

frequent /freequent/
Happening a lot or doing something
a lot ADJECTIVE
• **frequently** /freequentlee/ ADVERB

fresh /fresh/
1. In good condition because it was
recently made or prepared *I buy fresh
food.* 2. New or recent *Here's a fresh
piece of paper.* 3. Not tired ADJECTIVE

Ff

Friday /friedai/
A day of the week NOUN
▶ CALENDAR, page 13

fridge /frij/
A machine for keeping food cool
NOUN

friend /frend/
Someone you know well and like to
spend time with NOUN
• **friendly** /frendlee/ ADJECTIVE
• **friendship** /frendship/ NOUN

fries /friez/
Long thin chips NOUN PLURAL

fright /friet/
The feeling of fear or of being afraid
NOUN

• **frighten** /frieten/ VERB
• **frightened** /frietend/ ADJECTIVE
• **frightening** /frietening/ ADJECTIVE

fringe /frinj/
Hair cut short across the forehead
NOUN

frock /froc/
An old-fashioned word for a girl's
or a woman's dress NOUN

frog /frog/
A little green animal that jumps and
lives on land and in water NOUN

from /from/
1. Starting somewhere, or coming from
somewhere *Bee flew from the flower to
Inky's house.* 2. Because of something
Hinda's suffering from a bad headache.
3. Using something *Snake's house is built
from sticks and stones.* PREPOSITION

front /frunt/
1. The part of something that faces
forward *Here is the front of the house.*
2. The part of something that is at
the beginning *There is space at the
front of the book to write your name.* NOUN
• **front** /frunt/ ADJECTIVE *the front door*

frost /frost/
Tiny pieces of ice that cover things
outside in cold weather NOUN
Look at the frost on the ground.
• **frost** /frost/ VERB
• **frosty** /frostee/ ADJECTIVE

froth /froth/
Small bubbles on top of a liquid NOUN
• **frothy** /frothee/ ADJECTIVE

frown /froun/
To move your eyebrows together and
make an unhappy or confused face VERB
• **frown** /froun/ NOUN

froze /froaz/
PAST TENSE ▶ **freeze**
• **frozen** /froazen/
PAST PARTICIPLE ▶ **freeze**

fruit /froot/
Something that grows on a plant or tree
and contains seeds, such as apples and
oranges NOUN

125

Ff

fry /frie/
To cook or be cooked in hot oil or fat
VERB

fuel /fueel/
Something that you burn to provide heat
or power NOUN
Some cars use diesel for fuel.

full /fool/
With no more space left ADJECTIVE

full stop /fool stop/
A punctuation mark like a dot that you
put at the end of a sentence NOUN

fumes /fuemz/
Air that has a bad or strong smell or
that is poisonous NOUN PLURAL

fun /fun/
Enjoyable or amusing NOUN

funeral /fueneral/
An occasion when people bury a dead
person NOUN

funfair /funfeer/
Somewhere outside with games and
things to ride on NOUN

fungi /funggee/
NOUN PLURAL ▶ **fungus**

fungus /funggas/
A very simple type of plant such as a
mushroom NOUN
■ **fungi** /funggee/ PLURAL

funnel /funel/
1. A chimney for letting out smoke
2. A narrow tube with a wide top for
pouring liquids NOUN

funny /funee/
1. Amusing 2. Strange ADJECTIVE

fur /fer/
The thick hair that covers some animals
NOUN
• **furry** /ferree/ ADJECTIVE

furious /fyooreees/
Very angry ADJECTIVE

furnished /fernisht/
Containing furniture ADJECTIVE

furniture /fernicher/
Things in a room such as tables and
beds that can be moved around NOUN

further /ferther/
1. Another way of saying more *I can't
help you any further.* 2. Another way of
saying farther ADVERB, ADJECTIVE

furthest /ferthest/
Another way of saying farthest
ADJECTIVE, ADVERB

fuse /fuez/
1. A piece of wire that should break and
stop the power if something electrical
goes wrong 2. The part of a bomb that
controls when it explodes NOUN

fuss /fus/
1. Worrying and wasting time
2. **make a fuss** To complain NOUN
• **fussy** /fusee/ ADJECTIVE

future /fuecher/
The time yet to come NOUN
• **future** /fuecher/ ADJECTIVE

fuzzy /fuzee/
1. Not very clear *The photos were fuzzy.*
2. With lots of thick soft hair ADJECTIVE

Gg

gadget /gajit/
A small machine or object that does something useful NOUN
A bottle opener is a gadget for taking off bottle tops.

gale /gail/
A very strong wind NOUN

gallery /galɛree/
An art gallery is a place where people go to see pieces of art such as paintings NOUN

gallon /galɛn/
A measurement for liquids NOUN

gallop /galɛp/
The way a horse runs so fast that sometimes its feet are all off the ground at the same time NOUN

• **gallop** /galɛp/ VERB

game /gaim/
1. Something you play for fun that has rules and a winner *I love the game of chess.* 2. When two people or teams play against each other *We played a game of hockey.* 3. Wild animals that are hunted for sport NOUN

gander /gander/
A male goose NOUN

gang /gang/
A group of people who do things together NOUN
He was attacked by a gang of boys as he walked down the street.

gangster /gangster/
A violent criminal NOUN

gap /gap/
A space inside something or between two things NOUN

Snake has a gap between his teeth.

gape /gaip/
1. To look and open your mouth in surprise 2. To come open VERB

garage /garahj/
1. A place where cars are kept or repaired 2. A place where people buy fuel for cars NOUN

garden /gardɛn/
A piece of land with grass where flowers and trees are grown NOUN
• **gardener** /gardner/ NOUN

garlic /garlic/
A plant like a little onion with a very strong taste NOUN
▶ FRUIT AND VEGETABLES, page 15

Gg

gas /gas/
1. A substance like air that is not solid or liquid, and can be poisonous
2. A substance like air that is burnt for cooking and heating NOUN
• **gasman** /gasman/ NOUN
• **gasworks** /gaswerks/ NOUN

gash /gash/
A deep cut NOUN
• **gash** /gash/ VERB

gasp /gasp/
To breathe in quickly because you are surprised or having trouble breathing VERB
• **gasp** /gasp/ NOUN

gate /gait/
A type of door built in a fence or an outside wall NOUN

gather /gather/
1. To come together *The children gathered around the fire to keep warm.* 2. To collect *Bee gathers pollen from the flowers.* VERB

gave /gaiv/
PAST TENSE ▶ **give**

gaze /gaiz/
To look at someone or something for a long time VERB
• **gaze** /gaiz/ NOUN

gear /gier/
The part of a car that uses the power from the engine to make the wheels go around NOUN

geese /gees/
NOUN PLURAL ▶ **goose**

gem /jem/
A beautiful stone used as a jewel NOUN

general[1] /jenerel/
1. Describing only the main things about something 2. Including all or most things, or shared by all or most people 3. Dealing with different things *general knowledge* ADJECTIVE
• **generally** /jenerelee/ ADVERB

general[2] /jenerel/
An important person in the army who is in charge of all the soldiers NOUN

generous /jeneres/
1. Willing to help or give things to people
2. Larger than usual *Inky gave Snake a generous amount of cake.* ADJECTIVE

genius /jeeneees/
Someone who has a very high level of intelligence or skill NOUN

gentle /jentel/
1. Very kind and calm
2. Not strong or violent but slight *There was a gentle breeze.* ADJECTIVE
• **gently** /jentlee/ ADVERB

gentleman /jentelmen/
A polite word for a man, especially someone who is always good and polite NOUN
■ **gentlemen** /jentelmen/ PLURAL

geography /jeeogrefi/
The study of the countries of the world, including things such as rivers, mountains and cities NOUN
• **geographical** /jeeegraficel/ ADJECTIVE

germ /jerm/
Germs are very tiny creatures that cause disease NOUN

Gg

gesture /jescher/
A movement of your body or hands that helps you express what you mean **NOUN**

get /get/
1. To have, receive or be given something *I hope I don't get a cold.* 2. To bring or take something *I'm going back to get my umbrella.* 3. To become *Snake was getting hungry.* 4. To go into a certain position, or to go somewhere *Get up!* · *I must get to school.* **VERB**
■ **got**

ghost /goast/
The spirit of a dead person that some people believe they can see or feel **NOUN**

giant /jieent/
A very big and tall man in stories **NOUN**

· **giant** /jieent/ **ADJECTIVE**

gift /gift/
1. A present 2. A natural quality or skill someone has **NOUN**

gigantic /jiegantic/
Very big **ADJECTIVE**

giggle /gigel/
To laugh in a quiet and nervous way, especially when you cannot control your laughing **VERB**
· **giggle** /gigel/ **NOUN**

gill /gil/
The gills on a fish are the parts it uses to breathe **NOUN**

ginger[1] /jinjer/
Orange-brown in colour **ADJECTIVE**

ginger[2] /jinjer/
The root of a plant with a very strong taste **NOUN**

gingerbread /jinjerbred/
A cake or biscuit that has ginger in it, sometimes in the shape of a little man **NOUN**

giraffe /jiraf/
An animal with a very long neck and long legs that comes from Africa **NOUN**
▶ **ANIMALS**, page 16

girl /gerl/
A female child **NOUN**

girlfriend /gerlfrend/
Someone's girlfriend is the girl or woman they are going out with **NOUN**

give /giv/
1. To let someone have something *He gave me some flowers for my birthday.* · *Could you give me some information?* 2. To do something or make someone feel something *You gave me a shock.* **VERB**
■ **gave, given**

glad /glad/
Happy about something **ADJECTIVE**
· **gladly** /gladlee/ **ADVERB**

gladiator /gladeeaiter/
In Roman times, a gladiator was a man who fought against other men or wild animals in an arena, and was watched by lots of people **NOUN**

Gg

glance /glans/
To look at something or someone quickly
VERB
• **glance** /glans/ **NOUN**

gland /gland/
Glands are special parts of the body that make chemicals or substances **NOUN**

glass /glas/
1. A hard material that you can see through, used for making things such as windows 2. A container made of glass that is used for drinking **NOUN**

glasses /glasez/
Two pieces of special glass fixed into a frame that you wear over your eyes to see better **NOUN PLURAL**

glide /glied/
To move smoothly and quietly, and without much effort **VERB**

glider /glieder/
A light plane that has no engine **NOUN**

glimpse /glimps/
A very quick look at something or someone **NOUN**
I managed to catch a glimpse of her before she disappeared.

glitter /gliter/
To shine with lots of small flashes of light
VERB *The diamonds glittered in the light.*

globe /gloab/
1. An object shaped like a ball with a map of the world on it 2. A word meaning the whole world **NOUN**

• **global** /gloabel/ **ADJECTIVE**

gloom /gloom/
A feeling of sadness **NOUN**
• **gloomy** /gloomee/ **ADJECTIVE**

glorious /glorreees/
Excellent or beautiful **ADJECTIVE**
The weather was glorious.

glossy /glosee/
Shiny and smooth **ADJECTIVE**

glove /gluv/
Something that covers and protects your hand, with separate parts for each finger
NOUN

glow /gloa/
To shine with a gentle and steady light without any flames **VERB**
• **glow** /gloa/ **NOUN**

glue /gloo/
A sticky substance for joining things together **NOUN**
• **glue** /gloo/ **VERB**

glum /glum/
Looking sad, and not saying very much
ADJECTIVE

glutton /gluten/
Someone who eats too much **NOUN**

go /goa/
1. To move from one place to another *Let's go!* 2. To become *My dad's going bald.* 3. To work properly *The clock has stopped going.* 4. To disappear *Has the pain gone?* 5. **go on** To start or continue something *Go on with the story.* **VERB**
■ **goes, went, gone**

goal /goal/
1. In sports like football, the goal is the place between two poles where the ball must go to score a point 2. If someone scores a goal, they get a point when they hit the ball into the goal 3. Something good you hope to do or get in the future
My goal is to be a teacher. **NOUN**

Gg

goat /gɒat/
An animal like a sheep but with horns
NOUN

gobble /gobəl/
To eat food quickly and noisily **VERB**

goes /gɒaz/
▶ **go** **VERB**

goggles /gogəlz/
Special glasses that you wear to protect
your eyes from things like dust or water
NOUN PLURAL

gold[1] /gɒald/
A metal used for making jewellery **NOUN**

gold[2] /gɒald/
Made of gold or having the bright yellow
colour of gold **ADJECTIVE**
• **golden** /gɒaldən/ **ADJECTIVE**

goldfish /gɒaldfish/
A little orange fish people keep as a pet
NOUN

golf /golf/
A game where people use sticks called
clubs to hit little white balls into holes
NOUN

gone[1] /gon/
PAST PARTICIPLE ▶ **go**

gone[2] /gon/
Later than a certain time **PREPOSITION**
It's gone midnight.

good[1] /good/
1. Pleasant or helpful or kind *Inky is a
good friend.* 2. Of high standard *That's a
good score.* 3. Behaving right *The children
were good when you were out.* **ADJECTIVE**
■ better, best

good[2] /good/
for good For always **NOUN**
Our teacher has left for good.

goodbye /goodbie/
A word you say to someone when you
leave them **INTERJECTION**

goose /goos/
A bird like a big duck **NOUN**
■ **geese** /gees/ **PLURAL**

gorgeous /gorjəs/
Very pleasant or beautiful **ADJECTIVE**

gorilla /gərilə/
A very big and strong ape that lives in
Africa **NOUN**

got /got/
PAST TENSE ▶ **get**

gown /goun/
A long dress or robe for special occasions
NOUN

Gg

grab /grab/
To take something quickly and sometimes violently VERB

graceful /graisfel/
Very pleasant and attractive because of smooth and gentle movements ADJECTIVE
a graceful dancer

grade /graid/
A number or letter that shows how good something is NOUN
Bee got a good grade for her work.

gradual /grajꝏel/
Happening one bit at a time, or very slowly ADJECTIVE
• **gradually** /grajꝏelee/ ADVERB

graduate /grajꝏait/
To finish your studies and get your certificate VERB
• **graduate** /grajꝏet/ NOUN

grain /grain/
1. The seeds of a plant like wheat or rice, or one single seed 2. A grain of salt or sand is one tiny hard piece of it NOUN

gram /gram/
A tiny unit for measuring weight NOUN

grammar /gramer/
The rules for how to use words in writing and speaking NOUN
• **grammatical** /grematicel/ ADJECTIVE

gran /gran/
Short for grandmother NOUN

grand /grand/
1. Impressive and important *What a grand building!* 2. Pleasant *We'll have a grand day out.* ADJECTIVE

grandchildren /grandchildren/
Granddaughters and grandsons
NOUN PLURAL

granddaughter /grandawter/
The daughter of someone's son or daughter NOUN

grandfather /grandfahther/
The father of someone's mother or father NOUN
• **grandad** /grandad/ NOUN
• **grandpa** /granpah/ NOUN

grandmother /grandmuther/
The mother of someone's mother or father NOUN
• **grandma** /grandmah/ NOUN
• **granny** /granee/ NOUN

grandparents /grandpeerents/
Grandmothers and grandfathers
NOUN PLURAL

grandson /grandsun/
The son of someone's son or daughter
NOUN

grape /graip/
Grapes are little round fruits that grow on a vine and that can be used for making wine NOUN
▶ FRUIT AND VEGETABLES, page 15

graph /graf/
A drawing with lines that show how numbers or measurements are related to each other NOUN

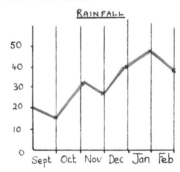

graphics /grafics/
Pictures and drawings on a computer
NOUN PLURAL

Gg

grasp /grasp/
1. To take something with your hand and hold it tightly 2. To understand something **VERB**

grass /gras/
A plant with thin green leaves that covers the ground in gardens and fields **NOUN**

grasshopper /grashoper/
An insect with long back legs that jumps and makes a high noise **NOUN**
▶ **INSECTS**, page 14

grateful /graitfel/
Knowing that someone has helped you, and wanting to thank them for it **ADJECTIVE**

grave /graiv/
A hole in the earth where a dead person is buried **NOUN**
• **graveyard** /graivyard/ **NOUN**

gravy /graivee/
A sauce made of liquid that comes from meat as it cooks **NOUN**

graze /graiz/
1. To hurt the surface of your skin by rubbing it against something 2. If animals graze, they eat grass **VERB**

grease /grees/
1. The soft fat from animals that comes from cooking meat 2. An oily substance, for example for making machines work better **NOUN**
• **grease** /grees/ **VERB**
• **greasy** /greesee/ **ADJECTIVE**

great /grait/
1. Excellent *The party was great fun!*
2. Very big 3. Important *This is a great day for our school.* **ADJECTIVE**

greed /greed/
When people want more money or food than they need **NOUN**
• **greedy** /greedee/ **ADJECTIVE**

green /green/
The colour of growing grass **NOUN, ADJECTIVE**

greengrocer /greengrouser/
Someone who has a shop selling fruit and vegetables **NOUN**

greenhouse /greenhous/
A building made of glass where people grow plants **NOUN**

greet /greet/
To be friendly to someone when you meet them, for example by saying hello or smiling **VERB**
• **greeting** /greeting/ **NOUN**

grew /groo/
PAST TENSE ▶ **grow**

grey /grai/
A colour that can be made by mixing black and white. Grey is the colour of the sky on a rainy day **NOUN, ADJECTIVE**

Gg

grief /greef/
Very great sadness NOUN

grill¹ /gril/
To cook food by putting it very close to the heat VERB

grill² /gril/
The part of a cooker where food is grilled NOUN

grim /grim/
Sad and unpleasant ADJECTIVE
The news is grim.

grin /grin/
A very big and wide smile NOUN
• **grin** /grin/ VERB

grind /griend/
To break something into tiny pieces or crush something into a powder VERB
  ■ **ground**

grip /grip/
To hold something very tightly VERB
• **grip** /grip/ NOUN

groan /groan/
To make a long low sound when you are in pain or unhappy VERB
• **groan** /groan/ NOUN

gross /groas/
Very rude or unpleasant ADJECTIVE
I can't eat that food, it looks gross.

ground¹ /ground/
The surface of the land, or the soil under it NOUN

ground² /ground/
PAST TENSE ▶ **grind**

group /groop/
Several people or things together NOUN

grow /groa/
1. To get bigger and develop *He's growing into a big boy.* 2. To put things in the soil and take care of them, such as plants and vegetables 3. To get bigger in amount or in number *My fears are growing.* VERB
  ■ **grew, grown**
• **grown-up** /groan up/
  An adult person NOUN
• **growth** /groath/ NOUN

growl /groul/
To make a deep noise like a dog when it is angry VERB

grown /groan/
PAST PARTICIPLE ▶ **grow**

grub /grub/
A young insect like a fat worm NOUN

grubby /grubee/
Another word for dirty ADJECTIVE

gruesome /groosem/
Another word for horrible ADJECTIVE

gruff /gruf/
1. Unfriendly and rude *He has a gruff manner.* 2. If a voice is gruff, it is deep and rough ADJECTIVE

grumble /grumbel/
To keep complaining about something VERB

grumpy /grumpee/
In a bad mood, or always complaining ADJECTIVE

grunt /grunt/
A low deep sound like the sound of a pig NOUN
• **grunt** /grunt/ VERB

guarantee /garentee/
To promise that something will happen VERB

Gg

guard[1] /gard/
To protect a person, place or thing VERB

guard[2] /gard/
1. A person who guards things or people
2. A person in charge of a train NOUN

guess /ges/
To give an answer or an opinion about something without knowing all the details VERB
I don't know the answer, I'm only guessing.
• **guess** /ges/ NOUN
• **guesswork** /geswerk/ NOUN

guest /gest/
1. Someone who stays in your home or in a hotel 2. Someone who is invited somewhere such as a party NOUN

guide[1] /gied/
To show someone the way, or show them how to do something VERB

guide[2] /gied/
1. A person or a book that guides you
2. A Guide is a girl who belongs to a group called the Guides NOUN

guilty /giltee/
1. If someone is guilty of a crime, they have done that crime 2. If you feel guilty, you feel sad because you have done something wrong ADJECTIVE

guinea pig /ginee pig/
A little furry animal with no tail that people keep as a pet NOUN

guitar /gitar/
A musical instrument with a long neck and strings that you play with your fingers NOUN

gull /gul/
A big sea bird NOUN

gulp /gulp/
To swallow something quickly VERB
• **gulp** /gulp/ NOUN

gum /gum/
1. The flesh around your teeth 2. A soft sweet you chew for a long time but do not swallow NOUN

gun[1] /gun/
A weapon that fires bullets NOUN

gun[2] /gun/
gun down To shoot someone with a gun VERB
• **gunfire** /gunfieer/ NOUN
• **gunpowder** /gunpouder/ NOUN

gush /gush/
To flow out quickly and strongly VERB
Water gushed out of the broken pipe.

gust /gust/
The wind when it blows suddenly with strength NOUN

guts /guts/
The inside parts of an animal or person NOUN PLURAL

gutter /guter/
The edge of a roof or road where rain water flows away NOUN

gym /jim/
1. A big room for doing exercises
2. The exercises that people do in a gym NOUN

Hh

habit /habit/
Something you do lots of times almost without thinking about it NOUN

had /had/
PAST TENSE ▶ **have**
I had a pet dog.

haddock /hadɘc/
A fish that lives in the sea NOUN

■ **haddock** /hadɘc/ PLURAL

hail /hail/
Frozen rain that falls down like little pieces of ice NOUN
• **hail** /hail/ VERB

hair /heer/
The thin threads that grow on your head and body NOUN
• **hairbrush** /heerbrush/ NOUN
• **haircut** /heercut/ NOUN
• **hairy** /heɘree/ ADJECTIVE

hairdresser /heerdreser/
Someone who cuts your hair, washes it and arranges it NOUN

half /haf/
One of two parts of something that are equal NOUN

■ **halves** /havz/ PLURAL
• **halfway** /hafwai/ ADVERB

hall /hawl/
1. The space behind the front door of a house 2. A big room where people meet together 3. A big important building NOUN
• **hallway** /hawlwai/ NOUN

Halloween /halɘɑeen/
The night of 31 October when some children dress to look like witches or ghosts, and go to people's houses asking for sweets NOUN

halt /hawlt/
Another word for stop INTERJECTION
• **halt** /hawlt/ VERB

halves /havz/
NOUN PLURAL ▶ **half**

ham /ham/
Meat from the leg of a pig NOUN

hamburger /hamberger/
Minced meat made into a round flat shape NOUN

hammer /hamer/
A tool for hitting nails or for breaking things into pieces NOUN
• **hammer** /hamer/ VERB

hamster /hamster/
An animal like a mouse with no tail that people keep as a pet NOUN

Hh

hand[1] /hand/
1. The part of your body at the end of your arm that you use for taking and holding things 2. One of the long thin parts of a clock that point to the time **NOUN**

hand[2] /hand/
To give something to someone **VERB**
Inky handed Snake an egg sandwich.
• **handbag** /handbag/ **NOUN**
• **handcuff** /handcufs/ **NOUN**
• **handful** /handfool/ **NOUN**

handicap /handeecap/
1. If a person has a handicap, they cannot use a part of their body properly because of illness or injury 2. Something that stops a person doing something easily or in the usual way **NOUN**
• **handicapped** /handeecapt/ **ADJECTIVE**

handkerchief /hangkerchif/
A piece of cloth for wiping your nose **NOUN**

handle[1] /handel/
The part of something you hold with your hand **NOUN**

handle[2] /handel/
1. To hold something in your hands or touch it 2. To control something **VERB**
• **handlebars** /handelbarz/ **NOUN PLURAL**

handshake /handshaik/
When two people shake each other's hand when they meet or agree something **NOUN**

handsome /hansem/
Nice or attractive, usually used to describe a man or boy **ADJECTIVE**

handwriting /handrieting/
The way someone writes with a pen or pencil **NOUN**

handy /handee/
1. Useful 2. Nearby and easy to get to *Snake and Bee always keep their handkerchiefs handy.* **ADJECTIVE**

hang[1] /hang/
To fix something so it can still move, but does not touch the ground **VERB**
■ **hung**

hang[2] /hang/
To kill someone by hanging them from a rope around their neck **VERB**

hanger /hanger/
Something with a special shape for hanging clothes on **NOUN**

happen /hapen/
1. To start to exist and continue for a little while before stopping *The accident happened last week.* 2. To be affected by something *What would happen to Phonic if you unplugged him?* **VERB**

happy /hapee/
Having feelings of great pleasure **ADJECTIVE**
• **happiness** /hapeenes/ **NOUN**

harbour /harber/
A safe place on the coast for boats to stop **NOUN**

hard[1] /hard/
1. Very stiff when you touch it 2. Not easy *This is a hard question.* **ADJECTIVE**
• **harden** /harden/ **VERB**

137

Hh

hard[2] /hard/
Using a lot of effort ADVERB
Inky hit the ball hard.

hardly /hardlee/
Another way of saying only just ADVERB
Bee is so tired she can hardly fly.

hardware /hardweer/
1. Tools and useful things used in the house or garden 2. The solid parts of a computer such as the case or monitor NOUN

hare /heer/
An animal like a big rabbit that can run very fast NOUN

harm /harm/
To hurt someone or damage something VERB
• **harm** /harm/ NOUN
• **harmful** /harmfel/ ADJECTIVE
• **harmless** /harmles/ ADJECTIVE

harmonica /harmonice/
A small musical instrument you play by blowing through it NOUN

harness /harnes/
1. Straps made of leather that go over the head of a horse to control it
2. Straps fixed around a person to keep them in place *A safety harness is used to save people from falling.* NOUN

harp /harp/
A big musical instrument with a frame shaped like a triangle that has strings across it NOUN

harsh /harsh/
1. Very difficult for people to live in *The winter is always harsh.* 2. Not at all pleasant *He has a harsh voice.* ADJECTIVE

harvest /harvest/
The time when crops are taken from the fields NOUN

has /haz/
▶ **have** VERB
She has red hair.

haste /haist/
Doing things quickly NOUN
• **hasty** /haistee/ ADJECTIVE

hat /hat/
A type of clothing you wear on your head NOUN

hatch[1] /hach/
To break out of an egg VERB
The chicks are hatching.

hatch[2] /hach/
A small square opening between two rooms NOUN

hate /hait/
To not like someone or something at all VERB
• **hate** /hait/ NOUN

haul /hawl/
To pull something very hard VERB

Hh

haunt /hɑwnt/
If a ghost haunts somewhere, it appears there many times VERB
• **haunted** /hɑwntid/ ADJECTIVE

have /hav/
1. To own or do something *I have a dog called Spot.* • *I'm having a party next week.*
2. **have to** If you have to do something, you feel you should do it or someone makes you do it *You have to go to school.*
3. Used with other verbs to show that an action has happened *Snake has finished his work.* VERB
■ **has, had, had**

hawk /hɑwk/
A big bird that eats smaller birds and animals NOUN

hay /hai/
Dry grass that is cut and used to feed animals NOUN
• **hay fever** /hai feever/ NOUN
• **haystack** /haistac/ NOUN

hazy /haizee/
Not clear ADJECTIVE

he /hee/
A male person or animal that someone has already mentioned in the sentence
PRONOUN *Gus can run fast, he won the race.*

head /hed/
1. The top part of your body that has your brain, eyes and nose in it ▶ PARTS OF THE BODY, page 18
2. Another word for your brain or mind 3. The person in charge *What's the name of your head teacher?* NOUN
• **headache** /hedaic/ NOUN
• **headband** /hedband/ NOUN
• **headlights** /hedliets/ NOUN
• **headmaster** /hedmaster/ NOUN
• **headmistress** /hedmistres/ NOUN
• **headphones** /hedfoanz/ NOUN

heading /heding/
Something written above some writing, often at the top of a page NOUN

headlice /hedlies/
Tiny insects that live in people's hair
NOUN PLURAL

headway /hedwai/
If you make headway, you make progress towards getting something done NOUN

heal /heel/
If something like a cut or injury heals, it gets better VERB

health /helth/
Keeping your body well and in good condition NOUN
• **healthy** /helthee/ ADJECTIVE

heap /heep/
A big pile of things, often an untidy pile
NOUN
• **heap** /heep/ VERB

hear /hier/
1. To use your ears to take sounds into your brain 2. To be told something such as news *We heard that school would be closed next Tuesday.* VERB
■ **heard**
• **hearing** /hiɛring/ NOUN
• **hearing aid** /hiɛring aid/ NOUN

heard /herd/
PAST TENSE ▶ **hear**

heart /hart/
The organ in your chest that pumps blood around your body NOUN
• **heart attack** /hart ɛtac/ NOUN
• **heartbeat** /hartbeet/ NOUN

heat[1] /heet/
The warm feeling that comes from something hot NOUN

Hh

heat[2] /heet/
To make something hotter, or become hotter VERB
- **heater** /heeter/ NOUN
- **heating** /heeting/ NOUN

heavy /hevee/
1. If something is heavy, it weighs a lot
2. Used to say there is a lot of something
We've had heavy snow today. ADJECTIVE
- **heavily** /hevilee/ ADVERB

hectic /hectic/
Very busy ADJECTIVE

hedge /hej/
A row of bushes that grow very close together NOUN

hedge

hedgehog

hedgehog /hejhog/
A small brown animal that has a body covered in sharp needles NOUN

heel /heel/
The back part of your foot NOUN

hefty /heftee/
Big and heavy ADJECTIVE
Inky was trying to carry a hefty suitcase.

height /hiet/
How high or tall someone or something is NOUN

held /held/
PAST TENSE ▶ **hold**

helicopter /helicopter/
A flying machine with big metal blades on top that turn around to make it move in the air NOUN

hello /heloa/
A word you use when meeting or calling someone INTERJECTION

helmet /helmet/
A hard hat, usually of metal or plastic, for protecting your head NOUN

help /help/
To do something for someone to make things easier for them VERB
Can you help Bee find her hive?
- **help** /help/ NOUN
- **helper** /helper/ NOUN
- **helpful** /helpfel/ ADJECTIVE

helpless /helples/
If someone is helpless, they cannot take care of themselves ADJECTIVE

hen /hen/
A female chicken NOUN

her[1] /her/
A female person or animal who has already been mentioned in a sentence
PRONOUN *Where is Inky, can you see her?*

her[2] /her/
Belonging to a female person or animal already mentioned *Inky found her glasses.*
ADJECTIVE

herb /herb/
A small plant used in cooking or medicines NOUN

herd /herd/
A group of animals of the same type
NOUN *Here comes a herd of cattle.*

here /hier/
1. In or to the place where you
are *Come here!* 2. Happening now
Great, summer is here! ADVERB

hero /hierഗ/
1. A person who you admire and respect
2. The main person in a story NOUN
• **heroic** /herഗic/ ADJECTIVE
• **heroine** /herഗin/ NOUN

hers /herz/
Belonging to a female person or animal
already mentioned in the sentence
PRONOUN *This isn't my hat, it's hers.*
• **herself** /herself/ PRONOUN

hesitate /hezitait/
To stop saying or doing something for a
moment because you are nervous or not
sure VERB
• **hesitation** /hezitaishen/ NOUN

hexagon /hexegen/
A shape that has six sides NOUN
▶ **SHAPES**, page 17

hey /hai/
A word you can use to call out to
someone to get their attention
INTERJECTION

hibernate /hiebernait/
To go to sleep for the whole winter VERB

hiccup /hicup/
A sharp, sudden swallowing sound made
in your throat after eating or drinking
too quickly NOUN
• **hiccup** /hicup/ VERB

hid /hid/
PAST TENSE ▶ **hide**
• **hidden** /hiden/
PAST PARTICIPLE ▶ **hide**

hide /hied/
1. To put something or someone where
no one can see them 2. To go where no
one can see you *Snake was hiding from
Bee again.* VERB
■ **hid, hidden**
• **hideaway** /hiedewai/ NOUN
• **hide-out** /hied out/ NOUN

hideous /hideees/
Very ugly or bad ADJECTIVE
a hideous scar

high[1] /hie/
1. Far from or far above the ground
That's a high wall. 2. Very big in numbers
or amount *This car can go at a high speed.*
3. Very good *High quality shoes cost more.*
ADJECTIVE
• **highchair** /hie cheer/ NOUN
• **high school** /hie scool/ NOUN

high[2] /hie/
Doing something a long way above the
ground ADVERB
The plane was flying high in the sky.

highlight /hieliet/
To make something obvious or easy to
see VERB

hijack /hiejac/
To take control of something by force,
usually a plane VERB
• **hijack** /hiejac/ NOUN
• **hijacker** /hiejacer/ NOUN

Hh

hike /hiek/
A long walk in the countryside NOUN
• **hike** /hiek/ VERB

hill /hil/
Land that is higher than the land around it NOUN
• **hilly** /hilee/ ADJECTIVE

him /him/
A male person or animal that someone has already mentioned in the sentence
PRONOUN *Can you see him?*
• **himself** /himself/ PRONOUN

Hindu /hindoo/
Someone who believes in the main religion of India NOUN

hinge /hinj/
A piece of metal made of two parts that is fixed to a door and its frame so it can open and close NOUN

hint /hint/
Information that helps you find an answer, without giving the answer itself
NOUN *Phonic gave Bee a hint to help her answer the question.*
• **hint** /hint/ VERB

hip /hip/
The place where your leg joins your body
NOUN

hippopotamus /hipepotemes/
Or **hippo** /hipoa/ A very big animal that lives in Africa with thick skin and short legs NOUN

his /hiz/
Belonging to a male person or animal already mentioned in the sentence
ADJECTIVE *Snake is eating his dinner.*

hiss /his/
To make a noise that sounds like the letter S repeated lots of times VERB
Snake was hissing as he went slowly home.
• **hiss** /his/ NOUN

history /histree/
All the things that happened in the past
NOUN
• **historical** /historicel/ ADJECTIVE

hit /hit/
To touch someone or something using a lot of force VERB
Inky hit the ball with a bat.
■ **hit**
• **hit** /hit/ NOUN

hive /hiev/
A place where bees live NOUN

hoarse /hors/
If you are hoarse or you have a hoarse voice, you cannot speak clearly because you have a sore throat ADJECTIVE

hobble /hobel/
To walk with difficulty VERB

hobby /hobee/
Something you like doing when you have free time NOUN

hockey /hocee/
A game between two teams that is played with sticks and a ball NOUN

hold /hoald/
1. To put your hand around something
2. To keep something or someone in a certain place *They held him prisoner.*
3. To contain *This glass can hold a whole bottle of milk.* VERB
■ **held**

Hh

hold-up /hoald up/
1. Something that causes things to go slow *There's a traffic hold-up in town.*
2. When someone tries to steal from a place using a gun *There was a hold-up at the bank today.* NOUN
• **hold up** /hoald up/ VERB

hole /hoal/
An empty or open space in something that is solid NOUN
Dig a hole in the ground.

holiday /holidai/
1. A day off from school or work
2. The time you go away somewhere to enjoy yourself *Where are you going for your holidays this year?* NOUN

hollow /holoa/
Something that is hollow has an empty space inside it ADJECTIVE
The log of this tree is hollow.

holly /holee/
An evergreen tree that has prickly leaves and red berries NOUN

holy /hoalee/
Connected with religion ADJECTIVE

home[1] /hoam/
1. The place where you live
2. A special place where people go to be cared for *My granny lives in an old people's home.* NOUN

home[2] /hoam/
In or to the place where you live ADVERB
We're going home now.
• **homeless** /hoamles/ ADJECTIVE

homework /hoamwerk/
School work that you must do at home NOUN

homophone /homefoan/
A word that sounds the same as another word but has a different spelling or meaning NOUN
Knight and night are homophones.

honest /onest/
Always telling the truth and behaving properly ADJECTIVE

honey /hunee/
The thick yellow substance that bees make NOUN
• **honeycomb** /huneecoam/ NOUN

honeymoon /huneemoon/
The special holiday people have after they get married NOUN

honk /hongk/
1. The loud noise made by a car horn
2. The sound made by a goose NOUN
• **honk** /hongk/ VERB

honour /oner/
A sign of great respect NOUN

hood /hood/
The part of a coat you wear over your head NOUN

• **hooded** /hoodid/ ADJECTIVE

hoof /hoof/
The hard foot of an animal like a horse or cow NOUN
■ **hoofs** /hoofs/ or **hooves** /hoovz/
   PLURAL

143

Hh

hook /hʊk/
A curved piece of metal or plastic for hanging things from NOUN
a coat hook

hoop /hoop/
A big ring made of something like wood or plastic NOUN

hooray /hoorai/
A word people shout to show they are happy about something INTERJECTION

hoot[1] /hoot/
The sound made by an owl or a car horn NOUN

hoot[2] /hoot/
1. To make a sound like an owl
2. To press a car horn so that it makes a noise VERB

hooves /hoovz/
NOUN PLURAL ▶ **hoof**

hoover /hoover/
To clean a carpet or the floor with a hoover, a machine that sucks up dirt VERB

hop /hop/
1. To jump up and down on one foot
2. To get on something to go somewhere
You can hop on a bus to go to town. VERB

hope[1] /hoap/
To really want something to be true or something to happen VERB
I hope it's going to be a nice day tomorrow.

hope[2] /hoap/
1. The feeling that you want something good to happen or believe it will happen
2. The chance of something happening
There's no hope the weather will be good tomorrow. NOUN

- **hopeful** /hoapfəl/ ADJECTIVE
- **hopefully** /hoapfəlee/ ADVERB
- **hopeless** /hoapləs/ ADJECTIVE

hopscotch /hopscoch/
A game played by children jumping between squares marked on the ground NOUN.

horizon /həriezən/
The place in the distance where the sky and the earth seem to meet NOUN

We could see a ship on the horizon.

horizontal /horizontəl/
Lying flat from left to right ADJECTIVE

horn /horn/
1. One of the hard pointed parts that grow on the heads of some animals *Goats have two short horns.*
2. The part in a car that you press to make a warning noise NOUN

horrible /horəbəl/
1. Very bad, or frightening 2. Very rude or nasty to people ADJECTIVE

horror /horer/
1. A strong feeling of fear or shock caused by something bad
2. A badly behaved person NOUN

horse /hors/
A big animal that people ride on or that is used for pulling things NOUN
- **horse chestnut** /hors chesnut/
  A big tree that grows shiny brown nuts inside a prickly covering NOUN
- **horseshoe** /horsshoo/ NOUN

Hh

hose /hoʊz/
A long tube of rubber or plastic for carrying water NOUN

hospital /hɒspitel/
A place where sick or injured people go to get better NOUN

hot /hɒt/
At a high temperature ADJECTIVE

hot dog /hɒt dɒg/
A long bread roll that has a hot sausage inside it NOUN

hotel /hoʊtel/
A building where people pay to eat and sleep for a short time NOUN

hot-water bottle /hɒt wɔːter bɒtel/
A kind of rubber bag that people fill with hot water to keep their bed warm NOUN

hound /hoʊnd/
A dog used for hunting NOUN

hour /oʊer/
A measurement of time. There are 60 minutes in an hour and 24 hours in a day NOUN

house /hoʊs/
The building where someone lives NOUN
• **housework** /hoʊswerk/ NOUN

hover /hover/
To stay in one place in the air VERB

The helicopter hovered above the trees.

how[1] /hoʊ/
1. Used to ask in what way something is done *How do you spell snake?*
2. Used to ask about the size or amount of something *How big was that fish?*
3. Used to ask about the way someone is feeling *How are you today?* ADVERB

how[2] /hoʊ/
Used for explaining the way of doing something, or of giving a fact
CONJUNCTION *This is how we spell comb.*

however /hoʊever/
Used for adding something to the sentence that seems surprising ADVERB
John is my best friend. However, he can be annoying sometimes.

howl /hoʊl/
To make a long loud noise like a baby crying or a dog VERB
• **howl** /hoʊl/ NOUN

hug /hug/
To put your arms around someone and press them tightly to show you like them or love them VERB

• **hug** /hug/ NOUN

huge /hueʤ/
Very big ADJECTIVE

hum /hum/
To sing a tune with your lips closed VERB

human /huemen/
Connected with people ADJECTIVE
the human body
• **human being** /huemen beeing/
A person NOUN

145

Hh

humid /huemid/
Hot and wet ADJECTIVE
humid weather

humour /huemer/
A sense of humour is a special quality that makes people see the funny side of things NOUN

hump /hump/
A lump on the back of a camel or a person NOUN

hunch /hunch/
A strong feeling that something is true or something will happen NOUN

hung /hung/
PAST TENSE ▶ **hang**[1]

hunger /hungger/
A feeling you have when you do not have enough food NOUN
• **hungry** /hunggree/ Needing more food to eat ADJECTIVE

hunt /hunt/
To try and find or catch something VERB
Can you hunt for some information on this?
• **hunt** /hunt/ NOUN
• **hunter** /hunter/ NOUN

hurl /herl/
To throw something using a lot of strength VERB

hurray /herai/
A word that people shout out to show they are very happy about something INTERJECTION

hurricane /huricen/
A very strong wind that can damage trees and buildings NOUN

hurry[1] /huree/
To do something or go somewhere quickly VERB
Hurry up, Bee, or we'll be late.

hurry[2] /huree/
If you are in a hurry, you are doing something or going somewhere quickly NOUN

hurt /hert/
1. To make someone feel pain
2. To feel pain in your body VERB
▪ hurt
• **hurtful** /hertfel/ ADJECTIVE

husband /huzbend/
A man who is married to a woman NOUN

hush /hush/
A word used to tell people to be quiet INTERJECTION

hut /hut/
1. A shed made of wood 2. A small house or shelter, built in a simple way NOUN

hutch /huch/
A cage made of wood for keeping small animals in NOUN

Dad made a hutch for the rabbit.

hyena /hieeene/
A wild animal that looks like a dog NOUN

hygiene /hiejeen/
Keeping things very clean NOUN
• **hygienic** /hiejeenic/ ADJECTIVE

hymn /him/
A song of praise NOUN

hyphen /hiefen/
A small line used to join words together, for example in the word well-known NOUN

I /ie/
A word you use when you are talking about yourself PRONOUN
I am rather tired today.

ice /ies/
Water that is frozen NOUN
• **ice cube** /ies cueb/ NOUN

iceberg /iesberg/
A very large lump of ice that floats in the sea NOUN

ice cream /ies creem/
A cold food made from frozen cream NOUN

ice-skate /ies skait/
A special type of shoe for moving on ice NOUN
• **ice-skating** /ies skaiting/ NOUN

icing /iesing/
A sweet mixture covering the top of a cake NOUN

icon /iecon/
A tiny picture or sign on a computer screen NOUN

icy /iesee/
Very cold, or covered in ice ADJECTIVE
This road is icy.

idea /iedie/
A plan or a picture that you have in your mind NOUN

ideal /iediel/
Perfect in every way ADJECTIVE
This would be an ideal spot to have a picnic.
• **ideally** /iedieli/ ADVERB

identical /iedenticel/
The same in every way ADJECTIVE

Jim and Tim are identical twins.

identify /iedentifie/
To recognize something or someone, and describe exactly what they are VERB
• **identification** /iedentificaishen/ NOUN

idiot /ideeet/
A person who does stupid things NOUN

idle /iedel/
1. Not doing anything *The computer printer is idle now.* 2. Lazy *He's an idle boy.* ADJECTIVE

if /if/
Used when you talk about something that is not certain or that might happen CONJUNCTION
If it rains, we won't go on our picnic.

Ii

Ii

igloo /igloo/
A small round house made from blocks
of snow NOUN

ignorant /ignerent/
Not knowing very much ADJECTIVE

ignore /ignor/
To pay no attention to something
or someone VERB
He ignored me when I called to him.

ill /il/
Not feeling well ADJECTIVE
• **illness** /ilnes/ NOUN

illegal /ileegel/
Against the law ADJECTIVE

image /imij/
A picture of something NOUN

imagination /imajinaishen/
The power to create images and ideas
in your mind NOUN

imagine /imajin/
1. To make a picture of something in
your mind *Imagine being on the beach.*
2. To think something is true *I imagine
Snake will be hungry by now.* VERB
• **imaginable** /imajinebel/ ADJECTIVE
• **imaginary** /imajineree/
Not real ADJECTIVE

imitate /imitait/
To copy what someone else does VERB

immediate /imeedeeet/
Happening at once, with no delay
ADJECTIVE *I got an immediate answer
to my question.*
• **immediately** /imeedeetlee/ ADVERB

imp /imp/
In stories, an imp is a badly behaved
little creature with magical powers NOUN

impact /impact/
When one thing comes into contact with
or hits something else NOUN

impatient /impaishent/
Wanting something now, without having
to wait ADJECTIVE
• **impatience** /impaishens/ NOUN
• **impatiently** /impaishentlee/ ADVERB

important /importent/
1. Something important matters very
much *Learning to read is very important.*
2. An important person or thing has a
lot of influence and respect *The queen
bee is a very important bee.* ADJECTIVE
• **importance** /importens/ NOUN

impossible /imposibel/
Used to mean something that cannot be
done or just cannot happen ADJECTIVE

impress /impres/
To make someone think you are good at
something VERB
• **impression** /impreshen/ NOUN

impressive /impresiv/
Very big or special in some way
ADJECTIVE

improbable /improbebel/
Not likely to happen or be true ADJECTIVE

improve /improov/
To make something better VERB
• **improvement** /improovment/ NOUN

Ii

in /in/
1. Used to show where someone or something is *Inky is in the box.*
2. Used to show when something happened *Bee started to learn to read in May.* PREPOSITION

incapable /incaipəbəl/
Not able to do something ADJECTIVE

inch /inch/
A measurement of length. There are twelve inches in a foot NOUN

incident /insidənt/
Something that happens NOUN

include /incloͻd/
To make something or someone belong VERB *Can we include Snake and Bee in our group?*
• **included** /incloͻdid/ ADJECTIVE
• **including** /incloͻding/ PREPOSITION

incorrect /incərect/
Wrong, or with mistakes ADJECTIVE

increase /increes/
To get bigger, or to make something bigger VERB
• **increase** /ingcrees/ NOUN

incredible /incredibəl/
Surprising and almost unbelievable ADJECTIVE

indeed /indeed/
Another word for certainly or really
ADVERB *That was very good indeed!*

independent /indəpendənt/
Not controlled by anyone else ADJECTIVE

index /index/
A long list of the things mentioned in a book showing what pages they are on NOUN

index finger /index fingger/
The finger that is next to your thumb NOUN

indicate /indicait/
1. To show something 2. To give a signal *He indicated which way he would go.* VERB

indigo /indigoͻ/
A dark purple-blue colour
NOUN, ADJECTIVE

Ii

individual[1] /indivijꭥꭥl/
Belonging to, or for one person **ADJECTIVE**
This is Snake's individual homework book.
• **individually** /indivijꭥꭥlee/ **ADVERB**

individual[2] /indivijꭥꭥl/
One particular person **NOUN**
He's a nasty individual.

indoors /indoꭨz/
Inside a house or a building **ADVERB**
• **indoor** /indoꭨ/ **ADJECTIVE**

industry /indꭩstree/
1. Work done in factories
2. A trade or type of work **NOUN**
• **industrial** /indꭩstreeꭩl/ **ADJECTIVE**

inevitable /inevꭩtꭩbꭩl/
Certain to happen **ADJECTIVE**

inexcusable /inekscuezꭩbꭩl/
If something is inexcusable, it is so
bad that you cannot forgive someone
for doing it **ADJECTIVE**

infant /infꭩnt/
A baby or young child **NOUN**

infect /infect/
To pass an illness to someone **VERB**

infection /infecshꭩn/
An illness caused by germs **NOUN**
• **infectious** /infecshꭩs/ **ADJECTIVE**

inferior /infiꭨeeeꭨ/
Not as good as something else **ADJECTIVE**

infested /infestid/
Full of something that is not wanted
ADJECTIVE *The carpet is infested with fleas.*

inflate /inflait/
To fill something with air or gas so that
it gets bigger **VERB**

inflict /inflict/
To make someone suffer something
painful or unpleasant **VERB**
It is wrong to inflict pain on someone.

influence /inflooꭩns/
The power to make other people behave
in the way you want **NOUN**
Inky has a good influence over her friends.
• **influence** /inflooꭩns/ **VERB**
• **influential** /inflooꭩnshꭩl/ **ADJECTIVE**

info /infoꭩ/
Short for information **NOUN**

inform /infoꭨm/
To tell someone about something **VERB**

informal /infoꭨmꭩl/
Normal and relaxed **ADJECTIVE**

information /infꭩmaishꭩn/
Facts and details about something **NOUN**

ingenious /injeeneꭩs/
Very clever and original **ADJECTIVE**

inhabitant /inhabitꭩnt/
Someone who lives somewhere **NOUN**

inhale /inhail/
To breathe in **VERB**

inhaler /inhailꭨ/
A tube with medicine in it that people
use to help them breathe **NOUN**

initials /inishꭩlz/
The first letters of all your names
NOUN PLURAL *Inky Mouse's initials are I.M.*

injection /injecshꭩn/
When medicine is put into your body
with a needle **NOUN**

Ii

injure /injer/
To hurt something or someone VERB
• **injured** /injerd/ ADJECTIVE
• **injury** /injeree/ NOUN

ink /ingk/
A special liquid used for writing NOUN

inn /in/
A small hotel or place where people drink alcohol NOUN

inner /iner/
The inner part of something is the part that is further in and close to its middle ADJECTIVE

innocent /inesent/
Not guilty of doing something ADJECTIVE
• **innocence** /inesens/ NOUN

inquisitive /inquizetiv/
Interested, full of questions ADJECTIVE

insane /insain/
Crazy, not thinking or acting in a normal way ADJECTIVE

insect /insect/
A little creature with six legs and sometimes with wings NOUN

insert /insert/
To put something into something else
VERB   Inky inserted the key into the door.

inside¹ /insied/
In something and completely surrounded by it PREPOSITION, ADVERB
Put the card inside the envelope. • Go inside.

inside² /insied/
The inner part of something NOUN
The inside of an orange is very juicy.

insist /insist/
To refuse to change your mind about something or about doing something
VERB   I insist on seeing the manager.
• **insistent** /insistent/ ADJECTIVE

inspect /inspect/
To examine something carefully VERB
• **inspection** /inspecshen/ NOUN

install /instawl/
To put something in place and make it ready for use VERB
We've installed a new game on the computer.

instance /instens/
An example of something NOUN

instant /instent/
A moment in time NOUN
The accident happened in an instant.

instead /insted/
In place of something else ADVERB
There are no oranges, have an apple instead.

instruct /instruct/
To tell or show someone how to do something VERB
• **instructions** /instrucshenz/
  NOUN PLURAL

instrument /instrement/
1. Something for making musical sounds
A guitar is a musical instrument.
2. A tool used for doing a particular thing
scientific instruments NOUN

insult /insult/
To say rude and nasty things to someone
VERB
• **insult** /insult/ NOUN
• **insulting** /insulting/ ADJECTIVE

Ii

intelligent /intelijent/
Quick to learn and understand things
ADJECTIVE
• **intelligence** /intelijens/ NOUN

intend /intend/
To plan to do something VERB

intention /intenshen/
What you have decided to do NOUN

intentional /intenshenel/
Deliberately done, not by accident
ADJECTIVE
• **intentionally** /intenshenelee/ ADVERB

interactive /interactiv/
If a computer program is interactive, there is communication between the computer and the person using it
ADJECTIVE

interest[1] /intrest/
1. The feeling you have when you want to know more about something or someone 2. Your interests are the things you like doing NOUN

interest[2] /intrest/
If something or someone interests you, you want to know more about them VERB
• **interesting** /intresting/ ADJECTIVE

interfere /interfier/
To get involved in something that is nothing to do with you VERB

international /internashenel/
Connected with different nations
ADJECTIVE *The World Cup is an international competition.*

Internet /internet/
The Internet is a system where computers around the world can be connected to each other for sharing information NOUN

interrupt /interupt/
To make someone stop what they are doing for a short while VERB
Don't interrupt Inky while she's talking.
• **interruption** /interupshen/ NOUN

interval /intervel/
1. A period of time between two things
2. A short pause between each part of a play or game *There was an interval halfway through the play.* NOUN

into /intoo/
1. To the inside of something *Put your books into your bags.* 2. To a different place, or a different type of thing
The caterpillar changed into a butterfly.
PREPOSITION

introduce /intredues/
1. If you introduce someone to someone else, you tell them each other's names when they meet for the first time *Let me introduce you to Bee.* 2. To do something new or differently *The factory introduced a new method for building cars.* VERB
• **introduction** /intreducshen/ NOUN

invade /invaid/
To go somewhere and try to take control of it by force VERB
The country was invaded by a large army.
• **invasion** /invaizhen/ NOUN

invent /invent/
To make or do something in a way that has never been done before VERB
Who invented the telephone?
• **invention** /invenshen/ NOUN

investigate /investigait/
To try and find out exactly what happened VERB
• **investigation** /investigaishen/ NOUN

invisible /invizibel/
If something is invisible, you cannot see it ADJECTIVE

Ii

invite /inviet/
To ask someone if they want to go somewhere **VERB**
Inky invited Bee and Snake to a party.
• **invitation** /invitaishen/ **NOUN**

involve /involv/
To include something or someone **VERB**
The music teacher was trying to involve all the students in the singing.

iron[1] /ieen/
1. A type of metal 2. A flat metal tool that is heated and used to make clothes smooth **NOUN**

iron[2] /ieen/
To make clothes smooth using an iron **VERB**
• **ironing** /ieening/ **NOUN**
• **ironing board** /ieening bord/ **NOUN**

irregular /iregyeler/
Not smooth or even, and without any regular pattern **ADJECTIVE**
an irregular shape

irritate /iritait/
1. To make someone angry 2. To hurt a part of your body slightly *This rash is irritating my skin.* **VERB**
• **irritable** /iretebel/ **ADJECTIVE**
• **irritating** /iritaiting/ **ADJECTIVE**

is /iz/
▶ **be** **VERB**

island /ielend/
A piece of land with sea all around it **NOUN**

isolated /ieselaitid/
1. Far away from anything else *It was an isolated house, a long way from any other buildings.* 2. Not connected *It was an isolated event.* **ADJECTIVE**

it /it/
Something that someone has already mentioned in the sentence **PRONOUN**
Sam likes his book, it is really interesting.

itch /ich/
If something itches like your arm or clothes, you get a feeling that makes you want to scratch your skin **VERB**
• **itch** /ich/ **NOUN**
• **itchy** /ichee/ **ADJECTIVE**

item /ietem/
One of the things in a group **NOUN**

its /its/
Belonging to a thing or animal already mentioned in the sentence **ADJECTIVE**
The dog was wagging its tail.
• **itself** /itself/ **PRONOUN**

it's /its/
Short for 'it is' or 'it has' **CONTRACTION**

ivory /ieveree/
A type of bone that comes from the tusks of an elephant **NOUN**

ivy /ievee/
A climbing plant that grows on walls and trees **NOUN**

Jj

jab[1] /jab/
To push something pointed into something
VERB *He jabbed me with a pencil.*

jab[2] /jab/
An injection to stop you getting sick NOUN
a flu jab

jackal /jacel/
A wild animal like a dog NOUN

jacket /jacit/
A short coat NOUN

jaguar /jagueer/
A big wild cat like a leopard NOUN

jail /jail/
A place where criminals are locked up
NOUN
• **jail** /jail/ VERB

jam[1] /jam/
A food made from cooking fruit and
sugar together NOUN

jam[2] /jam/
1. To press something tightly into a small
space *Snake jammed lots of papers into his
bag.* 2. To make something stop working
because it is stuck *I can't open the drawer,
it's jammed.* VERB

jangle /janggel/
To make a ringing sound when small
things knock together VERB
*We could hear his keys jangle as he
got nearer.*
• **jangle** /janggel/ NOUN

January /janueeree/
The first month of the year NOUN
▶ CALENDAR, page 13

jar /jar/
A container used for keeping food in,
usually made of glass NOUN
a jam jar

jaw /jaw/
The bones in your mouth that hold your
teeth NOUN

jazz /jaz/
A type of music with a strong regular
pattern of sounds NOUN

jealous /jeles/
Unhappy because you want something
that another person has ADJECTIVE
• **jealousy** /jelesee/ NOUN

jeans /jeenz/
Blue trousers made of cotton NOUN PLURAL

jeep /jeep/
A type of car for driving where there are
no roads NOUN

jeer /jier/
To shout rude things at someone VERB
• **jeer** /jier/ NOUN

jelly /jelee/
A type of soft sweet food that shakes
when you move it NOUN

jellyfish /jeleefish/
A sea animal with a clear body you can
see through NOUN

jerk /jerk/
1. A sudden movement you make quickly
2. Another word for a stupid person NOUN

jersey /jerzee/
Something you wear over a shirt or blouse to keep the top of your body and arms warm NOUN

jet /jet/
1. A plane with a very powerful engine 2. A stream of water or gas that comes out of a small hole NOUN

Jew /joo/
A person who believes in the Jewish religion based on part of the Bible and the laws and written words of rabbis NOUN
• **Jewish** /jooish/ ADJECTIVE

jewel /jooel/
A beautiful and valuable stone that people wear for decoration NOUN
• **jeweller** /jooeler/ NOUN
• **jewellery** /jooelree/ NOUN

jigsaw puzzle /jigsaw puzel/
A picture cut into small pieces that you put back together for fun NOUN

jingle /jinggel/
1. A kind of ringing sound when metal objects like keys knock against each other 2. A short song NOUN

job /job/
1. Work that people do to get money 2. Something you have to do *Washing the dishes is a job I don't like.* NOUN

jockey /jocee/
Someone who rides a horse in a race NOUN

jog /jog/
1. To knock against something *Don't jog my elbow!* 2. If you jog someone's memory, you remind them of something 3. To run at a slow steady speed VERB
• **jogging** /joging/ NOUN

join /join/
1. To fix things together 2. To come together *Here is where the river joins the sea.* 3. To become part of a group of people *Snake will join the class soon.* 4. To take part in something *We all joined in the singing.* VERB

joint /joint/
1. A place where two things fit together 2. A part of your body where two bones meet *The elbow is a joint in the middle of your arm.* 3. A piece of meat for cooking *We're having a joint of beef for dinner.* NOUN

joke /joak/
Something you say or do that makes people laugh NOUN
• **joker** /joaker/ NOUN

jolly[1] /jolee/
Another word for happy ADJECTIVE

jolly[2] /jolee/
Another word for very ADVERB
We had a jolly good time.

journalist /jernelist/
A person who gets news and writes about it in newspapers NOUN

journey /jernee/
When you travel from one place to another NOUN

joy /joi/
A feeling of being very happy NOUN
• **joyful** /joifel/ ADJECTIVE

joystick /joistic/
In computer games, a joystick is a handle you use to control the way things move on your screen NOUN

Jj

Jj

judge[1] /juj/
1. An important person in a court who decides how criminals should be punished 2. A person who decides who is going to be the winner in a competition or a race **NOUN**

judge[2] /juj/
1. To decide who will be the winner in a competition or race 2. To give an opinion about something **VERB**
• **judgement** /jujment/ **NOUN**

jug /jug/
A container with a handle for pouring liquids such as water **NOUN**

juggle /jugel/
To keep several things in the air at once by quickly catching and throwing each one **VERB**
• **juggler** /jugler/ **NOUN**

juice /joos/
The liquid that comes out of fruit or vegetables **NOUN**
orange juice
• **juicy** /joosee/ **ADJECTIVE**

July /joolie/
The seventh month of the year **NOUN**
▶ **CALENDAR**, page 13

jumble[1] /jumbel/
Lots of things that are all mixed up **NOUN**

jumble[2] /jumbel/
To mix things up **VERB**

jumbo /jumboa/
Another way of saying very big **ADJECTIVE**
a jumbo jet

jump /jump/
To push yourself off the ground and into the air **VERB**
• **jump** /jump/ **NOUN**

jumper /jumper/
Something you wear to keep your body and arms warm **NOUN**

June /joon/
The sixth month of the year **NOUN**
▶ **CALENDAR**, page 13

jungle /junggel/
A very thick forest with lots of trees and plants growing close to each other. Jungles grow only in hot parts of the world **NOUN**

junior[1] /jooneeer/
Younger than someone, or having a lower job than someone **ADJECTIVE**

junior[2] /jooneeer/
A young person between the ages of seven and eleven at school **NOUN**

junk /jungk/
Things that people do not use or want any more **NOUN**

just /just/
1. Exactly *That's just what I was looking for.* 2. A short time ago *Snake has only just arrived.* 3. Only *Bob is just a little boy.* 4. Doing something, but nearly failing to do it *I just managed to catch the train.* **ADVERB**

justice /justis/
1. The way criminals are judged in courts and punished 2. When all people are treated well and in the same way **NOUN**

jut /jut/
To stick out slightly **VERB**
The end of the pipe juts out of the wall.

kangaroo /kanggeroo/
An animal with two big long legs that moves by jumping. Kangaroos live in Australia NOUN

kebab /kibab/
A food made up of little pieces of meat and vegetables that are cooked on a stick NOUN

keen /keen/
Really happy about doing something
ADJECTIVE *Bee is keen to learn new things.*

keep /keep/
1. To have something and not give it back or throw it away 2. To stay the same *I just can't keep warm.* 3. To make someone or something stay somewhere *Our teacher kept us in school for an extra 15 minutes.* 4. To put something in the same place again and again *I keep my pens in this box.* 5. To have something and take care of it *Lots of people keep pets.* 6. To do something again and again *Don't keep doing that!* VERB

kennel /kenel/
A small house for a dog NOUN

kerb /kerb/
The edge of the pavement NOUN

ketchup /kechup/
A red sauce made from tomatoes that you eat with food NOUN

kettle /ketel/
A metal or plastic container for boiling water NOUN

key[1] /kee/
1. A small piece of metal used to turn a lock 2. The keys on a computer keyboard are the buttons with letters, numbers and signs on them that you press with your finger NOUN

key[2] /kee/
If you key something in, you type it on your computer keyboard VERB
• **keyhole** /keehoal/ NOUN

keyboard /keebord/
A computer keyboard is a piece of flat plastic with keys on it for typing things into a computer NOUN

kick /kic/
To hit something or someone with your foot VERB
• **kick** /kic/ NOUN

kid[1] /kid/
1. A young goat 2. Another word for a child or young person NOUN

kid[2] /kid/
Another way of saying 'to joke' VERB
Are you kidding?

kidnap /kidnap/
To use force to take someone away VERB

Kk

kidney /kidnee/
Your two kidneys are parts of your body that take waste liquids away from your blood **NOUN**

kill /kil/
To make someone or something die **VERB**
• **killer** /kiler/ **NOUN**

kilogram /kilegram/
Or **kilo** /keeloa/ A unit for measuring weight **NOUN**

kilometre /kilemeeter/
A unit for measuring length **NOUN**

kilt /kilt/
A type of heavy skirt that men from Scotland sometimes wear as part of their traditional clothing **NOUN**

kind¹ /kiend/
Helpful and friendly **ADJECTIVE**

kind² /kiend/
A thing or person that belongs to a certain type or group **NOUN**
What kind of food does Snake like?
• **kindly** /kiendlee/ **ADVERB**
• **kindness** /kiendnes/ **NOUN**

king /king/
An important man who is the head of a country usually because he is the son of the person who ruled the country before **NOUN**

kingdom /kingdem/
A country ruled by a king or queen **NOUN**

kiosk /keeosk/
A small place where people sell things such as newspapers and sweets **NOUN**

kiss /kis/
To touch your lips against someone or something you like **VERB**
• **kiss** /kis/ **NOUN**

kitchen /kichen/
A room where people cook food **NOUN**

kite /kiet/
A frame covered in paper or plastic that flies in the air on a long string **NOUN**

kitten /kiten/
A young cat **NOUN**

kiwi /keewee/
1. A type of bird from New Zealand that cannot fly 2. A type of soft fruit **NOUN**

Kk

knack /nac/
An ability to do something well **NOUN**

knee /nee/
The joint in the middle of your leg
NOUN
▸ **PARTS OF THE BODY**, page 18

kneel /neel/
To sit with your knees on the ground
VERB
■ **knelt**

knew /nue/
PAST TENSE ▸ **know**

knickers /nicerz/
Underwear for girls and women,
worn under a skirt or trousers
NOUN PLURAL

knife /nief/
A sharp piece of metal used for cutting
NOUN
■ **knives** /nievz/ **PLURAL**

knight /niet/
A man who rode a horse and fought
for his king in early times **NOUN**

knit /nit/
To make clothes out of wool using
knitting needles **VERB**
• **knitting** /niting/ **NOUN**
• **knitting needle** /niting needel/ **NOUN**

knives /nievz/
NOUN PLURAL ▸ **knife**

knob /nob/
1. A round handle that you turn to open
or close a door 2. A round switch that
you turn on a machine **NOUN**

knock /noc/
To hit or touch something **VERB**
Inky knocked over a bottle of ink by accident.
• **knock** /noc/ **NOUN**

knot[1] /not/
The lump where something like string
or rope is tied together **NOUN**.

knot[2] /not/
To tie something like rope or string
together to form a knot **VERB**

know /noa/
1. To have learned something and
remember it *Do you know how to
swim?* 2. To have met a person or
been somewhere before **VERB**
■ **knew, known**
• **knowledge** /nolij/ **NOUN**

known /noan/
PAST PARTICIPLE ▸ **know**

knuckle /nucel/
Your knuckles are the joints in your
fingers **NOUN**

koala /koaahle/
A small animal like a bear with thick
furry ears that climbs trees. Koalas live in
Australia **NOUN**

Koran /kerahn/
The Koran is the holy book of the
Muslims **NOUN**

Ll

label /laibel/

A piece of paper or plastic with some information on it that explains something NOUN *Inky put a label on her suitcase in case it got lost.*
• **label** /laibel/ VERB

lace[1] /lais/

1. A string for fastening your shoes
2. A pretty material like a net with patterns in it NOUN

lace[2] /lais/

To pull a string through a row of holes and tie a knot VERB
Can you lace up your shoes?

lack /lac/

To not have something you need VERB
• **lack** /lac/ NOUN

lad /lad/

Another word for a boy NOUN

ladder /lader/

A frame with steps used to climb up and reach things in high places NOUN

lady /laidee/

A polite word for a woman NOUN

ladybird /laideeberd/

A tiny round insect that is red with black spots NOUN
▶ **INSECTS**, page 14

laid /laid/

PAST TENSE ▶ **lay**[1]

lain /lain/

PAST PARTICIPLE ▶ **lie**[3]

lake /laik/

A big area of water with land all around it NOUN

lamb /lam/

1. A young sheep 2. Meat that comes from a young sheep NOUN

lame /laim/

Not able to walk properly ADJECTIVE

lamp /lamp/

An object that gives you light NOUN
an oil lamp • an electric lamp
• **lampshade** /lampshaid/ NOUN

lance /lans/

A long thin weapon with a point at the end NOUN

land[1] /land/

1. The parts of the earth not covered by water 2. An old-fashioned word for a country NOUN

land[2] /land/

To come down from the air onto the ground VERB
When does our plane land?

landing /landing/

1. The floor at the top of the stairs, or between different sections of the stairs
Inky was waiting for Snake on the landing.
2. When a plane lands somewhere
What a smooth landing! NOUN

landlady /landlaidee/

A woman who owns a building and rents it out to other people NOUN

Ll

landlord /landlord/
A man who owns a building and rents it out to other people NOUN

landscape /landscaip/
The land you can see around you NOUN

lane /lain/
1. A narrow road, often in the countryside 2. A part of a main road that is divided by painted lines that show cars and other vehicles where they must travel 3. A long narrow section in a swimming pool or running track where the swimmers or runners must stay NOUN

language /languwij/
A particular way of speaking or writing NOUN *the French language*

lantern /lantern/
A little container with a light inside and a handle for people to carry NOUN

lap /lap/
The flat part of your body from your waist to your knees when you are sitting down NOUN
The baby was sitting on his mother's lap.

laptop /laptop/
A small computer that people can carry with them NOUN

larder /larder/
A small cool room or cupboard where food is kept NOUN

large /larj/
Something that is large has a great size or amount ADJECTIVE
Snake was eating a large egg sandwich.

lark /lark/
A little brown bird that sings NOUN

lasagne /lezanye/
Long flat pieces of pasta with meat or vegetables and a sauce NOUN

laser /laizer/
A machine that produces a very powerful line of light NOUN

lash /lash/
When someone is hit with a whip as a punishment NOUN

lasso /lasoo/
A long rope with a loop at the end used by cowboys for catching animals NOUN

• **lasso** /lasoo/ VERB

last[1] /last/
1. Coming after all the others *Come on Snake, you don't want to be the last one at the picnic!* 2. The one before this one, or the most recent one *What did you do last week?* ADJECTIVE

last[2] /last/
After all the others ADVERB
This time Bee came last.

last[3] /last/
The person or thing that comes after all the others PRONOUN
Hurry up, or you will be the last to arrive.

last[4] /last/
To continue, or to go on in the same way VERB *I hope this nice weather will last.*

Ll

late /lait/
1. After the usual or expected time *I went to bed late.* 2. Near the end of the day or the end of a period of time *I must leave now, it's late.* ADJECTIVE, ADVERB
- **latecomer** /laitcumer/ NOUN
- **lately** /laitlee/ ADVERB
- **later** /laiter/ ADJECTIVE
- **latest** /laitest/ ADJECTIVE

laugh /laf/
To make a sound with your throat and a very big smile when you think something is funny VERB
- **laughter** /lafter/ NOUN

launch /lawnch/
To send something on its way VERB *The rocket will be launched tomorrow.*
- **launch** /lawnch/ NOUN
- **launch pad** /lawnch pad/ NOUN

launderette /lawnderet/
A place with big washing machines where people can go to wash their clothes NOUN

laundry /lawndree/
1. Things such as clothes that are dirty and need to be washed 2. A place where people wash and iron things such as clothes NOUN

lavender /lavender/
A plant with purple flowers and a very sweet smell NOUN

law /law/
1. A rule that people must obey *There are lots of laws in our country.* 2. The law is all the rules together that people must obey *We would never break the law.* NOUN

lawn /lawn/
An area with short grass in someone's garden or in a park NOUN

lawnmower /lawnmoaer/
A machine for cutting grass on a lawn NOUN

lawyer /loier/
Someone who gives people advice about the law NOUN

lay¹ /lai/
1. If an animal such as a bird lays an egg, the egg comes out of its body 2. To put something or someone down 3. If you lay the table, you put things on it ready for a meal VERB
- **laid**

lay² /lai/
PAST TENSE ▶ **lie**³

layer /laier/
Something that covers a whole surface NOUN *There was a thick layer of dust on Snake's book.*

lazy /laizee/
Not working very hard or not making an effort ADJECTIVE

lead¹ /leed/
1. To go in front and show people the way 2. To go somewhere *This path leads straight to our school.* 3. To be in charge of a group VERB
- **led**
- **leader** /leeder/ NOUN

lead² /leed/
1. **in the lead** Ahead of everyone else in a race or competition 2. A strap for holding a dog NOUN

lead³ /led/
A soft but very heavy metal **NOUN**

leaf /leef/
Leaves are the flat green parts of a tree or plant that grow from the branches or the stem **NOUN**

■ **leaves** /leevz/ **PLURAL**

leaflet /leeflǝt/
A small sheet of paper with words printed on it that give people information about something **NOUN**
Here's a leaflet about the computer club.

league /leeg/
A group of sports teams that play games against each other **NOUN**

leak /leek/
A hole that appears in something and lets gas or liquid escape **NOUN**
• **leak** /leek/ **VERB**
• **leaky** /leekee/ **ADJECTIVE**

lean¹ /leen/
1. To rest on or against something
Lean the ladder on the wall. 2. To slope
Look how the trees lean in the wind. **VERB**
■ **leant** or **leaned**

lean² /leen/
Thin, without any fat **ADJECTIVE**
He's a tall lean athlete.

leant /lent/
PAST TENSE ▶ **lean**¹

leap /leep/
To jump high in the air **VERB**
■ **leapt** or **leaped**

learn /lern/
To become able to understand or do something **VERB**
Bee and Snake are learning to read.
■ **learnt** or **learned**
• **learner** /lerner/ **NOUN**

learnt /lernt/
PAST TENSE ▶ **learn**

least /leest/
1. Less than anyone or anything else
Mary has most, and John has least.
2. The smallest in size or importance
Peter has the most, and Sarah the least money. 3. **at least** Not less than a certain amount *We waited at least an hour.* **ADJECTIVE**, **PRONOUN**, **ADVERB**

leather /lether/
The skin from an animal that is used for making things such as shoes **NOUN**

leave /leev/
1. To go away from somewhere or something *What time do we leave?*
2. To let something or someone stay in a certain place or stay a certain way
Snake left his umbrella at Inky's house.
• *Inky left the door open.* 3. If you leave someone or something alone, you stay away from them *Leave me alone!* **VERB**
■ **left**

leaves /leevz/
NOUN PLURAL ▶ **leaf**

led /led/
PAST TENSE ▶ **lead**¹

ledge /lej/
A kind of shelf that sticks out from a wall
NOUN *a window ledge*

Ll

163

Ll

leek /leek/
A vegetable that tastes like an onion. It is long and white, and has flat green leaves **NOUN**
▶ **FRUIT AND VEGETABLES**, page 15

left¹ /left/
The opposite side to the right side **NOUN**

left² /left/
On the same side as your left hand **ADJECTIVE** *Take a left turn at the traffic lights.*

left³ /left/
Towards the left **ADVERB**
I turned left.

left⁴ /left/
PAST TENSE ▶ **leave**

leftovers /leftoaverz/
Food that has not been eaten during a meal **NOUN PLURAL**
• **leftover** /leftoaver/ **ADJECTIVE**

leg /leg/
One of the two parts of your body that you use for walking **NOUN**
▶ **PARTS OF THE BODY**, page 18

legal /leegel/
1. To do with the law *These are legal papers.* 2. Allowed by law **ADJECTIVE**

legend /lejend/
A very old and well-known story that may or may not be true **NOUN**
Do you know the legend of King Arthur?

lemon /lemen/
A small fruit with a yellow skin and a sour taste **NOUN**
▶ **FRUIT AND VEGETABLES**, page 15

lemonade /lemenaid/
A sweet drink made from lemons with lots of bubbles in it **NOUN**

lend /lend/
To let someone use something of yours that they must give back later **VERB**
Inky lent Snake her pen.
■ **lent**

length /length/
1. The amount that something measures from one end to the other 2. The amount of time something takes **NOUN**

lengthen /lengthen/
To make or become longer **VERB**

lens /lenz/
A piece of glass for making things look bigger or smaller used in things such as glasses and cameras **NOUN**

lent /lent/
PAST TENSE ▶ **lend**

lentil /lentel/
A small round seed that can be cooked and eaten **NOUN**

leopard /leperd/
A wild animal like a very big cat with spots on its body **NOUN**

less /les/
Not as much **ADJECTIVE, ADVERB, PRONOUN**

lesson /lesen/
A period of time when someone teaches you something **NOUN**
What time is our dance lesson?

Ll

let /let/
1. To give someone permission to do something 2. To take no action to stop something from happening *Don't let that fall off the table.* 3. To let someone have something means to give it to them *Please let me have your pen.* 4. To let someone know something means to tell them *Can you let me know what happens?* 5. To let someone down means to disappoint them VERB
■ **let**

letter /leter/
1. A mark in writing that expresses one of the sounds of the alphabet *The word 'kite' begins with the letter 'k'.* 2. A written message that you put in an envelope and send to someone *Inky wrote a letter to her friend.* NOUN

• **letterbox** /leterbox/ NOUN

lettuce /letɐs/
A round vegetable made up of lots of green leaves that people eat in salads
NOUN ▶ FRUIT AND VEGETABLES, page 15

level[1] /level/
1. Completely flat 2. At the same height *The water is almost level with the top of the bucket.* ADJECTIVE

level[2] /level/
1. The height, amount or standard of something 2. A piece of ground, or a floor *The house is built on three levels.* NOUN

level crossing /level crosing/
A place where a road crosses a railway line NOUN

lever /leever/
A stick you move up or down to move something heavy or to make a machine work NOUN
We moved the rock using a long lever.

liar /lieer/
Someone who tells lies NOUN

library /liebrɐree/
A room or building where books are kept for reading NOUN

lick /lic/
To move your tongue over something
VERB *Harry was licking an ice cream.*

lid /lid/
A cover for something like a box or saucepan NOUN
Can you lift up the lid?

lie[1] /lie/
Something someone says that is not true
NOUN *She's always telling lies.*

lie[2] /lie/
To say things that are not true VERB
Stop lying!
■ **lied**

lie[3] /lie/
To be in a flat position VERB
■ **lay, lain**

lied /lied/
PAST TENSE ▶ **lie**[2]

life /lief/
1. The time when someone is alive, between their birth and their death
2. When someone or something is living *Is there life on Mars?* NOUN
• **lifetime** /lieftiem/ NOUN

Ll

lift¹ /lift/
To move something or someone to a higher position **VERB**

lift² /lift/
1. A machine for travelling between different floors in a big building
2. A drive in someone's car **NOUN**

light¹ /liet/
Something that shines and allows you to see things **NOUN**
The light from the sun was very strong.

light² /liet/
1. To make something burn *Bee and Snake lit a fire.* 2. To give a lot of light *All the fireworks lit up the sky.* **VERB**
- lit

light³ /liet/
1. Not weighing very much *Snake's school bag is very light.* 2. Not strong or dark in colour *Do you like my light blue dress?* 3. With lots of light from the sun *My bedroom is very light in the morning.*
ADJECTIVE
- **light bulb** /liet bulb/ **NOUN**
- **lightly** /lietlee/ **ADVERB**

lighthouse /liethous/
A tall thin building with a strong light that warns ships there is danger **NOUN**

lightning /lietning/
A bright flash of light in the sky during a thunderstorm **NOUN**

like¹ /liek/
1. Almost the same as something else
2. Used to describe something, or ask for a description of something *What is your teacher like?* **PREPOSITION**

like² /liek/
To think that someone or something is nice or good **VERB**
We all like chocolate.

likely /lieklee/
If something is likely, it will probably happen **ADJECTIVE**

lily /lilee/
A tall plant with big flowers **NOUN**

limb /lim/
An arm or a leg **NOUN**

limit /limit/
The biggest amount of something that is allowed **NOUN**
There are speed limits on all the roads.

limp /limp/
To walk with difficulty because you have a problem with your leg or your legs **VERB**

line /lien/
1. A long thin mark *Inky drew a line on the blackboard.* 2. A row of people or things *The children all stood in a line.*
3. A telephone wire 4. The tracks that a train travels on *The railway line goes from London to Brighton.* **NOUN**

liner /liener/
1. A big ship for passengers 2. A piece of plastic that protects the inside of something **NOUN**

linger /lingger/
To stay somewhere longer than you should **VERB**

link¹ /lingk/
1. A ring in a chain
2. A connection between things **NOUN**

Ll

link² /lingk/
To join together or connect things in some way **VERB**
The police think the two crimes are linked.

lino /lienɒa/
A smooth floor covering **NOUN**
We've got lino in the kitchen.

lion /lieɛn/
A big wild animal that is strong and kills other animals to eat. Lions live mainly in Africa **NOUN**

lip /lip/
Your lips are the soft edges of your mouth **NOUN** ▶ **PARTS OF THE BODY**, page 18
• **lipstick** /lipstic/ **NOUN**

liquid /liquid/
Anything that flows like water **NOUN**

list¹ /list/
Words or numbers that you write down underneath each other, usually on a piece of paper **NOUN**
a shopping list

list² /list/
To write things down in a list **VERB**

listen /lisɛn/
To pay attention so that you can hear something **VERB**
Listen to what the teacher is saying.

lit /lit/
PAST TENSE ▶ **light²**

litre /leeter/
A unit for measuring liquid **NOUN**

litter /liter/
1. Waste paper that is thrown away
2. A group of baby animals born at the same time *The cat has a litter of kittens.*
NOUN

little¹ /litɛl/
Very small **ADJECTIVE**
They live in a little house in the forest.

little² /litɛl/
Used when you mean a small amount of something **ADVERB**
Bee seems a little tired.

live /liv/
1. To have your home somewhere
Where do you live, Inky? 2. To be alive
Dickens lived in the nineteenth century.
3. To have a certain type of life
He lives like a king. **VERB**

lively /lievlee/
Happy and always doing things
ADJECTIVE *Julia is a very lively girl.*

liver /liver/
A big organ inside your body that cleans your blood **NOUN**

lizard /lizerd/
A crawling animal with four legs and a long tail like a small crocodile **NOUN**

llama /lahme/
An animal with thick hair, like a camel without humps. Llamas live in South America **NOUN**

Ll

load[1] /loɑd/
An amount of something that can be carried in one go **NOUN**
Can you carry this load of bricks?

load[2] /loɑd/
1. To put things into or onto something
We loaded the truck with vegetables.
2. To put a computer program onto your computer **VERB**

loads /loɑdz/
Another word for lots **NOUN PLURAL**
Bee has made loads of mistakes in her homework.

loaf /loɑf/
Bread that has been baked as one big piece **NOUN**
Let's go and buy a loaf of bread.
■ **loaves** /loɑvz/ **PLURAL**

lobe /loɑb/
The soft part at the bottom of your ear **NOUN**

lobster /lobster/
A sea animal with a shell and big claws **NOUN**

local /loɑcel/
Near, or connected with a particular area **ADJECTIVE** *Many children go to their local school.*

location /loɑcaishen/
The place where something is **NOUN**

loch /loc/
A loch is a lake in Scotland **NOUN**

lock[1] /loc/
Something opened with a key that is used to keep a door, drawer or box shut **NOUN**

lock[2] /loc/
1. To turn the key in a lock so that something cannot be opened *He locked the door when he left the house.* 2. To lock something somewhere is to put it there and turn the key in the lock *They locked the money in the safe.* **VERB**

locker /locer/
A small cupboard with a lock where you can keep things **NOUN**

locomotive /loɑcemoɑtiv/
The big engine that pulls a train **NOUN**

loft /loft/
The space under the roof of a building **NOUN**

log /log/
A thick piece of wood from a tree **NOUN**
a log cabin

lollipop /loleepop/
A hard sweet on a stick **NOUN**

lone /loɑn/
Not with anyone else **ADJECTIVE**
We saw a lone figure in the distance.

lonely /loɑnlee/
1. Unhappy because you are all alone
If you're feeling lonely, phone me and I'll come over. 2. Far away from other people *This is a lonely place.* **ADJECTIVE**

Ll

long¹ /long/
1. Measuring a big distance or amount of time *It was a long walk to the park. · An hour is too long to wait.*
2. Measuring a certain amount *The carpet is ten feet long.* **ADJECTIVE**

long² /long/
For a long time **ADVERB**
Have you been waiting long?

look¹ /look/
1. To turn your eyes so that you are aware of something or someone *Look out of the window.* 2. To have the appearance of something or someone *You look just like your grandfather.* 3. **look after** To be responsible for someone or something *I look after my pet cat.* 4. **look for** To try and find someone or something *I was looking for my keys.* **VERB**

look² /look/
1. When you see or look at something *Can I have a look at your book?*
2. The expression on someone's face *an angry look.* 3. Appearance *I don't like the look of those rain clouds.* **NOUN**

loop /loop/
A circular shape made in something like string **NOUN**
To tie a knot, first make a loop.

loose /loos/
1. Not tight *I like to wear loose clothes in the summer.* 2. Not fixed in its place *Snake has a loose tooth.* **ADJECTIVE**

lord /lord/
An important man who has a special title **NOUN**

lorry /loree/
A truck for carrying heavy goods **NOUN**

lose /looz/
1. To not have something any more and not know where it is *I have lost my keys again.* 2. To not win a game or a race
3. If you lose weight, you become thinner **VERB**
▪ **lost**
· **loser** /loozer/ **NOUN**
· **loss** /los/ **NOUN**
· **lost** /lost/ **ADJECTIVE**

lost /lost/
PAST TENSE ▶ **lose**

lot /lot/
1. **a lot of** or **lots of** Many or much of something *They have lots of animals on the farm.* 2. **a lot** Many times or very much *I visit my uncle a lot. · Snake likes Inky a lot.* **NOUN**

lotion /loashen/
A liquid people put on their skin **NOUN**

a suntan lotion

Ll

lottery /loteree/
A lottery is a game where people buy tickets with numbers on them. If your number is chosen you win money NOUN

loud /loud/
Making a lot of noise ADJECTIVE, ADVERB
Her teacher has a very loud voice.

lounge /lounj/
A room in your house where you can rest and watch TV NOUN

love /luv/
To like someone or something very much
VERB
• **love** /luv/ NOUN

lovely /luvlee/
Beautiful or very good ADJECTIVE
She's a lovely baby.

low[1] /loa/
1. Near the ground *Stand by the low wall.*
2. Very small in amount or in numbers
I can't hear the TV, the volume is too low.
3. Not very important *That is a low priority.* ADJECTIVE

low[2] /loa/
Doing something near to the ground
ADVERB *The planes were flying low.*

lower /loaer/
To move or bring something down to a lower level VERB
They lowered the flag.

loyal /loiel/
If you are loyal to someone or something, you always help and support them
ADJECTIVE *He is a loyal friend.*

luck /luc/
Good or bad things that happen by chance NOUN
He has had some bad luck recently.
• **luckily** /lucilee/ ADVERB
• **lucky** /lucee/ ADJECTIVE

ludo /loodoa/
A game people play on a board with counters and dice NOUN

luggage /lugij/
The suitcases and bags you carry with you when you travel NOUN

lullaby /lulebie/
A song you sing when children are going to sleep NOUN

lump /lump/
A piece of something with no particular shape NOUN
a lump of wood or coal
• **lumpy** /lumpee/ ADJECTIVE

lunar /looner/
Connected with the moon ADJECTIVE
a lunar landing

lunch /lunch/
A meal you eat in the middle of the day
NOUN
• **lunchbox** /lunchbox/ NOUN
• **lunch break** /lunch braik/ NOUN
• **lunchtime** /lunchtiem/ NOUN

lung /lung/
Your lungs are the two parts inside your body that you use for breathing
NOUN

luxury /lucsheree/
Something expensive or comfortable that people do not need but would like to have NOUN

Mm

mac /mac/
A thin coat that you wear to keep the rain out **NOUN**

macaroni /maceroanee/
Food made from little tubes of pasta **NOUN**

machine /mesheen/
Something with parts that move together to do a job **NOUN**
A washing machine cleans clothes.
• **machinery** /mesheeneree/ **NOUN**

mad /mad/
1. Very silly 2. Angry *Are you mad with me?* 3. If something or someone drives you mad, they are very annoying *That noise is driving me mad.* 4. Suffering from an illness of the mind **ADJECTIVE**
• **madness** /madnes/ **NOUN**

madam /madem/
A very polite name sometimes used when speaking to a lady **NOUN**

made /maid/
PAST TENSE ▶ **make**¹

made-up /maid up/
If a story is made-up, it is not true **ADJECTIVE**

magazine /magezeen/
A thin paper book with lots of pictures and stories that is sold every week or month **NOUN**

maggot /maget/
A little worm that will change into a winged insect **NOUN**

magic /majic/
A special power to make impossible things happen, or a clever trick **NOUN**
• **magical** /majicel/ **ADJECTIVE**

magician /mejishen/
A person who does clever tricks or makes impossible things happen by using special words or doing special actions **NOUN**

magnet /magnet/
A piece of metal that can pull other bits of metal towards it **NOUN**
• **magnetic** /magnetic/ **ADJECTIVE**

magnificent /magnifisent/
Very good because it is big and beautiful **ADJECTIVE**
The king lived in a magnificent palace.

magnify /magnifie/
To make something look bigger **VERB**

magpie /magpie/
A big black and white bird with a long tail **NOUN**

maid /maid/
A woman servant **NOUN**

Mm

maiden /maiden/
An old-fashioned word for a young girl
NOUN

mail[1] /mail/
1. Anything you send to someone by post
2. Anything you send to someone on a computer by email 3. A way of sending letters or packages by putting stamps on them and putting them in a postbox
Shall I send the letter by mail? NOUN

mail[2] /mail/
To send something by post to someone's house or by email to someone's computer
VERB

mailbox /mailbox/
A place on your computer where email messages are kept NOUN

main /main/
Most important ADJECTIVE
the main character in a play

mainly /mainlee/
Used when you talk about the most important part of something ADVERB
The fair was a success mainly due to everyone's hard work.

maisonette /maizenet/
A flat that has two floors and is a part of a much bigger house NOUN

maize /maiz/
A tall plant with big yellow seeds that people cook and eat NOUN

majesty /majestee/
A name used when speaking to a king or queen NOUN
Good morning, your Majesty.
• **majestic** /mejestic/ ADJECTIVE

major /maijer/
Very big or important ADJECTIVE
We have a major problem.

majority /mejoritee/
The biggest part of a group of people or things NOUN
The majority of our flowers are red.

make[1] /maik/
1. To perform an action or activity *Bee must make a decision.* • *Inky is making a cake.* 2. To cause something to happen *Bee's decision made Inky happy.* 3. To force someone to do something *They made me wait an hour.* 4. **make up** To invent something like a story *Is this story true or did you make it up?* 5. **make up** To be part of a group *Men make up less than half of all the teachers in our school.* VERB
■ **made**

make[2] /maik/
A certain type of thing made by one company NOUN
What make is your computer?

make-up /maik up/
Things such as lipsticks and powders that people put on their faces to make them look different NOUN

male /mail/
A boy or a man NOUN
• **male** /mail/ ADJECTIVE

mall /mawl/
Short for shopping mall, a big building with lots of shops in it NOUN

Mm

mammal /mamel/
Any animal, including human beings, where the females give birth to babies and the babies are fed with milk NOUN

man /man/
A human being who is male and an adult NOUN
■ **men** /men/ PLURAL

manage /manij/
1. To succeed in doing something difficult
It was hard, but we managed to win the game. 2. To be in charge of something
Who is going to manage our pop group?
VERB
• **manager** /manijer/ NOUN

mane /main/
The long hair on the neck of a horse or lion NOUN

mango /manggoa/
A big fruit with yellow flesh that grows in hot countries NOUN

maniac /maineeac/
Someone who behaves in a dangerous or a stupid way NOUN
He drives like a maniac.

manner /maner/
A way of behaving or doing things NOUN
Inky always explains the lesson in a very careful manner.

manners /manerz/
A polite way of behaving and speaking to others NOUN PLURAL
She has very good manners.

mansion /manshen/
A very big house NOUN

mantelpiece /mantelpees/
A shelf above a fireplace NOUN

many /menee/
Lots of people or things
ADJECTIVE, PRONOUN
There are many books in the library.
■ more, most

map /map/
A drawing of somewhere that shows where important things are and where roads and rivers go NOUN

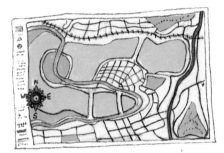

maple /maipel/
A tree that has pointed leaves and grows in Canada and other northern countries NOUN

marble /marbel/
A hard rock that is shiny when polished, used in building and to make statues NOUN

marbles /marbelz/
Little round balls of glass that children use in the game called marbles NOUN PLURAL

march /march/
To walk together in a group with regular steps VERB
Look at the soldiers marching past.
• **march** /march/ NOUN

March /march/
The third month of the year NOUN
▶ CALENDAR, page 13

margarine /marjereen/
A food you can use instead of butter, made from vegetable oil NOUN

173

Mm

margin /marjin/
The empty space around the edge of a page NOUN
Leave a margin on the left when you write in your book.

marigold /mareegoald/
A plant with gold or yellow flowers that have a strong smell NOUN

mark[1] /mark/
1. A spot or a dirty area that spoils something *There's a finger mark on my book.* 2. A number or letter that shows how good something is *Bee got a good mark for her work.* 3. A symbol on something to give you information *The mark on the pirate's map showed where the treasure was buried.* NOUN

mark[2] /mark/
1. To put or write a mark on something *I've marked the pages you have to read.* 2. To put a number or letter on someone's school work to show how good it is VERB

market /markit/
A place where people go to buy and sell things NOUN

marketplace /markitplais/
An open place in a town where people often meet for buying and selling NOUN

markings /markingz/
The shapes on the fur of an animal such as the zebra NOUN PLURAL
A tiger has striped markings.

marmalade /marmelaid/
A jam made from fruits such as oranges NOUN

maroon /meroon/
A dark red-brown colour NOUN, ADJECTIVE

marriage /marij/
The ceremony when a man and woman get married NOUN

married /mareed/
If someone is married, they have a husband or a wife ADJECTIVE

marrow /maroa/
A big dark green vegetable NOUN

marry /maree/
To become a husband or wife VERB

marshes /marshez/
Flat parts of the land that are wet and muddy NOUN PLURAL

marshmallow /marshmaloa/
A soft sweet that is white or pink NOUN

Mm

Martian /marshen/
Someone who comes from the planet
Mars in stories **NOUN**

marvel /marvel/
To be surprised and pleased by something
VERB

marvellous /marvles/
Really good **ADJECTIVE**
The weather is marvellous today.

mascot /mascot/
Something that brings good luck **NOUN**

mash /mash/
To crush food until it is soft **VERB**

mask /mask/
A cover for your face that hides it or
protects it **NOUN**

mass /mas/
1. A lump of something 2. A lot of
something *There's a mass of people
outside the school.* **NOUN**

massive /masiv/
Very big **ADJECTIVE**

mast /mast/
A long pole for the sails on a boat **NOUN**

master[1] /master/
1. An old-fashioned word for a male
teacher in a school 2. Someone who has
reached a high level of skill at something
She is a master of her craft. 3. Someone
who is in control of something *The owner
of a dog is its master.* **NOUN**

master[2] /master/
To learn how to do something **VERB**
*You need to master the basic skills
before moving on.*

masterpiece /masterpees/
Something of very high quality such as a
painting or piece of music **NOUN**

mat /mat/
A piece of strong material for covering
part of a floor **NOUN**
Don't forget to wipe your feet on the mat.

match[1] /mach/
1. A small thin piece of wood used for
lighting things such as a fire or candle
2. A game between two people or teams
The tennis match is today. 3. Something
similar to something else *It's an exact
match.* **NOUN**

match[2] /mach/
1. To be the same as something else
or similar in some way *His socks don't
match.* 2. To look good with something
else *Do these shoes match this dress?* **VERB**

mate /mait/
Another word for friend **NOUN**

material /metiereeel/
1. Cloth for making things such as
clothes 2. The basic things used to
make something *Bricks are a building
material used to make houses.* **NOUN**

mathematics /mathematics/
Or **maths** /maths/ The study
of numbers and shapes **NOUN**
• **mathematical** /mathematicel/
  ADJECTIVE

matter[1] /mater/
To be important **VERB**
It matters how you behave.

175

Mm

matter[2] /mater/
1. A subject or question that people talk about or write about *Kate isn't very interested in this matter.* 2. Used when you talk about what is wrong with someone or something *You look upset, what's the matter?* NOUN

mattress /matres/
The part of the bed that you sleep on NOUN

mature /mechooer/
1. Fully grown *Mature animals don't grow any bigger.* 2. Behaving in a sensible and grown-up way ADJECTIVE

mauve /moav/
A light purple colour NOUN, ADJECTIVE

maximum /maximem/
As big as something can be ADJECTIVE
• **maximum** /maximem/ NOUN

may /mai/
1. To be allowed *May I come in?*
2. You use may to mean that something is possible *I may go for a walk if it stops raining.* VERB
■ might

May /mai/
The fifth month of the year NOUN
▶ CALENDAR, page 13

maybe /maibee/
Used to mean that something could happen or be true but it is not certain ADVERB

mayonnaise /maienaiz/
A sauce made from eggs, oil and vinegar that people put on salads NOUN

mayor /meer/
An important person who is in charge of a town or city NOUN

maze /maiz/
Somewhere with lots of paths separated by bushes or walls that make it difficult to find a way out NOUN

me /mee/
A word you use when you talk about yourself PREPOSITION

meadow /medoa/
A field with grass and flowers NOUN

meal /meel/
1. The food that people eat at different times of the day *Breakfast is a meal.*
2. The occasion when you eat a meal *Snake's meal lasted two hours!* NOUN

mean[1] /meen/
1. To have a meaning *The red light means you must stop.* 2. To plan to do something *I meant to call you yesterday.* • *I didn't mean to hurt you.* 3. To be important or of great value *You mean a lot to me.* VERB
■ meant

mean[2] /meen/
1. Nasty or unkind 2. Not wanting to spend money or share things ADJECTIVE

meaning /meening/
The explanation for something NOUN
What's the meaning of this?

Mm

means /meenz/
1. A way of doing something *She tried every means to get there on time.*
2. **by means of** Using a particular way of doing something *I climbed up to the roof by means of a ladder.* **NOUN**

meant /ment/
PAST TENSE ▶ **mean**¹

meantime /meentiem/
The time between now and a particular time or event in the future **NOUN**

meanwhile /meenwiel/
1. During the time before something happens *Dad's not here yet. What shall I do meanwhile?* 2. While something else is happening *Snake was reading his book. Meanwhile Bee was writing.* **ADVERB**

measles /meezelz/
An illness when you get spots on your body and a high fever **NOUN**

measure¹ /mezher/
1. To find out the size or amount of something *The class measured their feet to see whose were biggest.* 2. To show a measurement *A clock measures time.* **VERB**

measure² /mezher/
1. An amount of something that can be measured *A foot is a measure of length.*
2. An action that people take to solve a problem *We must take measures to stop this happening again.* **NOUN**

measurement /mezherment/
The size, length or amount of something
NOUN *Do you know your chest measurement?*

meat /meet/
The flesh from animals or birds that people eat as food **NOUN**

mechanic /mecanic/
A person who repairs cars or machines
NOUN
• **mechanical** /mecanicel/ **ADJECTIVE**

mechanism /mecenizem/
The part of a machine that makes it work, or one of the parts that do a particular job **NOUN**
This mechanism turns the hands of the clock.

medal /medel/
A piece of metal on a ribbon given to someone for doing something special
NOUN

medical /medicel/
Connected with the treatment of illnesses
ADJECTIVE *Simon hurt himself but did not need medical treatment.*

medicine /medisen/
Something that you drink or eat to get better when you are sick **NOUN**
Have you taken your medicine?

medieval /medieevel/
Connected with the Middle Ages
ADJECTIVE

The castle dates from medieval times.

Mediterranean¹ /mediteraineeen/
Connected with the people or the countries around the Mediterranean Sea
ADJECTIVE

Mediterranean² /mediteraineeen/
The Mediterranean is the sea between the countries of Southern Europe, North Africa and the Middle East **NOUN**

Mm

medium /meedeeəm/
The middle size between small and big
ADJECTIVE

meet /meet/
1. To be in the same place as someone else either by plan or by chance *Bee went to meet her friend from the station.*
2. To speak to someone for the first time *I'm pleased to meet you!* 3. To come together *The two roads meet here.* VERB
■ met

meeting /meeting/
A group of people who gather together to talk about something NOUN
There's a meeting at the school tonight.

melon /melən/
A big round fruit that is soft and juicy inside, and has lots of seeds NOUN

▶ FRUIT AND VEGETABLES, page 15

melt /melt/
To make or go soft, and turn liquid VERB
The sun is melting the snow.

member /member/
Someone who belongs to a group NOUN
Snake and Bee are members of Inky's class.

memory /meməree/
1. Memory is the power people have to remember things *Ruth can remember when she was a baby. What a good memory she has!* 2. Something people remember *I have good memories of the days I was at school.* 3. The part of a computer where it stores information NOUN

men /men/
NOUN PLURAL ▶ **man**

menace¹ /menəs/
Someone or something dangerous NOUN
He's a real menace to the class.

menace² /menəs/
To behave in a threatening or frightening way VERB

mend /mend/
To repair something VERB

mental /mentəl/
1. Connected with the mind 2. Suffering from an illness of the mind ADJECTIVE

mention /menshən/
To talk about something or say something VERB *Inky mentioned that Bee and Snake were working very hard.*
• **mention** /menshən/ NOUN

menu /menuə/
1. A list of food that you can choose from 2. A list of choices on a computer screen NOUN

merchant /merchənt/
Someone who buys and sells things NOUN

mercy /mersee/
When you are kind and forgiving NOUN

mermaid /mermaid/
A woman in stories who has the tail of a fish instead of legs NOUN

Mm

merry /meree/
Another word for happy ADJECTIVE
Inky wished Snake a Merry Christmas.

merry-go-round /meree goa round/
A big machine at a fairground that goes
around and around. It has model horses
that people can ride on NOUN

mess¹ /mes/
1. If something is a mess or is in a mess,
it is dirty or untidy *Snake's room is in a
real mess.* 2. If someone is in a mess,
they have lots of problems NOUN
• **messy** /mesee/ ADJECTIVE

mess² /mes/
mess about If someone messes about,
they waste time or do silly things VERB

message /mesij/
Some information sent from one person
to another NOUN
Can you give Inky the message please?
• **messenger** /mesenjer/ NOUN

met /met/
PAST TENSE ▶ **meet**

metal /metel/
A hard, heavy substance NOUN
Iron and gold are types of metal.

meter /meeter/
A machine that measures how much of
something is used, such as a gas meter
NOUN

method /methed/
A way of doing something NOUN
*What method did you use to solve the
problem?*

metre /meeter/
A measurement of length. A metre is
made up of 100 centimetres NOUN

miaow /meeou/
The sound that a cat makes NOUN
• **miaow** /meeou/ VERB

mice /mies/
NOUN PLURAL ▶ **mouse**

Inky knows lots of other mice.

microphone /miecrefoan/
Something you use to record sounds or
to make sounds louder NOUN

microscope /miecrescoap/
Something that makes it possible to look
at very small things because it makes
them look bigger NOUN

microwave /miecrewaiv/
1. A type of oven used to cook food
quickly 2. A very small radio wave NOUN

midday /middai/
Midday is twelve o'clock in the middle of
the day NOUN
We're going to stop at midday for lunch.

middle /midel/
1. A position exactly halfway between
two points 2. The part of something that
is at an equal distance from all its edges
*The teacher stood in the middle of the
classroom.* NOUN
• **middle** /midel/ ADJECTIVE

midget /mijit/
A small person or thing NOUN

midnight /midniet/
Twelve o'clock at night NOUN

midway /midwai/
In a middle position between two things,
or halfway through a period of time
ADVERB

179

Mm

might[1] /miet/
You use might to mean that something is possible in the future or could have been possible in the past VERB
I might go out for a walk if it stops raining.
· I might have done it if I had more time.

might[2] /miet/
An old-fashioned word for strength NOUN
The giant used all his might to lift the stone.
· **mighty** /mietee/
Very strong or very big ADJECTIVE

mild /mield/
1. If something like an illness is mild, it is not very bad or serious 2. Not strong
This cheese has a mild taste. ADJECTIVE

mile /miel/
A unit for measuring length NOUN

milestone /mielstoan/
1. A big stone at the side of the road that shows how far it is to somewhere
2. An important event in someone's life
NOUN

milk /milk/
1. A white liquid that comes from cows and that people drink 2. A liquid for feeding babies that comes from mothers
NOUN

· **milkman** /milkmen/ NOUN
· **milk shake** /milk shaik/ NOUN
· **milky** /milkee/ ADJECTIVE

mill /mil/
1. A building with a big machine for crushing grain to make into flour
2. A little machine for crushing things such as pepper to make a powder NOUN
· **miller** /miler/ NOUN

millennia /mileneee/
NOUN PLURAL ▶ **millennium**

millennium /mileneem/
A period of a thousand years NOUN
■ **millennia** /mileneee/ PLURAL

millionaire /mileeeneer/
A very rich person who has a million pounds or more NOUN

mimic /mimic/
To copy the way someone does something
VERB
■ **mimicked**

mince /mins/
To cut meat into very small pieces VERB

mince pie /mins pie/
A little cake filled with small pieces of dried fruit NOUN

mind[1] /miend/
1. To be careful about something *Mind the step!* 2. To be worried or upset *Do you mind if I open the window?* 3. To take care of someone *Could you mind the baby while I go out?* VERB

mind[2] /miend/
1. Someone's brain or what they think about or pay attention to *I've changed my mind, I'm not going to the party now.*
2. To have something in mind means to have an idea about something or a plan
What dress did you have in mind? NOUN

mine[1] /mien/
Belonging to me PRONOUN
This book is mine.

mine² /mien/
1. A deep hole in the ground that people dig to find something like coal or gold
2. A good source of something *He's a mine of information!* NOUN

• **miner** /miener/ NOUN

mine³ /mien/
To dig deep into the ground to get something out VERB

mineral /minerel/
Things like coal or iron that people dig out of the ground NOUN

minibus /mineebus/
A kind of big car that can carry between about six and twelve people NOUN

minicab /mineecab/
A type of taxi NOUN

minimum /minimem/
The smallest amount NOUN
It takes a minimum of an hour to drive there.
• **minimum** /minimem/ ADJECTIVE

miniskirt /mineeskert/
A very short skirt NOUN

minor /miener/
Very small or not very important
ADJECTIVE *We have a minor problem.*

minority /mienoritee/
A very small part of a group of people or things NOUN
Only a minority of people behave like this.

mint /mint/
1. A sweet with a very strong taste
2. A plant with a strong smell that people use when they are cooking NOUN

minus /mienes/
1. Used to show that you are taking one number away from another number *Ten minus three is seven.* 2. Used to show numbers that are less than zero *One minus three is minus two.* 3. Used to show that a temperature is less than zero *Isn't it cold? It's minus three!* PREPOSITION

minus sign /mienes sien/
The symbol (−) that shows that one number should be taken away from another NOUN

minute /minit/
1. A part of an hour. There are 60 minutes in an hour *The train was five minutes late.* 2. Used to mean a short amount of time *Snake will be back in a minute.* NOUN

minute hand /minit hand/
The long hand on a clock that shows the minutes past or to the hour NOUN

miracle /miracel/
Something really good that happens that cannot be explained because it is so surprising or impossible NOUN
It's a miracle you were not hurt!
• **miraculous** /miracyeles/ ADJECTIVE

mirror /mirer/
A piece of glass with a special shiny surface that you can see yourself in NOUN

Mm

misbehave /misbehaiv/
To behave very badly VERB

mischief /mischif/
Bad behaviour that causes trouble for other people NOUN
The children are getting up to mischief again.
• **mischievous** /mischives/ ADJECTIVE

miser /miezer/
Someone who does not like spending money NOUN

miserable /mizerebel/
Very unhappy ADJECTIVE
• **misery** /mizeree/ NOUN

misfortune /misforchoon/
Another word for very bad luck NOUN

misplace /misplais/
To put something in the wrong place and not be able to find it VERB

miss¹ /mis/
1. To fail to get or do something *I was late so I missed the train. • It missed the target.* 2. To feel sad because someone or something is not there *I miss him when he goes away.* VERB

miss² /mis/
1. A word used to mean a girl or young woman *Can you tell me the time, miss?*
2. Used when speaking politely to a girl or woman who is not married
Good morning, Miss Smith. NOUN

missile /misiel/
A weapon like a rocket that can fly through the air and explode when it hits something NOUN

missing /mising/
Not able to be found ADJECTIVE
His coat is missing from the rack.

mission /mishen/
An important job that someone has been given to do NOUN
Your mission is to find the enemy's spaceship.

mist /mist/
A low thin cloud made up of tiny drops of water that makes it hard to see NOUN
• **misty** /mistee/ ADJECTIVE

mistake¹ /mistaik/
1. Something that is not correct
There's a spelling mistake in your work.
2. The wrong opinion or idea
It is a mistake to think that. NOUN

mistake² /mistaik/
If you mistake someone for somebody else, you are confused and think that the person is someone else VERB
Sorry, I mistook you for your sister.
■ **mistook, mistaken**
• **mistaken** /mistaiken/ ADJECTIVE

mister /mister/
Used when addressing or speaking politely to a man. In writing it is usually shortened to Mr NOUN
Hello, Mr Smith.

mistletoe /miseltoa/
A plant with little white berries that people use for Christmas decoration NOUN

mistook /mistook/
PAST TENSE ▶ **mistake**²

mistress /mistres/
1. An old-fashioned word for a woman teacher in a school 2. A woman in charge of other people *She is the mistress of the house.* NOUN

Mm

misunderstanding /misunderstanding/
When you think someone means something but they really mean something else **NOUN**
There was a misunderstanding. I thought she said the meeting was at two o'clock, not three o'clock.

mix /mix/
1. To put different things together so they make one thing *Mixing blue and yellow paint makes green.* 2. **mix up**
To get things confused with each other
Sorry, I mixed you up with your brother.
VERB
• **mixer** /mixer/ Something that mixes things together **NOUN**

mixture /mixcher/
Different things mixed together **NOUN**

moan /moan/
1. To make a low sound that expresses pain or sadness
2. To complain *Stop moaning!* **VERB**
• **moan** /moan/ **NOUN**

moat /moat/
A deep hole full of water going all the way around a castle **NOUN**

mobile¹ /moabiel/
Moving around, or able to move around
ADJECTIVE

mobile² /moabiel/
A mobile or mobile phone is a small phone you carry around with you **NOUN**

model /model/
1. A small copy of something *Do you like this model car?* 2. Someone or something that is so good that people copy them *He's a model teacher.* 3. Someone who wears new clothes to show to people *She's a fashion model.* **NOUN**

modern /modern/
1. Belonging to the time now *Your dress looks very modern.* 2. Very new, or using all the latest ideas or machines **ADJECTIVE**

moist /moist/
Slightly wet **ADJECTIVE**
Your cake is so moist, Inky.

mole /moal/
1. A dark spot on someone's skin
2. A small animal that lives under the ground **NOUN**

moment /moament/
1. A small amount of time *I'll be back in a moment.* 2. When something happens or starts happening *Just at that moment, in flew Bee.* **NOUN**

Monday /mundai/
A day of the week **NOUN**
▶ CALENDAR, page 13

money /munee/
The pieces of paper and coins with values printed on them that are used to buy things **NOUN**

Mm

monitor /moneter/
1. A child who helps the teachers at school 2. A small screen, like a TV screen, that shows information *A computer displays its information on a monitor.* **NOUN**

monk /mungk/
A religious man who lives in a building called a monastery **NOUN**

monkey /mungkee/
A furry animal with a long tail but with hands and feet like a man. Monkeys climb trees and live in hot countries **NOUN**
▶ **ANIMALS**, page 16

monotonous /menotenes/
If something is monotonous, it is not interesting because it has a pattern that is repeated many times **ADJECTIVE**
He speaks with such a monotonous voice.

monster /monster/
A big ugly creature that frightens people in stories **NOUN**

month /munth/
A period of time about four weeks long. There are twelve months in a year **NOUN**
January is the first month of the year.
• **monthly** /munthlee/ **ADJECTIVE**

monument /monyement/
Something that is built to remember an important person or event **NOUN**
Nelson's Column in London is a famous monument to Admiral Lord Nelson.

mood /mood/
The way someone feels **NOUN**
Inky is always in a good mood.
• **moody** /moodee/ **ADJECTIVE**

moon /moon/
The round object in the sky that shines at night and moves around the earth **NOUN**
• **moonlight** /moonliet/ **NOUN**

moose /moos/
A big animal like a deer that lives in North America **NOUN**

■ **moose** /moos/ **PLURAL**

mop /mop/
Something with a long handle used to clean floors **NOUN**
• **mop** /mop/ **VERB**

moped /moaped/
A kind of bicycle with a small engine **NOUN**

more /mor/
1. A bigger amount or number of something *There are more people in my class than in yours.* 2. Very much compared to something else *This exercise is more difficult than that one.*
ADJECTIVE, **ADVERB**, **PRONOUN**

morning /morning/
The first part of the day between the time it gets light and midday **NOUN**

mosque /mosc/
A building where Muslim people go to pray **NOUN**

Mm

mosquito /mosceetoa/
A little flying insect that bites and can make people sick NOUN
- **mosquitoes** /mosceetoaz/ or **mosquitos** /mosceetoaz/ PLURAL

moss /mos/
A soft green plant without any flowers NOUN
- **mossy** /mosee/ ADJECTIVE

most /moast/
1. More compared to anyone or anything else *Peter has most, and Jane has least.*
2. The biggest in size or importance, or the biggest thing or amount *That's the most ice cream I've ever seen.* 3. Nearly all of something *I spend most of my time studying.* ADJECTIVE, PRONOUN, ADVERB
- **mostly** /moastlee/ ADVERB

moth /moth/
An insect like a butterfly that flies mainly at night NOUN

mothball /mothbawl/
A chemical shaped like a little ball that is put on clothes to keep the moths away NOUN

mother /muther/
A woman who has children NOUN

motion /moashen/
Another word for movement NOUN
The rolling motion of a boat.

motor /moater/
1. A machine that makes something work *The motor of the lawnmower is very noisy.* 2. Another word for a car NOUN
- **motor car** /moater car/ NOUN

motorbike /moaterbiek/
A vehicle like a big bicycle with an engine NOUN
- **motorcycle** /moatersiecel/ NOUN

motorist /moaterist/
Someone who drives a car NOUN

motorway /moaterwai/
A big road where traffic can move very fast NOUN

motto /motoa/
A few words that express a rule for how people should behave NOUN
Our school motto is 'Always help other people.'
- **mottoes** /motoaz/ or **mottos** /motoaz/ PLURAL

mould /moald/
1. A black or green substance that grows on food that has gone bad
Don't eat that, there's mould on it.
2. A container for making things in a particular shape. You pour a liquid into it until the liquid becomes hard NOUN
- **mouldy** /moaldee/ ADJECTIVE

moult /moalt/
If a bird or animal moults, it loses its old feathers or fur VERB

mountain /mounten/
A hill that is very high NOUN

mouse /mous/
1. A little furry animal with a long tail
2. A small object that you move around on your desk to help you work a computer NOUN
- **mice** /mies/ PLURAL
- **mousehole** /moushoal/ NOUN
- **mousetrap** /moustrap/ NOUN

moustache /mestash/
Hair that grows above a man's upper lip NOUN

185

Mm

mouth /mouth/
The part of your face that you use for talking or eating NOUN
▶ PARTS OF THE BODY, page 18
• **mouthful** /mouthfool/ NOUN
• **mouthwash** /mouthwosh/ NOUN

move /moov/
1. To go or take something from one place to another *I moved the computer screen so that I could see it more clearly.*
2. To travel, or to travel fast *The train is moving.* 3. To go to live in another home *We're going to move next week.*
VERB
• **movement** /moovment/ NOUN

movie /moovee/
A moving picture that you watch in the cinema or on television NOUN

mow /moa/
To cut grass with a lawnmower VERB
■ **mowed, mowed** or **mown**
• **mower** /moaer/ NOUN

mown /moan/
PAST PARTICIPLE ▶ **mow**

Mr /mister/
Short for mister, used when speaking politely to a man NOUN
Good morning, Mr Smith.

Mrs /misiz/
Used when speaking politely to a married woman NOUN
Good afternoon, Mrs Smith.

Ms /miz/
Used when speaking politely to a woman instead of Miss or Mrs NOUN
Good afternoon, Ms Smith.

much /much/
1. A big amount of something
2. Many times *He doesn't visit him much.*
ADJECTIVE, ADVERB, PRONOUN
■ more, most

muck /muc/
Another word for dirt or mud NOUN
• **mucky** /mucee/ ADJECTIVE

mud /mud/
Wet earth NOUN
Inky's boots are covered in mud.
• **muddy** /mudee/ ADJECTIVE

muddle[1] /mudel/
When people are confused NOUN
I'm in a bit of a muddle.

muddle[2] /mudel/
To get things confused or in a mess VERB
My papers are all muddled up.

mudguard /mudgard/
One of the curved pieces of metal or plastic on a bike or car that stop the mud splashing NOUN

muffin /mufin/
1. A little soft cake *Strawberry muffins are very tasty.* 2. A small round bread roll that people toast NOUN

mug[1] /mug/
A big cup with straight sides NOUN

mug[2] /mug/
To attack someone in the street and steal from them VERB
• **mugger** /muger/ NOUN

mule /muel/
An animal that has a donkey and a horse as its parents NOUN

multiply /multiplie/
To add a number a certain amount of times. Four multiplied by three (or 4 x 3) means you add up four a total of three times (4 + 4 + 4 = 12) VERB
• **multiplication** /multiplicaishen/ NOUN

mum /mum/
Another word for mother NOUN
• **mummy** /mumee/ NOUN

Mm

mumble /mumbəl/
To speak in a way that is not clear and is difficult to understand VERB

mumps /mumps/
An illness that makes your neck swell and become painful NOUN

munch /munch/
To eat something in a noisy way VERB

murder /merder/
The crime of killing someone NOUN
• **murder** /merder/ VERB
• **murderer** /merderer/ NOUN

murmur /mermer/
To say something quietly VERB

muscle /musəl/
One of the parts of your body under the skin that make the body move NOUN

museum /muezeeəm/
A building where important things from the past or scientific objects are kept. People go to museums to look at these things and study them NOUN

mushroom /mushroom/
A type of small plant you can eat, often shaped like an umbrella with a white top. A mushroom is a fungus NOUN

music /muezic/
1. Pleasant sounds made by instruments or voices 2. The way music is written down on paper *Inky can read music.* NOUN
• **musical** /muezicəl/ ADJECTIVE
• **musician** /muezishen/ NOUN

Muslim /moozlim/
A person who believes in the religion started by Mohammed NOUN

mussel /musəl/
A little sea animal that people can eat. It lives in a black shell that is made up of two parts NOUN

must /must/
1. To have to do something *You must leave now, it's getting dark.* 2. Used to show that something is likely, but not certain *Our teacher is late, he must be stuck in traffic.* VERB

mustard /musterd/
A yellow or brown sauce with a very strong taste NOUN

musty /mustee/
Smelling old and wet ADJECTIVE

mutter /muter/
To say something in a quiet voice that people cannot hear properly VERB

mutton /muten/
Meat that comes from sheep NOUN

my /mie/
Belonging to me ADJECTIVE
This is my book.
• **myself** /mieself/

mysterious /mestiereees/
Strange and difficult to understand ADJECTIVE

mystery /mistree/
Something that no one can explain NOUN
Nobody knows why he disappeared, it's a mystery.

myth /mith/
1. A story from long ago in history
2. Something that many people believe to be true, but is not NOUN

Nn

nag /nag/
To keep asking someone to do something they do not want to do **VERB**

nail /nail/
1. The thin hard part at the end of your finger or toe 2. A small thin pointed piece of metal that is hit with a hammer to join bits of wood together **NOUN**

naked /naikid/
With no clothes on **ADJECTIVE**

name[1] /naim/
The word or the words that people use to say who someone is or what something is **NOUN**

name[2] /naim/
1. To give someone or something a name *They named their son Jack.* 2. To say what something is *Can you name all the people in your class?* **VERB**

nap /nap/
A little sleep **NOUN**
Snake is tired. He's going to take a nap.
• **nap** /nap/ **VERB**

napkin /napkin/
A square piece of paper or cloth that you use when you are eating to keep your clothes and hands clean **NOUN**

nappy /napee/
A special type of paper or cloth that is put around a baby's bottom **NOUN**

narrow /naroa/
Measuring a very short distance from one side of something to the other compared to how long it is **ADJECTIVE**
a narrow street

nasty /nastee/
Another word for bad or unpleasant **ADJECTIVE** *Poor Robert has a nasty cough.*

nation /naishen/
A country and all the people living in it **NOUN**
• **national** /nashenel/ **ADJECTIVE**
• **nationality** /nashenalitee/ **NOUN**

native /naitiv/
Someone or something that comes from a certain country or place **NOUN**
She's a native of France.
• **native** /naitiv/ **ADJECTIVE**

natural /nacherel/
1. Normal *It's natural to be tired if you've been walking all day.* 2. Connected with nature *This lake is natural, not man-made.* **ADJECTIVE**
• **naturally** /nacherelee/ **ADVERB**

nature /naicher/
All the animals, plants, rivers, mountains and other things in the world that are not made by people **NOUN**

naughty /nawtee/
Behaving badly **ADJECTIVE**

Nn

near /nier/
Not far away from something or from a time or place PREPOSITION, ADJECTIVE
You're very near the edge of the cliff.
• **nearby** /nierbie/ ADVERB, ADJECTIVE
• **nearly** /nierlee/ Not completely but not far from something ADVERB
I'm nearly finished.

neat /neet/
Arranged or done in a very careful way ADJECTIVE *Bee's handwriting is neat.*
• **neatly** /neetlee/ ADVERB

necessary /neseseree/
If something is necessary, you have to do it or have it since there is no choice ADJECTIVE *Food is necessary.*

neck /nec/
The part of your body that joins your head to the rest of the body NOUN
▶ PARTS OF THE BODY, page 18
• **necklace** /necles/ A string of jewels, or a gold or silver chain, that is worn around the neck NOUN

nectarine /nectereen/
A fruit like a peach but with a smooth skin NOUN

need¹ /need/
To have to do or have something VERB
You need a raincoat if you go out in the rain.

need² /need/
1. Something that must be done
2. What someone needs, for example to be successful or healthy *All the children in the school have different needs.* NOUN

needle /needel/
1. A needle in sewing is a little thin piece of metal with a sharp point at one end and a hole at the other end for the thread 2. A thin pointed tube that is stuck into someone's body to give them a drug 3. A thin piece of metal that points to something such as a number, or the direction in a compass 4. Knitting needles are long plastic sticks that people use to knit with NOUN
• **needlework** /needelwerk/ NOUN

negative /negetiv/
Connected with the words 'no', 'not' or 'nothing'. For example, a negative answer means that the answer is 'no' ADJECTIVE

neglect /neglect/
1. To not give enough attention to something *If you neglect your work you'll fail the test.* 2. To not take care of someone or something properly *The rabbits were hungry because they had been neglected.* VERB
• **neglect** /neglect/ NOUN

neigh /nai/
To make the sound that a horse makes VERB

neighbour /naiber/
Someone who lives near you, usually in the same street NOUN

• **neighbourhood** /naiberhood/ NOUN

Nn

neither[1] /niether/
Not one thing or person or the other
ADJECTIVE, CONJUNCTION, PRONOUN
Neither Snake nor Bee can go with Inky.

neither[2] /niether/
Used to mean 'not also' or 'and not'
ADVERB *If you don't go, then neither will I.*

nephew /nefue/
The son of your brother or sister NOUN

nerve /nerv/
1. Your nerves are tiny parts in your body like very thin strings that carry feelings and messages 2. You use nerves to mean that you are very nervous about something *I have exams tomorrow, I'm a bundle of nerves.* NOUN

nervous /nerves/
Worried or frightened about something
ADJECTIVE *Thunderstorms make me nervous.*

nest /nest/
A place where birds live or where insects such as ants live NOUN

net /net/
1. Strings twisted together in a special way to make a cloth with lots of spaces in between *There are lots of fish in my net.* 2. Another word for the Internet NOUN

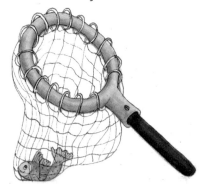

netball /netbawl/
A game where two teams of people throw a ball and try to get it into a high net NOUN

never /never/
Not at any time ADVERB
Inky's never been to Scotland.

new /nue/
1. Made or started only a short time ago *My bike is new.* 2. Not seen or known before *Inky has plenty of new ideas.* 3. Never been used before *Start writing on a new page.* ADJECTIVE

news /nuez/
New information about what is happening to someone or something NOUN *Good news! Inky is having a party!*
• **newspaper** /nuezpaiper/ NOUN

newsagent /nuezai jent/
A shop where people can buy newspapers and other things NOUN

newt /nuet/
An animal like a very small lizard that lives in and around water NOUN

next /next/
1. Without anything coming in between *I can hear a strange noise in the next room.* 2. After this one, or straight afterwards *I'll see you next week.* • *What happens next?* ADJECTIVE, ADVERB

nib /nib/
The pointed part at the end of a pen NOUN

nibble /nibel/
To eat something with very small bites VERB *Inky Mouse usually nibbles her food.*

Nn

nice /nies/
1. Good or pleasant *The weather is really nice today.* 2. Kind *My teacher has always been nice to me.* **ADJECTIVE**
• **nicely** /nieslee/ **ADVERB**

nickname /nicnaim/
A name people sometimes give to someone instead of their real name **NOUN** *Mike is a nickname of Michael.*

niece /nees/
The daughter of your brother or sister **NOUN**

night /niet/
1. The time when it is dark, between the evening and the next morning 2. The time in the evening before you go to bed *We went out last night.* 3. The time when people sleep *Did you have a good night?* **NOUN**

• **nightdress** /nietdres/ **NOUN**
• **nightfall** /nietfawl/ **NOUN**
• **night-time** /niet tiem/ **NOUN**

nightmare /nietmeer/
A frightening dream **NOUN**

nil /nil/
Another word for nothing or zero **NOUN**

nimble /nimbel/
Moving quickly and easily **ADJECTIVE**

nit /nit/
The egg of a tiny insect that sometimes lives in people's hair **NOUN**

no /noa/
1. Used in an answer when you refuse something or do not agree with the question *No, thank you.* 2. Not any *The weather is no better today.* **ADVERB, ADJECTIVE**

nobody /noabedee/
Not a single person **PRONOUN**

nod /nod/
To bend your head forward and up and down, as a way of saying yes **VERB**
• **nod** /nod/ **NOUN**

noise /noiz/
A sound, usually a loud one **NOUN**
• **noisy** /noizee/ **ADJECTIVE**

none /nun/
1. Not a single one *None of my friends can swim.* 2. Not any part of something *I had none of the cake.* **PRONOUN**

nonsense /nonsens/
Used to mean words that make no sense **NOUN** *Don't talk nonsense!*

noodles /noodelz/
Long thin pieces of pasta **NOUN PLURAL**

noon /noon/
Twelve o'clock in the middle of the day **NOUN**

Nn

no one /noʊ wun/
Not a single person PRONOUN

nor /nor/
Used to mean 'and not' or 'not also'
CONJUNCTION, ADVERB
I can't swim, nor can I dance.

normal /normɛl/
1. Completely usual and as it should be
It's normal to get out of breath if you run.
2. Healthy and with nothing wrong with
you *He's just a normal two-year-old.*
ADJECTIVE
• **normally** /normɛlee/ ADVERB

north /north/
The direction on the left of the person
who is looking at the sun as it is rising.
The sun rises in the east NOUN

▶ WORLD MAP, page 14
• **north** /north/ ADJECTIVE, ADVERB

nose /noʊz/
The part of your face that you use for
smelling and breathing NOUN
▶ PARTS OF THE BODY, page 18
• **nosebleed** /noʊzbleed/ NOUN

nostril /nostril/
Nostrils are the two openings at the end
of your nose NOUN

nosy /noʊzee/
Interested in other people or events that
are nothing to do with you ADJECTIVE

not /not/
1. A word used to change the meaning
of something to the opposite meaning
I am not coming to your party, I'm afraid.
2. Used instead of a word to mean the
opposite *Are you coming or not?* ADVERB

note[1] /noʊt/
1. A short letter 2. Something written
down to remind someone about
something 3. A certain musical sound
4. A piece of paper used as money
Here's a ten-pound note. NOUN

note[2] /noʊt/
1. To write something down so you will
remember it 2. To pay attention to
something VERB
• **notepad** /noʊtpad/ NOUN
• **notepaper** /noʊtpaiper/ NOUN

nothing /nuthing/
1. Not a single thing *There's nothing to
see.* 2. **nothing like** Very different from
someone or something PRONOUN, ADVERB

notice[1] /noʊtis/
To see something, or sometimes to hear
or smell it VERB
Did you notice where I left my keys?

notice[2] /noʊtis/
1. Something that gives information
to people *The teacher stuck an important
notice to the classroom door.* 2. If you do
not take any notice of something, you
do not pay attention to it NOUN
• **noticeable** /noʊtisɛbel/ ADJECTIVE
• **noticeboard** /noʊtis bord/ NOUN

nought /nawt/
The number zero, written 0 NOUN

noun /noun/
A word used in grammar as the name of
a person, place or thing NOUN
The words 'pen' and 'ink' are nouns.
▶ PARTS OF SPEECH, pages 6 and 7

Nn

nourish /nurish/
To give someone or something food to keep them healthy VERB

novel /novel/
A book containing a long story that someone has made up NOUN
She loves reading novels.
• **novelist** /novelist/ NOUN

November /noavember/
The eleventh month of the year NOUN
▶ CALENDAR, page 13

now /nou/
1. At this time, not in the past or the future 2. **now that** Because *Now that you can cook, you can bake me a cake.*
ADVERB, CONJUNCTION

nowhere /noaweer/
Not in or to any place ADVERB
We have nowhere to go.

nude /nued/
Wearing no clothes ADJECTIVE, NOUN

nuisance /nuesens/
Something or someone that annoys you NOUN

numb /num/
When you cannot feel anything in a part of your body ADJECTIVE
It's so cold my fingers are numb.

number[1] /number/
1. A word or sign showing how many *1, 2, 3, 4 are numbers.* 2. A number used for showing something such as a position, or as a way of recognizing something *What is your phone number?* 3. An amount of things or people *There are a number of books that Bee would like to read.* NOUN

number[2] /number/
To give numbers to something such as the pages of a book VERB

nun /nun/
A religious woman who is a member of a group of women that live in a building called a convent NOUN

nurse /ners/
Someone who takes care of people who are sick, usually in a hospital NOUN

nursery /nerseree/
1. A bedroom for a baby 2. A place that takes care of children during the day NOUN

nursery rhyme /nerseree riem/
A poem or song for children NOUN

nut /nut/
A seed inside a hard shell. Nuts grow on trees NOUN

nylon /nielon/
A strong material used for making clothes NOUN

Oo

oak /oak/
A big tree that has acorns as its fruit
NOUN

oar /or/
A long pole with a flat part at the end for rowing a boat NOUN

oases /oaaiseez/
NOUN PLURAL ▶ **oasis**

oasis /oaaisis/
A place in a desert with water and trees
NOUN
■ **oases** /oaaiseez/ PLURAL

oats /oats/
The seeds of a plant used for making porridge or for feeding animals like horses NOUN PLURAL

obey /oabai/
To do what someone tells you to do VERB

object[1] /object/
A thing that you can touch NOUN

object[2] /ebject/
To disagree with something VERB

oblong /oblong/
A shape that is long but not very wide, especially one that has square ends
ADJECTIVE ▶ SHAPES, page 17

oboe /oaboa/
A musical instrument shaped like a tube that is played by blowing through the top NOUN

observe /ebzerv/
1. To watch someone or something carefully 2. To notice something
Snake observed that there were plenty of egg sandwiches for the picnic. VERB

obsessed /obsest/
Thinking about someone or something all the time ADJECTIVE
Snake is obsessed with food.

obstacle /obstecel/
Something that blocks your way, or makes it difficult for you to do something NOUN

obtain /ebtain/
To get something VERB

obvious /obveees/
Easy to see or understand ADJECTIVE
• **obviously** /obveeeslee/ ADVERB

occasion /ecaizhen/
1. A special event like a birthday
We're going to have a party for the occasion.
2. Used when talking about a time that something happens *On this occasion we're going to learn about the letter P.* NOUN

Oo

ocean /oashən/
1. The water that covers most of the earth 2. One of the big seas such as the Pacific Ocean **NOUN**

o'clock /əcloc/
Used with a number to show the hour when telling the time **ADVERB**
It's seven o'clock.

octagon /octəgən/
A shape that has eight sides **NOUN**
▶ **SHAPES**, page 17

October /octoaber/
The tenth month of the year **NOUN**
▶ **CALENDAR**, page 13

octopus /octəpəs/
A sea creature with eight long arms called tentacles **NOUN**

■ **octopuses** /octəpəsəz/ **PLURAL**

odd /od/
1. Another word for strange or unusual 2. Describing two things that should be the same but are not *He is wearing odd socks.* 3. A number that cannot be divided exactly by two, such as 1, 3, 5 or 7 **ADJECTIVE**

of /ov/
1. Belonging to or connected with *the top of my head* 2. Made from something *a house of bricks.* 3. Containing something *Here's a bag of apples.* 4. From something *We're within 20 miles of London.*
PREPOSITION

off /of/
1. Away from a place *Zack rode off on his bike.* 2. Not connected to something, or taken away from something *The door knob fell off.* 3. Not being used *The light is off.* · *Can you turn the television off?* 4. Bad-smelling and too old to eat *This fish is off.* **ADVERB, ADJECTIVE**

offend /əfend/
To make someone angry or upset **VERB**

offensive /əfensiv/
Rude or upsetting to people **ADJECTIVE**

offer[1] /ofer/
1. To say you are ready to do something for someone *I offered to help them.*
2. To hold something out for someone to take if they want it *Inky offered Snake and Bee some chocolates.* **VERB**

offer[2] /ofer/
1. Something you say you are ready to give to someone or do for someone
2. An amount of money you are ready to give someone for something **NOUN**

office /ofis/
A place where people work sitting at desks **NOUN**

officer /ofiser/
1. A policeman or a policewoman
2. Someone with an important job, for example in the army **NOUN**

official /əfishəl/
Accepted by important people in the government, or done as part of an important job **ADJECTIVE**
The President made an official visit to Russia.
· **officially** /əfishəlee/ **ADVERB**

often /ofən/
1. Lots of times *I often play the guitar.*
2. Usually *Bee often stays in the hive when it's raining.* **ADVERB**

Oo

ogre /oʊger/
In stories, an ogre is an ugly giant
NOUN

oil /oil/
1. A liquid from plants or animals used for cooking food 2. A liquid from plants or animals that people rub into their skin 3. A thick liquid from the ground that people burn for heat or use for making machines work better **NOUN**
• **oily** /oilee/ **ADJECTIVE**

ointment /ointment/
A substance from oil that people rub onto their skin **NOUN**

OK /oʊkai/
Or **okay** /oʊkai/ Another word for all right **ADJECTIVE, ADVERB, INTERJECTION**

old /oʊld/
1. Made or born a long time ago *She's an old woman.* 2. From your past *This is my old school.* 3. If you are a certain number of years old, that is what your age is *Inky is six years old.*
ADJECTIVE

old-fashioned /oʊld fashend/
Not modern any more **ADJECTIVE**
an old-fashioned dress

olive /oliv/
1. The small green or black fruit of the olive tree 2. A green colour **NOUN**

omelette /omlet/
Eggs mixed together and cooked in a frying pan **NOUN**

on /on/
1. Showing where something or someone is *My house is on the opposite side of the street.* 2. Connected to something *The handle is on the door.* 3. Being used *The light is on.* 4. Showing when something is *It all happened on Saturday.* 5. Showing how something is done *We came here on the train.* 6. Further forward *We must go on.* 7. About *Ia book on history.*
PREPOSITION

once /wuns/
1. One time only *I only saw it once.*
2. At some time in the past *We lived i n a big house once.* 3. **at once** At the same time *They all started talking at once.*
4. **at once** Immediately *When I heard the news, I left at once.* **ADVERB**

one[1] /wun/
1. The number one 2. A single person or thing *I saw one cat.* 3. Used when you talk about a certain time in the past or the future *One day I will be able to read.*
ADJECTIVE, NOUN

one[2] /wun/
1. Used when you talk about something already mentioned *I've bought a blue dress and a red one.* 2. **one another** Used to mean that every person in a group does something to the others *The boys were throwing pencils at one another.* **PRONOUN**

onion /unyen/
A round vegetable with lots of layers and a very strong taste **NOUN**
▶ **FRUIT AND VEGETABLES**, page 15

only[1] /oʊnlee/
1. Just the amount you mention *She only has four pages to read.* 2. In no other place, or at no other time *That could only happen in Spain in the summer.* 3. A short time ago *Bee has only just arrived.* **ADVERB**

only[2] /oʊnlee/
The one single thing or person ADJECTIVE
Bee found the only open flower on the bush.

only[3] /oʊnlee/
Another way of saying but CONJUNCTION
I'd help you, only I have to go home now.

onto /ontoʊ/
Used when talking about something or someone that moves to somewhere else
PREPOSITION *I jumped off the wall onto the ground.*

onwards /onwerdz/
Continuing from a certain place or time
ADVERB *from tomorrow onwards*

ooze /oʊz/
To flow out of somewhere slowly VERB

opaque /oʊpaic/
If something is opaque, you cannot see through it ADJECTIVE

open /oʊpɛn/
1. To change position, or the position of something, so that someone or something can come in or go out *Open the door, please.* 2. To pull the parts of something away so that you can see inside *He opened the book and started to read.* VERB
• **open** /oʊpɛn/ ADJECTIVE

opening /oʊpɛning/
A hole or space in something NOUN
Bee flew through the opening in the fence.

operate /opɛrait/
1. To be in charge of a machine and make it work 2. If doctors operate on you, they cut your body open and do something to make you healthy again VERB
• **operation** /opɛraishɛn/ NOUN
• **operator** /opɛraiter/ NOUN

opinion /ɛpinyɛn/
What someone thinks about something
NOUN

opportunity /opertuɛnɛtee/
A time when it is possible to do something NOUN
the opportunity to learn how to read

opposite /opɛzit/
1. As different from something as possible *Good is the opposite of bad.*
2. Facing something, or on the other side *Who lives in the house opposite?*
ADJECTIVE, PREPOSITION
• **opposite** /opɛzit/ NOUN

optician /optishɛn/
Someone who checks people's eyes and sells glasses to them NOUN

or /or/
1. A word that shows a choice between two or more things *Do you want an apple or a pear?* 2. Another way of saying 'and not' *You shouldn't eat or drink in here.* 3. Another way of saying 'if not' *Hurry up or you'll be late.* CONJUNCTION

orange[1] /orinj/
A round fruit with lots of juice and an orange-coloured skin NOUN
▶ **FRUIT AND VEGETABLES**, page 15

orange[2] /orinj/
A colour that is in between red and yellow NOUN, ADJECTIVE

orchard /orcherd/
A place where fruit trees are grown NOUN

Oo

orchestra /orcistrə/
A big group of musicians that play lots of different instruments together **NOUN**

order[1] /order/
1. The careful way things are arranged *The names on the list are in alphabetical order.* 2. Something someone tells you to do *Inky gave Snake an order.* 3. The things you ask to buy from a restaurant or shop *The waiter will take your order.* **NOUN**

order[2] /order/
1. To tell someone to do something 2. To tell someone you want to buy something, such as food in a restaurant *I ordered a cup of coffee.* **VERB**

ordinary /ordinəree/
Not special in any way but completely normal or usual **ADJECTIVE**

organ /orgən/
1. A musical instrument like a piano with big pipes that the sound comes out of 2. A part of your body that does a special job, like your heart or lungs **NOUN**

organization /orgəniezaishen/
A group of people or a business **NOUN**

organize /orgəniez/
To make plans or arrangements for something **VERB**
Inky is busy organizing her birthday party.

oriental /orientəl/
Connected with countries like China and Japan **ADJECTIVE**

origin /orijin/
The beginning of something, or where it comes from **NOUN**
What's the origin of the word sandwich?

original[1] /erijenəl/
Something original existed at the beginning **ADJECTIVE**
These are the original windows.

original[2] /erijenəl/
The real thing, not a copy of it **NOUN**
This is a copy of a famous painting. The original is in the museum.

ornament /ornəmənt/
A beautiful object in your house or garden **NOUN**

orphan /orfən/
A child whose mother and father are both dead **NOUN**

ostrich /ostrich/
A big bird with long legs and a long neck that can run fast, but cannot fly **NOUN**
▶ ANIMALS, page 16

other /uther/
1. A word you use to mean the second of two things *I'm looking for my other shoe.* 2. Used when talking about what is left when you have mentioned similar things *John and Peter will stay here, and the other boys will come with me.* **ADJECTIVE, PRONOUN**

otherwise /utherwiez/
1. If not *Be quiet, otherwise I can't hear what the teacher is saying.* 2. Except for something *I have a cold but otherwise I'm OK.* **ADVERB**

Oo

otter /oter/
An animal with fur that swims and eats fish **NOUN**

ought /awt/
1. Used to say it is right or sensible to do something *You ought to go now if you want to get home before dark.* 2. Used to say something will probably happen or be true *Snake ought to be here soon.* **VERB**

ounce /ouns/
A measure of weight **NOUN**

our /ouer/
Belonging to us **ADJECTIVE**
This is our school.
• **ours** /ouerz/ **PRONOUN**
• **ourselves** /ouerselvz/ **PRONOUN**

out /out/
1. Not inside something *We left the cat out.* 2. Not at home *Sorry, Bee is out.*
3. Taken away from something *I took my keys out of my pocket.* **ADVERB, ADJECTIVE**

outdoors /outdorz/
Outside a house or building **ADVERB**
• **outdoor** /outdor/ **ADJECTIVE**

outer /outer/
The outer part of something is the part that is furthest from the centre **ADJECTIVE**

outfit /outfit/
Clothes that you wear together, usually for a special purpose like a wedding **NOUN**

outing /outing/
A short trip you make away from your home or school **NOUN**
We went on an outing to the museum.

outlaw /outlaw/
Another word for a criminal **NOUN**

outline /outlien/
1. A line that you draw around the edge of something to show its shape
2. The main ideas of something **NOUN**

outside¹ /outsied/
Not in something such as a building or box **PREPOSITION, ADVERB**
Outside it was raining.

outside² /outsied/
The outer part of something **NOUN**
The outside of the bus was very dirty.

outstanding /outstanding/
Another word for excellent **ADJECTIVE**

oval /oavel/
Shaped like an egg or a long kind of circle **ADJECTIVE**
• **oval** /oavel/ **NOUN**

oven /uven/
The box-like part inside a cooker, used to bake food **NOUN**

over /oaver/
1. Higher than something *There was a lamp hanging over the table.* 2. To the other side of something *Inky climbed over the wall.* 3. On or in something *I spilled water over the carpet.* • *We want to travel all over Europe.* 4. Because of something *The dogs were fighting over a juicy bone.*
5. More than something *Snake has over 20 books.* 6. Finished *The game is over.* **PREPOSITION, ADVERB**

overalls /oaverawlz/
Loose clothing put on over other clothes to keep them clean **NOUN PLURAL**

overboard /oaverbord/
Into the sea from a boat **ADVERB**
Someone fell overboard.

Oo

overcame /ōavercaim/
PAST TENSE ▶ **overcome**

overcoat /ōavercoat/
A long thick coat that people wear in cold weather NOUN

overcome /ōavercum/
To fight against something and win VERB
Can you overcome your fear?
■ **overcame, overcome**

overcrowded /ōavercroudid/
With too many people ADJECTIVE
overcrowded buses and trains

overflow /ōaverfloa/
If something like a river overflows, there is so much water that it comes over the edges VERB

overhear /ōaverhier/
To hear something that other people are saying to each other, not to you VERB
■ **overheard**

overjoyed /ōaverjoid/
Very happy about something ADJECTIVE

overlap /ōaverlap/
To cover one part of something with part of something else VERB
The tiles on the roofs overlap.

overlook /ōaverlook/
1. To forget to pay attention to something obvious 2. To ignore something like someone's mistake VERB

overnight /ōaverniet/
For the whole night ADVERB
We stayed there overnight.

overseas /ōaverseez/
In or to a different country ADVERB

oversleep /ōaversleep/
To sleep for too long and wake up late VERB
■ **overslept**

overtake /ōavertaik/
To go past something that travels more slowly VERB
■ **overtook, overtaken**

overwork /ōaverwerk/
To work too much VERB

owe /ōa/
If someone owes money, they still have that money to pay VERB

owl /oul/
A bird with big eyes that flies at night NOUN

own[1] /ōan/
1. Belonging to someone and to nobody else *Is this your own bike? · Yes, it's my own.* 2. **on your own** By yourself, not with anyone else *Seth walks to school on his own.* ADJECTIVE, PRONOUN

own[2] /ōan/
To have something that belongs to you VERB *His dad owns this house.*
• **owner** /ōaner/ NOUN

ox /ox/
A big male cow for doing heavy work on farms NOUN
■ **oxen** /oxen/ PLURAL

oxygen /oxijen/
A gas in the air that people and animals need to breathe NOUN

oyster /oister/
A sea animal that lives inside two big flat shells. Pearls come from oysters NOUN

Pp

pace /pais/
The speed someone walks at or does something **NOUN**

pack¹ /pac/
1. To put things into a bag, box or some other kind of container 2. To put lots of people into something like a bus or room *They packed 50 students into the classroom.* **VERB**

pack² /pac/
1. Things put together that people give or sell *I've sent you an information pack.* 2. A bag that people carry on their shoulders 3. A group of animals that hunt together, such as wolves **NOUN**

package /pacij/
Things packed together and sent by post **NOUN**

packed /pact/
Very full **ADJECTIVE**
The bus was packed with people.

packet /pacit/
A little box or bag, or some other kind of container **NOUN**
a packet of crisps

pad /pad/
1. Something soft and thick that people use to protect something or clean something *They put a pad over his wound.* 2. Pieces of paper fixed together for writing on **NOUN**

paddle /padel/
1. To walk around in water that is not deep 2. To move a boat along using a short pole that is wide at one end, called a paddle **VERB**
• **paddle** /padel/ **NOUN**
• **paddling pool** /padeling pool/ **NOUN**

page /paij/
1. A single sheet of paper *Who has torn a page out of my book?* 2. One side of a sheet of paper **NOUN**

paid /paid/
PAST TENSE ▶ **pay**

pail /pail/
Another word for a bucket **NOUN**

pain /pain/
The feeling you get when a part of your body hurts you **NOUN**
• **painful** /painfel/ **ADJECTIVE**

paint¹ /paint/
1. A liquid that you put on something to give it a colour 2. Paints are little pieces of hard paint or small tubes of paint **NOUN**

paint² /paint/
1. To put paint on something to change its colour 2. To colour or make a picture with paint **VERB**
• **paintbox** /paintbox/ **NOUN**
• **paintbrush** /paintbrush/ **NOUN**
• **painter** /painter/ **NOUN**
• **painting** /painting/ **NOUN**

Pp

pair /peer/
1. Two things of the same type *I've bought a new pair of shoes.* 2. A single thing made up of two parts that are just like each other *Do you have a pair of scissors?* NOUN

pal /pal/
Another word for a friend NOUN

palace /pales/
A big house where a king or queen lives NOUN

pale /pail/
Light in colour, or lighter in colour than usual ADJECTIVE
You look pale, did something frighten you?

palm /pahm/
1. The inside part of your hand
2. A tree with long leaves but no branches that grows in hot countries NOUN

pan /pan/
A round metal container with a handle, used for cooking NOUN

pancake /pancaik/
A flat cake that is round and thin, cooked in a frying pan NOUN

panda /pande/
A big black and white animal that looks like a bear NOUN

pane /pain/
A sheet of glass in a window NOUN

panic /panic/
To become frightened and behave in a way that is not sensible VERB
■ panicked
• **panic** /panic/ NOUN

pant /pant/
To breathe quickly and noisily VERB
The dog was panting in the heat.

pantomime /pantemiem/
A play for children with music and jokes done at Christmas time NOUN

pantry /pantree/
A little room in a house where people keep food NOUN

pants /pants/
Underwear for boys and men, worn under trousers NOUN PLURAL

paper /paiper/
1. Thin sheets of material used for many things such as for writing or drawing on *I wrote my address on a piece of paper.*
2. Another word for newspaper NOUN
• **paperclip** /paiperclip/ NOUN

parachute /pareshoot/
A very large piece of cloth that people use if they jump out of a plane so that they can land slowly and safely NOUN

paragraph /parəgraf/
A group of sentences NOUN

parallel /parəlel/
Next to each other, going in the same direction and keeping the same distance apart ADJECTIVE
Railway lines are parallel lines.

paralysed /parəliezd/
Not able to move ADJECTIVE

parcel /parsel/
Things packed together and sent by post NOUN

pardon[1] /pardən/
1. A polite way of saying sorry to someone 2. A polite way of asking someone to say something again INTERJECTION

pardon[2] /pardən/
1. To let someone go free and not punish them 2. To tell someone you are not angry even though they have behaved badly 3. **pardon me** A polite way of saying sorry VERB

parent /peərent/
Your parents are your mother and father NOUN

park[1] /park/
1. A big area of land in a town with grass and trees where people can walk, run and play games 2. A car park is a place where people leave their cars NOUN

park[2] /park/
To leave a car somewhere for a certain amount of time VERB
• **parking** /parking/ NOUN
• **parking meter** /parking meeter/ NOUN

parlour /parler/
An old-fashioned word for a room in a house where people sit and relax NOUN

parrot /parət/
A big bird with a curved beak and feathers that have lots of colours. People can teach parrots to talk NOUN

part /part/
1. A piece of something, not the whole of it *My bicycle has lots of moving parts.* • *This part of town is noisy.* 2. The words and actions of one of the characters in a play *Inky is going to play the part of the queen.* 3. **take part** To do something along with other people *All the children took part in the singing.* NOUN

participate /partisipait/
Another way of saying to take part in something VERB
I want you to participate in the lesson.

particular[1] /perticyeler/
1. A particular thing or person is the one you are talking about *What were you doing on that particular day?* 2. Special, or different from normal *Do you want anything particular to eat?* ADJECTIVE

particular[2] /perticyeler/
in particular Used to give special importance to something. Another way of saying most of all NOUN
We're all hungry, Snake in particular.

partly /partlee/
Not completely but just a little ADVERB
It's partly my fault.

Pp

partner /partner/
1. Someone you do something with, like play games or dance 2. Someone who is married to someone, or who lives with them NOUN

party /partee/
An occasion when people come together to enjoy themselves NOUN

a birthday party

pass /pas/
1. To go from one place to another *Can you let me pass?* 2. To give something to someone *Can you please pass me the salt?* 3. To go up to something or someone, and then go past *A car passed us doing 60 miles an hour.* 4. To be successful in an exam or test VERB
• **pass** /pas/ NOUN

passage /pasij/
1. A long narrow way between rooms or buildings 2. A short part of a book or something written NOUN

passenger /pasinjer/
Someone who travels in a car, train or plane NOUN

passport /pasport/
A special document with your name and picture in it, used when you travel to another country NOUN

password /paswerd/
1. A secret word you have to type into a computer before you can use it 2. A secret word you have to tell someone before they will let you go into a special place NOUN

past[1] /past/
1. Further than something, or on the other side of something *Our school is past the hospital.* • *He ran past me.* 2. After, when you are talking about the time on the clock *It's half past six.*
PREPOSITION, ADVERB

past[2] /past/
Used when talking about things that have already happened ADJECTIVE
Snake's eaten a lot of cake in the past week.

past[3] /past/
The past is the time before now NOUN
All this happened in the past.

pasta /paste/
Food made from flour, water and usually eggs that comes in different shapes NOUN

paste[1] /paist/
1. Any soft substance that is mixed together 2. A type of glue for sticking things NOUN

paste[2] /paist/
1. To stick paper to something with glue 2. To copy words on a computer screen from one place to another VERB

pastry /paistree/
1. A type of little cake 2. Flour, fat and water mixed together and used to make food such as pies NOUN

pat /pat/
To touch something gently with your hand VERB
• **pat** /pat/ NOUN

Pp

patch /pach/
1. A small part of an area that is different from the rest *There were icy patches on the road.* 2. A piece of cloth you put over a hole in clothes 3. A piece of cloth someone puts over their eye when it has been hurt NOUN
• **patch** /pach/ VERB

path /path/
A narrow way that people walk along, for example in a park or forest NOUN

pathetic /pethetic/
1. Making you feel sorry for someone or something 2. Bad or useless *Your drawing is pathetic!* ADJECTIVE

patient[1] /paishent/
1. Able to wait a long time for something without getting angry 2. Able to stay calm if something bad keeps happening *Our teacher is patient with all the naughty boys in the class.* ADJECTIVE
• **patience** /paishens/ NOUN

patient[2] /paishent/
Someone who is taken care of by a doctor or dentist NOUN

pattern /patern/
The shapes and colours that are arranged on something in a certain way and are often repeated NOUN
Her dress had a pretty pattern on it.

pause /pawz/
To stop doing something for a short time before you start doing it again VERB
Inky paused and then started speaking again.
• **pause** /pawz/ NOUN

pavement /paivment/
A path at the side of a road that people walk on NOUN

paw /paw/
The foot of an animal such as a cat or dog NOUN

pay /pai/
1. To give someone money in return for something *Snake paid for his ice cream.*
2. **pay attention** To listen to or watch or think about something carefully VERB
■ **paid**
• **pay** /pai/ NOUN
• **payment** /paiment/ An amount of money that someone pays NOUN

PC /pee see/
Short for 'personal computer', a type of small computer NOUN

pea /pee/
Peas are round green seeds that grow in a seed case called a pod. People cook and eat peas NOUN
▶ FRUIT AND VEGETABLES, page 15

peace /pees/
1. When there is no war in a country
2. When everywhere is quiet *Inky loves the peace of the countryside.* NOUN
• **peaceful** /peesfel/ ADJECTIVE

peach /peech/
A soft round fruit with lots of juice and a yellow-coloured skin. It has a big stone in its centre NOUN
▶ FRUIT AND VEGETABLES, page 15

Pp

peacock /peecoc/
A big bird with green and blue feathers and a tail that it can spread like a fan **NOUN**

peak /peek/
The pointed part at the top of a mountain **NOUN**

peanut /peenut/
A little oval nut with a soft shell that grows under the ground **NOUN**

pear /peer/
A fruit like an apple but softer and narrow at the top **NOUN**
▶ **FRUIT AND VEGETABLES**, page 15

pearl /perl/
A yellow-white jewel that is small and round **NOUN**

pebble /pebəl/
A little smooth round stone found on beaches and at the bottom of rivers **NOUN**

peck /pec/
If a bird pecks something, it bites or hits it quickly with its beak **VERB**

peculiar /pəcueleeer/
Strange or unusual **ADJECTIVE**

pedal /pedəl/
A thing you press with your foot to make something work, for example on a bicycle or piano **NOUN**
• **pedal** /pedəl/ **VERB**

pedestrian /pədestreeən/
Someone who walks along the street **NOUN**

peek /peek/
To look at something quickly **VERB**
He peeked inside to see what was there.
• **peek** /peek/ **NOUN**

peel[1] /peel/
The skin of a fruit **NOUN**

peel[2] /peel/
1. To take the skin off a fruit or vegetable
2. To have your skin come off in small pieces **VERB**

peep /peep/
To look at something quickly, for example through a hole or over a wall **VERB**
• **peep** /peep/ **NOUN**

peg /peg/
1. A small hook of wood, plastic or metal that you use for hanging things on *Put your coat on the peg.* 2. A small piece of plastic or wood for fastening wet clothes to a washing line **NOUN**

pelican /pelicən/
A big bird that lives near water. It has a kind of bag under its beak where it keeps the fish it catches **NOUN**

pen /pen/
1. A long thin object filled with ink and used for writing 2. A place with a fence around it where farmers keep animals **NOUN**

penalty /penəltee/
A punishment for doing something wrong **NOUN**

Pp

pence /pens/
NOUN PLURAL ▶ **penny**

pencil /pensil/
A thin object made of wood with a
special substance in the middle, used
for writing and drawing NOUN
· **pencil sharpener** /pensil sharpner/
NOUN

pen friend /pen frend/
Or **pen pal** /pen pal/ Someone usually
in another country that you write letters
to so you can get to know them and be
their friend NOUN

penguin /penggwin/
A big black and white sea bird that uses
its wings to swim instead of fly. Penguins
live in the Antarctic NOUN

peninsula /peninsyeler/
A long piece of land that is almost
completely surrounded by water NOUN

penknife /pennief/
A little knife with blades that fold into
the handle NOUN
■ **penknives** /pennievz/ PLURAL

penny /penee/
A British coin. There are a hundred
pence in a pound NOUN
■ **pence** /pens/ PLURAL

pen pal /pen pal/
Someone usually in another country that
you write letters to so you can get to
know them and be their pal NOUN

pension /penshen/
Money someone gets when they do
not work any more because they have
reached a certain age or they are sick
NOUN

people /peepel/
Men, women and children NOUN PLURAL

pepper /peper/
A powder that people put on food to
give it a strong taste NOUN

perch /perch/
A stick that a bird stands on NOUN
· **perch** /perch/ VERB

perfect /perfect/
As good as something can be, without
any faults ADJECTIVE

perform /perform/
1. To do something special for the people
watching, like play music 2. To do a
particular action *The doctor performed a
difficult operation.* VERB
· **performance** /performens/ NOUN

perfume /perfuem/
A liquid with a very nice smell that girls
and women put on their skin NOUN

perhaps /perhaps/
Used to mean that something could
happen or be true, but it is not certain
ADVERB

peril /peril/
Another word for danger NOUN

207

Pp

period /piɛreeəd/
1. An amount of time 2. A part of the school day where you study a certain subject *We have a French period next.* NOUN

perm /perm/
Hair made curly using chemicals NOUN

permanent /permənənt/
Lasting for ever, or a very long time
ADJECTIVE

permission /permishən/
The words that allow you to do something NOUN

permit /permit/
1. To let someone do something
2. To let something happen VERB

persist /persist/
To keep doing something for a long time
VERB

person /persən/
A person is a man or woman, or a boy or girl NOUN

persuade /perswaid/
To try to get someone to do something by giving them good reasons why they should VERB
Dad persuaded me to go for a walk.

pest /pest/
1. Someone who annoys you *Don't be a pest!* 2. An insect or little animal that eats things like your plants or food NOUN

pester /pester/
To annoy someone when you keep on asking them to do things VERB

pet /pet/
An animal that you keep in your house and take care of NOUN

petal /petəl/
The small coloured parts of a flower that make up the flower itself NOUN

petrol /petrəl/
The liquid that is put into car engines to make them go NOUN
• **petrol station** /petrəl staishən/ NOUN

petticoat /peticoat/
A kind of thin skirt that girls or women use as underwear NOUN

pew /puɛ/
A long seat made of wood in a church
NOUN

phantom /fantəm/
Another word for a ghost NOUN

pharmacist /farməsist/
Someone who prepares and sells medicines NOUN
• **pharmacy** /farməsee/ NOUN

phone[1] /foan/
Short for telephone NOUN

phone[2] /foan/
To talk to someone using a phone VERB
• **phone book** /foan book/ NOUN
• **phone box** /foan box/ NOUN

phonic /fonic/
Connected with sound ADJECTIVE

photocopy /foatoacopee/
To make a copy of what is on a piece of paper using a special machine called a photocopier VERB
• **photocopy** /foatoacopee/ NOUN

photograph /foategraf/
Or **photo** /foatoa/ A picture you take using a camera NOUN

Pp

photographer /fɐtogrɐfer/
Someone who takes photos NOUN
• **photography** /fɐtogrɐfee/ NOUN

phrase /fraiz/
A small group of words NOUN

physical /fizicɐl/
Connected with the body ADJECTIVE
physical exercises

piano /peeanɒa/
A big musical instrument with black and
white bars called keys that you press
with your fingers to make sounds NOUN
• **pianist** /peeanist/ NOUN

pick /pic/
1. Another word for choose *Which dress
shall I pick?* 2. To break a flower off the
plant where it is growing 3. **pick up**
To take something up from where it
is *Inky picked up her book from the table.*
4. **pick up** To collect someone from
where they are waiting *Dad picked up
the children from school.* VERB

picnic /picnic/
A special meal you take somewhere to
eat outside NOUN

picture /piccher/
1. Something someone draws or paints,
or a photo someone takes 2. What you
see on a television, cinema or computer
screen 3. Another word for a film
NOUN

pie /pie/
A food made with fruit or meat that is
covered in pastry and cooked in the oven
NOUN

piece /pees/
1. A part of something, not the whole
of it *Would you like another piece of cake?*
2. A single thing of a certain kind
Take another piece of paper. NOUN

pier /pier/
Something built out from the land to the
sea with small buildings and shops on it
where people go to enjoy themselves and
play games NOUN

pierce /piers/
To make a small hole in something VERB

pig /pig/
An animal with a long nose, short legs
and a smooth fat body, that is usually
pink NOUN

pigeon /pijen/
A grey bird that is fat and lives in towns
NOUN

pigsty /pigstie/
A place where pigs live NOUN

pile /piel/
A lot of things that are on top of each
other NOUN
I put the clothes in a pile on the bed.

pill /pil/
A small hard type of medicine that you
swallow NOUN

pillow /pilɒa/
A square of cloth with soft material
inside that you put your head on in
bed NOUN

pilot /pielɐt/
Someone who operates a plane
and makes it go somewhere NOUN
• **pilot** /pielɐt/ VERB

Pp

pimple /pimpɛl/
A spot on your skin, like a tiny red bump
NOUN

pin /pin/
A short thin piece of metal with a point.
It is usually used for holding pieces of
cloth together when someone is sewing
NOUN
• **pin** /pin/ VERB

pinch[1] /pinch/
To squeeze someone's skin between your
finger and thumb VERB
• **pinch** /pinch/ NOUN

pinch[2] /pinch/
1. When you pinch someone's skin
2. A small amount of something NOUN

pineapple /pienapɛl/
A big fruit with a thick brown skin
shaped like an oval. Inside it is yellow
and juicy NOUN

ping-pong /ping pong/
A game like tennis played on the top of
a table with a small net and bats NOUN

pink /pingk/
A light red colour. The colour between
red and white NOUN, ADJECTIVE

pint /pient/
A measurement for liquids NOUN

pip /pip/
Pips are little hard seeds in fruit such as
apples or oranges NOUN

pipe /piep/
1. A tube for carrying water or gas in a
building or under the ground 2. A little
tube that some people use for smoking
tobacco *John's dad smokes a pipe.* NOUN

pirate /pierɛt/
A sailor who attacks other ships and
steals things from them NOUN

pistol /pistɛl/
A small gun that can be held in one
hand NOUN

pit /pit/
A big hole in the ground NOUN

pitch /pich/
A small area of land where people play
sports, such as a football pitch NOUN

pity /pitee/
Feeling sorry for someone because
they are unhappy or suffering NOUN
• **pity** /pitee/ VERB

pizza /peetsɛ/
A kind of flat round bread cooked with
cheese, tomatoes and sometimes meat or
other vegetables on top NOUN

place[1] /plais/
1. Any point or piece of land where
someone or something can be
2. Someone's house *Come over to play
at my place.* NOUN

place[2] /plais/
To put something somewhere VERB
Place your books on the table.

plague /plaig/
A disease that kills many people and
spreads very quickly NOUN

Pp

plaice /plais/
A type of flat sea fish **NOUN**

■ **plaice** /plais/ **PLURAL**

plain[1] /plain/
1. Simple and ordinary *Her dress was very plain.* 2. Clear and easy to understand *Inky's instructions are always very plain.*
ADJECTIVE

plain[2] /plain/
A big flat area of land **NOUN**

plaits /plats/
Long bunches of hair on either side of the head that have been twisted together **NOUN PLURAL**

plan[1] /plan/
1. A method for doing something that you have thought about carefully *Snake has a plan for learning to read more quickly.* 2. Something you intend to do *My plan is to stay here until my dad gets back.* **NOUN**

plan[2] /plan/
1. To think about how to do something carefully and in detail before doing it *We've planned our trip to the mountains.* 2. To think and talk about something you really want to do *I plan to go to university.* **VERB**

plane /plain/
Short for aeroplane, a vehicle with wings and an engine that flies in the air **NOUN**

planet /planit/
A big round object in space that moves around a star **NOUN**
Earth is a planet that moves around the sun.

plank /plangk/
A long flat piece of wood **NOUN**

plant[1] /plant/
Anything that grows in the earth and has roots and leaves. A plant is much smaller than a tree **NOUN**

plant[2] /plant/
To put something in the earth so that it will grow **VERB**

plaster /plaster/
1. A small piece of thin material that you stick over a cut or injury on your skin 2. A special hard material put on a broken leg or arm to hold it in place **NOUN**

plastic /plastic/
A strong but light material that is made with chemicals. People can use plastic for very many things **NOUN**
We keep our plastic toys in a plastic box.

plate /plait/
A flat round dish for eating food **NOUN**

platform /platform/
The place beside a railway track where you get on and off the train **NOUN**

play[1] /plai/
1. To do certain things you like doing, such as using your toys 2. To take part in a game or sport 3. To use a musical instrument *Can you play the piano?* 4. To act as a character in a play *Can I play Cinderella?* **VERB**

Pp

play[2] /plai/
1. A story for acting on a stage
2. The time when children play
It's time for play! NOUN
• **player** /plaier/ NOUN
• **playful** /plaifel/ ADJECTIVE

playground /plaiground/
A place where children play at school or in a park NOUN

• **playgroup** /plaigroop/ NOUN
• **playpen** /plaipen/ NOUN
• **playschool** /plaiscool/ NOUN
• **playtime** /plaitiem/ NOUN

pleasant /plezent/
1. Used to say that something is nice or that you like it *Our town is very pleasant.*
2. Friendly or kind to something
Inky is always pleasant to me. ADJECTIVE

please[1] /pleez/
1. Used to ask for something politely
Could I have a cup of coffee, please?
2. Used to say yes to something
Yes, please. I'd love a cup of coffee.
INTERJECTION

please[2] /pleez/
To make someone happy VERB
You can't please everybody!
• **pleased** /pleezd/ ADJECTIVE

pleasure /plezher/
A feeling of being very happy NOUN
Learning gives Bee and Snake great pleasure.

plenty /plentee/
A lot of something, and all that you need PRONOUN
There's plenty of time, we won't be late.

plimsolls /plimselz/
Soft shoes made of a strong cloth called canvas that have rubber soles
NOUN PLURAL

plot[1] /plot/
1. A secret plan to do something bad
2. The main story in a book or film around which everything else happens
3. A small piece of land NOUN

plot[2] /plot/
To plan to do something bad VERB

plough /plou/
A machine on a farm that is pulled over the earth to break it up for planting seeds NOUN
• **plough** /plou/ VERB

plug /plug/
1. A small plastic object with little metal bars sticking out. Plugs are used to connect electrical things to the electricity to make them work 2. A piece of rubber that covers the bath or sink hole to stop the water from going out NOUN
• **plughole** /plughool/ NOUN

plum /plum/
A small round fruit with a smooth skin and a stone in its centre NOUN

Pp

plumber /plumer/
Someone who repairs or connects water pipes, baths, sinks and toilets **NOUN**

plump /plump/
Another word for fat **ADJECTIVE**

plunge /plunj/
1. To fall suddenly *A car plunged into the river.* 2. To push something into something else very hard *Seb plunged his penknife into the tree.* **VERB**

plural /plooerel/
Used to talk about more than one thing or person **NOUN**
Books is the plural of book.
• **plural** /plooerel/ **ADJECTIVE**

plus /plus/
1. A word you use to show that you are adding one number to another number *Four plus two is six.* 2. Another way of saying 'and also' *There are four people in our family, plus the dog.* 3. Another word for the plus sign **PREPOSITION**

plus sign /plus sien/
A little cross (+) that is the sign that you are adding something up **NOUN**

p.m. /pee em/
Used to show the time in the afternoon. It is short for 'post meridiem', which means 'after midday'
Dinner is at 7 p.m.

poach /poach/
1. To cook an egg in boiling water without the shell 2. To steal animals or hunt them when you do not have permission **VERB**

pocket /pocit/
A small cloth bag for carrying things that is fixed into clothes like trousers or a jacket **NOUN**

poem /poaem/
Words arranged in patterns of short lines that often end with words that rhyme **NOUN**
• **poet** /poaet/
Someone who writes poems **NOUN**
• **poetry** /poaetree/ **NOUN**

point[1] /point/
1. The sharp end of something, like a knife 2. A dot on paper such as a decimal point 3. An exact place or moment in time 4. A single number you get in a game or competition when you do something good. The numbers are added up at the end of the game to make your score 5. The reason for something *There's no point going out if it's raining.* **NOUN**
• **pointed** /pointid/ **ADJECTIVE**
• **pointless** /pointles/
Without any meaning **ADJECTIVE**

point[2] /point/
1. To show where something is by holding your finger out towards it 2. To move something so that it is facing in the direction of something else *He pointed the way with his stick.*
3. **point out** To show or tell someone about a particular thing *The teacher pointed out the important questions.* **VERB**

poison /poizen/
A substance that kills people or makes them very sick if they swallow it **NOUN**
• **poisonous** /poizenes/ **ADJECTIVE**

poke /poak/
To push something or someone with your finger or with something long like a stick **VERB**

polar bear /poaler beer/
A big white bear that lives near the North Pole **NOUN**

Pp

pole /poal/
A long round stick usually made of wood
NOUN *a telegraph pole*

police /pelees/
The men and women who make sure people obey the law, and who deal with crimes and accidents **NOUN**
• **policeman** /peleesmen/ **NOUN**
• **police officer** /pelees ofeser/ **NOUN**
• **policewoman** /peleeswoomen/ **NOUN**

polish /polish/
Something people rub on a surface to make it shiny **NOUN**
• **polish** /polish/ **VERB**

polite /peliet/
Well-behaved towards other people
ADJECTIVE

pollen /polen/
A powder in flowers that helps make seeds **NOUN**
Bee collects pollen from the flowers.

pollute /peloot/
To make things such as the air or water very dirty and dangerous
VERB
• **pollution** /pelooshen/ **NOUN**

pond /pond/
A small area of water that has often been made by people **NOUN**

pong /pong/
Another way of saying a bad smell **NOUN**

pony /poanee/
A kind of small horse **NOUN**

ponytail /poaneetail/
Hair tied at the back of your head in a single bunch **NOUN**

pool /pool/
1. Another word for a swimming pool, a big hole specially built and filled with water for people to swim in 2. A pool of water is a small area where the water is not moving 3. A game like snooker **NOUN**

poor /por/
1. Not having much money 2. A place that has people living there who do not have much money *Our town is very poor.*
3. Used to show you feel sorry for someone *Poor Alex, he's always late!*
4. Not very good *The results were very poor.* **ADJECTIVE**

pop[1] /pop/
1. Modern music with a simple pattern of sounds that lots of young people like to listen to *Have you ever been to a pop festival?* 2. A loud quick sound like a balloon that bursts **NOUN**

pop[2] /pop/
1. To come or go somewhere quickly *Dad has just popped out to get some bread.*
• *I'll just pop in for a minute.* 2. Another way of saying put *He popped the cakes into the microwave.* **VERB**
• **pop group** /pop groop/ **NOUN**
• **pop star** /pop star/ **NOUN**

popcorn /popcorn/
Grains of a plant called maize that are heated until they go pop **NOUN**
■ **popcorn** /popcorn/ **PLURAL**

Pp

poppy /popee/
A plant with a long thin stem and a big red flower NOUN

popular /popyeler/
Liked by lots of people ADJECTIVE

population /popyelaishen/
All the people who live in a country or place NOUN

porch /porch/
The part of a building at the front door that is built like a little shelter with a roof NOUN

pork /pork/
The meat that comes from pigs NOUN

porridge /porij/
A soft food made from oats with water or milk NOUN

port /port/
1. A town that has a place where boats can stop 2. The place itself where boats stop and where they can be safely left NOUN

portable /portebel/
Able to be moved or carried around easily ADJECTIVE

porter /porter/
Someone who carries your luggage, for example at an airport NOUN

portion /porshen/
1. A part of something 2. An amount of food for one person NOUN

portrait /portret/
A painting, drawing or photo of a person NOUN

posh /posh/
1. Smart and expensive *Have you ever been to a posh restaurant?* 2. Speaking in a way that people from a high social class often do ADJECTIVE

position /pezishen/
1. The place where someone or something is 2. The correct place where something should be *If everyone is in position, we can start the dance.* NOUN

positive /pozetiv/
1. Certain about something
2. A positive answer means that the answer is 'yes' ADJECTIVE

possible /posebel/
1. If something is possible, it could happen *It's possible it might rain tonight.*
2. Used when you ask someone politely to do something *Would it be possible for you to get me some shopping?* ADJECTIVE

Pp

possibly /poseblee/
Another way of saying maybe **ADVERB**
• **possibility** /posebiletee/ **NOUN**

post[1] /poast/
1. A way of sending people letters or packages by putting stamps on them and putting them in a postbox *Shall I send the letter by post?* 2. Anything you send to someone by post 3. A pole made of wood or metal that is fixed into the ground **NOUN**

post[2] /poast/
To send a letter or package by post **VERB**
• **postbox** /poastbox/ **NOUN**

postage /poastij/
The money people pay to send something by post **NOUN**
• **postcard** /poastcard/ **NOUN**
• **postcode** /poastcoad/ **NOUN**
• **postman** /poastmen/ **NOUN**
• **post office** /poast ofis/ **NOUN**
• **postwoman** /poastwoomen/ **NOUN**

poster /poaster/
A big notice or picture for advertising something or for decorating a room **NOUN**

postpone /poastpoan/
To change the time that something happens to a later time **VERB**

pot /pot/
A container for cooking things in, or for putting things in like a plant or paint **NOUN**

potato /petaitoa/
A vegetable that grows under the ground that people cook and eat **NOUN**
■ **potatoes** /petaitoaz/ **PLURAL**
▶ **FRUIT AND VEGETABLES**, page 15

potter /poter/
Someone who makes things from clay **NOUN**

pottery /poteree/
Things made from baked clay **NOUN**

potty /potee/
A plastic container that very little children use as a toilet **NOUN**

pouch /pouch/
1. A little bag for keeping things in
2. A kind of pocket of skin at the front of a kangaroo's body for carrying a baby kangaroo **NOUN**

pounce /pouns/
To suddenly jump on something, usually from a hidden place **VERB**

pound /pound/
1. A measure of weight 2. A unit of money in the UK and some other countries. There are a hundred pence in a pound **NOUN**

pour /por/
1. To flow from one container to another one, or to make something do this
2. To rain heavily **VERB**

powder /pouder/
A substance like dust made up of tiny grains **NOUN**

power /pouer/
1. The ability to do something, or being allowed to do something *The police have the power to arrest you.* 2. Being in control of people because you have influence *The President has a lot of power.* **NOUN**
• **powerful** /pouerfel/ **ADJECTIVE**

Pp

practical /practicəl/
1. Good at solving problems or doing useful things *She's a practical person.*
2. Likely to be successful *That's a practical plan.* 3. Another way of saying useful *Shorts are practical in hot weather.* **ADJECTIVE**

practically /practiclee/
Another word for almost **ADVERB**
Bee has practically finished her book.

practice /practis/
Something you do lots of times to get knowledge and skill from it **NOUN**
You need a lot of practice when you're learning French.

practise /practis/
To do something lots of times so that you can get knowledge and skill from it **VERB**

praise /praiz/
To say very nice things about someone or something **VERB**
• **praise** /praiz/ **NOUN**

pram /pram/
A kind of bed on wheels for pushing a baby when you are out walking **NOUN**

prawn /prawn/
A little sea animal with a shell that goes pink when cooked **NOUN**

pray /prai/
To speak to God, often using the special words of a prayer **VERB**
• **prayer** /preer/ **NOUN**

precious /preshəs/
1. Worth a lot of money and very beautiful *She wore many precious jewels.*
2. Not to be wasted because there is not enough of it *Water is precious in the desert.* **ADJECTIVE**

predict /predict/
To say that something will happen in the future **VERB**

prefect /preefect/
An older pupil in a school who helps the teacher **NOUN**

prefer /prefer/
To like something or someone better than something else **VERB**
Bradley prefers the guitar to the flute.

prefix /preefix/
A letter or some letters that are added at the beginning of a word to change its meaning. For example, 'un' can be added to 'happy' to make 'unhappy' **NOUN**

pregnant /pregnənt/
Expecting a baby **ADJECTIVE**

prehistoric /preehistoric/
From a very long time ago, before anything was written down **ADJECTIVE**

prepare /prepeer/
To make something ready, or to get ready for something **VERB**
Snake's preparing a surprise for Inky.
• **preparation** /preperaishen/ **NOUN**
• **prepared** /prepeerd/ **ADJECTIVE**

preposition /prepezishen/
A word like 'on', 'to' or 'by' used to show the connection between one noun or pronoun and another. Prepositions often describe where someone or something is or where they are moving towards **NOUN**
▶ **PARTS OF SPEECH**, pages 6 and 7

Pp

prescription /prescripshen/
A piece of paper with the name of a medicine on it that a doctor gives to a patient to take to a chemist NOUN

present[1] /prezent/
1. Something that someone gives to you, usually for a special occasion like a birthday 2. The time now *I'm thinking about the present. I'm not worrying about the future.* NOUN

present[2] /prezent/
1. Belonging to the time now *At the present time, he's in France.* 2. In a certain place *Is Oliver present at school today?* ADJECTIVE
• **presence** /prezens/ NOUN

present[3] /prezent/
1. To give someone something *Inky presented Bee with a prize for hard work.*
2. To show someone something *Don't forget to present your tickets.* 3. To be in charge of a TV or radio programme VERB
• **presentation** /prezentaishen/ NOUN

preserve /prezerv/
1. To keep something safe, or stop something from being destroyed
2. To stop food from going bad VERB

president /prezident/
1. The person in charge of a country like the USA that does not have a king and queen 2. Someone in charge of a club or organization NOUN

press[1] /pres/
1. To push something against something *I pressed my nose against the window.*
2. To push something with your finger *I pressed the button.* VERB

press[2] /pres/
The press means newspapers and magazines NOUN

pressure /presher/
The force when something presses on something NOUN

pretend /pretend/
To behave as if something is true when it is not VERB
He pretended to be a cowboy.

pretty[1] /pritee/
Very nice to look at ADJECTIVE
What a pretty baby!

pretty[2] /pritee/
1. Not very much or too much but still quite a lot *It's pretty late!* 2. Another way of saying very *Learning to speak French is pretty difficult.* ADVERB

prevent /privent/
To stop something happening, or to stop someone doing something VERB

previous /preeveees/
Happening before something ADJECTIVE
What did you do on the previous day?

prey /prai/
Animals that another animal hunts and kills for food NOUN

price /pries/
The amount you pay for something NOUN

prick /pric/
1. To hurt someone with something sharp such as a needle 2. To make little holes in something *Prick the potatoes before putting them in the oven.* VERB

Pp

prickles /pricelz/
Sharp points on a plant or animal's skin
NOUN PLURAL
• **prickly** /priclee/ **ADJECTIVE**

pride /pried/
The feeling of being proud, or very happy because you think someone or something is good **NOUN**

priest /preest/
A man who does religious duties **NOUN**

primitive /primetiv/
Very simple compared to modern times
ADJECTIVE *They lived in primitive huts.*

primrose /primroaz/
A little plant that grows wild and has yellow flowers **NOUN**

prince /prins/
The son of a king and queen **NOUN**

princess /prinses/
The daughter of a king and queen **NOUN**

print[1] /print/
1. To make lots of copies of something such as a book 2. To make a copy of something on paper using a machine 3. To write words without joining the letters *Please print your name here.* **VERB**

print[2] /print/
1. The type of letters used for printing something *This book has large print for people who can't see very well.* 2. A mark left somewhere *Is this your hand print?* 3. Another word for a photo **NOUN**

printer /printer/
1. A machine connected to your computer that makes copies of pictures and documents 2. A person who does printing
NOUN
• **printout** /printout/ **NOUN**

prison /prizen/
A place where criminals are locked up
NOUN
• **prisoner** /prizener/ **NOUN**

private /prievet/
Connected with people's feelings, or with secret things about people **ADJECTIVE**

prize /priez/
Something you get for good work, or for winning in a game or competition **NOUN**

probability /probebilitee/
The chances of something happening, or something that is almost certain to happen **NOUN**
• **probably** /probeblee/ **ADVERB**

probable /probebel/
Almost certain to happen **ADJECTIVE**

problem /problem/
1. Something bad or difficult that needs to be understood and solved 2. A question that needs an answer **NOUN**

process /proases/
The actions needed to do something
NOUN *Learning to read is a slow process.*

Pp

procession /prəseshən/
Lots of people or vehicles moving slowly
in a line NOUN

produce[1] /prədues/
1. To make something, or to make
something happen *Inky is a good
teacher, she produces excellent results.*
2. To show something *You have to
produce your passport.* 3. To grow
something *Canada produces lots of
wheat.* VERB
• **production** /prəducshən/ NOUN

produce[2] /produes/
Something grown, for example on a farm
NOUN

product /product/
Something made in a factory or grown
on a farm NOUN

profession /prəfeshən/
Someone's job that needs lots of
education and training NOUN

program[1] /prɒagram/
A computer program is software that
contains instructions for performing
actions on a computer NOUN

program[2] /prɒagram/
To give a computer instructions so
that it will perform certain actions
VERB

programme[1] /prɒagram/
1. A show that you watch or listen to
on television or radio 2. A plan made
up of a number of different actions
3. Sheets of paper that describe
what happens in a play or concert
NOUN

programme[2] /prɒagram/
To do things to a machine so it works in
a certain way VERB
I've programmed the video to record the film.

progress /prɒagres/
make progress 1. To get better at
doing something *Bee is making progress
with her reading.* 2. To get closer to the
time when something will be finished
NOUN

project /project/
1. A subject a student works on that
needs a lot of studying *Bee is doing
a project on the history of the alphabet.*
2. Something that people work on
that takes a lot of time NOUN

projector /prəjecter/
A machine for making a film appear on
screen NOUN

promise /promis/
1. To tell someone you will definitely
do something or give them something
Snake promised to help Bee with her reading.
2. To tell someone that something will
certainly happen *You promised the photos
would be ready today.* VERB
• **promise** /promis/ NOUN

promising /promising/
1. Likely to be successful in the future
2. Likely to be good in the future
The weather looks promising for tomorrow.
ADJECTIVE

pronoun /prɒanoun/
In grammar, a pronoun is a word that
people use instead of a noun such as
'I', 'you', 'he', 'she', 'we', 'they' NOUN
▶ PARTS OF SPEECH, pages 6 and 7

Pp

pronounce /prɘnouns/
To say a word in the correct way VERB
You pronounce the word car 'c-ar'.
• **pronunciation** /prɘnunsiaishɘn/ NOUN

proof /proof/
Information that shows something is definitely true NOUN

propeller /prɘpelɘr/
The blades on a plane or ship that go around and make it move NOUN

proper /propɘr/
1. Right or correct *Is this the proper way to do it?* 2. Real *A sandwich isn't a proper meal.* ADJECTIVE
• **properly** /propɘrlee/ ADVERB

property /propɘrtee/
1. Things that belong to people
2. Land or buildings, or one building *Alice's dad owns a property in Spain.* NOUN

proportion /prɘporshɘn/
1. A part of something 2. The size or amount of one thing compared to something else *The proportion of girls in the class compared to boys has gone up.* NOUN

propose /prɘpouz/
1. To suggest something
2. To intend to do something VERB

protect /prɘtect/
To keep something or someone safe from harm VERB
• **protection** /prɘtecshɘn/ NOUN

proud /proud/
Happy because you think someone is good, or something they have done is good ADJECTIVE
Molly is so proud of her little baby sister.

prove /proov/
To use information to show that something is true VERB

provide /prɘvied/
1. To give someone what they need
2. To give someone something *The hotel provides meals.* VERB

prowl /proul/
To move around somewhere quietly, either to hunt or to do something bad VERB

prune /proon/
A dried plum NOUN

pub /pub/
A place where people can buy drinks with alcohol in them, and sit and talk to their friends NOUN

public[1] /public/
Connected with, or open to, ordinary people ADJECTIVE
a public park

public[2] /public/
1. The public are ordinary people
2. **in public** Done so that anyone can see it NOUN

publish /publish/
1. To produce something like a book or magazine and make it available to other people 2. To print a letter in a newspaper or magazine for everybody to read VERB

pudding /pooding/
1. A sweet dish that can be made from many things that people often eat at the end of a meal *rice pudding* 2. A dish made with meat or vegetables *steak and kidney pudding.* NOUN

Pp

puddle /pudəl/
A little pool of water on the ground NOUN

puff /puf/
1. To breathe noisily such as when you run 2. To blow air or smoke out of the mouth VERB
• **puff** /puf/ NOUN

pull /pool/
1. To move something towards you or in a certain direction *Pull the handle to open the door.* • *I pulled my socks up.* 2. To move something on wheels along behind you *The railway engine pulled the train.* VERB
• **pull** /pool/ NOUN

pulse /puls/
The regular beat of your blood being pumped around the body by your heart NOUN

pump /pump/
A machine people use to make liquids or gasses come out of something or go into something NOUN
a bicycle pump
• **pump** /pump/ VERB

pumpkin /pumpkin/
A very big round orange fruit that grows on the ground NOUN

punch /punch/
1. To hit someone with your hand, with your fingers closed 2. To make a hole in something using a machine VERB
• **punch** /punch/ NOUN

punctual /puncchooəl/
1. Arriving somewhere at the expected time *Snake and Bee are always very punctual for their lessons.* 2. Happening at the expected time ADJECTIVE
• **punctually** /puncchooəlee/ ADVERB

punctuate /puncchooait/
To add punctuation marks to your writing VERB
• **punctuation** /puncchooaishen/ NOUN

punctuation mark
/puncchooaishen mark/
A special sign used in writing such as a comma, full stop and question mark NOUN

puncture /pungccher/
A hole in a tyre NOUN

punish /punish/
To make someone suffer because they have done something wrong VERB
• **punishment** /punishmənt/ NOUN

pupil /puepəl/
A child who is studying in a school NOUN

puppet /pupit/
A kind of doll that you can make move, either by using strings or by putting your hand inside it NOUN

puppy /pupee/
A young dog NOUN

Pp

pure /pyooer/
1. Not mixed with other things *I drink pure orange juice.* 2. Very clean *Bee loves the pure sea air.* 3. Another word for complete *It was pure chance I bumped into him.* **ADJECTIVE**

purple /perpel/
The colour made when red and blue are mixed together **NOUN, ADJECTIVE**

purpose /perpes/
1. The reason for something *What's the purpose of your visit?* 2. **on purpose** Doing something because you want to do it *Did Nicole knock over the ink on purpose or by accident?* **NOUN**
• **purposely** /perpeslee/ **ADVERB**

purr /per/
The low sound a cat makes in its throat when it is happy **NOUN**
• **purr** /per/ **VERB**

purse /pers/
A little bag for carrying money **NOUN**

push /poosh/
1. To use force to move something away from you, or to move it in a certain direction *Push the door to open it.* 2. To move something on wheels along in front of you *Dad was pushing the buggy.* 3. To push a button is to put your finger on it hard, for example to make a machine work 4. To make people move out of the way with your arms *Stop pushing!* **VERB**
• **push** /poosh/ **NOUN**

pushchair /pooshcheer/
A folding chair with wheels for pushing a baby in **NOUN**

puss /poos/
Another word for a cat **NOUN**
• **pussy cat** /poosee cat/ **NOUN**

put /poot/
1. To move something to a certain place 2. To make someone go into another place, or change someone's situation *The news put me into a good mood.* 3. To write *Sam put the address down in his book.* 4. **put off** To change the time of something to a later time *The meeting has been put off until tomorrow.* 5. **put on** To wear something *Put on your coat, it's cold outside.* 6. **put on** To switch something on *It's dark, can you put the light on?* 7. **put out** To stop something burning or shining *Put the fire out.* **VERB**
■ put

puzzle[1] /puzel/
1. Something hard to understand 2. A game where you solve problems or answer questions 3. A jigsaw puzzle is a picture cut into small pieces that you put back together for fun **NOUN**

puzzle[2] /puzel/
If something puzzles you, you are confused because you do not understand it **VERB**
• **puzzled** /puzeld/ **ADJECTIVE**
• **puzzling** /puzeling/ **ADJECTIVE**

pyjamas /pejahmez/
Loose clothes that people wear to sleep in, made up of trousers and a jacket **NOUN PLURAL**

pylon /pielon/
A tall tower built out of metal that carries electric wires **NOUN**

pyramid /piremid/
A pointed shape or big stone building that has four sides, and the shape of each side is a triangle **NOUN**

Qq

quack /quac/
The sound made by a duck **NOUN**

quad /quod/
One of four children who were born at the same time to the same mother **NOUN**

quail /quail/
A small bird that people sometimes eat **NOUN**

qualification /quolificaishen/
Someone's qualifications are the exams they have passed **NOUN**
• **qualified** /quolified/ **ADJECTIVE**

quality /quoletee/
How good or bad something is **NOUN**

quantity /quontetee/
How much there is, or how many there are, of something **NOUN**

quarrel /quorel/
An argument you have with someone because you are angry **NOUN**
• **quarrel** /quorel/ **VERB**

quarter /quorter/
One of four parts of something that are equal **NOUN**

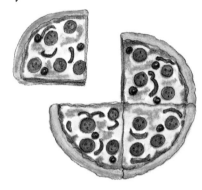

queen /queen/
An important woman who is the head of a country or who is married to a king **NOUN**

quench /quench/
If someone quenches their thirst, they stop themselves feeling thirsty by drinking something **VERB**

quest /quest/
A long search for something **NOUN**

Qq

question /queschen/
1. Something that you ask someone
2. A problem that needs to be solved
NOUN

- **question** /queschen/ VERB

question mark /queschen mark/
A punctuation mark (**?**) that people use at the end of a sentence to show they are asking a question NOUN

queue /cue/
A row of people waiting for something NOUN
- **queue** /cue/ VERB

quick /quic/
1. Happening or moving fast 2. Lasting a very short time *I had a quick look.*
ADJECTIVE
- **quickly** /quiclee/ ADVERB

quicksands /quicsandz/
Wet sands that people will sink into if they walk on them NOUN PLURAL

quiet /quieet/
1. Not making a lot of noise 2. Without much happening *Yesterday was very quiet in school.* ADJECTIVE
- **quiet** /quieet/ NOUN
- **quietly** /quieetlee/ ADVERB

quilt /quilt/
A thick cover for a bed NOUN

quin /quin/
One of five children born at the same time to the same mother NOUN

quit /quit/
To stop doing something and go away VERB

quite /quiet/
Not very much or too much but still quite a lot ADVERB
It's quite dark outside.

quiver /quiver/
If something quivers, it shakes very slightly VERB

quiz /quiz/
A competition where people answer questions NOUN
- **quizzes** /quiziz/ PLURAL

quotation /quoataishen/
A word or a sentence that someone has said before, for example one that has come out of a book NOUN

quotation marks /quoataishen marks/
Punctuation marks (**' '** or **" "**) that are put around words to show that someone is speaking NOUN PLURAL

Rr

rabbit /rabit/
A small furry animal with long ears
NOUN

rabbit

raccoon

raccoon /racoon/
A small animal that lives in trees. It has white stripes on its face and tail **NOUN**

race /rais/
A competition to see who or what is the fastest **NOUN**
• **race** /rais/ VERB
• **racing** /raising/ **NOUN**
• **racing car** /raising car/ **NOUN**

racist /raisist/
Someone who does not like people who are different from them **NOUN**

rack /rac/
A kind of frame or shelf for keeping things in **NOUN**
a magazine rack

racket /racit/
1. A round piece of wood with strings and a handle for hitting a ball in tennis
2. Another word for a loud noise **NOUN**

radiator /raideeaiter/
A flat metal object for heating a room that is connected by pipes going under the ground **NOUN**

radii /raidiie/
NOUN PLURAL ▶ radius

radio /raideeoa/
1. Special equipment for listening to radio programmes 2. A special system for sending sound over a long distance **NOUN**

radius /raidies/
The distance from the centre of a circle to the edge of the circle **NOUN**
■ **radii** /raidiie/ **PLURAL**

raft /raft/
A kind of boat made from pieces of wood tied together **NOUN**

rag /rag/
A little piece of cloth, usually for cleaning things **NOUN**

rage /raij/
A strong feeling of anger that makes you want to say or do bad things **NOUN**

raid /raid/
1. An attack by soldiers 2. An attack by criminals *There was a bank raid last night.*
3. An unexpected visit by the police **NOUN**
• **raid** /raid/ VERB

rail /rail/
1. A bar fixed onto something for holding on to 2. A bar for hanging things on *Put your towel on the rail.*
3. Rails are the metal bars that trains run on **NOUN**

railings /railingz/
The railings of a fence are the metal bars that make up the fence **NOUN PLURAL**

Rr

railway /railwai/
1. The tracks that a train runs on
2. Travelling by train **NOUN**

rain /rain/
Water that falls from the clouds in small drops **NOUN**
• **rain** /rain/ **VERB**
• **raincoat** /raincoat/ **NOUN**
• **rainforest** /rain forest/ **NOUN**
• **rainstorm** /rainstorm/ **NOUN**
• **rainy** /rainee/ **ADJECTIVE**

rainbow /rainboa/
A big curve of different colours that appears in the sky when it rains and the sun is shining at the same time **NOUN**

raise /raiz/
1. To lift something *Raise your arm if you have the answer.* 2. To increase something *Don't raise your voice.* **VERB**

raisin /raizen/
A dried grape that is used in cooking or can be eaten as a snack **NOUN**

rake /raik/
A garden tool with big metal teeth and a long handle **NOUN**
• **rake** /raik/ **VERB**

ran /ran/
PAST TENSE ▶ **run**

ranch /ranch/
A big farm where people keep animals such as cows or sheep **NOUN**

rang /rang/
PAST TENSE ▶ **ring**²

range /rainj/
1. A lot of different things *They sell a wide range of dresses.* 2. The distance that can be covered by a sound, or the distance you can see something *I can't hear the music. We're out of range.* **NOUN**

rapid /rapid/
Happening fast **ADJECTIVE**

rare /reer/
Not happening often or not seen often **ADJECTIVE** *It's a rare bird.*
• **rarely** /reerlee/ **ADVERB**

rascal /rascel/
Someone who behaves badly **NOUN**

rash /rash/
Little red spots on the skin **NOUN**

raspberry /razberee/
A little soft red fruit that people eat. Raspberries grow on bushes **NOUN**
▶ **FRUIT AND VEGETABLES**, page 15

rat /rat/
An animal like a big mouse with a long tail **NOUN**

Rr

rate /rait/
1. The rate of something is the speed it happens at 2. An amount of money that someone is paid for doing something NOUN

rather /rather/
1. Not very much or too much but still quite a lot *Inky is rather tired today.*
2. If someone would rather do something, they want to do that thing most *Snake would rather have his lunch now than wait till later.* ADVERB

rattle /ratəl/
1. A baby's toy that makes the noise you hear when things knock against each other 2. The noise of things knocking against each other NOUN

rattlesnake /ratəlsnaik/
A poisonous snake that makes a noise with its tail like a rattle NOUN

rave /raiv/
To be very excited about something and keep on talking about it VERB

raven /raivən/
A big bird that has shiny black feathers NOUN

raw /raw/
1. Not cooked 2. If someone's skin is raw, it is red and it hurts them ADJECTIVE

ray /rai/
A line of light that shines from something such as the sun NOUN

razor /raizer/
A special tool with a blade for getting rid of hair, for example on a man's face NOUN

reach[1] /reech/
1. To get somewhere *Bee hasn't reached Inky's house yet.* 2. To move your hand towards something to touch it *Can you reach the ceiling?* VERB

reach[2] /reech/
out of reach Too far away to reach NOUN

react /reeact/
If you react to something, you behave in a certain way because of it VERB
• **reaction** /reeacshen/ NOUN

read[1] /reed/
To look at words that are written down and be able to say and understand what they mean VERB
■ **read**
• **reader** /reeder/ NOUN
• **reading** /reeding/ NOUN

read[2] /red/
PAST TENSE ▶ **read**[1]

ready /redee/
1. Wanting to do something *I'm ready for bed now.* 2. Able to do something else because you have finished everything you needed to do *Snake is ready so Inky can start the lesson.* ADJECTIVE

real /reeəl/
1. Something real actually exists and has not been imagined by someone *Are dragons real?* 2. Based on facts and not on what people think *Tell me the real reason.* ADJECTIVE

Rr

reality /reealetee/
Things as they are, not things that people imagine NOUN

realize /reealiez/
To know and understand something VERB
I realize it's very late.

really /reealee/
1. Another way of saying very *That's really good.* 2. Definitely *I really don't know how to say this word.* 3. Another way of saying very much *That really hurt me.* ADVERB

rear /rier/
The back part of something NOUN
• **rear** /rier/ ADJECTIVE

reason /reezen/
Why someone did something or why something happened NOUN
Do you know the reason why Bee is late?
• **reasonable** /reezenebel/ ADJECTIVE

recall /recawl/
Another way of saying remember VERB
Do you recall the lesson we did yesterday?

receipt /reseet/
A piece of paper that someone gives you saying they have received something from you NOUN

receive /reseev/
To take something that someone gives to you VERB

receiver /reseever/
The part of a phone that you hold next to your ear and mouth NOUN

recent /reesent/
Happened or started a short time ago
ADJECTIVE *Here's a recent photo of Inky.*
• **recently** /reesentlee/ ADVERB

receptionist /resepshenist/
Someone who welcomes people when they go into an office or a hotel NOUN

recipe /resepee/
The instructions for making different types of food such as cakes with a list of the things you need to make them NOUN

recite /resiet/
To learn something like a poem and then say it out loud for people to hear VERB

reckon /recen/
Another way of saying think VERB
Do you reckon mice can see in the dark?

recognize /recegniez/
1. To know who someone is because you have seen them before *Of course, I recognize you.* 2. To know what something is because you have learned it or heard it or seen it before *Do you recognize this tune?* VERB

recommend /recemend/
1. To suggest that someone does something because you think they should
2. To say nice things about something or someone in case people find that useful
Snake recommended a good restaurant. VERB
• **recommendation** /recemendaishen/
NOUN

229

Rr

record[1] /record/
1. The best someone has ever done. If you break a record, you do better than someone else 2. If someone keeps a record of something, they write it down 3. A round and flat piece of plastic that music can be stored on NOUN

record[2] /record/
1. To store sounds and pictures on something like a tape or disc
2. To write something down VERB

recorder /recorder/
1. A tape recorder is something that stores sounds, and a video recorder is something that stores sounds and pictures
2. A musical instrument that looks like a pipe that people make sounds out of when they blow into it NOUN

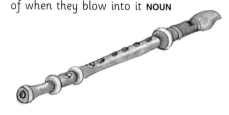

recover /recuver/
1. To get better after an illness
2. To get something back VERB
• **recovery** /recuveree/ NOUN

rectangle /rectanggel/
A shape that has four straight sides. Two of the sides are usually longer than the other two NOUN
▶ SHAPES, page 17

red /red/
The colour of blood NOUN, ADJECTIVE

reduce /redues/
To make something smaller VERB
They're reducing their prices.
• **reduction** /reducshen/ NOUN

reed /reed/
A kind of grass that grows in wet places NOUN

reel /reel/
A round object that you can wind things around such as cotton or a film NOUN

referee /referee/
A person in charge of a game in certain sports like boxing or football NOUN

reflect /reflect/
1. To send light rays back from a surface *The window reflected the sunlight into my eyes and I couldn't see.* 2. To show the image of something, like water or a mirror does *Inky saw her own face reflected in the pond.* VERB
• **reflection** /reflecshen/ NOUN

refresh /refresh/
1. To make someone feel less hot or tired *I took a cool shower to refresh me.*
2. If someone refreshes your memory, they tell you something you have forgotten VERB

refuse /refuez/
1. To say you will not do something
2. To say no to something that someone wants to give you VERB
• **refusal** /refuezel/ NOUN

region /reejen/
A big part of a country or the world NOUN
• **regional** /reejenel/ ADJECTIVE

register /rejister/
A list of names and other details NOUN
Has the teacher taken the register yet?

Rr

regular /regyeler/
1. With the same amount of time or space in between its parts *It happened at regular intervals.* 2. A regular shape is a shape that has sides that are equal 3. Happening all the time or always happening at the same time *Inky makes regular visits to the dentist.* 4. Another way of saying usual or normal *Our teacher wasn't wearing his regular glasses.* ADJECTIVE
• **regularly** /regyelerlee/ ADVERB

rehearse /rehers/
To practise for a play or concert VERB
• **rehearsal** /rehersel/ NOUN

reign /rain/
The reign of a king or queen is the time when they are king or queen of a certain country NOUN
• **reign** /rain/ VERB

reindeer /raindier/
A big wild animal like a deer with very big horns on its head like branches. Reindeer live in very cold areas NOUN

■ **reindeer** /raindier/ PLURAL

reins /rainz/
Leather straps for controlling a horse or for a young child who has just started walking NOUN PLURAL

rejoice /rejois/
To show how very happy you are
VERB

related /relaitid/
1. Connected in some way to something else 2. Being part of the same family
ADJECTIVE
• **relation** /relaishen/ Someone who belongs to your family NOUN
• **relative** /reletiv/ Another word for relation NOUN

relax /relax/
To rest and feel happy or less worried
VERB
• **relaxation** /reelaksaishen/ NOUN
• **relaxed** /relaxt/ ADJECTIVE
• **relaxing** /relaxing/ ADJECTIVE

release /relees/
To let someone or something go free
VERB
• **release** /relees/ NOUN

reliable /relieebel/
1. Well-known for being good and working well *This is a reliable computer.* 2. Able to be trusted *Bee is very reliable, she always works hard.* ADJECTIVE

relief /releef/
The happy feeling you get when something bad has ended or when something bad does not happen NOUN
• **relieved** /releevd/ ADJECTIVE

religion /relijen/
Religion is what people believe in, such as a faith in God NOUN
• **religious** /relijes/ ADJECTIVE

rely /relie/
rely on To be sure someone or something will do what you want them to VERB

Rr

remain /rəmain/
1. To stay in the same place *Can you remain in your seats for another five minutes?* 2. To be left over after other things have gone *One last thing remains for me to say.* VERB
• **remaining** /rəmaining/ ADJECTIVE

remarkable /rəmarkəbel/
Really good and surprising ADJECTIVE *Bee has made remarkable progress.*

remember /rəmember/
1. To know something from the past and be able to bring it into your mind *I remember your name from last time.*
2. If you remember to do something, you do it because you keep it in mind that you must do it *Inky remembered to take her umbrella.* VERB

remind /rəmiend/
To make someone think of something VERB *There's no need to remind Snake about lunch, he always remembers.*
• **reminder** /rəmiender/ NOUN

remove /rəmoov/
To take something away VERB
• **removal** /rəmoovel/ NOUN

rent /rent/
Money you pay someone for staying in their house or for using something that belongs to them NOUN
Dad rented a car when we went to Ireland.
• **rent** /rent/ VERB

repair /rəpeer/
To take something broken and put it back together or make changes to it so it works again VERB
A man came and repaired our TV.
• **repair** /rəpeer/ NOUN

repeat /rəpeet/
To say or do something again VERB
• **repeat** /rəpeet/ NOUN
• **repetition** /repətishən/ NOUN

replace /rəplais/
1. To put something back where it was before *Bee replaced the book on the shelf.*
2. To take someone else's place *Our teacher is really good, no one can replace her.* VERB

reply /rəplie/
Something you say or write or do when someone asks you something or makes a suggestion NOUN
Inky is still waiting for a reply to her letter.
• **reply** /rəplie/ VERB

report[1] /rəport/
To tell someone about something VERB

report[2] /rəport/
1. A description about something or news about something 2. A school report is a piece of paper from your school that tells your parents how well you are doing NOUN

represent /rəprəzent/
To be a sign or a symbol of something else VERB
On the map blue represents the sea.

reptile /rəptiel/
A type of animal like a snake or crocodile. Reptiles have cold blood, hard skin and lay eggs NOUN

reputation /repuətaishən/
The opinion that people have about someone or something, and about how good they are NOUN

request /rəquest/
To ask for something in a polite way VERB
• **request** /rəquest/ NOUN

Rr

rescue /rescue/
To save someone or something from
harm or danger VERB

*The fire fighters rescued two children from
the burning house.*

• **rescue** /rescue/ NOUN

resemble /rezembel/
To be like someone or something,
or to look like them VERB

reserve /rezerv/
1. Another way of saying keep
This space is reserved for our teacher's car.
2. To arrange to have something you
want such as a hotel room for the
time that you want it VERB
• **reservation** /rezervaishen/ NOUN

reserved /rezervd/
If someone is reserved, they are quiet
and shy ADJECTIVE

residence /rezidens/
The place where someone lives NOUN

resident /rezident/
Someone who lives somewhere NOUN

resist /rezist/
1. To fight against something 2. To stop
yourself doing something *Snake couldn't
resist eating those delicious chocolates.* VERB

respect /respect/
To have a very good opinion of someone
because you think they have good
qualities VERB
• **respect** /respect/ NOUN

responsible /responsebel/
1. If someone is responsible for something,
they have caused it *Who's responsible for
this mess?* 2. In charge of something
Bee is responsible for the pens and pencils.
ADJECTIVE
• **responsibility** /responsebiletee/ NOUN

rest[1] /rest/
1. To stop doing something like working
2. If you rest something on something,
you put it there *I rested my elbows on the
table.* VERB

rest[2] /rest/
1. A quiet time when you have stopped
doing something and you can relax
2. The rest of something is what is left
over *Bee ate a quarter of the pie and Snake
ate the rest.* NOUN

restaurant /resteront/
A place where people go to buy a meal
and eat it sitting at a table NOUN

restore /restor/
To repair something so that it is as good
as new VERB

233

Rr

result /rezult/
1. Something that happens because of something else *The result of your hard work is that you will be able to read!*
2. The final points or score you get at the end of a competition 3. Your exam results are the marks you get in an exam **NOUN**

retire /retieer/
To stop working because you have reached a certain age **VERB**
• **retirement** /retieerment/ **NOUN**

return /retern/
1. To go back or come back to a place *Inky returned to her mousehole.* 2. To give something back *Don't forget to return my book.* **VERB**
• **return** /retern/ **NOUN**

reveal /reveel/
To show something that was hidden **VERB**

reverse /revers/
1. To change the order of something such as the letters in a word so they go backwards 2. To go backwards in a car **VERB**

revise /reviez/
To go over your notes and study them before a test or exam **VERB**
• **revision** /revizhen/ **NOUN**

revolve /revolv/
To go around and around **VERB**

reward /reword/
1. Something you get for doing something good such as hard work 2. Money people get for giving information to the police, or for finding something and giving it back **NOUN**
• **reward** /reword/ **VERB**

rhinoceros /rienoseres/
A very big animal with thick skin and one or two horns on its nose **NOUN**

rhombus /rombes/
A diamond shape with four sides that are straight and as long as each other **NOUN**
▶ **SHAPES**, page 17

rhubarb /roobarb/
A plant with thick pink stems that people cook and eat **NOUN**

rhyme[1] /riem/
A word with an ending that sounds the same as another word, such as 'sad' and 'mad' **NOUN**

rhyme[2] /riem/
If words rhyme, they end with the same sound **VERB**

rhythm /rithem/
A pattern of sounds in music that is regular **NOUN**

rib /rib/
Your ribs are the curved bones that protect your chest **NOUN**

ribbon /riben/
A narrow piece of thin cloth that people use for decorating their hair or tying around presents **NOUN**

rice /ries/
Rice is made up of white or brown grains from a plant. People boil it and eat it when it is soft **NOUN**

rich /rich/
1. A rich person has lots of money
2. A rich place such as a country is where there are lots of rich people **ADJECTIVE**
• **riches** /richiz/ **NOUN**

rid /rid/
get rid of To take or throw something away that you do not want any more **ADJECTIVE**

ridden /ridən/
PAST PARTICIPLE ▶ **ride**[1]

riddle /ridəl/
A difficult and often funny question that you have to guess the answer to **NOUN**

ride[1] /ried/
1. To sit on an animal or a bike and make it move *Have you ever ridden a bicycle?* 2. If you ride on something, you travel that way *She rode on a horse.* **VERB**
■ **rode, ridden**

ride[2] /ried/
1. A journey somewhere, for example on a horse or a bicycle 2. A machine that people ride on at an amusement park *We loved the rides at Disneyland.* **NOUN**
• **rider** /rieder/ **NOUN**
• **riding** /rieding/ **NOUN**

ridiculous /rədicyələs/
If something is ridiculous, it is very silly or looks very silly **ADJECTIVE**

right[1] /riet/
1. With no mistakes *Bee gave the right answer.* 2. Used for talking about something that should be done *Snake made the right decision.* 3. If you say someone is right, you mean what they say is true and based on facts 4. Another way of saying good *That hat doesn't look right with those shoes.* **ADJECTIVE**

right[2] /riet/
1. Exactly at a certain place, or all the way around a certain place *Inky was standing right in front of me.* 2. Immediately *I want you to tell me right now.* **ADVERB**

right[3] /riet/
The opposite side to the left side **NOUN**

• **right** /riet/ On the same side as your right hand **ADJECTIVE** *Take a right turn.*
• **right** /riet/ Towards the right **ADVERB** *Turn right at the traffic lights.*
• **right-handed** /riet handid/ Using your right hand for writing and other things **ADJECTIVE**

ring[1] /ring/
1. A little circle of metal that people wear on their finger 2. A mark shaped like a circle *Snake drew a ring in the sand.* 3. The sound made by a bell **NOUN**

ring[2] /ring/
1. If you ring a bell, you make a noise with it 2. If a phone or bell rings, it makes its usual noise 3. To phone someone 4. **ring off** To stop speaking to someone on the phone **VERB**
■ **rang, rung**

rink /ringk/
A place where people go skating on ice or with roller skates **NOUN**

rinse /rins/
To wash something in clean water or with another liquid that makes it clean **VERB**
• **rinse** /rins/ **NOUN**

Rr

Rr

rip /rip/
1. To tear 2. If you rip something out or away, you take it away using a lot of strength *Someone has ripped a page out of Bee's book.* VERB
• **rip** /rip/ NOUN

ripe /riep/
Ripe fruit or vegetables are ready to eat ADJECTIVE *Green bananas are not ripe.*

ripple /ripel/
A little wave on the surface of the water NOUN

rise¹ /riez/
1. To move upwards or go higher *Smoke rises into the air.* 2. To get bigger, when talking about amounts or numbers *Prices are starting to rise.* 3. If the sun rises, it comes into the sky in the morning VERB
■ **rose, risen**

rise² /riez/
1. A bigger amount of money that someone gets in their job
2. A bigger amount of anything NOUN

risen /rizen/
PAST PARTICIPLE ▶ **rise**¹

risk /risk/
1. The chance that something bad or dangerous could happen to you *If Bee is angry, there's a risk she could sting you!*
2. **take a risk** To do something even though something bad could happen NOUN
• **risky** /riskee/ ADJECTIVE

rival /rievel/
Someone who tries to beat you, for example in competitions or sports NOUN

river /river/
A long line of water that flows across the land NOUN
• **riverside** /riversied/ NOUN

road /road/
A long piece of ground with a hard surface for cars, buses and other vehicles to travel on NOUN

• **roadside** /roadsied/ NOUN
• **roadsign** /roadsien/ NOUN

roam /roam/
To walk or travel around but not in a particular direction VERB

roar /ror/
To make a loud sound like a lion VERB
• **roar** /ror/ NOUN

roast /roast/
To cook food like chicken in an oven or in front of a fire VERB

rob /rob/
To steal from someone or something VERB *The thieves robbed the bank.*
• **robber** /rober/ NOUN
• **robbery** /roberee/ NOUN

robin /robin/
A little brown bird that is common in Europe. The male robin has a red neck and front NOUN

Rr

robot /roʊbot/
A machine controlled by computer that can move and perform actions NOUN

rock[1] /roc/
1. The stone that the earth is made of, or a big lump of this stone 2. Rock or rock music is a kind of music with a loud pattern of sounds 3. A very hard sweet shaped like a stick NOUN
• **rocky** /rocee/ ADJECTIVE

rock[2] /roc/
To move something backwards or forwards, or from side to side VERB
Mum was rocking the baby to sleep.

rocket /rocit/
1. A big machine like a long tube that is fired into space. Rockets can carry people or things, or can be used as weapons for destroying things 2. An object shaped like a small tube with chemicals in it that people fire into the air for fun. A rocket is a firework NOUN

rod /rod/
A long thin stick NOUN
a fishing rod

rode /roʊd/
PAST TENSE ▶ **ride**[1]

rodent /roʊdent/
The name for small animals like mice and rats that have front teeth that are long and sharp NOUN

rogue /roʊg/
Someone who behaves badly or dishonestly NOUN

role /roʊl/
The words and actions of one of the characters in a play NOUN

roll[1] /roʊl/
1. To turn around and around like a wheel along the ground, or turn something in this way 2. **roll up** To roll something such as a carpet into the shape of a tube VERB

roll[2] /roʊl/
1. Something like a piece of paper in the shape of a tube 2. A small of amount of baked bread usually in a round shape NOUN

roller skate /roʊler skait/
A shoe with four little wheels fixed to the bottom NOUN

Roman /roʊmen/
Someone who lived a long time ago in ancient Rome NOUN
• **Roman** /roʊmen/ ADJECTIVE

romantic /roʊmantic/
Romantic means connected with love
ADJECTIVE *He gave me some roses. How romantic!*

roof /roʊf/
The top part of something like a building or a car NOUN

rook /roʊk/
A big black bird like a crow NOUN

room /roʊm/
1. A section of a house or building with its own walls and door
2. If there is room, there is enough space for something or someone
Can you move along? I have no room. NOUN
• **roomy** /roʊmee/ ADJECTIVE

237

Rr

roost /roost/
A place where birds rest NOUN

rooster /rooster/
A male chicken NOUN

root /root/
The part of a plant or tree that grows under the ground NOUN

rope /roap/
Thick string that is twisted together NOUN

rose¹ /roaz/
A beautiful flower with a nice smell NOUN

rose² /roaz/
PAST TENSE ▶ **rise**¹

rosy /roazee/
Another way of saying pink ADJECTIVE

rot /rot/
To go bad slowly, or to make something do this VERB
• **rotten** /roten/ ADJECTIVE

rotate /roatait/
To turn around like a wheel VERB

rough /ruf/
1. Not flat and smooth 2. Mostly but not completely correct *Give me a rough idea of your plan.* 3. Violent or using too much strength *Stay away from those rough boys in your class.* ADJECTIVE

roughly /ruflee/
1. Another way of saying about *There are roughly ten apples in each bag.* 2. With too much violence or strength *The children were playing too roughly.* ADVERB

round¹ /round/
Shaped like a circle or a ball ADJECTIVE

round² /round/
1. If something moves round, it moves like a circle or a wheel 2. If you show someone round or hand something round, you take someone to lots of places or hand something to lots of people 3. Spread out in the shape of a circle *Children, please gather round.* ADVERB

round³ /round/
1. Going all the way on the outside of something in a circular movement *The earth goes round the sun.* 2. In all parts of something *Have you ever been round France, Inky?* PREPOSITION

roundabout /roundebout/
A big circle for cars to drive around where three or more roads join each other NOUN

238

Rr

rounders /roʊnderz/
A game played by two teams with a bat and ball. Players have to run around four sides of a square NOUN

route /roʊt/
A way of getting from one place to another, for example a road that cars travel on or a path that planes follow NOUN

routine /roʊteen/
Someone's routine is the normal way they do things NOUN

row[1] /roʊ/
1. A line of people or things 2. If things happen a few times in a row, it means they happen one after the other without anything in between *Bee got the right answer four times in a row.* NOUN

row[2] /roʊ/
To move a boat through the water using long poles called oars VERB
• **rowing** /roʊing/ NOUN

row[3] /roʊ/
1. A noisy argument with someone
2. Another word for noise NOUN

royal /roɪel/
Connected with a king or queen ADJECTIVE

rub /rub/
1. To move one thing against another
2. **rub out** To get rid of something written in pencil by using a rubber VERB

rubber /ruber/
1. A substance from a tree that grows in hot countries, used to make things like car tyres 2. A little piece of rubber for getting rid of pencil marks NOUN
• **rubbery** /ruberee/ ADJECTIVE

rubbish /rubish/
1. Waste material that people throw away 2. If you say something like a book or an idea is rubbish, you mean it is very bad or silly NOUN

ruby /roobee/
A jewel that has a dark red colour NOUN

rucksack /rucsac/
A bag that people carry on their back NOUN

rudder /ruder/
The flat part fixed to the back of a ship for making it move in different directions NOUN

rude /rood/
Behaving in a way that is not polite ADJECTIVE *Snake is never rude to his teacher.*

rug /rug/
A small carpet NOUN

rugby /rugbee/
A sport that people play with a ball shaped like an egg NOUN

ruin[1] /rooin/
To destroy or spoil something completely VERB

ruin[2] /rooin/
The ruins of a building are the parts left when the rest has been destroyed NOUN

rule[1] /rool/
1. Information that tells you what you are allowed to do and what you are not allowed to do 2. **break the rules** To do something you are not allowed to do NOUN

239

Rr

rule² /rool/
If someone like a king or queen rules, they have the power to control a country VERB
Queen Victoria ruled for a long time.

ruler /rooler/
A flat and narrow piece of plastic, wood or metal to measure things or to draw straight lines NOUN

rumble /rumbel/
A long low sound that continues for a while like the sound of thunder NOUN

run /run/
1. To move very quickly on your feet
2. If a machine runs, it goes or works *Don't leave the engine running too long.*
3. To be in charge of something, like an office 4. If a tap or nose runs, water or liquid comes out of it 5. To go *The road runs along the railway track.* 6. To not have any more of something left *Sorry, we've run out of pens.* 7. If someone gets run over, they are hit by a car VERB
■ ran, run

• **run** /run/ NOUN
• **runner** /runer/ NOUN
• **running** /runing/ ADVERB
• **runny** /runee/ ADJECTIVE

rung /rung/
PAST PARTICIPLE ▶ **ring**²

runway /runwai/
A type of big wide road that planes use for taking off and landing NOUN

rush¹ /rush/
To do something or go somewhere very quickly VERB
Bee had to rush as she was late.

rush² /rush/
When people move quickly NOUN
There was a rush for the door.
• **rushed** /rusht/ ADJECTIVE

rust /rust/
A light brown substance on metal that happens when the metal gets wet NOUN
• **rust** /rust/ VERB
• **rusty** /rustee/ ADJECTIVE

rustle /rusel/
To make the noise of leaves or papers rubbing against each other VERB
• **rustle** /rusel/ NOUN

rye /rie/
The seeds of a plant that people use for making a type of bread NOUN
• **rye bread** /rie bred/ NOUN

Ss

sack /sac/
A big bag made of cloth or strong paper for carrying heavy things like coal or potatoes **NOUN**

sacrifice /sacrifies/
1. A gift that is offered to God
2. When you give up something you want or like for someone else **NOUN**
• **sacrifice** /sacrifies/ **VERB**

sad /sad/
If you are sad, you have no feelings of pleasure, usually because something bad has happened **ADJECTIVE**

• **sadly** /sadlee/ **ADVERB**
• **sadness** /sadnes/ **NOUN**

saddle /sadel/
A leather seat on a bike or on the back of a horse for people to ride on **NOUN**

safe¹ /saif/
1. Without danger *The streets are safe in this part of town.* 2. Free from harm *Inky feels safe in her mousehole.* **ADJECTIVE**
• **safely** /saiflee/ **ADVERB**
• **safety** /saiftee/ **NOUN**

safe² /saif/
A big metal box where people keep money or valuable things to protect them **NOUN**

said /sed/
PAST TENSE ▶ **say**

sail¹ /sail/
1. A big piece of cloth on a boat that catches the wind and moves the boat along 2. **set sail** To start to go somewhere in a boat **NOUN**

sail² /sail/
1. To go somewhere in a boat *Inky has sailed to many countries.* 2. To control a boat so that it goes somewhere **VERB**

• **sailing** /sailing/ **NOUN**

sailor /sailer/
Someone who works on a boat or ship **NOUN**

saint /saint/
A very good and holy person in the Christian church **NOUN**

salad /saled/
A dish of raw vegetables such as lettuce and tomatoes, often with other things added **NOUN**
• **salad dressing** /saled dresing/
A liquid for putting on salads **NOUN**

salami /selahmee/
A big sausage with a strong taste that people eat cold **NOUN**

salary /saleree/
The money people get for doing their job **NOUN**

241

Ss

sale /sail/
1. When something is sold for money *Their house is for sale.* 2. A time when shops sell things for a special price that is lower than usual NOUN

salmon /samen/
A big sea fish with pink flesh and silver skin NOUN
■ **salmon** /samen/ PLURAL

salt /sawlt/
A white substance with a strong taste that is put on food to make it taste better NOUN
• **salty** /sawltee/ ADJECTIVE

salute /seloot/
When a soldier puts his hand against his head as a sign of respect or greeting NOUN
• **salute** /seloot/ VERB

same /saim/
When two or more things are no different from each other
ADJECTIVE, PRONOUN, ADVERB
Bee and Inky had bought the same hat.

sample /sampel/
A little part of something that shows what the rest of it is like NOUN

sand /sand/
A yellow substance like powder that is made up of very tiny pieces of stone. It is found in deserts and on beaches NOUN

• **sand castle** /sand casel/ NOUN
• **sandy** /sandee/ ADJECTIVE

sandpaper /sandpaiper/
A strong paper that has a rough surface with sand on it for rubbing wood to make it smooth NOUN

sandwich /sanwij/
Two pieces of bread with food in between NOUN *a cheese sandwich*

sane /sain/
A sane person is normal and healthy in their mind ADJECTIVE

sang /sang/
PAST TENSE ▶ **sing**

sank /sangk/
PAST TENSE ▶ **sink**[1]

sat /sat/
PAST TENSE ▶ **sit**

satellite /sateliet/
An object in space that moves around a planet NOUN

satisfactory /satisfacteree/
Good enough for something ADJECTIVE
Bee's work is always very satisfactory.
• **satisfaction** /satisfacshen/ NOUN

satisfy /satisfie/
If someone or something satisfies you, it makes you happy VERB

satsuma /satsoome/
A type of small orange with a soft skin NOUN

saturated /sacheraitid/
Another way of saying very wet ADJECTIVE

Saturday /saterdai/
A day of the week NOUN
▶ CALENDAR, page 13

sauce /saws/
A liquid that people cook and then put on food to give it a certain taste NOUN

Ss

saucepan /sɑwspɛn/
A metal container with a handle for cooking things in NOUN

saucer /sɑwsɛr/
A small curved plate that people put under a cup NOUN

sausage /sosij/
A thin tube with food inside such as meat and spices NOUN

savage /savij/
Cruel and violent ADJECTIVE
a savage dog

save /saiv/
1. To take someone away from danger *They managed to save the man who fell into the sea.* 2. If you save something such as time, you are happy because you use less of it *Bee saves time getting around by flying.*
3. **save up** To put some money somewhere and keep adding more until you have enough to buy something
4. To make your computer keep certain information so you can find it and use it again VERB

They managed to save the man who fell into the sea.

savings /saivingz/
The money you have put somewhere such as in a bank NOUN PLURAL

saw¹ /sɑw/
A tool with a sharp blade for cutting wood NOUN

saw² /sɑw/
PAST TENSE ▶ **see**

sawdust /sɑwdust/
Tiny pieces of wood like dust that are left over when wood is cut with a saw NOUN

saxophone /saxɛfɔɑn/
A musical instrument with a straight metal tube that is shaped like a letter U at the bottom NOUN

say /sai/
1. If you say something, you use words *Bee said she was tired after flying home.*
2. To give information about something *What time does the clock say?* VERB
■ **said**

saying /saiing/
Something that people often say that most people believe is true NOUN

scald /scɑwld/
To burn your skin with a hot liquid VERB

scale /scail/
1. The scale of something is the size of it *What is the scale of the problem?*
2. Marks on something like a thermometer for measuring NOUN

scales /scailz/
1. A machine for weighing people or things 2. Little flat pieces of skin on the body of a fish or snake NOUN PLURAL

243

Ss

scanner /scaner/
A machine that copies words or pictures on paper on to your computer NOUN

scar /scar/
A mark left when a cut has got better NOUN
• **scar** /scar/ VERB

scarce /sceers/
If something like food is scarce, there is not enough of it ADJECTIVE

scarcely /sceerslee/
Almost not ADVERB
Inky's leg is so painful she can scarcely walk.

scare /sceer/
To frighten VERB
• **scare** /sceer/ NOUN
• **scared** /sceerd/ ADJECTIVE
• **scary** /sceeree/ ADJECTIVE

scarecrow /sceercroa/
Something that looks like a person that people make and put in a field to frighten the birds NOUN

scarf /scarf/
A piece of cloth people wear around the neck or head to keep warm or to look nice NOUN
■ **scarves** /scarvz/ or **scarfs** /scarfs/ PLURAL

scarlet /scarlet/
A bright red colour NOUN, ADJECTIVE

scarves /scarvz/
NOUN PLURAL ▶ **scarf**

scatter /scater/
To throw things around in lots of different places VERB

scene /seen/
1. The place where something happens
This was the scene of the accident.
2. The part of a book or film where a certain action happens NOUN

scenery /seeneree/
All the things like land and rivers you can see around you NOUN

scent /sent/
The nice smell of something NOUN
Bee loves the scent of roses.

scheme /sceem/
A plan for doing something NOUN

school /scool/
A place where children go to learn things NOUN
• **schoolboy** /scoolboi/ NOUN
• **schoolgirl** /scoolgerl/ NOUN
• **schoolteacher** /scoolteecher/ NOUN

science /sieens/
Knowing things from studying nature NOUN
• **scientific** /sieentific/ ADJECTIVE
• **scientist** /sieentist/ NOUN

Ss

scimitar /simiter/
A sword with a curved blade that is wider near the point of the blade NOUN

scissors /sizerz/
A tool for cutting paper made up of two blades fixed to handles NOUN PLURAL

scone /scon/
A little round cake that people often eat with jam and cream NOUN

scoop /scoop/
A kind of deep spoon for picking up food such as ice cream NOUN
• **scoop** /scoop/ VERB

scooter /scooter/
1. A type of bicycle with an engine and a low seat that has less power than a motorcycle 2. A toy with two wheels and a tall handle that you stand on with one foot and push along with the other NOUN

score[1] /scor/
To win a point or goal in a game or sport VERB

score[2] /scor/
The number of points someone scores in a game or sport NOUN

scorpion /scorpeeen/
An animal that looks like a big insect. It has a long curved tail with a poisonous sting at the end NOUN

scoundrel /scoundrel/
Someone who behaves dishonestly NOUN

Scout /scout/
A boy who belongs to a group called the Scouts NOUN

scramble /scrambel/
To climb and crawl using your hands and feet VERB

scrambled egg /scrambeld eg/
Egg that is mixed together and cooked in a pan NOUN

scrap /scrap/
A small piece of something NOUN
a scrap of paper

scrapbook /scrapbook/
A book with empty pages where you can stick things like pictures NOUN

scrape /scraip/
To take away something from a surface by rubbing something sharp over it VERB
Scrape the carrots before you eat them.

scratch /scrach/
1. To make a mark or cut on something
Snake scratched poor Phonic with his pencil.
2. To rub your skin because it itches VERB
• **scratch** /scrach/ NOUN

scream /screem/
To make a loud noise, for example because you are frightened or hurt VERB
• **scream** /screem/ NOUN

screech /screech/
To make a loud noise that is not pleasant VERB
• **screech** /screech/ NOUN

screen /screen/
1. A computer or television screen is the flat glass part that you look into
2. The big white area where you watch the film in a cinema 3. Something like a thin wall you can move and put around things to protect them NOUN

245

Ss

screw /scroo/
A small pointed piece of metal that people put into wood with a screwdriver to join the wood to something NOUN
• **screw** /scroo/ VERB
• **screwdriver** /scroodriever/ A tool with a kind of blade for turning screws to make them go into wood NOUN

scribble /scribel/
To write something quickly or in a careless way VERB
• **scribble** /scribel/ NOUN

scroll /scroal/
To move the words on a computer screen up or down so you can read them VERB
• **scrollbar** /scroalbar/ A tool for scrolling through words on a computer screen NOUN

scrub /scrub/
To rub something with a hard brush to make it clean VERB

scuffle /scufel/
A short fight between people that is not very serious NOUN

sculpture /sculpcher/
A statue or something special carved out of wood or stone NOUN

sea /see/
1. A very big area of water with land around most of it 2. The water that covers most of the earth NOUN
• **sea bed** /see bed/ The ground at the bottom of the sea NOUN
• **seafood** /seefood/ NOUN
• **seagull** /seegul/ A big bird that lives near the sea NOUN
• **seahorse** /seehors/ A small fish with a head that looks slightly like a horse's head NOUN
• **seashore** /seeshor/ NOUN
• **seasick** /seesic/ Sick when you travel by boat ADJECTIVE

seal[1] /seel/
1. A sea animal that eats fish and lives on land and in the sea 2. A round piece of wax used in the past to seal letters NOUN

seal[2] /seel/
To close something tightly VERB

seam /seem/
A line where two pieces of cloth are joined together NOUN

search /serch/
1. If you search for something or someone, you try to find them
2. If you search someone, you look in their pockets and clothes to find something VERB
• **search** /serch/ NOUN

seashell /seeshel/
The shell of some types of sea animals NOUN

seaside /seesied/
The part of a town next to the sea where people go for their holidays NOUN

season /seezen/
1. Spring, summer, autumn, winter are the four seasons of the year
2. A period in the year when something happens *Now is the rainy season.* NOUN

Ss

seat /seet/

A place where you sit, such as a chair or a place on a bus **NOUN**

• **seatbelt** /seet belt/ **NOUN**

seaweed /seeweed/

A plant that grows in the sea **NOUN**

second¹ /secend/

Next, coming after the first one
ADJECTIVE, **ADVERB**

second² /secend/

The thing or person that comes after the first one **PRONOUN**, **NOUN**

I was the second in the class to finish my painting.

• **second-hand** /secend hand/

Not new and already used **ADJECTIVE**
second-hand clothes

second³ /secend/

1. A very small part of a minute.
There are 60 seconds in every minute
2. A very short amount of time *Bee will be back in a second.* **NOUN**

• **second hand** /secend hand/

The short hand on a clock or watch that shows the seconds **NOUN**

secret¹ /seecret/

1. Something that only one person or a few people know about
2. **keep a secret** To not tell anyone about something **NOUN**

secret² /seecret/

If something is secret, only a few people know about it, and they do not tell anyone else **ADJECTIVE**

secretary /secreteree/

Someone who works in an office and does things like typing letters and answering the phone **NOUN**

section /secshen/

A part of something **NOUN**
This section of the road is always very busy.

see /see/

1. To look at someone or something
2. To understand *Yes, I see what you mean.*
3. To find out, or know about something
Let's wait and see what happens. 4. To meet someone *Come and see me after the lesson.*
VERB

■ **saw, seen**

seed /seed/

Something little and hard that comes from a plant and grows into a new plant **NOUN**
Inky planted sunflower seeds in her garden.

seek /seek/

To try to find something **VERB**
■ **sought**

seem /seem/

To look as if something is true **VERB**

seen /seen/

PAST PARTICIPLE ▶ **see**

seesaw /seesaw/

A long board that is fixed to the ground in the middle. Someone sits at either end to make it move up and down **NOUN**

Ss

seize /seez/
To take something quickly and violently
VERB

seldom /seldəm/
Not often ADVERB

select /select/
To choose something VERB
Would you like to select another chocolate?
• **selection** /selecshən/ NOUN

self /self/
What somebody is like NOUN
I'm glad Snake is back to his usual self.

selfish /selfish/
Only thinking about yourself and not caring about other people ADJECTIVE

sell /sel/
To give something to someone for money
VERB
■ **sold**
• **seller** /seler/ NOUN

semicircle /semeesercel/
A shape that looks like half a circle NOUN
▶ SHAPES, page 17

send /send/
To make something or someone go somewhere VERB
Inky sent a letter to her cousin in New York.
■ **sent**
• **sender** /sender/ NOUN

senior /seeneeer/
1. Older than someone 2. Having a higher job than someone ADJECTIVE
• **senior citizen** /seeneeer sitizen/
An older person, for example someone over 65 NOUN

sensational /sensaishenel/
Really good, interesting and exciting
ADJECTIVE

sense /sens/
1. Intelligence and understanding
Bee had the sense not to go out in the rain. 2. The meaning of something
3. **make sense** To be clear and easy to understand *Sentences should make sense.* 4. The five senses are the ways that people can see, smell, hear, feel and taste things *Inky has a very good sense of smell.* NOUN

sensible /sensebel/
1. Wise or good to do *It's sensible to wait for the rain to stop before we go out.*
2. A sensible person is someone who is intelligent and understands about things *Bee and Snake are always very sensible.*
ADJECTIVE

sensitive /sensetiv/
1. Easily upset or hurt 2. If something like your skin is sensitive, it can feel pain easily ADJECTIVE

sent /sent/
PAST TENSE ▶ **send**

sentence /sentens/
A group of words that starts with a capital letter and finishes with a full stop. Sentences should have meaning and include a verb NOUN

separate[1] /sepret/
Not connected to anything ADJECTIVE

separate[2] /seperait/
To divide or keep two or more things apart VERB
The teacher separated the two boys because they were talking.
• **separation** /seperaishen/ NOUN

September /september/
The ninth month of the year NOUN
▶ CALENDAR, page 13

Ss

sergeant /sarjent/
A person in the army or the police who is in charge of other people NOUN

serial /siꝝeeꝛl/
A story on television or in a magazine that is told in several parts NOUN

series /siꝝeez/
A number of things that follow one another NOUN
■ **series** /siꝝeez/ PLURAL

serious /siꝝeeꝛs/
1. Very bad *My friend had a serious accident.* 2. If someone is serious, for example in their work, they are very careful 3. If someone looks serious, they look as if they are worried ADJECTIVE
• **seriously** /siꝝeeꝛslee/ If someone is seriously hurt, they are very hurt ADVERB

serpent /serpent/
A big snake NOUN

servant /servꝛnt/
Someone who works in someone else's house doing things such as cleaning and cooking NOUN

serve /serv/
1. To give someone food or drink
2. If someone serves you in a shop or restaurant, they bring you the things you ask for 3. **serve a purpose** To be useful VERB

service /servis/
1. When someone helps you, for example in a hotel or restaurant *The service is really good here.* 2. If you talk about a bus or train service, you mean the normal journeys made by that bus or train NOUN

serviette /serveeꝛt/
A square piece of paper or cloth for keeping your clothes and hands clean when you are eating NOUN

set[1] /set/
1. To put *Bee set her books down on the table.* 2. To become solid *Wait for the glue to set.* 3. **set out** To start *Bee set out to find Snake.* 4. **set fire to** To make something burn 5. If the sun sets, it goes down and disappears in the distance VERB
■ **set**

set[2] /set/
all set Completely ready ADJECTIVE
We're all set so let's go.

settee /setee/
A long seat with a back and arms where two or three people can sit NOUN

settle /setꝛl/
1. To put yourself into a nice comfortable position 2. To go and live somewhere *My parents settled in London.* 3. To decide something like an argument VERB

several /sevrꝛl/
Not very many but more than two or three ADJECTIVE, PRONOUN
Snake has already had several meals today!

severe /seviꝛr/
1. Very bad *There was a severe weather warning.* 2. Very strict ADJECTIVE
• **severely** /seviꝛrlee/ ADVERB

sew /soꝛ/
To use a needle and thread to join things together or repair things VERB
■ **sewed, sewn**
• **sewing** /soꝛing/ NOUN
• **sewing machine** /soꝛing mꝛsheen/ NOUN

sewn /soꝛn/
PAST PARTICIPLE ▶ **sew**

sex /sex/
Whether someone is a boy or girl NOUN
They had to put their name, age and sex on the form.
• **sexual** /sexuꝛl/ ADJECTIVE

249

Ss

shade /shaid/
1. A darker and cooler area where the sunlight cannot reach *Inky, Bee and Snake sat in the shade of the flower.* 2. A lighter or darker kind of the same colour *The quilt was made with lots of different shades of blue.* NOUN
• **shade** /shaid/ VERB
• **shady** /shaidee/ ADJECTIVE

shadow /shadoa/
The dark shape that is made when something or someone gets in the way of the light NOUN

shake /shaik/
1. To move up and down or from one side to the other very quickly, or move something in this way *Inky was shaking with cold.* 2. If two people shake hands when they meet, they take each other's hand and move it up and down VERB
■ shook, shaken
• **shake** /shaik/ NOUN
• **shaky** /shaikee/ ADJECTIVE

shaken /shaiken/
PAST PARTICIPLE ▶ **shake**

shall /shal/
A word you use to tell people what you will do in the future VERB
I shall see you tomorrow.

shallow /shaloa/
Not going very far down from the ground or from the top of something
ADJECTIVE
The swimming pool is shallow at this end.

shame /shaim/
1. If you say that something is a shame, you mean you are sad about it *What a shame you can't come to my party!* 2. An unhappy feeling people have when they think they have done something wrong NOUN

shampoo /shampoo/
A liquid people use to wash their hair NOUN
• **shampoo** /shampoo/ VERB

shape¹ /shaip/
What something looks like when you look at its outside edges. For example, shapes can be round or square, or they can look like stars or hearts NOUN

shape² /shaip/
To give an object a certain shape VERB

share¹ /sheer/
1. To use or have something at the same time as someone else *My brother and I share a room.* 2. To divide things between a group of people *Inky shared her pens with Snake and Bee.* VERB

share² /sheer/
A part of something you share with someone NOUN

shark /shark/
A very big fish with lots of sharp teeth and a fin shaped like a triangle on its back NOUN

Ss

sharp[1] /sharp/
1. With a thin edge that can cut things
2. With a thin point, like a pencil
3. Strong and sudden *I felt a sharp pain.*
4. Clear and easy to see or hear
The photo was sharp. **ADJECTIVE**

sharp[2] /sharp/
If you say something happens at eight o'clock sharp, you mean it happens exactly at that time **ADVERB**

sharpen /sharpen/
To make something like a pencil or knife sharper **VERB**
• **sharpener** /sharpener/ **NOUN**

shatter /shater/
To break into lots of tiny pieces, or break something in this way **VERB**

shave /shaiv/
To cut off hair with a sharp tool called a razor **VERB**
• **shave** /shaiv/ **NOUN**
• **shaving cream** /shaiving creem/ **NOUN**

shaver /shaiver/
A special electrical tool for getting rid of hair **NOUN**

shawl /shawl/
A piece of cloth that girls and women wear around their shoulders or over their head **NOUN**

she /shee/
A female person or animal that someone has already mentioned in the sentence **PRONOUN**

shed /shed/
A small building for storing things like garden tools, often built out of wood **NOUN**

sheep /sheep/
An animal that people get wool and meat from, and keep on farms **NOUN**

■ **sheep** /sheep/ **PLURAL**

sheet /sheet/
1. One of the big pieces of thin cloth that are put on beds 2. A flat piece of something like paper or glass *Snake needs a new sheet of paper to write on.* **NOUN**

shelf /shelf/
A long narrow board fixed to a wall or inside a cupboard for putting things on **NOUN**
■ **shelves** /shelvz/ **PLURAL**

shell /shel/
The hard part on the outside of an egg, animal or nut **NOUN**
• **shellfish** /shelfish/ A sea animal such as a lobster or crab that has a shell **NOUN**
■ **shellfish** /shelfish/ **PLURAL**

shelter[1] /shelter/
A building or a place with a roof that protects people from bad weather or from danger **NOUN**

shelter[2] /shelter/
1. To go somewhere that can protect you from something like rain 2. To protect someone from bad weather or from danger **VERB**

shelves /shelvz/
NOUN PLURAL ▶ **shelf**

251

Ss

shepherd /sheperd/
Someone who looks after sheep
NOUN

sheriff /sherif/
In the USA, a sheriff is the person in charge who makes sure people obey the law NOUN

sherry /sheree/
A type of dark brown wine NOUN

shield /sheeld/
Something carried in front of your body to protect it NOUN

shift /shift/
To move VERB
Bee shifted her head to see the blackboard.
• **shift** /shift/ NOUN

shin /shin/
The front part of your leg that goes from your knee to your foot NOUN

shine /shien/
1. To make a lot of light like the sun
2. If you shine a torch somewhere, you hold it and make the light go there *It's dark outside. Can you shine a light over here?* VERB
■ **shone**
• **shine** /shien/ NOUN
• **shiny** /shienee/ ADJECTIVE

ship /ship/
A very big boat NOUN
• **shipwreck** /shiprec/ NOUN
• **shipwrecked** /shiprect/ ADJECTIVE

shirt /shert/
Something you wear with buttons down the front that has sleeves and a collar NOUN
• **shirtsleeves** /shertsleevz/ NOUN

shiver /shiver/
To shake, usually because you are cold or frightened VERB
• **shivery** /shiveree/ ADJECTIVE

shock¹ /shoc/
1. When something bad happens, and you are surprised and upset *Inky got a real shock when she saw that Phonic was broken.* 2. **electric shock** A sharp pain you get if you touch a dangerous electric wire NOUN

shock² /shoc/
To really upset and surprise someone VERB
• **shocked** /shoct/ ADJECTIVE
• **shocking** /shocing/ ADJECTIVE

shoe /shoo/
Shoes are things you wear on your feet NOUN

shoelace /shoolais/
Shoelaces are thin strings for fastening your shoes NOUN

shone /shon/
PAST TENSE ▶ **shine**

Ss

shook /shʊk/

PAST TENSE ▶ **shake**

shoot[1] /shoot/

1. To hurt or kill using a gun or some other weapon like a bow and arrow *The police officer was shot in the leg.*
2. To fire bullets from a gun or arrows from a bow *Don't shoot!* 3. In sports, to kick or throw or hit the ball to try to score 4. To move very quickly *The flames shot up into the air.* VERB

■ **shot**

shoot[2] /shoot/

A young plant or bud NOUN

shop[1] /shop/

A place where people buy things NOUN

• **shopkeeper** /shopkeeper/ NOUN

shop[2] /shop/

To buy things at a shop VERB

• **shopper** /shoper/ NOUN

• **shopping** /shoping/ When people go to shops to buy things NOUN

shore /shor/

The land that goes along the edge of a sea or lake NOUN

short /short/

1. Measuring a small distance or amount of time *Bee flew for a very short time.*
2. **short of** Not having enough of something *I must go now, I'm short of time.*
3. If a word is short for another word, it is a way of saying the other word using fewer letters *Mike is short for Michael.*
ADJECTIVE

• **shortage** /shortij/ NOUN

shortly /shortlee/

Another way of saying soon ADVERB
Snake will be back shortly.

shorts /shorts/

Trousers with short legs above the knee
NOUN PLURAL

shot[1] /shot/

When someone fires a gun NOUN
We ran into the house when we heard shots.

shot[2] /shot/

PAST TENSE ▶ **shoot**[1]

should /shʊd/

1. Used to say it is right or sensible or important to do something *He should be more careful!* 2. Used to say something will probably happen or be true *I should be finished soon.* VERB

shoulder /shoalder/

The part of your body where your arm joins your body NOUN

shout /shout/

To say something in a very loud voice
VERB

• **shout** /shout/ NOUN

shove /shuv/

To push very hard VERB
Stop shoving!

• **shove** /shuv/ NOUN

shovel /shuvel/

A tool like a spade, that is curved for lifting things like earth or snow NOUN

Ss

show[1] /shoʊ/
1. If you show someone something, you let them see it *Show me your hands.*
2. To explain something *Show me how to write the letter Q.* VERB
■ **showed**, **shown**
• **showing** /shoʊing/ NOUN
• **show-off** /shoʊ of/ Someone who tries to make people think they are good or clever NOUN

show[2] /shoʊ/
A play or entertainment NOUN

shower[1] /shoʊer/
1. A water pipe with lots of holes in that you stand under to wash yourself
2. When you wash yourself in the shower *He likes to take a shower when he comes home from school.* 3. A short fall of rain *Bee was caught in a shower on her way home.* NOUN
• **showery** /shoʊeree/ ADJECTIVE

shower[2] /shoʊer/
To wash yourself under a shower VERB

shown /shoʊn/
PAST PARTICIPLE ▶ **show**[1]

shrank /shrangk/
PAST TENSE ▶ **shrink**

shred /shred/
To cut or tear something into little pieces VERB

shrewd /shrood/
Clever and able to give good opinions about things ADJECTIVE

shriek /shreek/
A loud shout in a very high voice NOUN
• **shriek** /shreek/ VERB

shrill /shril/
Sounding very high and loud, and unpleasant to listen to ADJECTIVE

shrimp /shrimp/
A little sea animal with lots of legs, that people can eat NOUN

shrink /shringk/
To get smaller, for example when someone washes clothes VERB
Inky's hat had shrunk.
■ **shrank**, **shrunk**

shrug /shrug/
To move your shoulders up and down to show that you do not know or do not care VERB

shrunk /shrungk/
PAST PARTICIPLE ▶ **shrink**

shudder /shuder/
To shake suddenly for a moment, for example because you are frightened VERB

shut /shut/
1. To close something
2. **shut up** To stop talking VERB
■ **shut**
• **shut** /shut/ ADJECTIVE

shy /shie/
1. Worried or frightened when you are with other people 2. An animal that is shy is frightened of people and tries to hide ADJECTIVE

sick /sic/
1. Not feeling well 2. **be sick** To have the food you have eaten come back up from your stomach and out of your mouth 3. **feel sick** To not feel well, or think you are going to be sick ADJECTIVE
• **sickness** /sicnes/ Illness NOUN

Ss

side /sied/
1. One of the edges on the outside of something *A square has four sides.*
2. A position on the left or right edge of something *I have a pain in my side.*
3. A flat surface *A cube has six sides.*
4. A group or team of people
5. Another word for a TV station
Which side is the news on? **NOUN**
• **sideways** /siedwaiz/ **ADVERB**

sideboard /siedbɔrd/
A piece of furniture where people keep things like plates and glasses **NOUN**

sieve /siv/
A container with lots of tiny holes for separating solid things from liquids or bigger lumps of powder from smaller ones **NOUN**

Pour the flour into the sieve.

sigh /sie/
To take a deep noisy breath, for example because you are very sad or very happy **VERB**
• **sigh** /sie/ **NOUN**

sight /siet/
1. When you can see things *Lots of people wear glasses to improve their sight.*
2. Something that people can see *We visited all the usual sights in New York.* **NOUN**

sign¹ /sien/
1. A notice that gives some information *Can you read that sign in the window?*
2. An action that tells you something *Bee waved to Inky as a sign that she had found Snake.* 3. A mark you write that has a certain meaning *Put a plus or minus sign next to the number.* **NOUN**

Bee waved to Inky as a sign that she had found Snake.

sign² /sien/
To write your name on a letter or document **VERB**

signal /signəl/
1. An action or sound that tells someone to do something *The teacher gave the signal and we all started jumping up and down.* 2. Signals are lights with different colours that tell car or train drivers when to stop and go **NOUN**
• **signal** /signəl/ **VERB**

signature /signəcher/
Someone's name that they write in their own special way **NOUN**

sign language /sien langgwij/
A special language for people who cannot hear. Instead of words people use their hands **NOUN**

signpost /sienpoast/
A notice next to a road with the name of a place written on it. It points in the direction of the place **NOUN**
• **signposted** /sienpoastid/ **ADJECTIVE**

Ss

Sikh /seek/

A person who believes in one of the main religions of India NOUN

silent /sielent/

Not making any noise ADJECTIVE
- **silence** /sielens/ NOUN
- **silently** /sielentlee/ ADVERB

silk /silk/

A thin shiny cloth for making things like scarves and ties. Silk is made by an insect called a silkworm NOUN
- **silkworm** /silkwerm/ NOUN
- **silky** /silkee/ ADJECTIVE

silly /silee/

Not very clever and not thinking about things carefully ADJECTIVE

That's a silly idea!

silver¹ /silver/

A metal used for making jewellery that has a light grey colour NOUN

silver² /silver/

Made of silver or having a light grey colour like silver ADJECTIVE
- **silvery** /silveree/ ADJECTIVE

similar /simeler/

Almost the same but not completely ADJECTIVE
- **similarity** /simelaretee/ NOUN

simple /simpel/

1. Easy to do or to understand
2. Ordinary *It's just a simple cold.*
3. Not very intelligent ADJECTIVE
- **simplicity** /simplisetee/ NOUN
- **simply** /simplee/ ADVERB

simplify /simplifie/

To make something easier to do or to understand VERB

sin /sin/

An action that people think is wrong and against their religion NOUN
- **sin** /sin/ VERB
- **sinful** /sinfel/ ADJECTIVE

since /sins/

1. You use since when you mean that something started to happen in the past and continues until now *It's a long time since we've been to Paris.* 2. From a certain time in the past *Since then, John has learned to read.* 3. Another word for because *I won't go out now since it's raining.* CONJUNCTION, PREPOSITION, ADVERB

sincere /sinsier/

If someone is sincere, they mean what they say ADJECTIVE

sing /sing/

To make music with your voice VERB
- ■ **sang, sung**
- **singer** /singer/ NOUN
- **singing** /singing/ NOUN

single /singgel/

1. One only *Snake didn't say a single word.* 2. A single ticket by train or bus lets you go somewhere but does not let you come back again 3. If someone is single, it means they are not married ADJECTIVE
- **single** /singgel/ NOUN

singular /singgyeler/

You use the singular when you are talking about one thing or person only NOUN *Book is the singular of books.*
- **singular** /singgyeler/ ADJECTIVE

sink¹ /singk/

1. To go down into the water and disappear *The boat hit the rocks and sank.* 2. To go down into a lower position or get lower *The sun is sinking in the sky.* VERB
- ■ **sank, sunk**

Ss

sink[2] /singk/

A big bowl with taps that is fixed to a wall in a kitchen or bathroom **NOUN**

sip /sip/

To drink something slowly a little bit at a time **VERB**

• **sip** /sip/ **NOUN**

sir /ser/

A polite word that people use sometimes when they are talking to a man **NOUN**

siren /sieren/

An object that makes a very loud sound and warns people about something **NOUN**

sister /sister/

A girl or woman who has the same mother and father as you **NOUN**

sit /sit/

To rest the lower half of your body on something like a chair or on the ground **VERB**

■ sat

• **sitting** /siting/ **ADJECTIVE**

site /siet/

1. A place on the Internet where you find information about something or someone 2. A place where something happened in the past 3. The land where something is built or is going to be built **NOUN**

situated /sichooaitid/

Used to explain where something is **ADJECTIVE**

The beehive is situated on the farm.

situation /sichooaishen/

The things that are happening at a certain time **NOUN**

We're in a difficult situation.

size /siez/

1. How big something is *Inky's pens come in all different sizes.* 2. A measurement for things, for example clothes or shoes *What size shoes do you take?* **NOUN**

skate[1] /skait/

1. A shoe with a long metal bar on the bottom for moving on ice 2. Another word for a roller skate **NOUN**

skate[2] /skait/

To move along with skates **VERB**

• **skating** /skaiting/ **NOUN**

skateboard /skaitbord/

A board with four wheels on the bottom that you ride on standing up **NOUN**

skeleton /skeleten/

The bones that support your body **NOUN**

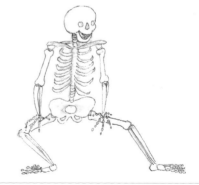

sketch /skech/

A drawing of something you do quickly and without all the details **NOUN**

• **sketch** /skech/ **VERB**

ski[1] /skee/

Skis are long thin pieces of wood or plastic or metal that people put on their feet to move quickly over the snow **NOUN**

Ss

ski[2] /skee/
To move over the snow with skis on
VERB

• **skiing** /skeeing/ NOUN

skid /skid/
To slip or slide along by accident VERB
The car skidded on the ice.
• **skid** /skid/ NOUN

skilful /skilfəl/
Able to do something well ADJECTIVE

skill /skil/
When you are good at doing something
that you have been trained to do NOUN

skin /skin/
1. The outer covering of your body
2. The outer part of some fruit and
vegetables, such as bananas NOUN

skinny /skinee/
Very thin ADJECTIVE
She's not as skinny as my sister.

skip[1] /skip/
1. To jump over a rope that you turn
around you, above your head and
under your feet 2. To move along
hopping on one foot and then on
the other 3. To miss something out
*We skipped page 20 of the book and
went straight to page 21.* VERB
• **skipping rope** /skiping roap/ NOUN

skip[2] /skip/
A very big metal container for rubbish
NOUN

skirt /skert/
A piece of clothing worn by girls and
women that hangs down loosely from
around the waist NOUN

skull /skul/
The bones in your head that protect your
brain NOUN

skunk /skungk/
A small black animal with a white stripe
down its body. It shoots a liquid with a
bad smell into the air if it is frightened
NOUN

sky /skie/
The space you can see a long way above
your head when you go outside and look
up NOUN

skyscraper /skiescraiper/
A very tall building, usually with offices
NOUN

slain /slain/
PAST PARTICIPLE ▶ **slay**

slam /slam/
1.To shut with a lot of force making
a loud noise, or shut something in this
way 2. To put something down or hit
something very hard *Dad slammed on
the brakes.* VERB
• **slam** /slam/ NOUN

Ss

slang /slang/
Slang means words or expressions that you should only use when talking to people you know well **NOUN**

slant /slant/
To lean over at an angle **VERB**
slanting handwriting

slap /slap/
To hit someone or something with your open hand **VERB**

slate /slait/
1. A kind of grey stone that breaks easily 2. Slates are small flat pieces of slate for covering roofs **NOUN**

slaughter /slawter/
To kill lots of people or animals **VERB**

slave /slaiv/
Someone who has to obey someone else because they belong to them **NOUN**

slay /slai/
To kill someone **VERB**
■ **slew, slain**

sledge /slej/
An object that you sit on to travel over snowy ground. Instead of wheels it has two long pieces of wood **NOUN**

sleep[1] /sleep/
To rest with your eyes closed and not know what is happening around you **VERB**
■ **slept**
• **sleepy** /sleepee/ **ADJECTIVE**

sleep[2] /sleep/
1. When you are sleeping, especially during the night *Bee needs more sleep than Snake.* 2. **sleep over** When you stay at someone's house all night and sleep there *Let's have a sleep over!* **NOUN**

sleeve /sleev/
Sleeves are the parts of a piece of clothing that cover your arms **NOUN**

sleigh /slai/
A large sledge pulled along by animals such as horses and reindeer **NOUN**

slender /slender/
Long and thin, or tall and thin **ADJECTIVE**
long slender fingers

slept /slept/
PAST TENSE ▶ **sleep**[1]

slew /sloo/
PAST TENSE ▶ **slay**

slice[1] /slies/
A thin piece of something like bread that someone has cut from a much bigger piece **NOUN**

slice[2] /slies/
To cut something like bread into thin pieces **VERB**

Ss

slid /slid/

PAST TENSE ▶ **slide**[1]

slide[1] /slied/

To move easily and smoothly, or move something in this way VERB

They slid down the slope on their skis.

■ slid

slide[2] /slied/

1. Something with steps up one side and a slope on the other that you slide down 2. A type of small photo that you shine a light through so you can see it on a screen 3. A small plastic clip that girls and women put in their hair to hold it in place NOUN

slight /sliet/

Very small ADJECTIVE

a slight problem

slightly /slietlee/

Only a little bit ADVERB

We're slightly late for school.

slim /slim/

Thin in a very pleasant way ADJECTIVE

slime /sliem/

Any thick wet substance that covers something NOUN

• **slimy** /sliemee/ ADJECTIVE

sling[1] /sling/

1. To throw something very hard 2. To put something somewhere so that it hangs down *Inky always slings her bag over her shoulder.* VERB

■ slung

sling[2] /sling/

If someone has their arm in a sling, they have a piece of cloth supporting it because it is hurt NOUN

slip[1] /slip/

1. To fall over because the ground is wet or greasy 2. To fall smoothly into a lower position *The glass just slipped out of my hand and fell on the floor.* 3. To go quietly without anyone seeing you *Snake slipped out of the classroom.* VERB

slip[2] /slip/

1. A little piece of paper

2. A slip or slip-up is a little mistake NOUN

slipper /sliper/

A soft shoe that people wear in their house NOUN

slippery /slipəree/

If something is slippery, it is difficult to walk on, or to hold because it is too smooth or wet or greasy ADJECTIVE

slit /slit/

To make a long thin cut in something VERB *Somebody's slit the tyres on the car.*

■ slit

• **slit** /slit/ NOUN

slither /slither/

To move along the ground smoothly or in a twisting way like a snake VERB

slog /slog/

To work really hard at something VERB

Ss

slope /slɒɒp/
1. A surface that is higher at one end than it is at the other 2. Another way of saying the side of a mountain or hill NOUN
• **slope** /slɒɒp/ VERB

slot /slot/
A little narrow hole for putting things into such as coins NOUN

slouch /slɒuch/
To sit or stand with your shoulders and head leaning forward in a lazy way VERB

slow[1] /slɒɒ/
1. Not moving or happening quickly
2. If a clock or watch is slow, the time it shows is earlier than it should be ADJECTIVE

slow[2] /slɒɒ/
To slow down is to go more slowly VERB
• **slowly** /slɒɒlee/ ADVERB

slug /slug/
A very small animal like a snail but without a shell. Slugs have soft bodies and move very slowly because they have no legs NOUN

slum /slum/
A house in bad condition that you find in a poor part of town. People use the word slums to mean the poor part of town NOUN

slung /slung/
PAST TENSE ▶ **sling**[1]

slush /slush/
Snow that is dirty and slowly becoming water NOUN

sly /slie/
Good at tricking people ADJECTIVE

smack /smac/
To hit someone with the flat part of your hand VERB
• **smack** /smac/ NOUN

small /smɑwl/
Not large or important ADJECTIVE

smart /smart/
1. Dressed in nice clothes 2. Very clever, and quick to learn things ADJECTIVE

smash /smash/
1. To break into lots of pieces
2. To hit something very hard
The truck smashed into a wall. VERB

smell[1] /smel/
What you notice about something when you breathe in through your nose NOUN
Your perfume has a sweet smell.

smell[2] /smel/
1. If something smells or if you smell something, you breathe in through your nose to notice it 2. To have a bad smell
The fruit was rotten and smelt awful. VERB
■ **smelt** or **smelled**

smile /smiel/
To make your mouth curve up to show you are happy VERB

• **smile** /smiel/ NOUN

Ss

smoke[1] /smoak/
The dark cloud that comes from something that is burning NOUN

smoke[2] /smoak/
To suck the smoke from a cigarette, cigar or pipe into the mouth VERB
- **smoker** /smoaker/ NOUN
- **smoking** /smoaking/ NOUN
- **smoky** /smoakee/ ADJECTIVE

smooth /smooth/
1. With no bumps or holes, and usually flat 2. A smooth ride or flight is pleasant because there are no bumps ADJECTIVE
- **smoothly** /smoothlee/ ADVERB

smudge[1] /smuj/
A dirty mark made by something like ink NOUN

smudge[2] /smuj/
To put a dirty mark on something VERB

smuggle /smugel/
To secretly take things into or out of a country VERB
- **smuggler** /smugeler/ NOUN
- **smuggling** /smugeling/ NOUN

snack /snac/
A little bit of food such as a sandwich that you eat between meals NOUN

snail /snail/
A very small animal with a shell and no legs that moves very slowly NOUN

snake /snaik/
An animal with a long body and smooth skin, and without any legs NOUN

snap[1] /snap/
To break with a sudden loud noise, or to break something in this way VERB

snap[2] /snap/
Snaps are pictures taken with a camera NOUN

snatch /snach/
To take something quickly with your hand VERB

sneak /sneek/
To move quietly, trying not to be seen by anyone VERB
Jack sneaked out of the classroom.

sneeze /sneez/
To make a loud noise when you suddenly blow air out through your nose VERB
- **sneeze** /sneez/ NOUN

sniff /snif/
1. To breathe in through your nose in a noisy way, usually with short breaths 2. To smell something and breathe in noisily at the same time VERB

snip /snip/
To cut something with scissors in one go VERB

snooker /snooker/
A game played on a big table where coloured balls are hit into holes with a long stick called a cue NOUN

Ss

snore /snɔr/
To make a loud breathing noise when
you sleep **VERB**
• **snore** /snɔr/ **NOUN**

snort /snɔrt/
To make a loud noise when you breathe
out through your nose **VERB**

snout /snɑut/
The long nose of an animal like a pig
NOUN

snow /snɒɑ/
Soft pieces of white ice that fall from
the sky **NOUN**

• **snow** /snɒɑ/ **VERB**
• **snowball** /snɒɑbawl/ **NOUN**
• **snowflake** /snɒɑflaik/ **NOUN**
• **snowman** /snɒɑman/ **NOUN**
• **snowstorm** /snɒɑstɔrm/ **NOUN**
• **snowy** /snɒɑee/ **ADJECTIVE**

snug /snug/
Feeling warm and comfortable and
protected, for example when you are
in bed **ADJECTIVE**

so /sɒɑ/
1. For this reason *It's late so we must
go home now.* 2. Another way of saying
very or very much because you are
giving great importance to a word in
the sentence *There are so many people
and there's so much noise.* 3. Also *You like
reading? So do I!* **ADVERB**, **CONJUNCTION**

soak /sɒɑk/
1. To make something or someone
very wet *The rain soaked Bee completely.*
2. To put something into liquid and
leave it there for a time **VERB**

The rain soaked Bee completely.

• **soaked** /sɒɑkt/ **ADJECTIVE**
• **soaking** /sɒɑking/ **ADJECTIVE**

soap /sɒɑp/
Something people use with water for
washing their body or other things.
Soap is usually hard but can also be
liquid **NOUN**
• **soapy** /sɒɑpee/ **ADJECTIVE**

soar /sɔr/
To go up quickly into the air or to a
higher level **VERB**

sob /sob/
To cry and breathe with short breaths
in a noisy way **VERB**

sober /sɒɑber/
1. If someone is sober, they have not
drunk too much alcohol 2. Serious and
quiet **ADJECTIVE**

society /sɒsieɹtee/
1. Everyone, when you talk about all
the people who live in a certain place
2. A small group of people interested
in the same thing **NOUN**

Ss

sock /soc/
Socks are things people wear on their feet inside their shoes NOUN

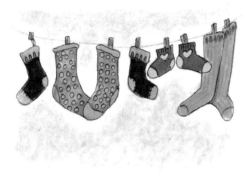

socket /socit/
An object with holes that a plug fits into to make electrical things work NOUN

sofa /soafe/
A soft and comfortable seat with a back and arms for two or three people NOUN

soft /soft/
1. Something soft can be pressed in easily when you touch it. Things like a cushion or a tennis ball are soft
2. A soft drink, like lemonade, does not contain any alcohol ADJECTIVE
• **soften** /sofen/
To make something soft VERB

software /softweer/
All the programs in a computer that make it work NOUN

soggy /sogee/
Very wet and soft ADJECTIVE
soggy ground

soil /soil/
The substance that plants grow in that covers the surface of the earth NOUN

solar /soaler/
Connected with the sun ADJECTIVE

solar system /soaler sistem/
Our solar system is made up of the sun and all the planets that go around it NOUN

sold /soald/
PAST TENSE ▸ **sell**

soldier /soaljer/
A man or woman who belongs to an army NOUN

sole /soal/
The flat part at the bottom of your foot or shoe NOUN

solid /solid/
1. Hard, not a liquid *My ice cream is frozen solid.* 2. With no empty spaces inside, and not made up from other pieces joined together *Inky's table top is made from a solid block of wood.* 3. Strong and not likely to break *Snake's chair is very solid.* ADJECTIVE

solution /selooshen/
The answer to a problem NOUN

solve /solv/
To find the answer to a problem VERB

some[1] /sum/
1. Used to mean a number of things or an amount of something *Snake ate some cake.* 2. A word you use if you talk about someone or something but you do not say exactly who or what *That happened some time last year.* ADJECTIVE

some[2] /sum/
Part of a bigger number of things or a bigger amount of something PRONOUN
I only drank some of the coffee.

someone /sumwun/
Or **somebody** /sumbodee/ A person you talk about but you do not say exactly who PRONOUN

Ss

somersault /sumersawlt/
When you make your body into a ball shape and roll it along the ground or through the air NOUN

something /sumthing/
A thing you talk about but you do not say exactly what it is PRONOUN

sometime /sumtiem/
At some time in the future or the past ADVERB

sometimes /sumtiemz/
On some occasions but not all the time ADVERB

somewhere /sumweer/
In some place but you do not say where ADVERB

son /sun/
The male child of a mother or father NOUN

song /song/
Words that you sing NOUN

soon /soon/
After a small amount of time ADVERB
Inky will begin the lesson soon.

sooner /sooner/
Earlier than something, or more quickly ADVERB
Can't you finish any sooner?

soot /soot/
The black powder that is left when people burn something like coal NOUN

sorcerer /sorserer/
A person who does magic NOUN

sore[1] /sor/
Painful ADJECTIVE

sore[2] /sor/
An area of your skin that is painful, for example because you have an illness there caused by germs NOUN

sorrow /soroa/
A feeling of being very sad NOUN

sorry /soree/
1. Sad about something you have done or something that has happened
2. Used when you want someone to forgive you for something you have done *Sorry, I won't be naughty again.*
3. Used when you want someone to repeat something *Sorry, can you say your name again?* ADJECTIVE

sort[1] /sort/
A thing or person that belongs to a certain type or group NOUN
What sort of weather did you have today?

sort[2] /sort/
1. To arrange things neatly in a certain way *Snake sorted out the books into four piles.* 2. **sort out** To find an answer to a problem VERB

sought /sawt/
PAST TENSE ▶ **seek**

soul /soal/
1. The part of a person that is not their body, that some people believe lives after they die 2. Another word for a person *There wasn't a soul in the park.* NOUN

265

Ss

sound¹ /sound/
Something you can hear NOUN

sound² /sound/
1. Used to describe the way something or someone seems to you *You sound as if you're tired.* 2. To make a noise VERB

soup /soop/
A food that is liquid made from cooking things such as vegetables or meat together NOUN

sour /souer/
Tasting bitter like a lemon ADJECTIVE

source /sors/
Where something comes from NOUN

south /south/
The direction opposite north NOUN

▶ WORLD MAP, page 14
• **south** /south/ ADJECTIVE, ADVERB

souvenir /soovenier/
Something you buy that makes you think about a place or an event NOUN
We brought back a souvenir from Wales.

sow /soa/
To plant seeds in the ground VERB
■ sowed, sown

space¹ /spais/
1. An empty place for something
There's plenty of space for you at the table.
2. The very big area outside the earth where the sun, moon, planets and stars are *The rocket went up into space.* NOUN

space² /spais/
To arrange things so there is a space between them VERB

space bar /spais bar/
A bar on a computer keyboard that you press to make a space in between the words on the screen NOUN

spaceship /spaisship/
A big machine like a long tube that carries people and things into space NOUN
• **space station** /spais staishen/ NOUN
• **spacesuit** /spaissoot/ NOUN

spacing /spaising/
The amount of space between things such as words on a page NOUN

spade /spaid/
A tool with a long handle and a flat metal part at the end for digging the earth NOUN

spaghetti /spegetee/
Food made from long pieces of pasta like string NOUN

spank /spangk/
If you spank a child, you hit them with the flat part of your hand on their bottom VERB
• **spanking** /spangking/ NOUN

Ss

spanner /spaner/
A metal tool that fits around pieces of metal called nuts and turns them to make them tighter or looser NOUN

spare[1] /speer/
1. Kept in case you need the same thing again *I always have a spare pair of glasses.*
2. **spare time** Time when you do not have to work and you can do what you like ADJECTIVE

spare[2] /speer/
To have enough of something so that you can give some of it away VERB
Inky grew so many beans she had plenty to spare for her friends.
• **spare** /speer/ NOUN

spark /spark/
A tiny piece of something burning, for example something that jumps suddenly out of a fire NOUN

sparkle /sparkel/
To shine with flashes of light like a diamond VERB
• **sparkle** /sparkel/ NOUN

sparrow /sparoa/
A small brown bird like a finch NOUN

spat /spat/
PAST TENSE ▶ **spit**

speak /speek/
1. To say words 2. **speak a language**
To know how to use a language and say words in it *Inky might teach Snake and Bee how to speak French.* VERB
■ **spoke, spoken**
• **speaker** /speeker/ NOUN

spear /spier/
A long thin weapon with a point at the end that was used in the past for throwing NOUN

special /speshel/
1. Better and more important than what is usual *Today is a special day, it's my birthday.* 2. Different from normal, and belonging to one person or group *We all have our own special way of writing our names.* ADJECTIVE

specially /speshelee/
Used as another way of saying most of all or for a certain reason ADVERB
I bought this book specially for John.

speck /spec/
A tiny spot of something like dirt NOUN

spectacle /spectecel/
Something exciting that people can watch NOUN

spectacles /spectecelz/
Another word for the glasses that you wear on your eyes NOUN PLURAL

spectacular /spectacyeler/
Very big or good or important ADJECTIVE

speech /speech/
1. The words someone speaks in front of a lot of people 2. The power to be able to speak NOUN

speed[1] /speed/
How quickly or slowly something moves or happens NOUN

speed[2] /speed/
1. To move fast
2. **speed up** To move faster VERB
• **speedy** /speedee/ ADJECTIVE

speeding /speeding/
A crime when someone drives a car too fast NOUN

spell[1] /spel/
To say or write the correct letters in a word in the correct order VERB
■ **spelt** or **spelled**
• **spelling** /speling/ NOUN

Ss

spell[2] /spel/
If someone like a magician puts a spell on someone, they say special words and magic things happen **NOUN**

spelt /spelt/
PAST TENSE ▶ **spell**[1]

spend /spend/
1. To pay out money to buy things
Snake likes to spend money on food.
2. **spend time** To stay somewhere or do something for a period of time
We spent a week in New York. **VERB**
■ **spent**

sphere /sfier/
A round shape like a ball **NOUN**
▶ SHAPES, page 17

spice /spies/
A powder made from plants that people add to food to give it more taste **NOUN**
• **spicy** /spiesee/ **ADJECTIVE**

spider /spieder/
A little animal like an insect with eight long legs. Spiders spin webs to catch their food **NOUN**

spike /spiek/
A thin piece of metal with a point, for example on the top of an iron fence **NOUN**

spill /spil/
If a liquid spills, or if you spill it, some of it or all of it suddenly comes out of its container **VERB**
I spilt the tea all over the carpet.
■ **spilt** or **spilled**

spin /spin/
1. To turn around and around very quickly, or turn something in this way
2. To make threads, like a spider does when it makes its web **VERB**
■ **spun**

spinach /spinij/
A vegetable with dark green leaves that are cooked and eaten **NOUN**

spine /spien/
The line of bones that goes down the middle of your back **NOUN**

spiral /spierøl/
A shape with lots of circles that wind around and around inside each other **NOUN**

a spiral staircase

spire /spieer/
The pointed top on a church tower **NOUN**

spirit /spirøt/
1. A person's spirit is the part of them that lives after they die 2. Evil spirits are imaginary creatures like ghosts that have the power to do bad things **NOUN**

spit /spit/
1. If someone spits, they shoot some watery liquid out of their mouth *It's very rude to spit.* 2. If it is spitting, there are a few drops of rain falling **VERB**
■ **spat** or **spit**
• **spit** /spit/ **NOUN**

spiteful /spietfel/
Deliberately nasty to people to try to upset them ADJECTIVE

splash /splash/
1. If a liquid splashes somewhere, lots of it goes onto something or hits something noisily *My coffee splashed onto the carpet.*
2. If you splash in the water, you make a noise as you move around hitting the water VERB
• **splash** /splash/ NOUN

splendid /splendid/
Very very good ADJECTIVE

splinter /splinter/
A thin piece of wood or glass that has broken off from something and is sharp and dangerous NOUN
Be careful not to get a splinter in your finger.

split /split/
1. To break something or divide it into smaller parts *Our teacher split the class into two.* 2. To make a thin cut in something, or to get a thin cut *The bag was so full that it just split.* VERB
■ **split**
• **split** /split/ NOUN

spoil /spoil/
1. To do something that will annoy or ruin what someone else is doing *The rain spoiled our day at the seaside.*
2. If someone spoils a child, they let them do everything they want, and this makes them behave badly VERB
■ **spoiled** or **spoilt**

spoilsport /spoilsport/
Someone who spoils someone else's fun NOUN

spoilt[1] /spoilt/
Or **spoiled** /spoild/ A spoilt child always gets what they want and behaves badly ADJECTIVE

spoilt[2] /spoilt/
PAST TENSE ▶ **spoil**

spoke /spoak/
PAST TENSE ▶ **speak**

spoken[1] /spoaken/
Spoken English is the sort of English people say and not write ADJECTIVE

spoken[2] /spoaken/
PAST PARTICIPLE ▶ **speak**

sponge /spunj/
A piece of soft material with lots of holes that people use for sucking up water, and for washing and cleaning things NOUN

spooky /spookee/
Another word for frightening ADJECTIVE

spoon /spoon/
Something you use for eating liquids such as soup. Spoons have a little bowl at one end and a long handle NOUN

sport /sport/
A game people or groups play to try and win. Sports are usually played outside and involve a lot of physical activity NOUN
• **sportsman** /sportsmen/ NOUN
• **sportswoman** /sportswoomen/ NOUN
• **sporty** /sportee/ ADJECTIVE

sports /sports/
Connected with sport such as a sports field or club ADJECTIVE

Ss

Ss

spot¹ /spot/
1. Another word for place *Let's look for a nice spot for our picnic.* 2. A tiny red bump on your skin 3. A little round shape that has a different colour to the rest of something *Catherine wore a beautiful dress with flowers and green spots.* 4. A dirty mark on something *There's a spot of grease on my shirt.* NOUN

spot² /spot/
To notice someone or something VERB

spotted /spotid/
Covered with little round shapes, like the fur of some animals ADJECTIVE
• **spotty** /spotee/ ADJECTIVE

spout /spout/
The small tube on some containers like a kettle that you pour the water through NOUN

sprain /sprain/
To accidentally twist your ankle or wrist too far so that they hurt VERB

sprang /sprang/
PAST TENSE ▶ **spring**²

spray¹ /sprai/
To make lots of tiny drops of liquid come out into the air like a thin cloud VERB

spray² /sprai/
1. A can or bottle with a liquid in it that you spray into the air *We need some insect spray.* 2. A thin cloud made up of tiny drops of a liquid NOUN

spread /spred/
1. To smooth something on a surface, or put something over it to cover it *I like to spread butter on my bread.* • *Dad spreads the newspaper all over the table.* 2. If something like a fire spreads, it moves and covers a bigger amount of space 3. If something like an illness spreads, it affects more and more people VERB
■ **spread**

spring¹ /spring/
1. One of the seasons in the year. In the spring the flowers and trees start to grow again and lots of baby animals are born ▶ CALENDAR, page 13 2. A thin piece of curved wire that always goes back to its normal shape after you press or pull it *Some of the springs in Inky's mattress are broken.* 3. Water that comes up from under the ground and makes a small river or pool NOUN

spring² /spring/
To move quickly, or to jump up quickly VERB
■ **sprang, sprung**

sprinkle /springkel/
To scatter tiny amounts of something all over something else VERB
Snake sprinkles lots of salt over his dinner.

Ss

sprout[1] /sprout/
Sprouts are little hard round vegetables made up of lots of leaves **NOUN**

sprout[2] /sprout/
To start to grow **VERB**

sprung /sprung/
PAST PARTICIPLE ▶ **spring**[2]

spun /spun/
PAST TENSE ▶ **spin**

spy /spie/
Someone who tries to get secret information about things or people **NOUN**
• **spy** /spie/ **VERB**

square /squeer/
1. A shape that has four straight sides, all of the same length, and four corners ▶ **SHAPES**, page 17 2. A big open space in a town, that has the shape of a square *Trafalgar Square* **NOUN**
• **square** /squeer/ **ADJECTIVE**

squash[1] /squosh/
To push down on something or hit it so hard that it gets flatter **VERB**
A machine was used to squash old cars.

squash[2] /squosh/
1. A game that people play where they hit a ball against a wall using something with strings and a handle, called a racket 2. A drink made from fruit juice, sugar and water **NOUN**
• **squashed** /squosht/ **ADJECTIVE**

squeak /squeek/
To make a high noise that is not very loud **VERB** *The other mouse squeaked at Inky.*
• **squeak** /squeek/ **NOUN**

squeeze /squeez/
1. To press something hard 2. To press your body hard so that it goes through or into a small space **VERB**
• **squeeze** /squeez/ **NOUN**

squid /squid/
A sea animal with ten long arms that people eat as food **NOUN**

squint[1] /squint/
When someone's eyes look in different directions **NOUN**

squint[2] /squint/
To close your eyes slightly to see better **VERB**

squirrel /squirel/
A grey or red-brown animal with a long thick tail. Squirrels live in trees and eat nuts **NOUN**

squirt /squert/
To make a thin flow of a liquid come out of something suddenly **VERB**
Bee squirted the water pistol at Snake.

stab /stab/
To push a knife or something sharp into something or someone **VERB**

stable[1] /staibel/
A building where people keep horses or sometimes other farm animals **NOUN**

stable[2] /staibel/
Staying the same and not likely to change **ADJECTIVE**

stack[1] /stac/
A lot of things that are on top of each other **NOUN**
There's a stack of books on Inky's desk.

Ss

stack[2] /stac/
To put lots of things on top of each other VERB

stadium /staideeem/
A big building where people come to watch sports NOUN
a football stadium

staff /staf/
All the people who work together in a place like an office or hospital NOUN

stag /stag/
A male deer that has big horns on its head like branches NOUN

stage /staij/
1. The part of a theatre where people act in plays, or where they play music, sing or dance 2. A part of someone's journey 3. A certain time for something, such as a stage in someone's life NOUN

stagecoach /staijcoach/
A vehicle with wheels pulled by horses that was used in past times to carry people and letters NOUN

stagger /stager/
1. To have trouble walking or standing and to look as if you might fall over
2. If someone is staggered by something, they are very surprised VERB

stain /stain/
A dirty mark that is accidentally put on something NOUN
• **stain** /stain/ VERB

stair /steer/
Stairs are flat pieces of wood or stone that you walk up or down when you want to go to a different level NOUN
• **staircase** /steercais/ NOUN

stale /stail/
Not fresh. Stale food is not good to eat because it is old ADJECTIVE

stalk /stawk/
A long thin part of a plant that stands upright and joins the flowers or the fruit to the rest of the plant NOUN

stammer /stamer/
To have difficulty saying words. People who stammer often repeat a sound in a word a lot of times VERB
• **stammer** /stamer/ NOUN

stamp[1] /stamp/
1. A little piece of paper with a picture that you stick on an envelope or package so it can be sent through the post 2. A block of wood or metal with a pattern that you put into ink and press onto something like paper to leave a mark *a rubber stamp* 3. A mark made on something with a stamp *Inky has a stamp in her passport from Argentina.* NOUN

stamp[2] /stamp/
1. To put your foot down on the ground making a lot of noise 2. To press a mark onto a piece of paper with ink and usually a rubber stamp VERB

Ss

stand[1] /stand/
1. To have your feet on the ground while your body and legs are straight
2. To be somewhere, or to put something somewhere *Our house stands at the bottom of a hill. · Can you stand my umbrella in the corner?* 3. If you say you cannot stand someone or something, it means you really do not like them or you really do not like doing it *Bee can't stand being late.*
4. If letters stand for something, that is what they mean *US stands for United States.* VERB
■ **stood**

stand[2] /stand/
1. A table where people show their things in an exhibition 2. An object for holding things *I left my umbrella in the umbrella stand.* NOUN

standard /standerd/
Normal or typical ADJECTIVE
These hats come in standard sizes.

stank /stangk/
PAST TENSE ▶ **stink**

staple /staipel/
A little piece of wire that you press through a few sheets of paper to hold them together. You use a stapler to make the staple go into the paper NOUN

star[1] /star/
1. A point of bright light in the sky at night. Stars are balls of hot gas
2. A shape that looks like a ball with five or more regular points sticking out of it *Inky gave Bee and Snake a star for good work.* ▶ SHAPES, page 17 3. A famous person such as an actor or sportsman NOUN

star[2] /star/
If someone stars in a film, they are the main actor in it VERB

stare /steer/
To look at someone or something for a long time without turning your head away VERB

starfish /starfish/
A flat sea animal that has the shape of a star NOUN

starling /starling/
A small bird with dark feathers NOUN

start[1] /start/
1. To do something that you were not doing before *We start school at nine o'clock.*
2. To happen at a certain time and continue for a while *Lessons will start again this afternoon.* 3. If a machine starts or you start it, you make it work *Dad couldn't start the car.* VERB

start[2] /start/
1. The very first part of something
2. The place where a journey or race starts NOUN

Ss

startle /startel/
To frighten a person or animal suddenly
VERB

starve /starv/
To suffer or die because there is not
enough food to eat VERB
• **starving** /starving/ ADJECTIVE

state /stait/
1. What someone or something is like
These roads are in a bad state. 2. A nation
or country *the United States of America*
3. A part of some countries like the USA
the State of Florida NOUN

station /staishen/
1. A place where trains or buses stop so
that people can get on and off *Meet us
at the railway station.* 2. A place where a
certain kind of work takes place, such as
a police station or a radio station NOUN

stationary /staisheneree/
Not moving ADJECTIVE
a stationary car

stationery /staisheneree/
Things you need for writing such
as paper, pens and ink NOUN

statue /statue/
An image of a person or animal made
out of stone or another hard material.
Statues are usually very big NOUN

stay /stai/
1. To live in a place for a little while *We
stayed in Paris for two days.* 2. To continue
as someone or something was before
I'm tired but I'll try and stay awake.
VERB
• **stay** /stai/ NOUN

steady /stedee/
1. Not moving much *If you're a painter,
you need a steady hand.* 2. Changing
slowly but all the time *a steady increase.*
3. Keeping at the same level *You have a
steady heartbeat.* ADJECTIVE

steal /steel/
To take something that belongs to
someone else VERB
■ **stole, stolen**

steam /steem/
A thin cloud made up of tiny drops of
water when the water is boiled
NOUN

steamroller /steemroaler/
A vehicle with very wide heavy wheels
for making roads flat when people build
or repair the roads NOUN

steel /steel/
A very strong metal made mainly from
iron NOUN

steep /steep/
Sloping very quickly ADJECTIVE
We live at the bottom of a steep hill.

steer /stier/
To control the direction of something like
a car or bicycle VERB
• **steering wheel** /stiering weel/ NOUN

stem /stem/
The long middle part of a plant that
stands upright. The flowers and the
leaves grow from the stem NOUN

Ss

step¹ /step/
1. When you put one leg in front of the other to walk or run *The baby took her first few steps.* 2. A flat piece of wood or stone that you walk up or down to go to a different level **NOUN**

step² /step/
1. To put one leg in front of the other as you walk or run *I stepped onto the bus.* 2. To walk *Please step this way.* **VERB**

stereo /stereeoɑ/
A machine for listening to CDs, cassettes and the radio where the sound comes from two different objects, called speakers **NOUN**
• **stereo** /stereeoɑ/ **ADJECTIVE**

stethoscope /stethescoɑp/
Something a doctor uses to listen to your heart beating **NOUN**

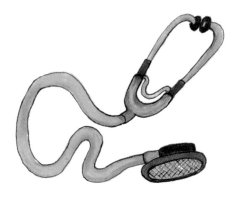

stew /stue/
A dish of vegetables and meat or fish that people cook together with lots of liquid **NOUN**
• **stew** /stue/ **VERB**

stick¹ /stic/
A long thin piece of wood. There are lots of different kinds of sticks that people use for different things, such as walking sticks or hockey sticks or drumsticks **NOUN**

stick² /stic/
1. To fix something onto something else, usually with glue *Bee stuck the stamp onto the envelope.* 2. To become fixed to something or become fixed in one position *The egg stuck to the frying pan.* 3. If something sticks out, you can see the end of it because it goes further than the main part of something *Inky's feet stuck out underneath the blanket.* **VERB**
■ **stuck**

sticker /sticer/
A piece of paper with a picture that you stick onto something **NOUN**

sticky /sticee/
1. If something like jam or glue is sticky, it can easily become fixed to other things 2. Sticky objects are covered with something that makes them stick to other things *sticky labels* **ADJECTIVE**

stiff /stif/
1. Hard, and not easy to bend *This paper is very stiff.* 2. If a part of your body is stiff, or if you feel stiff, you have a slight pain in your muscle when you move that part of your body *I woke up today with a stiff leg.* 3. Not easy to move *This drawer is stiff.* **ADJECTIVE**

still¹ /stil/
1. Used to talk about something that is continuing until the present time and that has not changed or stopped *It's still raining.* 2. Used to mean that something is true even though you have just said something else that makes that seem surprising *It's late but we can still get home before it gets dark.* 3. More than something else, or more than before *This book is good but that one is better still.* **ADVERB**

still² /stil/
1. Not moving *Stand still for a moment!* 2. Quiet *The streets around our house are very still.* **ADJECTIVE**

Ss

stilts /stilts/
Two long poles with places for your feet that people use for walking high above the ground NOUN PLURAL

sting /sting/
If an insect or animal stings you, it pushes a pointed part of its body into your skin and causes you pain VERB
Bee can sting but she never does!
- ■ **stung**
- • **sting** /sting/ NOUN

stink /stingk/
To smell very bad VERB
This fish stinks!
- ■ **stank, stunk**
- • **stink** /stingk/ NOUN
- • **stinking** /stingking/ ADJECTIVE

stir /ster/
To move something soft or liquid around, usually with a spoon VERB

stitch[1] /stich/
1. Stitches are the loops of thread made in sewing or knitting 2. A way of using the needle when you sew or knit *Watch me do this stitch.* NOUN

stitch[2] /stich/
To join pieces of cloth together with a needle and thread VERB

stole /stoal/
PAST TENSE ▶ **steal**
- • **stolen** /stoalen/
  PAST PARTICIPLE ▶ **steal**

stomach /stumec/
1. The soft part of your body below your chest 2. The part inside your body where the food goes NOUN
▶ PARTS OF THE BODY, page 18

stone /stoan/
1. The hard substance that the earth is made of, or a little piece of it. Rocks are made of stone 2. A piece of stone that has a certain shape *a paving stone* 3. The big hard seed in some fruits like peaches NOUN
- • **stony** /stoanee/ ADJECTIVE

stood /stood/
PAST TENSE ▶ **stand**[1]

stool /stool/
A seat with three or four legs but with no back or arms NOUN

stoop /stoop/
1. To stand with your head and shoulders bent downwards 2. To bend your body downwards to do something VERB
- • **stoop** /stoop/ NOUN

Ss

stop /stop/
1. To not do something any more, or to make sure something or someone does not do something any more 2. To not move any more, or to make someone or something not move *I stopped the ball.*
VERB

stopper /stoper/
Something in the top of a bottle to stop the liquid coming out **NOUN**

store[1] /stor/
1. A very big shop selling lots of different things 2. An amount of something that people keep to use later **NOUN**

store[2] /stor/
To keep something somewhere **VERB**

storey /storree/
All the rooms on one level of a building **NOUN**

stork /stork/
A bird with very long legs and a long beak **NOUN**

storm /storm/
Very bad weather with lots of rain and strong wind **NOUN**
• **stormy** /stormee/ **ADJECTIVE**

story /storree/
1. A description of something that happens that can be imaginary or true *It's a story about a king in a country far away.* 2. Something said that is not true *My friend's always telling stories and I don't believe him.* **NOUN**
• **storybook** /storreebook/ **NOUN**

stove /stoav/
A big metal object for cooking food or keeping rooms warm **NOUN**

straight[1] /strait/
1. Going in one direction only *Can you draw a straight line, Bee?* 2. In the correct position and level or upright *The picture on the wall is crooked. Can you put it straight?* 3. Honest *Please give me a straight answer.* **ADJECTIVE**

straight[2] /strait/
1. Moving in one direction without turning *Bee was flying straight at Inky.* 2. Immediately, without doing anything else *I'm tired so I'm going straight to bed.* 3. Exactly *Alex was walking straight in front of me.* **ADVERB**
• **straight away** /strait ewai/ Immediately **ADVERB**
• **straighten** /straiten/ **VERB**

strain /strain/
1. To hurt yourself when you stretch or push too much 2. To try hard to do something difficult 3. To pour food through a strainer or sieve to separate the liquid from the solid part **VERB**
• **strainer** /strainer/ **NOUN**

strange /strainj/
1. Not normal, or different in some way *I heard a strange noise.* 2. A strange thing or person is something or someone you do not know *Have you ever lived in a strange country?* **ADJECTIVE**

Ss

stranger /strainjer/
1. Someone you do not know
2. Someone who does not know a place very well NOUN

strangle /stranggel/
To kill, or try to kill, someone by squeezing their throat so they cannot breathe VERB

strap /strap/
A narrow piece of material like cloth or leather that is fixed to something. People use straps for holding things or fastening things NOUN
• **strap** /strap/ VERB

straw /straw/
1. The dry yellow stems of plants such as wheat 2. A very thin tube of plastic or paper for drinking cold drinks such as lemonade NOUN

strawberry /strawberee/
A little soft red fruit with tiny seeds on its skin. Strawberries grow on a plant near the ground NOUN

stray[1] /strai/
To move away from the right road or path VERB

stray[2] /strai/
An animal that has become lost ADJECTIVE

stream /streem/
1. A small river 2. Something that keeps moving all the time like liquid from a pipe or cars on a road NOUN
• **stream** /streem/ VERB

street /street/
A road in a town with buildings in it NOUN

strength /strength/
1. The power to do physical things like moving and lifting 2. The power of something to move or hold something heavy or to be hit without breaking
The castle has walls of great strength. NOUN
• **strengthen** /strengthen/ VERB

stress /stres/
When you are worried because you have problems in your life such as too much work or not enough money NOUN

stretch /strech/
1. To pull something and make it longer or wider 2. To become longer or wider when pulled 3. To make your arms or legs straight and long, for example when you wake up 4. To go all the way somewhere
The forest stretches as far as the river. VERB

stretcher /strecher/
A piece of cloth with poles each side that people use for carrying someone who is injured or dead NOUN

strict /strict/
Having very strong rules and wanting people to obey them ADJECTIVE

strike[1] /striek/
1. To hit someone or something 2. To stop working because you are angry about something to do with your job VERB
■ struck

strike[2] /striek/
If someone in a factory or office is on strike they have stopped working because they are angry NOUN

Ss

string /string/
1. A long thin material made of substances called fibres that are twisted together. String is used for tying things
2. Strings are the long thin pieces of nylon or other materials on musical instruments like guitars. The strings make the sounds **NOUN**

strip[1] /strip/
1. To take off your clothes or someone else's clothes 2. To take away all the things that cover something *The wind stripped the leaves off the tree.* **VERB**

strip[2] /strip/
A long piece of something **NOUN**
a strip of cloth

stripe /striep/
A line that has a different colour to the areas next to it **NOUN**

stroke[1] /strɒak/
To move your hand gently up and down over something **VERB**
Our cat loves to be stroked.

stroke[2] /strɒak/
1. A stroke of luck is a sudden amount of luck that you have 2. A mark made with your pen or with a paintbrush
3. A sudden serious illness of the brain
NOUN

stroll /strɒal/
A slow walk somewhere that is very relaxing **NOUN**
• **stroll** /strɒal/ **VERB**

strong /strong/
1. Having a lot of power in your body
2. Done with a lot of power *The horse gave a strong kick.* 3. Not easy to break or damage *This is a strong chair.* 4. Good at something *Our team needs another strong player.* **ADJECTIVE**

struck /struc/
PAST TENSE ▶ **strike**[1]

struggle /strugel/
1. To try very hard to do something
2. To fight against someone or something
VERB
• **struggle** /strugel/ **NOUN**

stubborn /stubern/
Doing what you want to do and not wanting to change your ideas **ADJECTIVE**

stuck[1] /stuc/
Not able to move or continue **ADJECTIVE**
Inky's boots got stuck in the mud.

stuck[2] /stuc/
PAST TENSE ▶ **stick**[2]

student /stuedent/
Someone who studies at a university or school **NOUN**

studio /stuedeeɒa/
1. A place where people make radio or television programmes, or films
2. A room where a painter or a photographer works **NOUN**

Ss

study /studee/
To spend a lot of time learning about something, usually when you go to school or university VERB
• **study** /studee/ NOUN

stuff /stuf/
To push something into something else VERB *Snake stuffed his breakfast into his mouth.*

stuffy /stufee/
1. A stuffy room does not have enough air and is too warm 2. A stuffy nose is blocked up, usually because you have a cold ADJECTIVE

stumble /stumbel/
To fall over or almost fall VERB

stump /stump/
The part of a tree trunk that is left after the rest of the tree has been cut down NOUN

stung /stung/
PAST TENSE ▶ **sting**

stunk /stungk/
PAST PARTICIPLE ▶ **stink**

stupid /stuepid/
A stupid person is not intelligent or sensible, and does not think about things carefully ADJECTIVE
• **stupidity** /stuepidetee/ NOUN

stutter /stuter/
To repeat the sounds in words lots of times because you are nervous or have a problem VERB
• **stutter** /stuter/ NOUN

sty /stie/
A place where pigs live NOUN

style /stiel/
A way of doing or making things NOUN
a new hair style

subject /subject/
1. Something people talk about. If you change the subject, you want to talk about something else 2. Something you learn in school, like English or maths NOUN

submarine /submereen/
A kind of ship that travels under the sea NOUN

substance /substens/
A substance is any kind of thing that is in a liquid, solid or powder form NOUN
Don't drink that, it's a poisonous substance.

subtract /sebtract/
To take one number away from another number VERB
Can you subtract 18 from 23?
• **subtraction** /sebtracshen/ NOUN

suburb /suberb/
A suburb or the suburbs are an area with lots of houses just outside a big town NOUN

subway /subwai/
A tunnel under a street for people to walk through NOUN

succeed /secseed/
1. To do well in something, for example in school or in your job 2. To do something you wanted to do *Bee and Snake succeeded in learning to read.* VERB
• **success** /secses/ Doing well, or doing something you wanted to do NOUN
• **successful** /secsesfel/ ADJECTIVE

Ss

such /such/

1. A word you use to mean the certain kind of thing or person you are talking about   *Teachers such as Inky are hard to find.* 2. A word you use to give a special importance to something you are talking about   *Yesterday was such a rainy day!* · *Snake and Bee are such good students.*
ADJECTIVE

suck /suc/

1.To pull a liquid into your mouth with your breath   *Snake sucked the lemonade through a straw.* 2. To keep something like a sweet in your mouth without chewing it   *Snake was sucking a lollipop.* **VERB**

sudden /suden/

Happening quickly and without you expecting it **ADJECTIVE**
· **suddenly** /sudenlee/ **ADVERB**

suffer /sufer/

To feel pain or feel sad because something bad has happened **VERB**
Alice has toothache. She's suffering very much.

suffocate /sufecait/

To die because there is not enough air to breathe **VERB**

sugar /shooger/

A brown or white powder that people add to food and drinks to make them taste sweet **NOUN**

suggest /sejest/

To give someone an idea for something to think about **VERB**
I suggest we have a picnic.
· **suggestion** /sejeschen/ **NOUN**

suit[1] /soot/

A jacket and trousers or a jacket and a skirt made from the same cloth
NOUN

suit[2] /soot/

1. To be right or good for something   *This hot weather really suits me.* 2. To look good on someone   *That hat suits you, Inky!* **VERB**

That hat suits you, Inky!

· **suitable** /sootebel/ **ADJECTIVE**
· **suitably** /sooteblee/ **ADVERB**

suitcase /sootcais/

A container made of strong material with handles for carrying your clothes and things when you travel **NOUN**

sulk /sulk/

To be angry about something and refuse to talk to anyone **VERB**
· **sulky** /sulkee/ **ADJECTIVE**

sum /sum/

1. An amount of money 2. The total of things added together 3. If you do sums, you find out things with numbers **NOUN**

summer /sumer/

The hottest season in the year **NOUN**
▶ **CALENDAR**, page 13

sun /sun/

1. A very bright star that gives light and heat to the earth 2. The heat or light you get from the sun   *Bee doesn't like the sun very much.* **NOUN**
· **sunbathe** /sunbaith/ **VERB**
· **sunburnt** /sunbernt/ **ADJECTIVE**
· **sunlight** /sunliet/ **NOUN**
· **sunny** /sunee/ **ADJECTIVE**
· **sunshine** /sunshien/ **NOUN**
· **suntan** /suntan/ **NOUN**

Ss

Sunday /sundai/
A day of the week NOUN
▶ CALENDAR, page 13

sunflower /sunflouer/
A very tall plant with big round yellow flowers that make people think of the sun NOUN

sung /sung/
PAST PARTICIPLE ▶ **sing**

sunk /sungk/
PAST PARTICIPLE ▶ **sink**¹

sunrise /sunriez/
The time in the morning when the sun first comes into the sky NOUN

sunset /sunset/
The time in the evening when the sun goes down and disappears in the distance NOUN

super /sooper/
Very good ADJECTIVE

superior /soopiereeer/
Of higher quality than something or someone else ADJECTIVE
My friend's school is superior to mine.

supermarket /soopermarkit/
A big shop that sells food and other things for your home NOUN

supervise /sooperviez/
To make sure other people are doing things properly VERB

supper /super/
A meal you have in the evening NOUN

supply /seplie/
To give someone what they need VERB
Phonic supplies Inky with lots of information.
• **supply** /seplie/ NOUN

support¹ /seport/
1. To like someone or their ideas and want them to be successful *What team do you support?* 2. To help someone to be successful 3. To hold something up that is heavy *These boards support the roof.* VERB
• **supporter** /seporter/ NOUN

support² /seport/
The help you give people because you think what they are doing is good NOUN

suppose /sepoaz/
1. To think something is true or may be possible *Do you suppose Inky likes living in her mousehole?* 2. If you are supposed to do something, it means there is something someone expects you to do *Am I supposed to wait here?* 4. If something is supposed to be or do something, it means people expect it to be that way *Learning to ride a bike is supposed to be very hard.* VERB

sure /shor/
1. Believing something is completely true *I'm sure you are right.* 2. If something is sure to happen, it will definitely happen ADJECTIVE

surf /serf/
1. To ride on waves in the sea with a surf board 2. **surf the net** To spend time on the Internet looking for things NOUN

surface /serfes/
The part of something on the outside or the top NOUN

Ss

surgery /serjeree/
The room or place you go when you want to see a doctor or dentist NOUN

surname /sernaim/
The last part of your name that other people in your family also have NOUN

surprise[1] /serpriez/
Something you did not expect, or the feeling when this happens NOUN

Inky's present came as a complete surprise to Snake.

surprise[2] /serpriez/
If something surprises you, you were not expecting it VERB
Snake was really surprised when Inky gave him a present.
• **surprising** /serpriezing/ ADJECTIVE

surrender /serender/
To stop fighting and admit that you have been beaten VERB
• **surrender** /serender/ NOUN

surround /seround/
To go or be all the way around something or someone VERB
The building is surrounded by a fence.

survive /serviev/
To still be alive, or not be destroyed after something bad has happened VERB
Bee was in a crash but she survived.
• **survivor** /serviever/ NOUN

suspicious /sespishes/
1. Strange, or behaving in a way that makes you think something is wrong *I saw something suspicious today.* 2. Thinking that something might be wrong or that someone cannot be trusted *I heard a funny noise and I became suspicious.*
ADJECTIVE
• **suspicion** /sespishen/ NOUN

swallow[1] /swoloa/
To make food and drink go down your throat to your stomach VERB

swallow[2] /swoloa/
A little bird with a tail that is divided into two parts NOUN

swam /swam/
PAST TENSE ▶ **swim**

swamp /swomp/
Land that is covered with water where plants grow NOUN

swan /swon/
A big white bird with a long neck that is curved. Swans live near and on water
NOUN

swap /swop/
To give someone something in exchange for something they have VERB
• **swap** /swop/ NOUN

swarm /sworm/
A lot of bees, or other insects, flying together NOUN
• **swarm** /sworm/ VERB

Ss

sway /swai/
To move slowly from one side to the other
VERB *The trees were swaying in the wind.*

swear /sweer/
1. To say words that are bad and not polite *Bee and Snake never swear.*
2. To say to someone that you are telling the truth *I swear that I didn't do it.* **VERB**
- **swore, sworn**

sweat /swet/
If you sweat, little drops of liquid come onto your skin because you are hot or frightened **VERB**
- **sweat** /swet/ **NOUN**
- **sweaty** /swetee/ **ADJECTIVE**

sweater /sweter/
Something you wear over a shirt or blouse to keep the top of your body and arms warm. Sweaters are usually knitted. **NOUN**

sweep /sweep/
To clean the floor or something else with a broom **VERB**
- **swept**

- **sweep** /sweep/ **NOUN**

sweet[1] /sweet/
1. Tasting like sugar 2. Very nice and pleasant *What a sweet face!* **ADJECTIVE**

sweet[2] /sweet/
A small piece of sugary food **NOUN**
Snake loves sweets.

sweetcorn /sweetcorn/
The soft yellow seeds of the maize plant that people cook and eat **NOUN**

swell /swel/
To get bigger **VERB**
My leg has swollen.
- **swelled, swollen**
- **swelling** /sweling/ **NOUN**

swept /swept/
PAST TENSE ▶ **sweep**

swift /swift/
Another way of saying quick **ADJECTIVE**

swim /swim/
1. To move through the water using your arms and legs 2. If fish swim, they move in the water using their fins and tail **VERB**
- **swam, swum**
- **swimmer** /swimer/ **NOUN**
- **swimming** /swiming/ **NOUN**
- **swimming pool** /swiming pool/ **NOUN**

swing[1] /swing/
A seat that hangs down from chains on a metal bar where you sit and move yourself backwards and forwards **NOUN**

swing[2] /swing/
To move backwards and forwards or from one side to the other through the air **VERB**
The monkey was swinging through the air, going from branch to branch.
- **swung**

switch[1] /swich/
1. If you switch something on or off, you make it work or you stop making it work *Please switch Phonic off!* 2. Another way of saying change *Can we switch places?*
3. To put one thing in the place of another *Someone has switched our drinks. I have your coffee and you have my tea.* **VERB**

Ss

switch[2] /swich/
Something like a button that you press or move to make a machine or a light work **NOUN**

swollen[1] /swoalen/
Made bigger, usually because of an injury **ADJECTIVE**

Snake's tail was swollen after he shut it in the door.

swollen[2] /swoalen/
PAST PARTICIPLE ▶ **swell**

swoop /swoop/
To move suddenly down from the air, usually to attack something or to catch something **VERB**
The hawk swooped down on the poor robin.

swop /swop/
▶ **swap** **VERB**
• **swop** /swop/ **NOUN**

sword /sord/
A weapon with a long pointed blade that people hold by a small handle **NOUN**

swordfish /sordfish/
A big fish with a long pointed mouth like a sword. People eat swordfish **NOUN**

swore /swor/
PAST TENSE ▶ **swear**
• **sworn** /sworn/
PAST PARTICIPLE ▶ **swear**

swum /swum/
PAST PARTICIPLE ▶ **swim**

swung /swung/
PAST TENSE ▶ **swing**[2]

syllable /silebel/
A word or part of a word that has one vowel sound only **NOUN**
The word rabbit has two syllables.

symbol /simbel/
A shape that is a sign of something else **NOUN** *A star can be a symbol of happiness.*

sympathetic /simpethetic/
Understanding someone else's problems and being kind to them **ADJECTIVE**

synagogue /sinegog/
A building where Jewish people go to pray **NOUN**

syringe /sirinj/
A needle fixed to a tube for putting medicines into your body or for taking blood from your body **NOUN**

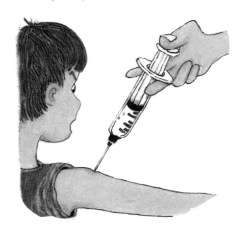

syrup /sirep/
A thick liquid made from sugar **NOUN**

Tt

table /taibəl/
A piece of furniture with a flat top and legs that people usually sit at NOUN
• **tablecloth** /taibəlcloth/ NOUN

tablespoon /taibəlspoon/
A big spoon for serving food NOUN

tablet /tablət/
A medicine that looks like a tiny round hard ball. If you take a tablet, you swallow it NOUN

table tennis /taibəl tenis/
A game like tennis but with a small bat, ball and net that two people play indoors on the top of a table NOUN

tackle /tacəl/
In sports, if a player tackles another player, they try to take the ball away from them VERB

tact /tact/
The ability to say or do things in a nice way, without being rude NOUN
• **tactful** /tactfool/ ADJECTIVE

tadpole /tadpoal/
A tadpole is a tiny baby frog or toad before its legs start to grow. It has a long tail and lives in water NOUN

tag /tag/
A piece of paper or plastic with information on it like a price or a name NOUN

tail /tail/
The long thin part that moves at the back of lots of animals like cats or mice or horses NOUN

tailor /tailer/
Someone who makes clothes such as trousers and jackets for men NOUN

take /taik/
1. To hold something or move it from one place to another *Don't forget to take your umbrella.* 2. To let someone come with you, for example in a car or walking *I'm taking the dog for a walk.* 3. To do a certain action *Do you want to take a shower?* 4. To go on something like a bus or train *I take the bus to school.* 5. If something takes up space or time, it fills it 6. If a plane takes off, it starts flying somewhere VERB
■ took, taken
• **take-off** /taik of/ NOUN

talcum powder /talcəm pouder/
A kind of powder that people put on a baby's body or their own body after a bath or shower NOUN

tale /tail/
Another word for a story NOUN

talent /talent/
When you are very good at something NOUN

talk /tawk/
To say things using words VERB
• **talk** /tawk/ NOUN
• **talkative** /tawkətiv/ Talking a lot ADJECTIVE

tall /tawl/
If someone or something is tall, their head or their top part is a long way from the ground **ADJECTIVE**

talon /talen/
Talons are the sharp claws of a bird such as an eagle **NOUN**

tambourine /tambereen/
An instrument like a small drum with little metal discs around the edge that you shake with your hand to make a ringing sound **NOUN**

tame[1] /taim/
A tame animal is happy to be near people and does not run away **ADJECTIVE**

tame[2] /taim/
To train an animal not to run away from people but to stay calm **VERB**

tan /tan/
1. The brown colour that the sun gives to people's skin 2. A light brown colour **NOUN**

• **tan** /tan/ **VERB**

tandem /tandem/
1. If people do something in tandem, they do it together and at the same time
2. A bicycle that two people ride at the same time **NOUN**

tangerine /tanjereen/
A fruit like a small orange with loose skin **NOUN**

tangled /tanggeld/
Twisted together and looking untidy **ADJECTIVE** *Comb your hair, James, it's all tangled.*

tank /tangk/
1. A big container for things like petrol or water 2. A fish tank is a container with glass sides for keeping fish in 3. A tank that soldiers use is a heavy vehicle with a gun on the top and metal belts over its wheels **NOUN**

tanker /tangker/
A ship or a truck that carries oil, petrol or other liquids **NOUN**

tanned /tand/
If someone is tanned, their skin has a brown colour because they have been in the sun **ADJECTIVE**

t

tantrum /tantrəm/
When someone suddenly behaves in an angry or bad way, usually shouting or crying **NOUN**

tap[1] /tap/
1. Something you turn to control water or gas flowing through a pipe
2. A knocking sound or action **NOUN**

tap[2] /tap/
To knock something gently once or a few times **VERB**
Is that Bee tapping on the window?

tap dancing /tap dansing/
Dancing where people wear special shoes with pieces of metal on the bottom that make a sound each time they touch the floor **NOUN**

tape[1] /taip/
1. A long thin plastic strip for recording sounds and pictures 2. A thin strip of sticky plastic for sticking things together **NOUN**

tape[2] /taip/
1. To record sounds and pictures with a tape 2. To stick things or tie things together using tape **VERB**

tape measure /taip mezher/
A strip of cloth or plastic or metal for measuring things **NOUN**

tar /tar/
A sticky black substance made from coal, used for making roads **NOUN**

tarantula /terantyoolə/
A type of large spider that is poisonous and lives in hot countries **NOUN**

target /targit/
Something you have to hit in a game such as darts or shooting **NOUN**

tart /tart/
A type of pie made with fruit or vegetables that has an open top **NOUN**

tartan /tartən/
Cloth made from wool with a pattern of lines and squares. People often wear tartan in Scotland **NOUN**

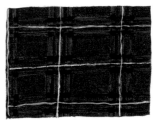

task /task/
A job that someone has to do **NOUN**

taste[1] /taist/
The feeling different foods give you when you put them in your mouth **NOUN**
This apple has a very nice taste.

taste[2] /taist/
1. If you taste something, you eat or drink it, and it gives you a certain feeling in your mouth *I can taste the salt in this soup.* 2. To eat or drink just a little amount of something to see what it is like *Can I taste your ice cream?* 3. If food tastes a certain way, that is the sense it gives people in their mouth *This orange tastes delicious.* **VERB**
• **tasty** /taistee/ **ADJECTIVE**

tattoo /tatoo/
A picture or pattern drawn on the skin using special inks **NOUN**
• **tattoo** /tatoo/ **VERB**

taught /tawt/
PAST TENSE ▶ **teach**

tavern /tavern/
An old-fashioned word for a pub **NOUN**

tax /tax/
Tax is money people have to pay to the people who control the country. Taxes pay for things like schools and police officers **NOUN**
• **tax** /tax/ **VERB**

Tt

taxi /taxee/
A car that takes people where they want to go, and they must pay the driver to take them NOUN

tea /tee/
1. A hot brown drink made from the leaves of the tea bush. People pour hot water onto the tea leaves or the teabags 2. A small meal that people eat in the afternoon or evening NOUN

- **teabag** /teebag/ A small bag made of paper with tea leaves in NOUN
- **teacup** /teecup/ NOUN
- **teapot** /teepot/ A container for making tea with a handle and a tube for pouring it NOUN
- **tea towel** /tee touel/ A little towel for drying dishes NOUN

teach /teech/
To get someone to learn something, for example in school VERB
Inky is teaching Bee and Snake how to read. · *Jack wants to teach English.*
■ **taught**
- **teacher** /teecher/ NOUN
- **teaching** /teeching/ NOUN

team /teem/
1. A group of people who play games or sports together against other people 2. A group of people who work together NOUN

tear[1] /tier/
Tears are drops of liquid that come from your eyes when you cry NOUN

tear[2] /teer/
1. To pull something and make it go into separate pieces, or make a hole in it 2. If something tears, it goes into separate pieces or a hole comes into it VERB
■ **tore, torn**

tear[3] /teer/
A hole in something like paper or cloth where someone has torn it NOUN

tease /teez/
To make friendly jokes to annoy someone about something VERB

teaspoon /teespoon/
A little spoon that you use for food or drink, for example for putting sugar into your tea NOUN

technical /tecnicel/
Connected with special knowledge of things such as machines that some people find hard to understand ADJECTIVE
My friend is a technical expert. · *This computer book is very technical.*

teddy bear /tedee beer/
A toy bear made from soft material NOUN

tedious /teedies/
Another word for boring ADJECTIVE

teenager /teenaijer/
A young person between the ages of 13 and 19 NOUN
- **teenage** /teenaij/ ADJECTIVE

289

Tt

teeny /teenee/
If you say something is teeny or teeny weeny, you mean it is very very small **ADJECTIVE**

tee shirt /tee shert/
▶ **T-shirt** NOUN

teeth /teeth/
NOUN PLURAL ▶ **tooth**
We brush our teeth twice a day.

telegraph pole /telegraf poal/
A tall pole that telephone wires are fixed to **NOUN**

telephone /telefoan/
A machine for talking to someone who is in a different place **NOUN**
• **telephone** /telefoan/ VERB
• **telephone book** /telefoan book/
  A book with all the telephone numbers in it **NOUN**
• **telephone box** /telefoan box/
  A little place in the street that contains a telephone **NOUN**
• **telephone call** /telefoan cawl/ **NOUN**
• **telephone directory** /telefoan dierecteree/ A telephone book **NOUN**

telescope /telescoap/
Something shaped like a long tube that people use to make things far away look bigger **NOUN**

television /televizhen/
1. A machine like a big box with a screen for watching television programmes 2. A special system for sending sound and pictures over a long distance **NOUN**

tell /tel/
1. To give someone some information *Tell me what happened.* 2. If someone tells you to do something, it means you must do it *The teacher told us to be quiet.* 3. To know something *Bee can tell when Snake is joking.* 4. If someone tells you off, they say they are angry with you for doing something wrong **VERB**
■ **told**
• **telling-off** /teling of/ **NOUN**

telltale /teltail/
A boy or a girl who tells a grown-up about something bad that someone else has done **NOUN**

telly /telee/
Another word for television **NOUN**

temper /temper/
1. If someone has a temper, they get angry quickly 2. If someone is in a temper, they are angry **NOUN**

temperament /temprement/
A person's normal sort of mood **NOUN**
Inky has a very calm temperament, she never gets excited.

temperature /temperecher/
1. A measurement showing how hot or cold something is *The temperature is too low to go outside.* 2. If you have a temperature, you are sick because your body is too hot **NOUN**

temple /tempel/
A building where people go to pray **NOUN**
a Hindu temple

temporary /tempərəree/
Lasting for a short time only ADJECTIVE

tempt /tempt/
To make someone want to do something or have something, often something bad VERB
• **temptation** /temptaishən/ NOUN
• **tempting** /tempting/ ADJECTIVE

tender /tendər/
1. If a part of your body is tender, it hurts when you touch it 2. Food that is tender is soft ADJECTIVE

tennis /tenis/
A game where you hit a ball over a net using something with strings and a handle called a racket NOUN

• **tennis court** /tenis cort/ The area where people play tennis NOUN

tenpin /tenpin/
Tenpins are standing sticks shaped like bottles that you knock over in the game of tenpin bowling. They are sometimes called skittles NOUN
• **tenpin bowling** /tenpin boaling/ NOUN

tense[1] /tens/
The tense of a verb is the form that shows when the action happens. The three main tenses are the past, present and future. For example, 'I see' is the present tense and 'I saw' is the past tense of 'to see' NOUN

tense[2] /tens/
Not relaxed because you are worried about something ADJECTIVE

tension /tenshən/
1. A feeling of being very worried or excited 2. Tension between people means that they do not like each other and often fight with each other NOUN

tent /tent/
A shelter made from a strong piece of cloth held up with poles and ropes. People use tents when they are camping NOUN

tentacle /tentəcəl/
Tentacles are the long thin arms of an octopus that it uses for moving and feeling NOUN

term /term/
1. A period of time that people divide the year into *The summer term was very long this year.* 2. A word or expression with a special technical meaning NOUN

terminal /termənəl/
1. A big building at an airport where people go when they get on or off a plane 2. A railway terminal is the last station on a line NOUN

terrace /terəs/
1. An area outside a building where people sit and eat 2. The terraces are steps at a football ground where people can stand while they watch the match NOUN

t

terrible /terebel/
Very bad ADJECTIVE
• **terribly** /teriblee/
Another way of saying very ADVERB
We're terribly late.

terrific /terific/
Very good ADJECTIVE
• **terrifically** /terificelee/
Another way of saying very ADVERB
She's terrifically happy.

terrify /terefie/
To make someone feel very frightened
VERB
• **terrified** /terefied/ ADJECTIVE
• **terrifying** /terefieing/ ADJECTIVE

territory /tereteree/
An area of land, for example in a
country or town NOUN

terror /terer/
A very strong bad feeling people have
when they are in danger NOUN

terrorist /tererist/
Someone who does bad things such as
killing people or bombing because they
believe they can change things in a
country NOUN

terrorize /tereriez/
To make someone very frightened VERB

test¹ /test/
1. A list of questions to answer about
a subject *Inky gave Snake a reading test.*
2. If someone has a test on part of their
body, such as an eye test, a doctor tries
to find out things about that part of the
body NOUN

test² /test/
1. To test someone is to try and find
out how much they know 2. To test
something is to try and find out things
about it VERB

text /text/
The written words in a book. The text
does not include pictures or notes NOUN

textbook /textbook/
A school book on a certain subject NOUN

than /than/
1. Used to compare things or to connect
two parts of a sentence *Does Bee work
harder than Snake?* • *We have more apples
than we need.* 2. Used with numbers to
show they are below or above other
numbers *Snake learned to read in less
than six months.* CONJUNCTION, PREPOSITION

thank /thangk/
To thank someone is to tell them you are
happy because they have done something
for you or given you something VERB

thanks /thangks/
A word that you say to people when you
thank them INTERJECTION
• **thanks** /thangks/ NOUN PLURAL

thank you /thangk yoo/
A polite way of thanking someone or of
saying yes INTERJECTION
Thank you, I'd love some cake.

that¹ /that/
1. Used for talking about something
you have already mentioned in the
sentence or something you can see
and point to but is not near you *I have
washed the car, you don't have to do that.*
• *That house is where I live.* 2. Also used
for talking about something that is not
happening now *That day I was very tired.*
3. Used for saying something about a
person or thing you are talking about
Snake likes books that are easy to read.
ADJECTIVE, PRONOUN
■ **those** /thoaz/ PLURAL

Tt

that² /that/

1. Used for saying what someone says or thinks or knows, or for expressing feelings *Dad thinks that we should go home now. · I'm sorry that I can't come tonight.*
2. Used for showing the result of something *It was so late that Bee fell asleep.* **CONJUNCTION**

thatch /thach/
A covering for a roof made from straw or reeds **NOUN**

thaw /thaw/
If snow or ice thaws, it turns into liquid because the weather gets warmer **VERB**
· **thaw** /thaw/ **NOUN**

the /thə/
A word used before a noun
DEFINITE ARTICLE *the girl, the boy, the house*

theatre /thiəter/
A place you go to see plays **NOUN**

theft /theft/
The crime of stealing something **NOUN**

their /theer/
Belonging to them **ADJECTIVE**
They've lost their pencils.

theirs /theerz/
If something is theirs, it belongs to them
PRONOUN *This dog is theirs.*

them /them/
People or things or animals that someone has already mentioned in the sentence
PRONOUN *We want to see the lions but we can't see them anywhere.*
· **themselves** /themselvz/ **PRONOUN**

theme /theem/
The main subject or idea of something such as a story **NOUN**
The theme of the party was Halloween.

theme park /theem park/
A big area that people pay to go into, with lots of machines they can ride on and games they can play **NOUN**

then /then/
1. At that time *Bee was just a baby then.* 2. Coming next, after something *First we eat, and then we look at our books.* 3. For that reason, or because of something someone has just said *If they went to the same school, then they must know each other.*
ADVERB

there /theer/
1. In or to that place *Put your books down there.* 2. You use 'there is' or 'there are' to mean that something exists or to tell someone about something. Also used to point to something *There are 26 letters in the alphabet. · There's my friend.*
ADVERB

therefore /theerfor/
A word that people sometimes use to mean 'for that reason' **ADVERB**
It was raining, therefore Bee took her umbrella.

Tt

thermometer /thermometer/
Something people use to measure
temperature, to see how hot or cold
it is NOUN

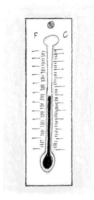

thesaurus /thesawres/
A book where words with similar
meanings are put together in groups
but the meanings are not given
NOUN

these /theez/
PRONOUN PLURAL ▶ **this**

they /thai/
People or things or animals that someone
has already mentioned in the sentence
PRONOUN
*The children played on the slide when they
went to the playground.*

thick /thic/
1. Having a big distance between the
two opposite sides of something *I've cut
the bread into thick slices.* 2. Made of lots
of things put close together or growing
close together *Thick smoke poured from
the building.* • *a thick forest* 3. Thick clothes
are made from heavy cloth and keep you
warm ADJECTIVE
• **thickness** /thicnes/ NOUN

thief /theef/
Someone who steals things NOUN
■ **thieves** /theevz/ PLURAL

thigh /thie/
Your thighs are the thick parts of your
legs above your knees NOUN

thimble /thimbel/
A little metal or plastic cover that people
wear on their finger to protect it when
they are sewing NOUN

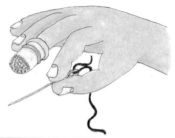

thin /thin/
1. A thin person has a body that does
not have much flesh 2. Having only a
little distance between the two opposite
sides of something *I prefer thin slices of
bread.* 3. Thin clothes are made from
light cloth that you can sometimes see
through ADJECTIVE
• **thinly** /thinlee/ ADVERB

thing /thing/
1. Something you can touch or
something you talk about when you
do not use its exact name *What's that
thing in your hand?* 2. Something you
do *Inky doesn't have many things to do.*
3. You use things to mean clothes
and other objects that belong to you
Don't leave your things on the floor. NOUN

think /thingk/
1. To have an idea in your mind about
something or someone *I think it's raining.*
• *What do you think of this book?* 2. If you
are thinking of doing something, you
really want to do it but you have not
decided yet 3. If you think about
someone, you pay attention to what
they want or need VERB
■ **thought**

Tt

thirst /therst/
When people do not have enough to drink NOUN

thirsty /therstee/
Needing something to drink ADJECTIVE

this /this/
1. Used for talking about something you have already mentioned or something you can see and point to that is near to you *Can you help me with this?* · *This house is where I live.* 2. Also used for talking about the present time *What shall we do this morning?* ADJECTIVE, PRONOUN
■ **these** /theez/ PLURAL

thorn /thorn/
A sharp point on the stem of some plants. Roses have thorns NOUN
· **thorny** /thornee/ ADJECTIVE

thorough /thure/
Complete and done properly so that nothing is left out ADJECTIVE
Inky is very thorough when she cleans her teeth.

thoroughly /thurelee/
1. Very much *Snake thoroughly enjoyed himself.* 2. Completely and properly *Bee has done all the exercises thoroughly.*
ADVERB

those /thoaz/
PRONOUN PLURAL ▶ **that**[1]

though /thoa/
Used for saying something that makes another part of the sentence surprising
CONJUNCTION, ADVERB
I'm not going to bed even though I'm tired.

thought[1] /thawt/
1. An idea in your mind *Have you any thoughts on that?* 2. Thinking deeply about something *After a lot of thought, they decided I was right.* NOUN

thought[2] /thawt/
PAST TENSE ▶ **think**

thoughtful /thawtfel/
Kind and paying attention to what people want or need ADJECTIVE

thoughtless /thawtles/
Not thinking of other people's feelings
ADJECTIVE

thrash /thrash/
To hit someone very hard VERB
· **thrashing** /thrashing/ NOUN

thread /thred/
A long thin piece of cotton for sewing pieces of cloth together. People put the thread through the top of the needle
NOUN

threat /thret/
When you tell someone that you are going to hurt them or do something they will not like NOUN

threaten /threten/
To frighten someone by saying you will do something nasty to them VERB

threw /throo/
PAST TENSE ▶ **throw**

thrill /thril/
A sudden, excited feeling NOUN
· **thrilled** /thrild/ ADJECTIVE
· **thrilling** /thriling/ ADJECTIVE

thrive /thriev/
To do well, and become big and strong
VERB

t

throat /throat/
The front part of your neck, and the part inside your body at the back of your mouth NOUN

throb /throb/
If a part of your body throbs, you get a pain in it that keeps coming and going all the time VERB

throne /throan/
A special chair for someone important like a king or a queen NOUN

through /throo/
1. From one side of something to the other *We walked through the tunnel.* 2. From the beginning to the end of something like a period of time *I slept through the film.* 3. Because of something *Beth missed a lot of school through being sick.* 4. Using a certain way of doing something *Snake bought some books through the Internet.* PREPOSITION, ADVERB

throughout /throoout/
All over something, or during all of a period of time PREPOSITION, ADVERB *Some animals hibernate throughout the winter.*

throw /throa/
1. To send something through the air using your hand *Throw the ball to me!* 2. To put, especially when you put something somewhere quickly *Can you throw your dirty clothes into the washing machine?* 3. **throw away** To take something and put it somewhere like a dustbin because you do not want it VERB
■ **threw, thrown**

thrush /thrush/
A small brown bird with spots on its front NOUN

thud /thud/
A kind of low sound made by things such as a heavy book or a person falling to the ground NOUN

thumb /thum/
The short thick finger at the side of your hand NOUN

thump /thump/
To hit something or someone with your closed hand VERB
• **thump** /thump/ NOUN

thunder /thunder/
The loud noise you hear in the sky during a storm. Thunder sometimes comes after a flash of lightning NOUN
• **thunder** /thunder/ VERB
• **thunderstorm** /thunderstorm/ NOUN

Thursday /therzdai/
A day of the week NOUN
▶ CALENDAR, page 13

tick¹ /tic/
1. To make a soft clicking sound like a clock or watch 2. To mark something with a tick to show it is correct or has been done VERB

tick² /tic/
A mark like this ✔ that shows someone's answer is correct, or someone has done something on a list of things to do NOUN

ticket /ticit/

1. A piece of paper that people pay for that lets them do something such as travel on a bus or train, or get into the cinema to see a film 2. A piece of paper people buy with a number on it that could win a prize *Have you bought your lottery ticket?* NOUN

tickle /ticel/

To touch someone very lightly with your fingers or with something like a feather and make them laugh VERB
• **tickle** /ticel/ NOUN

tide /tied/

The level of the sea that goes up and down at different times during the day NOUN *The tide was out so we could walk along the beach.*

tidy¹ /tiedee/

1. Carefully arranged with everything in the right place 2. If a person is tidy, they put things in the right place ADJECTIVE
• **tidiness** /tiedeenes/ NOUN

tidy² /tiedee/

To arrange things carefully somewhere such as a room VERB

tie¹ /tie/

1. To join the two ends of something together such as a piece of string and fix them with a knot *Can you tie your shoelaces?* 2. To fix things together using something such as string *Inky tied the three boxes with string.* VERB

tie² /tie/

A narrow piece of cloth with a knot in it that men and boys wear around their neck under the collar of their shirt NOUN

tiger /tieger/

A big wild animal with orange fur and black stripes. Tigers belong to the cat family and live mainly in Asia NOUN

tight¹ /tiet/

1. Tight clothes are clothes that people wear close to their body, or clothes that are not comfortable because they are too close to the body *These gloves are a little tight.* 2. Fixed in a position *I can't open the door. The handle is too tight.* 3. If something like string is tight, it is pulled hard so that it is straight ADJECTIVE

tight² /tiet/

Used to mean that you press hard on something ADVERB
I was holding her hand tight.
• **tighten** /tieten/
To make something tight VERB

297

Tt

tightrope /tietrᴐap/
A special rope or wire above the ground in a circus for acrobats to walk on **NOUN**

tights /tiets/
A piece of clothing worn by girls and women to cover their feet, legs and waist
NOUN PLURAL

tile /tiel/
Tiles are flat pieces of baked clay. People use tiles for covering walls, floors and roofs **NOUN**

till /til/
Up to a certain time
PREPOSITION, **CONJUNCTION**
Let's stay here till it stops raining.

tilt /tilt/
1. To move something so that one side is lower than the other 2. If something tilts, one side is lower than the other
The boat tilted on the high waves. **VERB**

The boat tilted on the high waves.

timber /timber/
Wood for making houses or furniture
NOUN

time¹ /tiem/
1. What people measure using the clock *Inky spends a lot of time teaching.*
2. A certain moment of the day on the clock *What time do you go to bed?*
3. A period when someone does something, or an occasion when something happens *Be more careful next time. · I rang the bell three times.* **NOUN**

time² /tiem/
To measure something using a clock or a watch **VERB**
Start running and I'll time you.
· **timer** /tiemer/ **NOUN**

times /tiemz/
Another way of saying multiplied by
PREPOSITION *Five times two equals ten.*

timetable /tiemtaibel/
A list of the times of something, such as school lessons or when buses come and go **NOUN**

timid /timid/
Shy and easily frightened **ADJECTIVE**

tin /tin/
1. A soft metal that is silver in colour
2. A metal container that you buy food in *Do you have any tins of beans?* **NOUN**
· **tinned** /tind/ **ADJECTIVE**

tingle /tinggel/
If a part of your body tingles, you have a feeling of slight sudden pains there **VERB**

tinsel /tinsel/
A type of decoration made from shiny threads. Tinsel is usually used to decorate Christmas trees **NOUN**

tiny /tienee/
Very very small **ADJECTIVE**

tip¹ /tip/
1. The very end of something long or big *the tip of an iceberg* 2. A little bit of useful information *Let me give you a few tips.* 3. A little bit of money that people give to someone who does things for them, like a waiter **NOUN**

tip² /tip/
1. If you tip something over or if something tips over, it falls *I accidentally tipped over a glass of water.* 2. If you tip something or it tips, it leans to one side *Don't tip your chair!* 3. To pour something from a container *Can you tip some cherries into everyone's bowl?* **VERB**

tipsy /tipsee/
A word that means slightly drunk **ADJECTIVE**

tiptoe¹ /tiptoa/
To stand on your toes and walk along quietly **VERB**

tiptoe² /tiptoa/
If you stand on tiptoe, you stand on your toes to look as if you are taller, or so you can see something **NOUN**

tired /tieərd/
Needing to rest or sleep **ADJECTIVE**
• **tiring** /tieəring/
Making you feel tired **ADJECTIVE**

tissue /tishoo/
1. A type of very thin paper 2. A thin piece of soft paper, for example for blowing your nose **NOUN**

titch /tich/
A word for someone very small **NOUN**

title /tietəl/
The title of a book, film, play or something similar is the name people give to it **NOUN**

to /too/
1. Used for showing that someone or something is going somewhere *Inky went back to her mousehole.* 2. Used for showing who gets or is given or is told something *Explain to Bee what you mean, Snake.* 3. Used for showing the position or direction of something *We turned to the right.* • *Snake's desk is to the left of Bee's.* 4. Used for showing how someone or something is treated *My teacher is always kind to me.* 5. Used as a sign that the next word is a verb *to go • to talk* **PREPOSITION**

toad /toad/
An animal like a big frog with rough brown skin **NOUN**

toadstool /toadstool/
A plant like a mushroom that grows wild and is poisonous **NOUN**

Tt

toast[1] /tɒɑst/
A slice of bread that is heated up until it turns brown and hard NOUN

toast[2] /tɒɑst/
To heat bread up until it is brown and hard VERB
• **toaster** /tɒɑster/ NOUN

tobacco /tɛbacɒɑ/
The dry leaves of the tobacco plant that are used to make cigarettes and cigars NOUN

toboggan /tɛbogɛn/
Another word for a sledge NOUN

today[1] /tɛdai/
1. On this day *Let's go swimming today.*
2. At the time happening now *Fashion today is very different from ten years ago.* ADVERB

today[2] /tɛdai/
Another way of saying this day NOUN
Today is my birthday.

toddler /todɛler/
A young child who is just learning to walk NOUN

toe /tɒɑ/
One of the long thin parts at the end of your foot NOUN
▶ PARTS OF THE BODY, page 18
• **toenail** /tɒɑnail/ NOUN

toffee /tofɛɑ/
A hard and sticky brown sweet made from sugar and butter NOUN

together /tɛgether/
You use together to mean at the same time or in the same place ADVERB
Let's all sing together. • *Snake and Inky went for a walk together.*

toil /tɒil/
To work very hard VERB

toilet /tɒilɛt/
1. A seat with a hole where people go to get rid of waste from their body
2. A room with a toilet in it NOUN

told /tɒɑld/
PAST TENSE ▶ **tell**

tomato /tɛmahtɒɑ/
A round red fruit that is very juicy. People eat them in salads or cook them as vegetables NOUN
▶ FRUIT AND VEGETABLES, page 15

tomb /tɒɑm/
A large place like a room where a dead person is buried NOUN

tomorrow[1] /tɛmorɒɑ/
On the day after today ADVERB
There's no school tomorrow.

tomorrow[2] /tɛmorɒɑ/
The day after today NOUN
Tomorrow it will be sunny.

ton /tun/
1. A measurement for weight
2. **tons of** Lots of *Bee and Snake have tons of things to read.* NOUN

tone /tɒɑn/
1. The sound of someone's voice, often showing a person's feelings *I don't like your angry tone!* 2. The sound made by something like a telephone or musical instrument NOUN

Tt

tongue /tung/
The long soft part inside your mouth that you use for tasting and speaking
NOUN

tonight /teniet/
The evening or the night of this day
ADVERB, NOUN *We're going to a restaurant tonight. • Tonight is Bee's birthday party.*

tonne /tun/
A measurement for weight NOUN

tonsillitis /tonselietes/
When your throat is very painful because the two little pieces of flesh at the back called your tonsils have an infection
NOUN

too /too/
1. Used to mean that something is so great or so much that something else is not possible *I'm too tired to play.*
2. More than something should be *Be quiet, you're too noisy.* 3. Used to include something or someone else in what you say *It's dark and it's late too.*
• *Can I come too?* ADVERB

took /took/
PAST TENSE ▶ **take**

tool /tool/
Something people hold in their hands for doing a certain kind of work, such as a hammer or a knife NOUN

tooth /tooth/
One of the hard white parts in your mouth for biting and chewing food NOUN
■ **teeth** /teeth/ PLURAL
• **toothbrush** /toothbrush/ NOUN

toothache /toothaic/
A painful feeling in one or more of your teeth NOUN

toothpaste /toothpaist/
The substance you put on your toothbrush for cleaning your teeth NOUN

top[1] /top/
1. The highest part of something
2. The end of something like a garden or street 3. A cover for a container like a bottle or box or pan *I've lost the bottle top.* 4. If someone wears a top, they wear something on the upper half of their body such as a T-shirt 5. A toy that spins around and around in one place NOUN

top[2] /top/
1. At the highest part of something *Knives and forks are in the top drawer.*
2. Used to mean the best or the highest or the most important of something *Bee won the top prize, and she's top of the class.* ADJECTIVE

topic /topic/
The subject someone is talking or learning about NOUN

topple /topel/
If something topples or topples over, it starts to move slightly from one side to the other and falls over VERB

torch /torch/
1. An electric light that you carry in your hand 2. A flame at the end of a piece of wood NOUN

tore /tor/
PAST TENSE ▶ **tear**[2]
• **torn** /torn/
PAST PARTICIPLE ▶ **tear**[2]

Tt

tornado /tɔrnaidoʊ/
A very strong wind that spins around as it moves along, and does a lot of damage NOUN

torpedo /tɔrpeedoʊ/
A kind of bomb shaped like a tube for destroying ships. It travels under the water NOUN

tortoise /tɔrtɐs/
A small animal with a thick shell that walks slowly along the ground NOUN

torture /tɔrcher/
To make someone suffer a lot of pain, usually to try and make them tell you something you want to know VERB
• **torture** /tɔrcher/ NOUN

toss /tos/
To throw something VERB
Can you toss me the ball?

total¹ /toʊtɐl/
The amount you get when you add things together NOUN
The numbers 6 and 8 make a total of 14.

total² /toʊtɐl/
1. A total number or amount or cost is what you get when you add things together 2. Complete *That man is a total stranger.* ADJECTIVE
• **total** /toʊtɐl/ VERB
• **totally** /toʊtɐlee/ Another way of saying completely ADVERB

touch /tuch/
1. To put your hand or a part of your body on someone or something
2. If something touches something else or if things are touching, there is no space between them *These chairs are so close they're touching.* VERB
• **touch** /tuch/ NOUN

tough /tuf/
1. Hard and strong *Phonic is made from a very tough plastic.* 2. If a person is tough, they are strong and successful even when a situation is difficult
3. Difficult *This problem is pretty tough.* ADJECTIVE

tour /tooer/
1. A journey where you go to lots of places 2. A short journey to visit different parts of a building *Inky took Snake and Bee on a tour of her mousehole.* NOUN
• **tour** /tooer/ VERB

tourist /tooerist/
Someone who travels to different places on vacation NOUN

tournament /tɔrnement/
A competition for lots of people where the winner of each game plays in the next game until there is one winner NOUN

tow /toʊ/
To pull something like a car or boat using a rope fixed to another car or boat VERB

towards /tewɔrdz/
1. Going in a certain direction *We're walking towards the forest.* 2. Near something *The letter C is towards the beginning of the alphabet.* 3. You use towards to show the way you treat someone or something *Inky is always kind towards Bee and Snake.* PREPOSITION

towel /toʊel/
A piece of soft cloth for wiping your hands or body until they are dry NOUN

Tt

tower /touer/
A tall narrow building or a tall narrow part of a building like a church NOUN

tower block /touer bloc/
A tall building with flats or offices in it NOUN

town /toun/
1. A place where thousands or millions of people live and work. Towns are much bigger than villages but smaller than cities 2. The main part of a town *Let's go into town tonight.* 3. The people who live in a town *The whole town came out to cheer our team.* NOUN

toy /toi/
Something that children play with like a doll or teddy bear or little train. Toys are often models of something real NOUN

trace¹ /trais/
1. To copy a picture using a special paper that you can see through, called tracing paper. You put the paper over it and go over the lines with a pencil 2. To find something you are looking for, such as a missing person or some information you want VERB
• **tracing paper** /traising paiper/ NOUN

trace² /trais/
1. A mark or sign of something that is left behind *Inky has left her mousehole and there's no trace of her.* 2. A very small amount of something *There is a trace of honey in the jar.* NOUN

track¹ /trac/
1. A path with lots of bumps in it *The car went slowly up the mountain track.* 2. A mark left behind by something like the feet of an animal or criminal, or the tyre of a car 3. A railway line 4. A piece of music on a CD or tape NOUN

track² /trac/
1. To follow someone or something by looking at their tracks 2. If you track someone down, you find them after looking for a long time VERB

tracksuit /tracsoot/
Loose warm clothes people wear to relax or do exercises NOUN

tractor /tracter/
A heavy vehicle for pulling things along on farms NOUN

trade¹ /traid/
1. The business of buying and selling things 2. The job that someone does *When Jim leaves school he will learn his trade as a plumber.* NOUN

trade² /traid/
If you trade something you have, you give it to someone, and they give you something else in exchange VERB

tradition /tredishen/
A way of doing things that has continued for a very long time NOUN

traffic /trafic/
The cars and other vehicles moving along the road at the same time. Heavy traffic means there are lots of them NOUN
• **traffic jam** /trafic jam/
A long line of cars and vehicles that cannot move NOUN

303

Tt

traffic lights /trafic liets/
The coloured lights that control the
traffic **NOUN PLURAL**

tragedy /trajedee/
Something very sad that happens **NOUN**
• **tragic** /trajic/ **ADJECTIVE**

trail /trail/
1. A path through the countryside or
forest 2. Things left behind by someone
or something after they have gone away
from a place *Snake left a trail of crumbs
from Inky's house.* **NOUN**

train¹ /train/
Railway carriages that are connected to
each other and pulled by an engine **NOUN**

• **train set** /train set/ A small model
train and track for children to play with
as a toy **NOUN**

train² /train/
1. To teach someone a job or skill
2. If someone trains, they learn a job
or practise a skill 3. To practise a sport
4. To teach someone how to play a
sport, or help them practise 5. To teach
an animal to obey you and to do things
VERB
• **training** /training/ **NOUN**

trainer /trainer/
1. A person who trains someone
2. Trainers are sports shoes you wear
to be comfortable or when you do sport
NOUN

tram /tram/
A big vehicle like a kind of small train
that travels along tracks in the street
NOUN

tramp /tramp/
A person with no home or job who goes
from one place to another begging for
food or money **NOUN**

trampoline /trampeleen/
A big piece of cloth fixed to a metal
frame with springs, for people to jump
up and down on **NOUN**

tranquil /trangquil/
Quiet and peaceful **ADJECTIVE**
a tranquil spot in the park

transfer /transfer/
To move something from one place to
another **VERB**

translate /translait/
To change the words in one language
to the words of another **VERB**
*Can you translate this sentence into
French, Inky?*

transparent /transparent/
If something is transparent, you can see
through it **ADJECTIVE**

transport /transport/
A way to travel from one place to
another such as by car or by train or
by plane **NOUN**
Do you have a means of transport?
• **transport** /transport/ **VERB**

T

trap¹ /trap/
1. Something people use to catch animals *Put the mouse trap over there.*
2. A bad thing someone does to catch or trick someone *The soldiers were caught in a trap.* **NOUN**

trap² /trap/
1. If you are trapped, you are not able to escape *Inky was trapped in her mousehole because the door was stuck.*
2. To stop a person or animal from escaping **VERB**

trapeze /trəpeez/
A bar held by a rope at each side that hangs from the ceiling and is used by acrobats, for example in a circus **NOUN**

trash /trash/
Waste material that people throw away **NOUN**

travel /travəl/
1. To go on a journey somewhere or visit different places *David would like to travel to Italy.* 2. To move somewhere *This car can travel really fast.* **VERB**
• **travel** /travəl/ Someone's travels are the journeys they make **NOUN**

tray /trai/
A flat piece of wood, plastic or metal for carrying food and the things you need to eat it with **NOUN**

treacle /treecəl/
A thick sticky sweet liquid for cooking or eating **NOUN**

tread /tred/
If you tread on something, you walk on it **VERB**
Ouch, you trod on my toe!
■ **trod, trodden**

treasure /trezher/
Lots of valuable things like gold or jewels **NOUN** *The children were digging for buried treasure.*

treat /treet/
1. To behave towards someone or something in a certain way *You should always treat people politely.* 2. If doctors treat you or your illness, they give you medicines and take care of you to try and make you better 3. To give or buy someone or yourself something nice to enjoy *Inky treated Snake and Bee to an ice cream.* **VERB**
• **treat** /treet/ **NOUN**
• **treatment** /treetmənt/ **NOUN**

tree /tree/
A very tall plant with lots of branches. It has a thick stem made of wood, called a trunk, and roots that go deep into the ground **NOUN**

tremble /trembəl/
To shake **VERB**
As you get old, your hands can start to tremble.

tremendous /tremendəs/
A word you use to mean very good or very big or very important **ADJECTIVE**
This is a tremendous book.

trespass /trespəs/
To go on land or into a building that belongs to someone else when you do not have their permission **VERB**

triangle /trieanggel/
A shape that has three straight sides and three angles **NOUN**
▶ **SHAPES**, page 17

Tt

tribe /trieb/
In certain countries a tribe is a group of families with the same race, language and religion NOUN

trick[1] /tric/
1. A bad thing people do to try and get something from someone or to make them suffer *The bully played a nasty trick on my friend.* 2. Something clever that someone does like magic, with other people watching *a magic trick.* 3. A special way of doing something *Here's a little trick that will help you when you cook eggs.* NOUN

trick[2] /tric/
To do a bad thing to someone, and make them believe something that is not true VERB

trickle /tricəl/
If a liquid trickles somewhere, it flows there slowly in a small thin flow VERB *The honey trickled out of the pot.*
• **trickle** /tricəl/ NOUN

tricky /tricee/
Another word for difficult ADJECTIVE
a tricky question

tricycle /triesicəl/
A bicycle with three wheels NOUN

trifle /triefəl/
A sweet food made from cake with fruit, jelly, custard and cream NOUN

trigger /trigər/
The small part on a gun that someone presses with their finger to make it fire a bullet NOUN

trim /trim/
To cut something slightly like hair or grass to make it look tidy VERB

trip[1] /trip/
When you travel from one place to another and back again NOUN
Tomorrow the whole class will be going on a trip to the zoo.

trip[2] /trip/
1. To fall over or almost fall over because your foot knocks against something 2. If someone trips you up, they make you fall or almost fall, usually when they put their foot in front of you when you are walking or running VERB

triplet /triplət/
One of three children born at the same time to the same mother NOUN

tripod /triepod/
A stand with three legs for keeping things such as cameras and telescopes steady NOUN

triumph /trieumf/
A great victory or success NOUN

trod /trod/
PAST TENSE ▶ **tread**
• **trodden** /trodən/
PAST PARTICIPLE ▶ **tread**

troll /trol/
A very ugly creature in stories that looks like a person and is usually very tall or very small NOUN

Tt

trolley /trolee/
A metal container with wheels for carrying things at a supermarket or airport **NOUN**

trombone /tromboan/
A musical instrument like a large trumpet with a long piece that slides in and out **NOUN**

trophy /troafee/
A prize, usually a silver cup, that people get when they win a sports event or competition **NOUN**

trot /trot/
If a horse trots, it moves quickly but it does not run **VERB**

trouble[1] /trubel/
1. Troubles are problems that make you worried 2. If you have trouble with something or someone, you have a problem with them 3. If you take the trouble to do something, you make a special effort *Inky took a lot of trouble explaining the 'th' sound.* **NOUN**

trouble[2] /trubel/
If something troubles someone, it makes them worried or causes them a problem **VERB**
• **troublemaker** /trubelmaiker/ **NOUN**

trousers /trouzerz/
Clothes you wear from your waist to your feet, with separate parts for each leg **NOUN PLURAL**

trout /trout/
A fish that lives in rivers that people eat **NOUN**
■ **trout** /trout/ **PLURAL**

trowel /trouel/
1. A tool with a short handle and a flat metal part at the end for digging small holes in the earth 2. A tool used to spread cement onto bricks **NOUN**

truck /truc/
A big vehicle for carrying heavy goods by road **NOUN**

true /troo/
Real or based on facts **ADJECTIVE**
What Bee says is true.

trumpet /trumpit/
A musical instrument made up of a metal tube curved around with a very wide end. People play it when they blow into the small end and press buttons on the top **NOUN**

truncheon /trunchen/
A short heavy stick that a police officer carries **NOUN**

trunk /trungk/
1. The trunk of a tree is the main stem that the branches grow from 2. The very long nose of an elephant **NOUN**

trunks /trungks/
The shorts that boys and men wear when they swim **NOUN PLURAL**

trust[1] /trust/
To believe someone is good and honest, and would not do anything bad **VERB**
Inky trusts Bee to do her homework on time.

trust[2] /trust/
A feeling that someone is good and honest **NOUN**

t

truth /trooth/
The real facts or what really happened
NOUN

try /trie/
1. If you try to do something, you do it and hope it will succeed *I'll try to phone you tomorrow if I can.* · *Snake tried to spell that word but he got it wrong.* 2. If you try something, you do something to find out what happens or if you like it *Can I try your bike?* 3. **try on** To put on clothes to see if you like them **VERB**
· **try** /trie/ **NOUN**

T-shirt /tee shert/
A thin shirt with no collar or buttons, and with short sleeves **NOUN**

tub /tub/
1. A container used for different things such as selling ice cream in or growing plants in 2. A big container for water for washing your body in **NOUN**

tubby /tubee/
A way of saying someone is a bit fat
ADJECTIVE

tube /tueb/
1. A long thin round object that is hollow, for example for carrying liquid or gas 2. A tube of something like toothpaste is a long narrow container that you squeeze to make the substance come out 3. Used to mean the trains in London that go under the ground **NOUN**

tuck /tuc/
1. To put something in a certain place because you think that it is a good or safe or comfortable place to put it *Inky tucked her book under her arm.*
2. To tuck something in means to put the end of it in somewhere to keep it neat and tidy *Tuck your shirt in before you go out!* 3. To tuck someone in is to make them comfortable in their bed before they go to sleep **VERB**

Tuesday /tuezdai/
A day of the week **NOUN**
▸ **CALENDAR**, page 13

tug /tug/
To pull hard on something with lots of little pulls **VERB**
Stop tugging at my coat sleeves!
· **tug** /tug/ **NOUN**

tulip /tuelip/
A flower that looks like a cup on a long stem. Tulips grow in spring **NOUN**

tumble /tumbel/
To tumble or to tumble down is to fall over **VERB**

tumble dryer /tumbel drieer/
A machine for drying clothes when they have been washed **NOUN**

tummy /tumee/
Another word for your stomach or the soft part of your body below your chest
NOUN

T

tuna /tuenə/
A large sea fish that people eat NOUN

tune /tuen/
A song or a group of musical sounds
NOUN

tunic /tuenic/
The top part of a uniform that people
like soldiers or police officers wear NOUN

tunnel /tunəl/
A long passage under the ground for
trains or cars NOUN

turban /terbən/
A long piece of cloth that men in some
religions wrap around their head. For
example, Sikh men wear turbans NOUN

turf /terf/
Short grass with a layer of earth under it
NOUN

turkey /terkee/
1. A bird like a big chicken that people
keep on farms 2. The meat from the
turkey that people eat. People often eat
turkey at Christmas NOUN

turn¹ /tern/
1. To go around in a circle, or to make
something do this 2. To change direction
or make something face in a different
direction *Inky turned Phonic so that Snake
and Bee could see him.* 3. If you turn a
page, you move it so you can read the
next page 4. To become something else
*Caterpillars turn into butterflies. · The leaves
turned red in October.* 5. Another way of
saying go *Let's turn back, I want to go
home.* 6. **turn down** To say you do not
want to accept something or someone
7. If you turn something on or off, you
make it work or you stop making it work
*Bee turned on the television. Snake turned off
the lights.* VERB

turn² /tern/
1. Someone's turn is the time when they
have to do something *It's your turn to
play now.* 2. A change of direction *The
bus made a right turn.* NOUN

turning /terning/
Another word for a road, especially a
small road that goes from a bigger road
NOUN

turnip /ternip/
A big round vegetable with a
light-coloured skin NOUN

turtle /tertəl/
A big animal with a thick shell that lives
in the sea but can also walk along the
ground NOUN

tusk /tusk/
Tusks are the long pointed teeth that
stick out of the mouths of an elephant
or walrus NOUN

tutor /tueter/
A teacher in a university or who gives
private lessons to students NOUN

Tt

TV /tee**vee**/
Another word for television **NOUN**

tweet /tweet/
The short high sound made by a bird
NOUN
• **tweet** /tweet/ **VERB**

tweezers /**twee**zerz/
A small tool made of two pieces of metal
that people use for pulling out small
objects like splinters or picking up small
things **NOUN PLURAL**

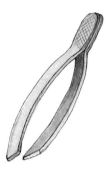

twice /twies/
Two times only **ADVERB**

twig /twig/
A little part of a branch from a tree
or bush **NOUN**

twilight /**twie**liet/
The part of the evening when it has
started to get dark **NOUN**

twin /twin/
Twins are children that are born at the
same time and have the same mother
NOUN *Tony is in the same class as his twin
brother.*

twinkle /**twing**kel/
If stars or lights twinkle, they shine then
stop shining and continue doing this all
the time.**VERB**

twirl /twerl/
To go around and around quickly in
circles, or to make something do this **VERB**

twist /twist/
1. To bend something until it does
not have its normal shape any more *My
bicycle wheel got twisted when I hit the tree.*
2. To turn something around and around
*You have to twist the top of the jar to open
it.* 3. If you twist a part of your body
like your ankle, you hurt it when you
bend it the wrong way **VERB**
• **twist** /twist/ **NOUN**

twister /**twis**ter/
Another word for a tornado or strong
wind that twists around as it moves
NOUN

twitch /twich/
To move suddenly with very small
movements **VERB**

type[1] /tiep/
A thing or person that belongs to a
certain group and has qualities that are
similar. Often used to describe or explain
something **NOUN**
What type of books do you like reading?

type[2] /tiep/
To write something using your computer
keyboard **VERB**
Bee typed in her name.
• **typing** /**tie**ping/ **NOUN**
• **typist** /**tie**pist/ **NOUN**

typewriter /**tie**prieter/
A machine people sometimes use to type
words straight onto a sheet of paper
NOUN

typical /**tip**icel/
Normal and just like other things of the
same kind **ADJECTIVE**
It's typical of Inky Mouse to be helpful.

tyre /tieer/
A rubber cover for the wheel of a bicycle
or car that is filled with air **NOUN**

Uu

ugly /uglee/
Not nice to look at **ADJECTIVE**

umbrella /umbrelɐ/
A folding frame with cloth over it that is fixed on to a stick. You hold an umbrella over your head when it rains **NOUN**

umpire /umpieer/
Someone who makes players obey the rules in sports like tennis or cricket **NOUN**

unable /unaibɐl/
If you say someone is unable to do something, you mean they cannot do it **ADJECTIVE**

unaware /unɐweer/
Not knowing something **ADJECTIVE**

unbearable /unbeerɐbɐl/
Very bad or making you suffer in a very bad way **ADJECTIVE**
The heat is unbearable.

unbelievable /unbɐleevɐbɐl/
A word you use to mean that something is really good or really bad **ADJECTIVE**
The music was unbelievable!

uncle /ungcɐl/
1. The brother of your father or mother
2. The husband of your aunt **NOUN**

uncomfortable /uncumftɐbɐl/
Stopping you from feeling good or relaxed **ADJECTIVE**
an uncomfortable chair

unconscious /unconshɐs/
If someone is unconscious, they do not know what is happening around them because they cannot see or hear, usually because they are hurt or sick **ADJECTIVE**

under /under/
1. In a lower place than something or covered by it Snake left his pen under his exercise book. 2. Less than something
All the children in the class are under ten.
PREPOSITION, ADVERB

underground[1] /underground/
Under the surface of the ground
ADJECTIVE, ADVERB

underground[2] /underground/
A railway that goes under the ground
NOUN

underline /underlien/
To draw a line under a word or words
VERB

underneath[1] /underneeth/
In a lower position to something
PREPOSITION, ADVERB
In our house the kitchen is underneath my bedroom.

Uu

underneath[2] /underneeth/
The underneath of something is the part that is under it NOUN
The underneath of the box is dirty.

understand /understand/
1. To know the meaning of something *Can you explain this word? I don't understand it.* 2. To know what someone means, how they are feeling or why they behave in a certain way *We can't understand their bad behaviour.* VERB
■ **understood**
• **understandable** /understandəbel/ ADJECTIVE

understanding /understanding/
1. What someone knows about something *Snake and Bee now have a good understanding of the alphabet.*
2. When you are kind to other people because you know how they feel *Bee is a bit slow sometimes. She needs Inky's understanding.* NOUN

understood /understood/
PAST TENSE ▶ **understand**

underwater /underwawter/
Under the surface of the water
ADJECTIVE, ADVERB

underwear /underweer/
The clothes you wear against your body under your normal clothes NOUN

undid /undid/
PAST TENSE ▶ **undo**

undo /undoo/
1. To open something so it is not closed any more 2. To make something looser so it is not tied or connected any more
To undo a belt or a knot. VERB
■ **undid, undone**

undone[1] /undun/
Not tied or connected any more
ADJECTIVE *Your button has come undone.*

undone[2] /undun/
PAST PARTICIPLE ▶ **undo**

undress /undres/
To take your clothes off, or to take them off someone else VERB
• **undressed** /undrest/ Without any clothes on ADJECTIVE

unemployed /unemploid/
An unemployed person has no job
ADJECTIVE

uneven /uneevən/
Not smooth or level or flat ADJECTIVE

unexpected /unekspectid/
Surprising because you did not know it was going to happen, or you do not know it will happen ADJECTIVE

unfair /unfeer/
Bad and wrong because people do not treat everyone the same ADJECTIVE

unfold /unfoald/
To open something so it is not folded any more VERB

unfortunate /unforchenet/
If someone is unfortunate, bad things happen to them by chance ADJECTIVE

unfortunately /unforchenetlee/
Used when you mean something bad happens ADVERB
Unfortunately, we missed the last train.

unfriendly /unfrendlee/
Not nice or kind ADJECTIVE

Uu

unhappy /unhapee/
1. Another way of saying sad
2. Not liking something or not liking what has happened *Snake was unhappy about missing school when he wasn't feeling well.* ADJECTIVE

unhurt /unhert/
Not injured or feeling any pain ADJECTIVE

unicorn /uenicorn/
An animal in stories that is like a horse with a horn on its head NOUN

uniform /ueniform/
Special clothes that some people have to wear, such as soldiers or schoolchildren NOUN

universe /uenivers/
All the planets and stars and everything that is in space NOUN

university /ueniversetee/
A place where students study after they leave school NOUN

unless /unles/
Used when you mean that something must happen before another thing can happen CONJUNCTION
I won't be able to spell this word unless you help me.

unlike /unliek/
Different from something or someone else PREPOSITION *Molly is unlike her sister.*

unlikely /unlieklee/
If something is unlikely, it will probably not happen ADJECTIVE
Snow is unlikely in the summertime.

unload /unload/
To take things out of something VERB

Inky and Snake unloaded the fruit from the truck.

unlock /unloc/
To open something by turning a key VERB

unlucky /unlucee/
1. If you are unlucky, bad things happen to you by chance 2. Used for talking about something that is thought to make bad things happen *His unlucky number is 13.* ADJECTIVE

unpack /unpac/
To take things out of a bag or other container VERB

unpleasant /unplezent/
1. Not nice or liked *This water has an unpleasant taste.* 2. Not friendly or kind to someone *Nicole is often unpleasant to me.* ADJECTIVE

unplug /unplug/
To take the plug out of something so it is not connected to the electricity any more VERB

unpopular /unpopyeler/
Not liked by many people ADJECTIVE

unreasonable /unreezenebel/
Not right or sensible or what it should be ADJECTIVE
This behaviour is completely unreasonable!

313

Uu

unscrew /unscroo/
To turn something until it comes off or is loose VERB
Unscrew the bottle top.

unsuccessful /unsecsesfel/
1. If someone is unsuccessful, they do not do well or get what they want
2. If something is unsuccessful, it does not give you what you want ADJECTIVE

unsuitable /unsootebel/
Not right or good for something
ADJECTIVE
This hat is unsuitable for the hot weather.

unsure /unshooer/
If you are unsure about something, there is something you do not know, for example you do not know if it is true or if you should do it ADJECTIVE
Bee was unsure how to spell finger.

untidy /untiedee/
1. Badly arranged with everything in the wrong place 2. If a person is untidy, they do not put things in the right place
ADJECTIVE

untie /untie/
To loosen, or take away a knot in something VERB

until /until/
1. Up to a certain time *On Sundays, Bee sleeps until eleven o'clock. • Let's stay here until it stops raining.* 2. Up to a certain place *Stay on the train until the last stop.*
PREPOSITION, CONJUNCTION

untrue /untroo/
Not real or based on facts ADJECTIVE

unused /unuezd/
1. Never used before 2. Not being used now *Don't throw away your unused tickets.*
ADJECTIVE

unusual /unuezhooel/
Not happening very often, or different in some way ADJECTIVE

unwell /unwel/
Another word for sick ADJECTIVE

unwise /unwiez/
Not sensible ADJECTIVE

up /up/
1. Towards a higher position or level, or in a higher position or level *Walk up the stairs.* 2. Not in bed any more *What time did you get up?* 3. Along *She lives up the street.* 4. Going near to someone or something *Inky went up to the window.*
5. If you say something is up to you, you mean you are the one who must decide about it *I'll leave the choice up to you.* ADVERB, PREPOSITION
• **uphill** /uphil/ ADVERB

upon /epon/
Another way of saying on PREPOSITION

upper /uper/
Higher in position than something else
ADJECTIVE
The upper part of the box has writing on it.

upright /upriet/
Straight up ADVERB, ADJECTIVE

Inky put the ladder in an upright position.

Uu

upset[1] /upset/

To make someone very sad or worried or slightly angry VERB

What you said has upset me

■ upset

upset[2] /upset/

Sad or worried or slightly angry

ADJECTIVE

upside down /upsied doun/

Turned around so that the top part is at the bottom ADVERB

You've hung the picture upside down!

upstairs /upsteerz/

To or on a higher level in a house or building that has stairs ADVERB

Inky went upstairs to get her book.

upwards /upwerdz/

Towards a higher position or level ADVERB

urgent /erjent/

Needing to be done quickly ADJECTIVE

us /us/

Used when you and other people are talking about yourselves PRONOUN

use[1] /uez/

1. If you use something, you do something with it for a particular reason *We use a fork to eat our food.* 2. To take a certain amount of something *I've used some of the paint but not all of it.* 3. To say or write something *Inky sometimes uses long words.* VERB

use[2] /ues/

1. When you use something or the way you use it *Computers have lots of different uses.* 2. **no use** Used to mean there is no reason for doing something because it probably will not happen *It's no use waiting any more, she won't come.* NOUN

used[1] /uezd/

If you buy a used car, someone has owned it before and driven it ADJECTIVE

used[2] /uest/

If you are used to something, you know all about it because you have done it or seen it or had it before ADJECTIVE

used to /uest too/

If something used to happen, it happened in the past lots of times VERB

We used to go for a walk on Sundays.

useful /uesfel/

If something is useful, it helps you in different ways ADJECTIVE

A dictionary can be very useful.

· *An umbrella is useful when it's raining.*

useless /uesles/

If something is useless, it does not help you because it cannot do what it is supposed to do ADJECTIVE

This radio is useless, it's broken.

usual /uezhooel/

1. If something is usual, it is what people do most often or what happens most of the time *It is usual to feel tired after running around the park.* 2. **as usual** Happening most of the time *As usual, we got to school late.* ADJECTIVE

usually /uezhooelee/

Used for talking about something that happens most of the time ADVERB

We usually go to school at eight o'clock.

315

Vv

vacant /vaicɛnt/
Another word for empty **ADJECTIVE**

vaccinate /vacsinait/
To use a needle to put something into your body that stops you getting an illness **VERB**
Have you been vaccinated against measles?

vacuum /vacuem/
To clean a carpet or the floor with a vacuum cleaner **VERB**

vacuum cleaner /vacuem cleener/
A machine people use for cleaning carpets and floors. It uses air to suck up the dirt and take it away **NOUN**

vague /vaig/
1. Not explained very clearly 2. Not very clear to see *I saw a vague shape in the distance.* 3. Not easy to understand or remember **ADJECTIVE**
• **vaguely** /vaiglee/ **ADVERB**

vain[1] /vain/
If someone is vain, they are too proud of themselves, and how they look **ADJECTIVE**

vain[2] /vain/
in vain Without any success, or for no reason **NOUN**
We waited in vain. She didn't come!

valentine /valɛntien/
1. A card or present sent to someone you love on Valentine's day (14 February)
2. The person you send a valentine to **NOUN**

valley /valee/
The low part of the land in between two hills or mountains **NOUN**

valuable /valyɛbɛl/
Worth a lot of money **ADJECTIVE**
This old book is very valuable.

value /value/
1. The amount of money something can be sold for *This jewel has a high value.*
2. How important something is
Learning to read is of great value. **NOUN**

vampire /vampieɛr/
In stories, a vampire is someone who has two long pointed teeth and drinks blood **NOUN**

Vv

van /van/
A vehicle like a big car or a small truck for carrying things **NOUN**

vandal /vandɛl/
Someone who damages things that belong to other people **NOUN**

vanilla /vɛnilɛ/
A special food taste that comes from the bean of a plant **NOUN**
vanilla ice cream

vanish /vanish/
To go away suddenly so you cannot see or find someone or something any more **VERB**
Where is Snake? He has just vanished!

varied /vɛɛrid/
Including lots of different things **ADJECTIVE**
The entertainment was very varied.

various /vɛɛreeɛs/
Used to mean different when talking about several things or people **ADJECTIVE**
There are various ways you can pronounce that word.

vase /vahz/
A container for flowers that have been cut from the plant **NOUN**

vast /vast/
Very very big **ADJECTIVE**

vault¹ /vawlt/
To jump over something by putting both your hands on it to lift yourself up **VERB**

vault² /vawlt/
1. A room with thick walls and a strong door where people keep money or valuable things to protect them
2. A room where people from the same family are buried **NOUN**

vegetable /vejɛtɛbɛl/
A plant or part of a plant that people use for food. Potatoes and cabbages are vegetables **NOUN**

vegetarian /vejɛteɛreeɛn/
A person who does not eat meat or fish **NOUN**

vehicle /veeicɛl/
A machine with wheels and an engine for taking people from one place to another **NOUN**

Cars, buses and trucks are different types of vehicle.

veil /vail/
A thin piece of cloth that some women wear over their face **NOUN**

vein /vain/
One of the very thin tubes that carry the blood around your body and to your heart **NOUN**

velvet /velvit/
A kind of cloth that is soft and thick on one side **NOUN**

317

Vv

venom /venəm/
The poison from some snakes, spiders and scorpions **NOUN**

ventriloquist /ventriləquist/
A person who can speak without moving the lips. Ventriloquists usually have a small dummy that they pretend is talking to them **NOUN**

verb /verb/
A word used in grammar to show what a person or thing does **NOUN**
Jump and sit are verbs.
▶ **PARTS OF SPEECH**, pages 6 and 7

verse /vers/
A part of a poem or song, or a few lines in a holy book **NOUN**

version /vershən/
1. A copy of something that is slightly different from the original *Snake downloaded the latest version of the software.* 2. Someone's description of something that happened, using their own words and ideas **NOUN**

versus /versəs/
A word that is sometimes used to mean against, especially in sports **PREPOSITION**

vertical /verticəl/
Standing upright **ADJECTIVE**

very¹ /veree/
Used to give more importance to another word, by saying it is more or greater in some way **ADVERB**
Snake is very tired. · Bee can fly very fast.

very² /veree/
1. Used for saying something is right at the end or beginning *Inky sat at the very back of the bus.* 2. This and no other *At that very moment the lights went out.*
ADJECTIVE

vessel /vesəl/
1. A boat or ship 2. A container for liquids **NOUN**

vest /vest/
Underwear to cover the top part of your body to keep you warm **NOUN**

vet /vet/
A doctor for animals **NOUN**

vibrate /viebrait/
To shake very fast with very small movements **VERB**

vicar /vicer/
A man who does religious duties in the Church of England **NOUN**

vicinity /vesinetee/
If somewhere is in the vicinity of something, it is near to it **NOUN**

vicious /vishes/
1. Very bad and cruel 2. A vicious animal attacks people and hurts them
ADJECTIVE

victim /victim/
1. Someone who has been hurt or killed by someone or in an accident or crime
2. Someone who has suffered because of someone or something *He was a victim of a racist remark.* **NOUN**

victory /victeree/
When people win in a competition or battle **NOUN**

Vv

video /videeɒɑ/

1. A film or programme that is recorded onto a special tape that people watch on television *We were watching Bee's birthday party on video.* 2. The plastic case and tape for recording and playing back television programmes and films 3. The machine for recording and playing back television programmes and films **NOUN**

view /vue/

1. When you can see something from somewhere *The trees spoil my view of the lake.* 2. The place you can see from somewhere, for example from a high place or a window *The view from the top of the building is very beautiful.* 3. Someone's views about something are what they think about it **NOUN**

Viking /vieking/

Vikings are a group of people who lived just over a thousand years ago. They came from the north and were good sailors and fighters **NOUN**

villa /vile/

A house, especially a big one, for example in a warm country or close to the sea **NOUN**

village /vilij/

A group of houses and buildings in the countryside **NOUN**

vine /vien/

A plant that grapes grow on **NOUN**

vinegar /viniger/

A liquid with a taste as strong as a lemon that is made from things like wine. People use vinegar to give taste to food **NOUN**

vineyard /vinyard/

A farm where vines are grown to produce grapes for making wine **NOUN**

violent /vieelent/

1. If someone is violent, they do things to hurt people or cause a lot of damage *He was a violent criminal.* · *a violent attack* 2. If something like a storm is violent, it has a lot of strength and can cause damage **ADJECTIVE**

· **violence** /vieelens/ **NOUN**

violet /vieelet/

A purple-blue colour **NOUN, ADJECTIVE**

violin /vieelin/

A musical instrument with strings that you hold under your chin. You pull a stick called a bow over the strings to make the sounds **NOUN**

virus /vieres/

1. A very tiny creature that makes people sick if it gets into the body 2. A computer program that causes damage to the information on your computer **NOUN**

visible /vizebel/

If something is visible, you can see it **ADJECTIVE**

Vv

visit /vizit/
1. To go and see someone
2. To go to a place **VERB**
• **visit** /vizit/ **NOUN**
• **visitor** /viziter/ **NOUN**

vital /vietel/
Very important **ADJECTIVE**

vitamin /vitemin/
A substance in food that your body
needs to keep it healthy **NOUN**

vixen /vixen/
A female fox **NOUN**

vocabulary /voacabyeleree/
All the words that you know **NOUN**

voice /vois/
The sound you make when you speak
NOUN

volcano /volcainoa/
A mountain that opens at the top and
sometimes throws hot and liquid rock
up into the air **NOUN**

volume /voluem/
1. The amount of sound that comes
out of something like a television
or radio *Can you turn the volume up?*
2. The amount of space that something
fills 3. A book, often one of several
books that together make a very long
book **NOUN**

volunteer /volentier/
1. Someone who does work but does not
want to be paid for it 2. Someone who
does something without someone telling
them to do it **NOUN**
• **volunteer** /volentier/ **VERB**

vomit /vomit/
To have the food you have eaten come
back up from your stomach and out of
your mouth **VERB**

vote /voat/
To say which person or thing you would
like to be chosen, for example by putting
a cross on a piece of paper or by putting
up your hand. The person or thing with
most votes wins **VERB**
• **vote** /voat/ **NOUN**
• **voter** /voater/ **NOUN**

voucher /voucher/
A piece of paper that people can use
instead of money **NOUN**
a gift voucher

vowel /vouel/
Vowels are the letters A, E, I, O, U **NOUN**

voyage /voiij/
A journey someone makes by boat or
into space **NOUN**

vulture /vulcher/
A very big bird that eats the bodies of
dead animals **NOUN**

Ww

waddle /wodǝl/
To walk like a duck, moving with short steps from side to side VERB

wade /waid/
To walk through water VERB

wafer /waifer/
A very thin biscuit that people often eat with ice cream NOUN

wag /wag/
If an animal such as a dog wags its tail, it moves it from one side to the other VERB

wages /waijiz/
Money that people get for working
NOUN PLURAL

wagon /wagen/
Or **waggon**. A vehicle with wheels pulled by horses that was mainly used in past times NOUN

wail /wail/
To make a long high sound when you are in pain or unhappy VERB

waist /waist/
The narrow part in the middle of your body above your hips NOUN

waistcoat /waistcoat/
Something people wear over a shirt. A waistcoat has buttons and no sleeves
NOUN

wait /wait/
1. To stay in the same place until someone comes or something happens *Inky was waiting for Snake before starting the lesson.* 2. To be expecting something soon *We're still waiting for our tickets.* VERB
• **wait** /wait/ NOUN

waiter /waiter/
A man who works in a restaurant and brings food or drinks to people's tables
NOUN
• **waitress** /waitrǝs/ NOUN

wake /waik/
1. If you wake or wake up, you stop sleeping 2. To wake someone up is to stop them sleeping VERB
■ **woke, woken**

walk[1] /wawk/
1. To move along the ground using your legs 2. If you walk a dog, you walk with it so that it gets some exercise VERB

walk[2] /wawk/
1. A journey you make when you walk somewhere, or the distance or the time it takes *It's a ten-minute walk to Snake's house.* 2. If you go for a walk, you walk somewhere because you like walking *Let's go for a walk in the park.* NOUN
• **walker** /wawker/ NOUN
• **walking** /wawking/ NOUN

wall /wawl/
1. The side of a room or a building
2. Something built usually out of bricks that goes around someone's land *There's a high wall around Inky's garden.* NOUN

321

Ww

wallaby /woləbee/
An animal like a small kangaroo NOUN

wallet /wolet/
A little folding case for carrying important documents and money NOUN

wallpaper /wowlpaiper/
Special paper people stick on the walls inside buildings to decorate them NOUN

walnut /wowlnut/
A nut you can eat that grows inside a hard shell. Walnuts are round but with lots of little lumps NOUN

walrus /wowlres/
A big sea animal like a seal with two very long pointed teeth called tusks NOUN

wand /wond/
A thin stick for doing magic tricks NOUN

wander /wonder/
1. To walk around but not in a particular direction *Some parents are wandering around the school.* 2. **wander off** To go away from the place where you are supposed to be VERB

want /wont/
1. If you want something, you have a feeling that you need to have it or do it *Do you want a cup of tea? · Snake's hungry, he wants to eat.* 2. If you want someone, you ask for them because you need to see them or speak to them *Inky wants you, Bee.* 3. To want someone to do something means that you are telling them to do it VERB

war /wor/
When two or more countries fight against each other NOUN

ward /word/
A big room in a hospital with beds for people who are sick NOUN

wardrobe /wordroab/
A big cupboard where you hang your clothes NOUN

warm¹ /worm/
When the temperature is not too high and it feels very pleasant ADJECTIVE

warm² /worm/
To make something warm VERB

Bee sat by the fire to warm up her wings.

• **warmth** /wormth/ NOUN

warn /worn/
To tell someone about something bad that might happen VERB
• **warning** /worning/ NOUN

Ww

warren /woren/
A place under the ground where lots of rabbits live **NOUN**

warrior /woreeer/
A soldier **NOUN**

warship /worship/
A big ship with lots of guns for fighting in a war **NOUN**

wart /wort/
A little hard lump on people's skin **NOUN**

was /woz/
PAST TENSE ▶ **be**

wash /wosh/
1. To clean something with water and usually soap 2. **wash up** To wash things like the plates, knives and forks after a meal **VERB**

• **wash** /wosh/ **NOUN**
• **washing** /woshing/ The dirty clothes that have to be washed **NOUN**

washbasin /woshbaisen/
A big bowl in a bathroom for washing your hands and face **NOUN**

washing machine
/woshing mesheen/
A machine for washing clothes **NOUN**

wasp /wosp/
An insect with a yellow and black body that has a sting **NOUN**
▶ INSECTS, page 14

waste /waist/
1. To use too much of something or use it badly *We don't have much water left. Don't waste it.* 2. If you say something is wasted, you mean it was not necessary to do something or use it *The whole morning has been wasted.* **VERB**

wastepaper basket
/waistpaiper baskit/
A container for rubbish such as pieces of paper you do not want **NOUN**

watch[1] /woch/
1. A small clock that people wear on their wrist 2. **keep watch** To pay a lot of attention to something or someone **NOUN**

• **watchstrap** /wochstrap/ **NOUN**

watch[2] /woch/
1. To keep looking at something or someone *Watch Bee, she's going to fly to the top of the tree!* 2. To pay attention to something that could be dangerous *Watch that loose step!* 3. To take care of someone or something *Can you watch the children?* **VERB**

water[1] /wawter/
The liquid that falls from the clouds as rain and makes rivers and seas. Water is used for drinking and washing **NOUN**

water[2] /wawter/
To pour water on plants to make them grow **VERB**
• **watering can** /wawtering can/ **NOUN**
• **water pistol** /wawter pistel/ **NOUN**

W

waterfall /wawterfawl/
A place where water falls off the edge of a cliff NOUN

watermelon /wawtermelen/
A big round fruit with a hard green skin. Watermelons are soft and red on the inside NOUN

waterproof /wawterproof/
Something waterproof does not allow water to go through it ADJECTIVE
a waterproof jacket

wave¹ /waiv/
1. An area of water that swells up on the surface of the sea 2. When you hold up your hand and move it from side to side *He gave me a little wave as he got on the train.* NOUN

wave² /waiv/
To move something like your hand or a flag from side to side, for example to say hello or goodbye VERB

wavy /waivee/
Wavy hair or a wavy line is not straight but has curves in it ADJECTIVE

wax /wax/
A soft substance made by bees and used for many things such as to make candles or to make furniture shine NOUN

way /wai/
1. How you do something *We like the way Inky sings that song.* 2. The line or direction that someone or something is moving in *Which way did he go?*
3. A road or path *Snake has lost his way.*
4. A distance *Our grandparents live a long way away.* 5. The space someone or something is using *You're in my way, Bee.*
NOUN

way out /wai out/
The door or place you go through to leave somewhere such as a building NOUN

WC /dubelue see/
Short for 'water closet', another word for a toilet NOUN

we /wee/
Used when talking about yourself and another person or other people PRONOUN
We are late for class today.

weak /week/
1. Not powerful or strong 2. Easy to break or damage *This part of the bridge is a bit weak.* 3. Not very good at something *She's a very weak player.*
ADJECTIVE
• **weaken** /weeken/ VERB
• **weakness** /weeknes/ NOUN

wealthy /welthee/
Having lots of money ADJECTIVE

weapon /wepen/
A thing such as a gun or knife that people can use to hurt other people
NOUN

wear /weer/
1. If you wear something such as clothes, you have them on your body *Inky was wearing a hat with flowers on it.* 2. If something wears out or you wear it out, you have used it so much that it cannot be used any more *My shoes are completely worn out.* VERB
■ **wore, worn**
• **wear** /weer/ NOUN

weary /wieree/
Another word for tired ADJECTIVE

weasel /weezel/
A small furry animal that eats eggs and other small animals NOUN

weather /wether/
The conditions in the air such as the temperature, rain, wind, snow or sun NOUN

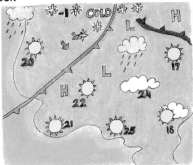

weave /weev/
To make cloth using a special machine that puts long threads over and under each other VERB
■ **wove, woven**

web /web/
1. The net made by a spider to catch insects 2. The Web is a very big collection of documents and pictures stored on computers all over the world. All the computers are connected to each other and make up the Internet NOUN

website /websiet/
A place on the Internet where you find information about something or someone NOUN

wedding /weding/
The ceremony when a man and a woman get married NOUN

Wednesday /wenzdai/
A day of the week NOUN
▶ CALENDAR, page 13

wee /wee/
A word that is sometimes used to mean little, especially in Scotland ADJECTIVE

weed /weed/
A plant that people do not want that grows very fast in places like gardens. People often pull them up NOUN

week /week/
A period of seven days NOUN
• **weekly** /weeklee/ Happening once every week ADJECTIVE

weekday /weekdai/
Any day of the week except Saturday and Sunday NOUN

weekend /weekend/
Used to mean Saturday and Sunday NOUN

weep /weep/
If you weep, tears come out of your eyes VERB
■ **wept**

Ww

weigh /wai/
1. To find out how heavy something or someone is 2. To have a certain weight
How much do you weigh? VERB

weight /wait/
1. How heavy something or someone is
2. Something very heavy NOUN

weird /wierd/
Very strange ADJECTIVE

welcome[1] /welcəm/
To be friendly to someone when they arrive somewhere VERB

welcome[2] /welcəm/
If you say someone is welcome, you mean you are happy to see them somewhere ADJECTIVE
You're always welcome in my home.
• **welcome** /welcəm/ NOUN

well[1] /wel/
1. If you do something well, you do it properly and in a very good way
I can swim very well. 2. Very much *Inky finished the lesson well before three o'clock.*
3. **as well as** Used to include something or someone else in what you say *Snake reads comics as well as books.* ADVERB
■ better, best

well[2] /wel/
If you are feeling well, you are healthy and not sick ADJECTIVE

well[3] /wel/
A deep hole in the ground that people get water from NOUN

wellington /welingtən/
Wellingtons are boots made of plastic or rubber that people use in the rain. They are called wellies for short NOUN

went /went/
PAST TENSE ▶ **go**

wept /wept/
PAST TENSE ▶ **weep**

were /wer/
PAST TENSE ▶ **be**

west /west/
The direction where the sun sets. If someone is looking north, the west is on their left NOUN
▶ WORLD MAP, page 14
• **west** /west/ ADJECTIVE, ADVERB

wet[1] /wet/
1. If something or someone is wet, there is water or liquid on them
2. Wet weather means there is a lot of rain ADJECTIVE

wet[2] /wet/
To make something wet VERB
■ wet or wetted

whack /wac/
To hit something very hard VERB
• **whack** /wac/ NOUN

Ww

whale /wail/
A big animal that lives in the sea and looks like a fish. Whales breathe air through a hole in the top of their head **NOUN**

what /wot/
1. Used in questions when you want information about something *What kind of food do you like?* 2. Used when you talk about a thing or idea and mention the thing or idea that it is *I know what he wants.* 3. Used when you are surprised, or when you do not hear something *What! You can't speak French!*
PRONOUN, **ADJECTIVE**

whatever /wotever/
1. Used to mean anything or any *Inky is good at whatever she does.* 2. Used to mean that nothing should change a particular situation *Whatever happens, we must not be scared.* PRONOUN, **ADJECTIVE**

wheat /weet/
A tall yellow plant with seeds that are crushed and made into flour to make bread **NOUN**

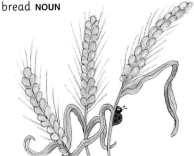

wheel[1] /weel/
1. An object shaped like a circle that goes around and makes things such as cars or bicycles move 2. Another word for the steering wheel inside a car for controlling which way it moves **NOUN**

wheel[2] /weel/
To push something with wheels along the ground **VERB**

wheelbarrow /weelbaroa/
A container with one wheel at the front and two handles at the back for carrying things outside such as earth or fallen leaves **NOUN**

wheelchair /weelcheer/
A special chair with wheels for people who cannot walk **NOUN**

when /wen/
1. At what time, or on which date *When are you leaving?* 2. Used to describe two situations happening at the same time *When the question is too hard, ask the teacher.* ADVERB, **CONJUNCTION**

whenever /wenever/
1. Used to mean every time something happens *Whenever I go to the park it rains.* 2. At any time *Come and see me whenever you like.* 3. Used to show that you do not know the time something will be *Whenever you leave, don't forget your umbrella.* **CONJUNCTION**

W **where** /weer/
Used to ask about or talk about the place something is in or has come from or is going to **ADVERB**, **CONJUNCTION**
Where are you going?

wherever /weɛrever/
1. Used to mean every place or any place *You can sit wherever you like.*
2. Used to show that you do not know where a place is *She lives in Sunnyville, wherever that is.* **CONJUNCTION**

whether /wether/
1. Used when you talk about two things and only one is true *I don't know whether he's staying in or going out.* 2. Also used to mean that it does not matter which of two things is true because that will not change what will happen *I will go, whether you stay at home or come with me.* **CONJUNCTION**

which /wich/
1. Used when talking about more than one thing and someone needs to choose one thing only *Which book do you like best?* 2. Also used to say something about a person or thing or fact that you are talking about *It's a song which lots of people have heard.* **ADJECTIVE**, **PRONOUN**

whichever /wichever/
1. Used for saying you can choose one person or thing or another, and it will not make any difference *Whichever road you take, you will still reach Inky's house.*
2. Used for choosing between two or more different things or people *There are three types of cake on the plate, take whichever one you like.* **PRONOUN**, **ADJECTIVE**

whiff /wif/
A slight smell of something **NOUN**

while¹ /wiel/
Used when talking about something that happens at the same time that something else is happening
CONJUNCTION *Bee was studying while Snake was eating his lunch.*

while² /wiel/
You use while to mean a certain amount of time, often a short amount **NOUN**
Can I stay a little while longer after class?

whimper /wimper/
If someone whimpers, they make sounds that show they are frightened or sad or something hurts them **VERB**

whip /wip/
A long piece of leather or rope with a handle that people use for hitting horses or other people **NOUN**
• **whip** /wip/ **VERB**

whirl /werl/
To go around and around in circles, or to make something do this **VERB**

whirlwind /werlwind/
A very strong wind that spins around as it moves along **NOUN**

whisk /wisk/
1. To mix something like eggs or cream very quickly 2. To take something away quickly *Before we had finished, he whisked the cups and saucers away.* **VERB**

whisker /wisker/
Whiskers are the long hairs that grow near the mouth of an animal like a cat, or the hairs on the side of a man's face **NOUN**

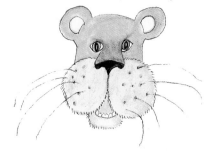

Ww

whisper /wisper/
To say something in a very quiet voice
so that other people cannot hear VERB
• **whisper** /wisper/ NOUN

whistle[1] /wisəl/
1. To make a high sound when you make
your breath come out hard through your
lips *My dad was whistling a tune.*
2. If something like a kettle whistles,
it makes a high sound VERB

whistle[2] /wisəl/
1. A little plastic or metal object that
makes a high sound when someone
blows on it 2. The sound of something
or someone whistling NOUN

white /wiet/
A very light colour like snow
NOUN, ADJECTIVE

whiteboard /wietbord/
A big white board that teachers write on
in classrooms NOUN

whizz /wiz/
To move very very fast VERB

who /hoo/
1. Used when you want to ask for
information about someone *Who do
you want to see?* 2. Used when you talk
about someone and mention what kind
of person they are *I know who you mean.*
3. Used when you talk about someone
and want to give more information
about them *I sent a letter to my aunt,
who lives far away.* PRONOUN

whoever /hooever/
Used to mean any person PRONOUN
*Whoever did this will be punished. • You can
bring whoever you like to your party.*

whole[1] /hoəl/
1. You use whole to mean all of
something *Bee and Snake spent the
whole day learning to read.* 2. Not broken
or with no parts missing *Snake ate
two whole apples and another half!*
ADJECTIVE

whole[2] /hoəl/
1. The whole of something means all
of it *It was hot the whole of the month.*
2. A whole is one thing made up of
different parts with no parts missing
Two halves make a whole. NOUN

whoops /woops/
Used when people make a mistake
or when a little accident happens
such as bumping into someone
INTERJECTION

whoosh /woosh/
To move very quickly and make a sound
like the wind blowing VERB
• **whoosh** /woosh/ NOUN, INTERJECTION

whose /hooz/
1. Used for showing that something
belongs to or is connected with something
else that you have already mentioned in
the sentence *I have a friend whose dad is
a doctor.* 2. Also used when you ask who
something belongs to or is connected with
Whose dog is this? ADJECTIVE, PRONOUN

why /wie/
Used when you ask for the reason for
something ADVERB, CONJUNCTION
*Why are you so sad? • I don't know why
he's late.*

329

W **wick** /wic/

A string running through the middle of a candle that you burn to get light NOUN

wicked /wicid/

Very bad ADJECTIVE

Their king was a wicked man.

wicket /wicit/

In cricket, a wicket is three pieces of wood stuck in the ground with another piece across the top that you try to hit with the ball NOUN

wide[1] /wied/

1. Measuring a very big distance from one side of something to the other compared to how long it is *I live on a wide street.* 2. Measuring a certain amount from one side to the other *The carpet is six feet wide.* 3. Very big *They sell a wide choice of hats.* ADJECTIVE

wide[2] /wied/

As much as possible ADVERB

When the dentist looks at your teeth, you must open your mouth wide.

widen /wieden/

To make something wider or bigger, or to become wider or bigger VERB

widow /widoa/

A woman whose husband has died NOUN

widower /widoaer/

A man whose wife has died NOUN

width /width/

The distance from one side to the other NOUN

wield /weeld/

If someone wields something like a hammer or sword, they carry it in their hand and use it VERB

wife /wief/

The woman a man is married to, who is her husband NOUN

■ **wives** /wievz/ PLURAL

wig /wig/

Hair that someone wears on their head that is not their own but is made by someone to look real NOUN

wiggle /wigel/

To make little movements from side to side like a worm moving along the ground VERB

• **wiggly** /wigelee/ ADJECTIVE

wigwam /wigwam/

A tent that Native Americans lived in during past times NOUN

Ww

wild /wield/

1. A wild animal or person lives away from people 2. A wild plant grows on its own in a natural way, and people do not take care of it 3. A wild area is a place where plants and animals live and grow on their own, and where there are no people ADJECTIVE

will[1] /wil/

1. A word you use to tell people what is going to happen in the future *We will finish the lesson at two o'clock.* 2. Used when asking someone to do something or have something *Will you help me?* VERB

will[2] /wil/

1. If you talk about someone's will to do something, you mean they really want to do it *I have the will to succeed.* 2. A document saying who is to have what when someone dies NOUN

willing /wiling/

If you are willing to do something, you are ready to do it and you want to do it ADJECTIVE

• **willingly** /wilinglee/ ADVERB

willow /wiloʊ/

A big tree with long thin leaves that usually grows near water NOUN

wilt /wilt/

If a plant wilts, it becomes weak and hangs downwards VERB

win /win/

1. To do better than everyone else in a game or race 2. To be stronger in a war or battle than the enemy 3. To get a prize *Bee won a prize for her reading.* VERB

■ **won**

• **win** /win/ NOUN

• **winner** /winer/ NOUN

wind[1] /wind/

The air that blows that you can feel on your body NOUN

Bee can't fly if there's too much wind.

• **windy** /windee/ ADJECTIVE

wind[2] /wiend/

1. To put something around something else, or to put things around each other lots of times *Wind the rope tightly.* 2. If a path winds, it bends from side to side as it goes along 3. If you wind something like a video, you move it backwards or forwards *Can you wind the video back to the beginning?* 4. To wind a clock is to turn a part of it to make it work VERB

■ **wound**

windmill /windmil/

A tall building with long pieces of wood at the front that turn in the wind. This usually makes a machine inside the building crush seeds to make flour NOUN

Ww

window /windoɑ/
A space in a wall with glass in it that lets light and air come into a room NOUN

• **windowpane** /windoɑpain/
The glass in a window NOUN
• **windowsill** /windoɑsil/
The little shelf under a window NOUN

windscreen /windscreen/
The front window of a car or truck NOUN

wine /wien/
A drink containing alcohol, made from grapes NOUN

wing /wing/
1. The wings of a bird or insect are the parts of its body that go up and down that it uses to fly 2. The wings of a plane are the long flat parts on each side that make it possible for it to fly NOUN

wink /wingk/
If someone winks, they close one of their eyes and then open it again quickly VERB

Snake winked at Bee.

winter /winter/
The coldest season in the year NOUN
▶ CALENDAR, page 13

wipe /wiep/
To clean something or make it dry when you rub it with a cloth or with something soft VERB
• **wipe** /wiep/ NOUN

wire /wieer/
A long very thin piece of metal you can bend NOUN

wise /wiez/
Very intelligent ADJECTIVE
• **wisdom** /wizdem/ Being wise NOUN

wish¹ /wish/
1. To want something *I wish we had a bigger house.* 2. If you wish someone something good like a happy birthday, you mean you hope they will have it *I wish you a Merry Christmas!* VERB

wish² /wish/
1. Something you want *I asked for a blue bike and I got my wish.* 2. **best wishes** Used for example at the end of a letter to mean you hope good things will happen to someone NOUN

witch /wich/
In stories, a witch is a woman with magic powers NOUN

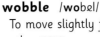

Ww

with /with/
1. If something or someone is with something else, they are together *I had my dog with me.* 2. Also used for saying that someone or something has something *I saw Snake with a sandwich in his mouth.* 3. Using something *Can you eat with chopsticks?* 4. Because of something *He was shaking with fear.* 5. Against someone *They were fighting with each other.* PREPOSITION

within /within/
1. During something *I'll be seeing her within the next day or two.* 2. Inside a place or less than a certain distance *The tennis ball must land within the lines.* PREPOSITION

without /without/
1. Not having something *Snake couldn't live without food for more than two hours!* 2. Not having someone with you *Hurry up or I'll go without you.* 3. Not doing something *You mustn't say things without thinking.* ADVERB

witness /witnes/
Someone who sees something important happen like an accident or crime and can describe what happened NOUN

wives /wievz/
NOUN PLURAL ▶ **wife**

wizard /wizerd/
In stories, a wizard is a man with magic powers NOUN

wobble /wobel/
To move slightly from one side to the other VERB
My tooth is starting to wobble.
• **wobbly** /woblee/ ADJECTIVE

woke /woak/
PAST TENSE ▶ **wake**
• **woken** /woaken/
PAST PARTICIPLE ▶ **wake**

wolf /woolf/
A wild animal like a big dog. Wolves live in groups called packs NOUN

■ **wolves** /woolvz/ PLURAL

woman /woomen/
A human being who is female and an adult NOUN
■ **women** /wimin/ PLURAL

wombat /wombat/
An animal like a small bear with a strong body and short legs that digs burrows. Wombats live in Australia NOUN

women /wimin/
NOUN PLURAL ▶ **woman**

won /wun/
PAST TENSE ▶ **win**

wonder[1] /wunder/
1. To say you want to know about something *I wonder what the time is.* 2. To show you have doubts about something *I sometimes wonder if he will pass his exam.* 3. To be surprised at something, usually because it is so beautiful or so good VERB

Ww

wonder[2] /wunder/
A feeling that shows you are surprised and very happy about something
NOUN

wonderful /wunderfel/
Really good ADJECTIVE
We had a wonderful time at the party.

wonky /wongkee/
Not straight, or shaking a little
ADJECTIVE

wood /wood/
1. The hard part from the trunk or branches of a tree 2. A little forest
NOUN
• **wooden** /wooden/
Made from wood ADJECTIVE

woodlouse /woodlous/
A tiny animal like an insect that lives in wet dark places in the house or garden
NOUN
■ **woodlice** /woodlies/ PLURAL

woodpecker /woodpecer/
A bird that makes holes in trees with its beak NOUN

woof /woof/
The sound a dog makes when it barks
NOUN

wool /wool/
The soft thick hair that grows on the body of sheep NOUN

• **woollen** /woolen/ or **woolly** /woolee/
Made from wool ADJECTIVE

word /werd/
1. A group of letters with a particular meaning and sound *What does the word 'wool' mean, Inky?* 2. A promise *I give you my word I will not be late.* 3. If you have a word with someone, you talk to them
NOUN

wore /wor/
PAST TENSE ▶ **wear**

work[1] /werk/
1. To spend time doing something *Inky has been working hard to teach Snake and Bee to read.* 2. To have a job that people pay you for *Miss Beech works as a teacher.* 3. If a machine works, all the parts of it move as they are supposed to 4. If something like a plan works, it succeeds 5. To work out something is to find what the correct answer is *Can you work out what eight plus twelve is?* VERB
• **worker** /werker/ NOUN
• **workman** /werkmen/ A man who works mainly using his hands NOUN
■ **workmen** /werkmen/ PLURAL

Ww

work² /werk/
1. Something you do that needs a lot of effort 2. Another word for a job or the place where you do it *He travels a long way to work.* **NOUN**

world /werld/
The planet that we live on, and all the people who live on the planet **NOUN**

worm /werm/
A little animal with a long thin body that has no bones or legs and lives under the ground **NOUN**

worn /wɔrn/
PAST PARTICIPLE ▶ **wear**

worry¹ /wuree/
1. To feel sad because you are thinking about a problem 2. To make someone feel sad because of a problem *I didn't want to worry you.* **VERB**

worry² /wuree/
1. A big problem 2. Used to mean being worried *Inky has a lot of worry at the moment.* **NOUN**

worse¹ /wers/
1. More bad than something else *My shoes are dirty, but your boots are worse.* 2. More sick than before *I'm feeling worse today. My head really aches.* **ADJECTIVE**

worse² /wers/
More badly than something else **ADVERB** *Does Snake sing worse than Bee?*

worship /wership/
A word than means praying together in a place like a school or church **NOUN**
• **worship** /wership/ VERB

worst¹ /werst/
Worse than anything else, most bad or badly **ADJECTIVE**, **ADVERB**

worst² /werst/
Something or someone that is worse than anything else **NOUN**

worth /werth/
1. If something is worth a certain amount of money, that is the true amount that people think they can sell it for *How much is your ring worth?* 2. If something is worth doing, there is a good reason for doing it *Of course, it's worth learning to read.* **ADJECTIVE**

worthwhile /werthwiel/
Worth doing because it is good or important **ADJECTIVE**

would /wood/
1. Used as the past tense of 'will' for talking about something that was going to happen *Snake said he would work harder.* 2. Used with 'if' to show something that could happen if something else was different *If I were rich, I would buy a big house.* 3. Used when you ask someone politely to do something *Would you help me, Bee?* 4. You use 'would like' as a polite way of saying you want something *I would like a cup of coffee.* **VERB**

wound¹ /woond/
Damage that is done to a part of someone's body **NOUN**
• **wound** /woond/ VERB
• **wounded** /woondid/ ADJECTIVE

wound² /wound/
PAST TENSE ▶ **wind**²

Ww

wove /wōav/

PAST TENSE ▶ **weave**

• **woven** /wōaven/

PAST PARTICIPLE ▶ **weave**

wrap /rap/

To put paper or cloth around something to cover it VERB

wrapper /raper/

A piece of paper or plastic that is wrapped around something NOUN

a sweet wrapper

wreath /reeth/

Flowers and leaves arranged in the shape of a ring NOUN

wreck[1] /rec/

To damage something badly or destroy it VERB

wreck[2] /rec/

Something so badly damaged that it cannot be used any more, such as a plane that has crashed or a ship that has hit rocks NOUN

wreckage /recij/

Pieces of something like a car or plane that have been damaged, for example in an accident NOUN

wren /ren/

A little brown bird with a short tail NOUN

wretched /rechid/

1. Very unhappy or sick
2. Of a very low quality ADJECTIVE

wriggle /rigel/

To make lots of little movements with your body, like a worm moving along the ground VERB

wring /ring/

To squeeze and twist something wet like a cloth to make the water come out VERB

■ **wrung**

wrinkle /ringkel/

Wrinkles are lines on people's skin, especially their face, as they get older NOUN

• **wrinkled** /ringkeld/ ADJECTIVE

wrist /rist/

The part of your body that joins your hand to your arm NOUN

• **wristwatch** /ristwoch/ NOUN

Xx

write /riet/

1. To make letters and words, usually with a pen or pencil *Bee and Snake are learning to read and write.* 2. To write something like a book or letter or song means that you put all the words together that make them 3. If you write to someone, you send them a message in a letter or email 4. To spell a word *You write 'knife' with a silent 'k'.* VERB

■ wrote, written

• **writer** /rieter/ NOUN
• **writing** /rieting/ NOUN

written /riten/

PAST PARTICIPLE ▶ **write**

wrong¹ /rong/

1. With mistakes *Snake gave the wrong answer.* 2. Used for talking about something that should not be done *I made the wrong decision.* 3. If you say someone is wrong, you mean what they say is not true or based on facts 4. If there is something wrong, it means there is a problem *What's wrong, Jack?* 5. Another way of saying bad *That blue looks wrong in your painting.* ADJECTIVE

• **wrongly** /ronglee/ ADVERB

wrong² /rong/

If you do something wrong, you do not do it correctly ADVERB

wrong³ /rong/

If someone does wrong, they do something they should not have done NOUN

wrote /roat/

PAST TENSE ▶ **write**

wrung /rung/

PAST TENSE ▶ **wring**

Xmas /exmøs/

Another way of writing Christmas NOUN

X-ray /ex rai/

A special picture that shows a part of the inside of something, usually of someone's body NOUN

• **X-ray** /ex rai/ VERB

xylophone /zielefoan/

A musical instrument with a row of metal bars that you hit with a little hammer to make the sounds NOUN

337

Yy

yacht /yot/
A big boat with sails that people sometimes use for racing **NOUN**

yak /yak/
An animal that looks like a large cow with long hair **NOUN**

yard /yard/
1. An area next to a building with a wall around it 2. A small area with no grass at the back of a house 3. A measurement of length **NOUN**

yawn /yawn/
To open your mouth wide and breathe in a lot, usually because you are tired **VERB**
• **yawn** /yawn/ **NOUN**

year /yier/
A period of twelve months or 52 weeks **NOUN**
• **yearly** /yierlee/
Happening once every year **ADJECTIVE**

yeast /yeest/
A substance put into bread to make it rise **NOUN**

yell /yel/
To say something in a very loud voice **VERB**
• **yell** /yel/ **NOUN**

yellow /yeloa/
The colour of a lemon or butter or the middle of an egg **NOUN, ADJECTIVE**

yes /yes/
Used in an answer to mean that what someone asks you is correct, or that you agree to do something, or give permission **ADVERB**
Yes, you can go out to play.

yesterday¹ /yesterdai/
On the day before today **ADVERB**
We went to the museum yesterday.

yesterday² /yesterdai/
The day before today **NOUN**
Yesterday was my birthday.

yet /yet/
1. Used to mean that something has not happened but will probably happen soon *Bee isn't here yet.* 2. Up until now *Today is the sunniest day we've had yet.* **ADVERB**

Yy

yew /ue/
A tree that stays green all year with dark green leaves and red berries **NOUN**

yield /yeeld/
1. To produce fruit or vegetables
2. To produce a useful result or information **VERB**

yoghurt /yogert/
Or **yogurt** /yogert/ A thick liquid made from milk that people eat, often with pieces of fruit in it **NOUN**

yolk /yoak/
The yolk of an egg is the middle part that is yellow **NOUN**

you /yoo/
Used to mean the person or people you are talking to or writing to **PRONOUN**
What are you doing, Inky?

young[1] /yung/
Born only a short time ago **ADJECTIVE**
• **youngster** /yungster/
A young person **NOUN**

young[2] /yung/
Another word for young animals or sometimes young people **NOUN**

your /yor/
Belonging to you **ADJECTIVE**
Is this your school?

yours /yorz/
If something is yours, it belongs to you
PRONOUN *This book is yours.*
• **yourself** /yorself/ **PRONOUN**
■ **yourselves** /yorselvz/ **PLURAL**

youth /yooth/
1. A young person 2. The time of your life when you are young **NOUN**

yo-yo /yoa yoa/
A little round toy fixed to the end of a string. You can make the yo-yo go up and down as you move the string **NOUN**

yuck /yuk/
A word that shows you think something is dirty or sticky or bad **INTERJECTION**
• **yucky** /yukee/ **ADJECTIVE**

Yuletide /yooltied/
An old-fashioned word for Christmas **NOUN**

yummy /yumee/
Something that is yummy tastes good **ADJECTIVE**

339

Zz

zebra /zebrɐ/
An animal like a horse with black and white stripes **NOUN**

zebra crossing /zebrɐ crosing/
A place on a road with black and white lines where cars must stop to let people cross **NOUN**

zero /ziɐroɑ/
The number 0 that means 'nothing' **NOUN**

zest /zest/
The outer skin of fruits like lemons or oranges. People use tiny pieces of zest in cooking to give the food more taste **NOUN**

zigzag /zigzag/
A line that keeps changing direction **NOUN**

• **zigzag** /zigzag/ **ADJECTIVE, VERB**

zip /zip/
Something used for opening and closing things like parts of clothes. It has two rows of pointed parts called teeth that fit into each other **NOUN**

• **zip** /zip/ **VERB**

zit /zit/
Another word for a spot on your skin like a tiny red bump **NOUN**

zone /zoɑn/
An area, usually where only certain things are allowed **NOUN**

Zz

zoo /zoo/

A place with lots of animals from different countries. People go there to look at them **NOUN**

zoom /zoom/

1. To move very fast 2. To zoom in on something means to make it look bigger with a camera **VERB**